AN **INTRODUCTION** TO THE **DARK SIDE** OF **INTERPERSONAL** COMMUNICATION

Megan R. Dillow

West Virginia University

cognella®

SAN DIEGO

For my dad—my favorite person and strongest supporter.

And with special thanks to Stephen Yoshimura,
who helped me get started,
and deepest gratitude to Todd Armstrong,
who helped me finish.

Bassim Hamadeh, CEO and Publisher
Todd R. Armstrong, Publisher
Michelle Piehl, Senior Project Editor
Abbey Hastings, Production Editor
Asfa Arshi, Graphic Design Assistant
Trey Soto, Licensing Specialist
Stephanie Adams, Senior Marketing Program Manager
Natalie Piccotti, Director of Marketing
Kassie Graves, Senior Vice President, Editorial
Jamie Giganti, Director of Academic Publishing

Printed in the United States of America.

 **cognella®** | ACADEMIC PUBLISHING

3970 Sorrento Valley Blvd., Ste. 500, San Diego, CA 92121

BRIEF CONTENTS

ABOUT THE AUTHOR

Megan **R. Dillow** (Ph.D., The Pennsylvania State University, 2006) is an associate professor in the Department of Communication Studies at West Virginia University. She teaches several courses at the undergraduate and graduate levels, including interpersonal communication, the dark side of interpersonal communication, persuasion, and communication theory. Her research primarily focuses on communication in close relationships—particularly communication surrounding dark side issues such as relational transgressions (e.g., opposite-sex infidelity, same-sex infidelity, deception, and destructive conflict) and how couples react to such negative relational events (e.g., forgiveness). She also studies uncertainty and information management processes, largely in the context of interpersonal relationships. Her secondary area of research is health communication, and (as co-principal investigator) she and some of her colleagues were recently awarded a grant from the National Science Foundation to study the impact of the COVID-19 pandemic in rural Appalachia, a project she was especially passionate about because she grew up and still resides in this area. She serves as a member of numerous editorial boards, has chaired the Interpersonal Communication Division of the National Communication Association, and recently served a five-year term as an associate editor for *Personal Relationships*. In 2020, she was named a Distinguished Research Fellow by the Eastern Communication Association. In 2021, she was the recipient of the Past Officers' Award from the Eastern Communication Association, and she was named a Research MVP by West Virginia University. In 2022, she was the recipient of the Eberly College Outstanding Teacher Award at West Virginia University.

DETAILED CONTENTS

PREFACE

This book emerged from the influence of two primary sources. On the one hand, the idea for an undergraduate-level dark side of interpersonal communication book has been percolating since graduate school, soon after I was first introduced to the dark side as an area of study. In this way, and as readers of this book will immediately see, I have been and continue to be strongly influenced by the pioneering work of William R. Cupach and Brian H. Spitzberg in this domain. Although they would deny it (and in fact, they already have denied it in their own published work), their synthesis of scholarly work under the umbrella of the "dark side" catalyzed this domain of study for so many scholars, and I pay tribute to them. As the founders of this area of inquiry, their graduate-level volumes on the dark side of interpersonal communication, of close relationships, and of relationship pursuit are the ultimate inspiration for and basis of this book. Without them, this book would not—could not—exist.

From a practical perspective, this book stemmed from my own personal need for a book that would be more appropriate for the undergraduate-level dark side of interpersonal communication course that I developed and continue to teach at West Virginia University. Of course, my own personal needs hardly seemed to warrant writing a book that only I would find useful. But as the dark side continues to grow in popularity as an area of scholarly inquiry, I found that more and more of my contemporaries at colleges and universities across the United States were creating undergraduate-level courses on the topic of the dark side, and they too were in need of a book that is targeted specifically toward undergraduate students. As such, what seemed to be a broader need for a book such as this was the impetus that finally encouraged me to write it. I do hope that my contemporaries and their students will find it valuable.

Overview of the Book

The approach taken in this book is one that applies a dark side "lens" to various experiences and events that are relatively common in interpersonal relationships, incorporating relevant theories and recent empirical research in my explication of these topics. Readers of this book will see that—while I and others recognize that nearly all interpersonal experiences and events have both bright and dark side elements—my goal in this book was necessarily to draw attention to the more negative aspects of these occurrences in an effort to better understand (and perhaps then to ameliorate) them.

After a general introduction to the dark side, several topics that may also be fruitfully examined from a bright side lens are considered (i.e., relational uncertainty, topic avoidance, and secret keeping). From there, we progress through arguably more severe experiences and events and potential responses in interpersonal relationships that are typically investigated from a dark side perspective (e.g., relationship transgressions, hurtful communication, jealousy, deception, infidelity, responses to transgressions, aggression and violence, obsessive relational intrusion, stalking, cyberstalking, teasing, bullying, cyberbullying, and destructive conflict). Along the way, where possible, we discuss ways to mitigate the incidence and/or effects of dark side events in interpersonal relationships.

Features of the Textbook

This book contains several useful pedagogical elements that are designed to be helpful to instructors and to assist students in understanding and applying the content of a dark side of interpersonal communication or close relationships course.

Unique and contemporary examples are provided throughout the book to engage students and facilitate their ability to understand and apply the material in a practical way.

Theory in Practice, **Mediated Contexts**, and **Flipping the Script boxes** are included in most chapters. These boxes complement the content of this book by identifying and discussing relevant theoretical perspectives, research related to social media and technology use, and pieces of commonsense information that are often taken for granted but in reality have been challenged by empirical research.

Discussion questions are also provided in every chapter. These may serve as a chapter summary and/or a way for students to test themselves, allowing students to know if they have mastered the more critical content in a particular chapter. These also serve as a resource for instructors in directing class discussion about important chapter content.

A **glossary** serves as a convenient resource, containing key terms/phrases to help ensure that students are able to identify and understand the central ideas of the book.

Acknowledgments

This book would not have been possible without the assistance and support of so many people, chief among them the members of the team I was lucky enough to work with at Cognella Academic Publishing: Todd Armstrong, Michelle Piehl, and Tony Paese. All of you were continuously supportive and endlessly helpful, and I could never thank you enough for believing in and sticking it out with me. Quite simply, this book would never have come to fruition without you.

I also owe a great debt of gratitude to the thorough and conscientious reviewers of this book: Lindsey S. Aloia (University of Arkansas), Kory Floyd (The University of Arizona), Sean M. Horan (Texas State University), Robin Kowalski (Clemson University), Kelly G. McAninch (University of Kentucky), Rachel M. McLaren (The University of Iowa), Joshua R. Pederson (The University of Alabama), Molly Reynolds (University of Kentucky), Jennifer A. Samp (University of Georgia), P. L. Secklin (Saint Cloud State University), Stephanie A. Tikkanen (Ohio University), and Steve Yoshimura (University of Montana). Your thoughtful, insightful, and encouraging feedback and suggestions certainly made this book better than it would have otherwise been, and I very much appreciate you.

Thank you also to Matthew M. Martin, who encouraged me to pursue this book and, as my department chair at the time, contributed in other instrumental ways to its completion. Finally, I have been so appreciative of the support of my family and friends while writing this book. You know who you are, and I am so fortunate to have you in my life.

Chapter 1

The Dark Side of Communication in Close Relationships

"*Imagine two porcupines huddled together in the cold of an Alaskan winter's night, each providing life-sustaining warmth to the other. As they draw ever closer together the painful prick from the other's quills leads them to instinctively withdraw—until the need for warmth draws them together again. This "kiss of the porcupines" is an apt metaphor for the human condition*" (Fincham, 2000, p. 2). The "kiss of the porcupines" also happens to be a fitting metaphor for this textbook. Despite the harm that others (e.g., romantic partners, spouses, friends, family members) so often cause to each other, whether intentionally or otherwise, people continue to seek interpersonal relationships with others.

Our involvement in interpersonal relationships with others allows us to meet some of our most fundamental human needs for affiliation and for survival, and to experience some of the greatest joys in life. This drive to form relationships with others has long been documented by scholars who study interpersonal and relational processes. For instance, the **belongingness hypothesis** has been posited, which in brief claims that people have an inherent and axiomatic "need to belong" and are rather quick to form social attachments to other people, and at the same time are rather reluctant to break those social bonds (Baumeister & Leary, 1995). "Belonging" or forming social attachments to others is associated with a variety of positives outcomes while a lack of social attachments is linked to a number of deleterious outcomes, both for psychological well-being and for physical health. Both anecdotal and empirical evidence make clear the importance of interpersonal connections with others in terms of satisfying basic human needs and wants.

Yet, paradoxically—as the vignette that opened this chapter illustrates—it is within these very interpersonal relationships that we are the recipient of some of the deepest hurts and most harmful behaviors we will ever experience (Fincham, 2000). We need each other, yet we will inevitably harm each other, given enough time. Opening ourselves up to others is a requirement of interpersonal relationships, yet doing so makes us vulnerable. Such negative, harmful, or otherwise disfavored events and experiences in interpersonal relationships are often studied under the moniker of the "dark side." In this chapter, the dark side of interpersonal relationships will be introduced, and some foundational material related to interpersonal communication and relational communication will be discussed. Various conceptualizations of the dark side will be debated, and the importance of the dark side of interpersonal communication as an area of study will be overviewed.

Dark Side of Interpersonal Relationships

Several decades ago, the dark side began to emerge as an established area of inquiry for communication scholars and scholars of other related disciplines, such as psychology and social psychology. Although our interactions and our close relationships with others serve basic need fulfillment functions and can be the source of much happiness and life satisfaction, things frequently go wrong and people regularly behave badly in these interactions/relationships (Fincham, 2000). Those closest to us, such as romantic partners and friends, often commit relationship transgressions or otherwise violate relational rules in a number of minor and major ways, including communicating hurtful messages (e.g., "I'm not attracted to you anymore"); keeping secrets from us; refusing to talk about certain topics with us; causing us to feel jealous (perhaps intentionally); behaving in a jealous manner toward us when jealousy is not warranted or justified; being deceptive; being unfaithful (e.g., committing sexual, emotional, or communicative infidelity); enacting revenge or refusing to grant forgiveness; perpetrating intimate partner violence; engaging in stalking or other unwanted/obsessive pursuit behaviors; enacting antisocial teasing or even bullying/cyberbullying; and engaging in patterns of destructive conflict (e.g., serial arguments, demand-withdrawal, the four horsemen of the apocalypse).

These transgressions, in addition to other individual experiences (e.g., the experience of relational uncertainty and rumination about negative events), can cause harm and perhaps irreparable damage to the people involved in the relationship and the relationship itself. Dark side research examines all these topics, including their antecedents and consequences, to try to better understand why and how problematic behaviors are enacted in close relationships, how people respond when they are faced with such events or experiences, and the implications of various types of bad behavior for the relationships in question. But before we dive into the dark side, let us take a moment to revisit some fundamental concepts that undergird the study of both the bright and dark sides of relationships.

Foundations of Interpersonal and Relational Communication

Comparatively speaking, the focused study of the dark side is still relatively new. In fact, research on relationships in general is fairly recent as compared to many other disciplines (even other related social sciences). The dark side is situated in the study of **interpersonal communication**, which is defined by some as the exchange of verbal and/or nonverbal messages between at least two people, regardless of the relationship between them. Note that there is a significant lack of consensus regarding this definition (Knapp & Daly, 2011). Some scholars argue that this conceptualization merely constitutes communication, and they would take this definition a step further by claiming that *interpersonal* communication is an effort to create a connection or bond with another person; an attempt to establish and navigate a relationship with another. Others have claimed that the degree to which communication is interpersonal or not has to do with the kind of information the interactants have about each other and use during message exchange (Miller & Steinberg, 1975). For instance, information that is psychological in nature is more personal/intimate, idiosyncratic, and explanatory in nature; it is therefore considered more interpersonal. Conversely, information that is sociological relies on demographic or cultural characteristics and is merely descriptive in nature; thus, it is less interpersonal (or it constitutes **impersonal communication**).

Research on interpersonal communication began to flourish in the 1960s, and by the 1970s it was a recognized area of study in the United States (Knapp & Daly, 2011). Scholarship from the early period of research on interpersonal communication revealed that people use interpersonal communication differently depending on the type of relationship they wish to establish and maintain with another. For example, communication in early relationships, or in relationships that we wish to keep from getting too close, is typically pretty superficial in nature and governed by social norms regarding appropriate self-disclosure (e.g., do not share too much too soon; Altman & Taylor, 1973). As relationships progress over time, communication naturally becomes more personal and intimate and those involved become closer, and social norms for appropriate self-disclosure become less important as the people in the relationship develop their own (usually implicit) rules for self-disclosure. As this example reflects, **interpersonal relationships** are characterized by at least three elements: (a) they are enduring, with repeated interactions over some period of time; (b) the people involved in them mutually influence each other—they are interdependent; and (c) the people involved have unique communication and other interaction patterns (Kelley, 1986).

Communication in an interpersonal relationship (e.g., with your roommate) differs in important ways from noninterpersonal or impersonal communication (e.g., communication with people according to their roles with no unique explanatory knowledge about them, such as fast-food workers, salespeople, bank tellers, teachers, and physicians). However, these types of relationships (e.g., with physicians or teachers) can become interpersonal in nature if you interact with these people repeatedly over time, your behaviors impact each other, and you interact with them in ways that transcend the role that they play in your life. Often, though, communication with people in these types of roles is done primarily (if not solely) for functional, instrumental reasons; reciprocal knowledge of each other is often superficial and merely descriptive; the influence that is exerted is often far more one-directional than it is mutual or reciprocal; the people involved in them often interact for only limited, temporary time periods; and the people involved in them are basically interchangeable (e.g., any bank teller or fast-food worker will do).

Much of the study of dark side relationship processes is often situated in the context of relationships that are close in nature (although there are exceptions to this; bullying, cyberbullying, violence, stalking, and other aggressive behaviors may be enacted by people we know but are not close with, or even by strangers). **Close relationships** include all the characteristics of interpersonal relationships identified previously, as well as several more: (a) the ability to meet important psychological and interpersonal needs, (b) a degree of emotional attachment and connection between the people involved, and (c) the perception of each other as difficult or impossible to easily replace. Our close relationships—those with romantic partners, close friends, and some family members—help us meet our needs to belong and to affiliate with others, our needs for intimacy and acceptance, and our needs to give and receive affection (Schutz, 1958). They also may help us reach our goals of self-fulfillment and achieving our full potential (Aron & Aron, 1986). We tend to view people with whom we are involved in close relationships as being irreplaceable (whereas you could buy your next vehicle from any salesperson, for example, and get basically the same results). In other words, in part because of our increased levels of emotional attachment to and connection with close others, we do not think they can easily (if at all) be replaced by another person. The exchange of verbal and nonverbal messages in the context of these kinds of close relationships is often referred to as **relational communication**.

Early work in the areas of interpersonal and relational communication largely focused on more positive and constructive behaviors, experiences, and events in close relationships, such as the benefits of physical attractiveness, the relationship between attitudinal similarity and liking, the development and maintenance of relationships, and affinity seeking (Barnlund, 1968; Bell & Daly, 1984; Berscheid & Walster, 1974; Byrne, 1971). Some research on what would now be termed the dark side was taking place in the early years of the study of interpersonal communication, of course, such as the study of deception (Knapp et al., 1974) and earlier work by psychologists on destructive obedience to authority and the Stanford prison experiment (Haney et al., 1973; Milgram, 1963). But this work was rather sporadic and disparate in nature, as scholars did not then have the nomenclature of the dark side. It was not until the 1990s that we really began to see focused research on behaviors, experiences, and events that can be damaging to people and the close relationships in which they are involved. Before that, with some exceptions (i.e., research on aggressive behaviors such as intimate partner violence), interpersonal and relationship scholars argued that we were "somewhat overbalanced in focusing on the positive" (Duck, 1994, p. 3; Kowalski, 2001).

In the communication discipline, the area we know today as the dark side was catalyzed when two founding scholars—William R. Cupach and Brian H. Spitzberg—edited the first dark side of interpersonal communication book in 1994. This edited book was revolutionary for would-be dark side scholars because, among other things, it labeled the dark side, laid out its basic parameters, and brought together various areas of formerly disjointed scholarly inquiry and united them under the rubric of the dark side. Within the communication discipline, this book and the scholars who edited it are primarily responsible for galvanizing the concerted study of all types of dark side issues. Because of Cupach and Spitzberg's pioneering work, the dark side is recognized today as a legitimate and distinct area of scholarly inquiry.

Conceptualizing the Dark Side

In 1994, Cupach and Spitzberg made a first attempt to identify the basic focus of the dark side as "social interaction that is difficult, problematic, challenging, dysfunctional, distressing, and disruptive" (p. vii). Given that research on these topics was still in its infancy, comparatively speaking, Cupach and Spitzberg were careful not to position this as *the* definition of the dark side, as any such definition could inadvertently serve to limit the study of concepts that might not be so obvious or easy to immediately characterize as dark in nature (e.g., incompetence, shyness). Later, Spitzberg and Cupach (1998) expanded their earlier musings to also include several other elements that are relevant to and characteristic of the dark side:

- Behaviors that violate, including betrayals, deviance, and other transgressions (e.g., infidelity, deception, secret keeping, obsessive relational intrusion, stalking, intimate partner violence, etc.), including features of human behavior/interaction that are rude and awkward and thereby disruptive. This category of behaviors encompasses a number of dark side issues that will be discussed throughout this textbook.

- Behaviors that exploit or objectify other people who have difficulty defending themselves (e.g., sexual harassment, bullying, cyberbullying).

- Aspects of human endeavor that are unappreciated, unfulfilled, and underestimated (e.g., unrequited love).

- Aspects of people and interactions that are unattractive, repulsive, and unwanted (e.g., social incompetence, love shyness).

- Paradoxical elements of people and interactions that are not always what they seem to be (e.g., the paradox that those we love most often hurt us the worst).

This list was inclusive and evocative, and it was perhaps most useful in terms of its effort to highlight the behavioral dimensions of the dark side. In the latter sense, this view of the dark side aligned closely with some work by social psychologist Robin Kowalski (1997) on **aversive interpersonal behaviors**. Like this behavioral approach to the dark side, aversive social behaviors were defined as those that deny people valued outcomes or cause people to experience adverse outcomes. Aversive interpersonal behaviors often deal with more mundane, everyday, "mean and nasty" things people do to each other that are relatively more minor in nature, in addition to acts that would be considered major violations of relational rules (Kowalski et al., 2003). For example, they include behaviors such as complaints, forgetting commitments, displaying arrogance, not listening, being too dependent, and swearing, in addition to extreme forms of aversive behavior (e.g., violence). Basically, anything experienced as aversive—anything that is not liked or wanted—could "count" as an aversive interpersonal behavior.

Any number of things might influence whether a particular behavior is experienced as aversive, including judgments of its appropriateness, intentionality, ambiguity, frequency, severity, and whether the behavior is committed in public or private (Kowalski, 2001). Although Kowalski's definition of aversive interpersonal behaviors shares some aspects in common with Spitzberg and Cupach's (1998) view of the dark side (in that they both identify behaviors that are dark or aversive in nature), work outside the communication discipline has largely proceeded independently and not always under the moniker of the dark side.

In 2007, Spitzberg and Cupach made their first attempt at conceptualizing the dark side in a more formal way. As comprehensive as their 1998 behavioral take on the dark side was, they recognized that it may not be possible for any conceptual taxonomy that attempts to delineate the behaviors or aspects of human interaction to be inclusive enough to house all of the topics that could be viewed from a dark side perspective. Further, Spitzberg and Cupach (2007) were dissatisfied with the ambiguity in some of these characteristics as well as the overlap between and among some of them. Thus, they offered a new perspective in 2007 that does not rely on such delineation of behaviors but instead focuses on dimensions of behavior.

Specifically, two behavioral dimensions are used to help categorize and classify behavior. The first dimension ranges from that which is typically perceived as appropriate to that which is perceived as inappropriate according to societal, cultural, and/or moral norms. Further, on the second dimension, behavior can range from that which is considered functionally productive to that which is considered functionally destructive with regard to a person's well-being or a relationship's quality and survival. Crossing these two dimensions results in four spheres of human behavior, as depicted by Spitzberg and Cupach (2007).

As you can see in Figure 1.1, three of these quadrants of human behavior (i.e., evil incarnate, what was once dark is now bright, and what was once bright is now dark) house behaviors that can be fruitfully viewed from a dark side perspective. It is obvious that behaviors that would be characterized as "evil incarnate" (i.e., both socially/culturally/morally inappropriate and functionally destructive) fall squarely within the purview of the dark side. However, not all dark side behaviors are solely or completely destructive or inappropriate in nature. In other words, some dark side behaviors can have bright elements (i.e., what was once dark is now bright)—and indeed, research would suggest some surprising bright side implications of a number of actions, events, and experiences typically (and sometimes exclusively) considered to be more dark side in nature. For instance, sexual infidelity is generally viewed as both inappropriate and destructive in societies where monogamy is overwhelmingly preferred over polyamory (such

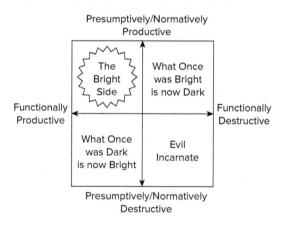

FIGURE 1.1   The Domains of the Dark Side

Adapted from: Brian H. Spitzberg and William R. Cupach, *The Dark Side of Interpersonal Communication*, p. 6. Copyright © 2007 by Taylor & Francis Group.

as the United States). But perhaps surprisingly, research has shown some positive (if unintended) outcomes that are sometimes associated with the commission of sexual infidelity, including realizing the importance of quality couple communication, increased assertiveness, valuing family more highly, taking better care of oneself, and developing a closer relationship with each other (Olson et al., 2002). Similarly, deception is often morally disdained, and there is a basic expectation of truthfulness in close relationships, although lies are often told in order to be polite or to ease social interaction (Vrij, 2007). In fact, if we insisted on being nothing but completely honest all the time, it would likely have negative implications for our close relationships with others.

Further, some behaviors may start off as bright in nature but devolve or otherwise morph into dark side behaviors (i.e., what was once bright is now dark). Social support has numerous benefits and is identified as a central aspect of close relationships such as friendships, yet both giving and receiving support can have negative implications. For example, the support you receive may be unhelpful; it may even place demands on you that you perceive as costs (Albrecht & Adelman, 1987; Barbee et al., 1998; Hays et al., 1994). For example, say you agree to help a family member financially while they are trying to kick a drug or alcohol addiction, but only if your family member agrees to commit to an in-patient rehabilitation program for at least 30 days. Your intentions in making this demand are obviously focused on what you believe to be the best interests of your family member; however, they may perceive such a contingent support attempt as ineffective due to the costs and restrictions that it imposes, and it may further strain the quality of your relationship.

Seeking and even receiving support from others has implications for impression management as well. Some people are reluctant to ask for help when they need it due to impression management concerns, and conversely, having support thrust upon you (e.g., another person's well-intentioned advice) when you do not need it and did not ask for it can be face threatening. For instance, a parent who continually inserts themselves in your life on the premise of helping you take care of things may be intended as helpful, but may be interpreted by you (and possibly by others around you) as an implication that you cannot manage things on your own. These **support dilemmas**, wherein the benefits of receiving social support are offset by the costs or drawbacks of doing so (Brashers et al., 2004), represent just one area in which typically bright communication can have important drawbacks. Spitzberg and Cupach (2007) put it best when they noted that dark clouds can have silver linings and silver clouds can have dark linings.

This expanded view suggests that conceptualizations of the dark side should not be based on identifying specific content or types of dark side behaviors, thus moving us away from earlier categorizations of behaviors like infidelity, jealousy, and deception as obviously (and only) dark in nature and behaviors like social support, relational maintenance, and affinity seeking as obviously (and only) bright in nature. Instead, the **dark side** functions more as a perspective or way of looking at things; it is a way of asking questions that draws attention to the inappropriate and destructive elements of all kinds of behaviors, even those that ostensibly begin as, are intended as, or are usually evaluated as positive. A dark side approach recognizes that "all social processes unfold in ways that produce both gains and losses, and gains that appear to be losses and losses that appear to be gains" (Spitzberg & Cupach, 2007, p. 8).

In keeping with this notion of the dark side as a perspective or lens through which to view relationship processes, this textbook examines a range of behaviors and experiences from a dark side perspective.

Importance of Dark Side Study

Why should scholars continue to explore the dark side? Why should members of the general public such as yourselves care about it? Now that you have a better understanding of what the dark side entails, undoubtedly you can come up with a few good reasons on your own! Although we might come up with reasons ad nauseam, some of the more important will be identified and discussed here. As other scholars have persuasively argued, one compelling reason for studying the dark side is because dark side events are so incredibly common as to be considered pervasive in close relationships. From scholarly and practical perspectives, dark side behaviors warrant continued study because they occur so frequently in close relationships. In line with Spitzberg and Cupach's conceptualization of the dark side as fundamental to interpersonal and close relationships, and to return to an idea that was introduced at the start of the chapter, the ones who love us most are virtually guaranteed to hurt us in big or small ways, even if they do so unintentionally (Fincham, 2000).

A second convincing reason for studying the dark side can be found in studies of the **negativity effect**, which suggests that negative aspects of social interaction have a stronger, longer lasting impact than the positive events that occur in interpersonal and close relationships (e.g., Kellermann, 1984; Rook, 1984, 1998). This tendency has been documented in relationships of all types, including (but not limited to) romantic relationships. Although dark side events are common, it is important to note that they do not tend to occur as frequently as more positive events and interactions in close relationships do; if they did, it is unlikely that we would wish to maintain such a dysfunctional relationship! But the point of the negativity effect is that when these negative events do occur, they are attended to much more closely and for longer periods of time than more positive events.

The insidiousness of negative events is such that some scholars have posited the existence of a **magic ratio**, which identifies the number of positive behaviors or interactions during conflict that is necessary to offset every negative behavior or interaction in order to maintain stability and relational harmony (the magic ratio is 5:1; Gottman, 1994). That is, research by John Gottman and his colleagues (mostly with spouses) has shown that five positive behaviors or interactions during conflict are necessary to counteract each negative behavior or interaction that is experienced. Further, he and his colleagues have argued that adherence to this magic ratio constitutes the difference between happy and unhappy couples. Given the magnitude of their effects, there is a clear need for scholars and students of the dark side to learn more about these dark side events and how to ameliorate them, both within the context of conflict and outside of it.

A third important reason to study the dark side has to do with people's general tendency to make sense of things using a series of bipolar ratings (e.g., Perlman & Carcedo, 2011). This argument is based on Charles Osgood et al.'s seminal work employing semantic differential tasks wherein people are asked to evaluate various concepts based on a set of verbal opposites (e.g., good–bad, strong–weak, active–passive). The argument here is that people naturally approach, interpret, understand, and respond to the world around us using such bipolar opposites, suggesting some innate and perhaps subconscious motivation to do so (Osgood, 1952; Osgood & Suci, 1955). Interestingly, the opposite pair of "bright–dark" showed up in Osgood's early research, confirming the presumption that people are predisposed to categorize stimuli as either bright or dark (and in many other ways as well).

As others have pointed out, both the negativity effect and our tendency to view and evaluate behaviors and events in dichotomous ways may be adaptive in nature (e.g., Gould, 2002; Perlman & Carcedo, 2011). Scholars of evolutionary theory would argue that paying particular attention to threats in our environment so that we can react appropriately to them is important for survival. Further, our tendency to see and make sense of the world around us via the use of dichotomous, bipolar evaluations may improve our ability to quickly categorize an event as threatening (or not) and respond appropriately to that event.

All of these represent good reasons for better understanding dark side events from both scientific and practical standpoints. The early research with bipolar ratings suggests the importance of understanding both ends of the bright and dark spectrum, as a better understanding of the dark side may help shed even more light on the bright side (and vice versa). To return to a previous example, understanding that there is a dark side of social support and why or under what conditions social support may have downsides in interpersonal and close relationships can enhance what scholars know about crafting and delivering effective support messages by reducing or eliminating that which people find problematic and focusing instead on what works. In short, it is important to understand both sides of the coin. Further, even if negative events and interactions are fewer in functional relationships than positive ones, they are still quite common—and yet they were comparatively neglected in favor of studying the bright side in the early years of interpersonal communication inquiry. Although we have gotten a good start, research on the dark side of interpersonal communication and close relationships still has some catching up to do. This work is made all the more imperative when considering the implications of the negativity effect for individual and relationship functioning.

Conclusion

As you have learned from this chapter, the dark side is a burgeoning area of inquiry that is situated within the larger study of interpersonal and relational communication. Although the study of interpersonal processes has been established for some time, only in the last few decades have scholars began to focus in a concerted way on the darker side of a variety of behaviors and events in close relationships, including their cognitive, emotional, communicative, and—in more recent research—physiological antecedents and consequences. Among other insights, this body of research has revealed that behaviors, experiences, or events in and of themselves are not necessarily dark or bright. Instead, these behaviors, experiences, and events typically have both dark *and* bright aspects.

Those who study relational processes through a dark lens are focused on the more negative, destructive, and challenging aspects of those experiences while still recognizing that they may have their bright components. As you have seen, learning about the dark side is important for academic and practical reasons because dark side events are common and can have long-lasting implications for individuals and their close relationships. In accordance, the bulk of this textbook is dedicated to explicating the dark nature of various behaviors and events in interpersonal and close relationships (particularly romantic relationships), identifying their causes and consequences, and when possible, discussing how to combat or mitigate the effect of these negative events in close relationships.

Discussion Questions

1. Distinguish among impersonal communication, interpersonal communication, and relational communication. In doing so, make sure to define and discuss interpersonal relationships and close relationships as well.

2. Based on what you learned from this chapter, discuss what the dark side is. How has it been conceptualized in the past, and how is it conceptualized today? Include related areas of inquiry (e.g., aversive interpersonal behaviors) as part of your discussion.

3. Identify and discuss the three major reasons studying the dark side is important and necessary. Which of these reasons do you find most compelling, and why? Can you think of two other reasons?

4. How might taking a dark side perspective have been/continue to be adaptive from an evolutionary perspective? Do you find this to be another compelling reason for studying the dark side? Why or why not?

Chapter 2

Relational Uncertainty

Carmen and Cesar have been involved in a romantic relationship for about 2 years. Both will be graduating from the university they attend this year, and after graduating Cesar will begin a job with his family's company in Chicago. He has asked Carmen to join him, and while she agreed to spend the summer after graduation with him in Chicago, she then plans to move to Seattle to attend graduate school next fall. As graduation nears, Carmen finds herself growing more and more insecure about the future of her relationship with Cesar. It seems as if their paths are leading away from each other, and although she loves Cesar, Carmen recognizes that the relational problems they've had are only likely to worsen once they're no longer geographically close. Carmen is not sure that she is willing or able to sustain a long-distance relationship, and she doubts that the relationship would be very satisfying for either of them even if she and Cesar attempted to continue it.

S ituations such as this scenario are common. At some point in a romantic relationship—whether early on when the relationship is in its initial development stages, or later when the relationship is comfortably established and stable, or even later as it is nearing its end—partners are bound to experience doubts and insecurities about the relationship at times. For example, Carmen is questioning whether she wants to continue her relationship with Cesar and what the quality of the relationship would be for both of them if she does attempt to sustain it. Such relational uncertainties are not uncommon, yet they can negatively impact cognitions, emotions, physiological responses, communicative behaviors, and relational outcomes. Ultimately, these insecurities impact the viability of the relationship.

In this chapter, we will examine relational uncertainty. We will delve into the factors that lead to more relational uncertainty, as well as the consequences of relational uncertainty in the context of close relationships. It is important to note that this concept is not solely or inherently dark in nature, and in fact may have bright aspects—especially when compared with other topics that are covered in this book (e.g., infidelity, stalking, intimate partner violence). In keeping with current conceptualizations of the dark side, as discussed in Chapter 1, this chapter will focus on the negative aspects of relational uncertainty while still recognizing that such experiences may also have more positive elements.

Uncertainty in Interpersonal Relationships

Uncertainty is an ideal concept to consider from both dark and bright perspectives. **Uncertainty**, generally, is thought of as the inability to understand, describe, explain, and/or predict another person's attitudes or behaviors (Berger & Calabrese, 1975). On the bright side, uncertainty can keep things interesting, as it helps to avoid the monotony that can accompany complete certainty and predictability about how another person will act, think, or feel in any given situation (Baxter, 1990). On the other hand, uncertainty often carries with it certain drawbacks. For example, discomfort, stress, and anxiety can arise when one is insecure about or uncomfortable with their lack of knowledge in a particular situation (Berger & Calabrese, 1975; Brashers, 2001). Further, in the context of close relationships, uncertainty can be perceived as problematic because it results in doubts not just about another's cognitions, emotions, and behaviors, but about one's own thoughts, feelings, and actions (Berger & Gudykunst, 1991). In other words, uncertainty can make it difficult for us to understand why someone feels or behaves a certain way, to predict how this person might feel or behave in future, and therefore to make decisions regarding how we should behave in order to achieve particular outcomes.

Beyond these general notions of uncertainty across contexts, three specific sources of uncertainty that arise in the context of close relationships have been identified, including self, partner, and relationship sources of relational uncertainty (Knobloch & Solomon, 1999). Here, **relational uncertainty** is an overarching umbrella term that comprises all three sources of doubt individuals may experience in the context of close relationships.

Self-uncertainty concerns the doubts or questions that an individual has about perceptions of their own involvement in and commitment to a close relationship with another person. **Partner uncertainty** entails a lack of confidence in an individual's perceptions of their partner's involvement in and commitment to the relationship. Self-uncertainty and partner uncertainty each have three subdimensions: desire, evaluation, and goals. Individuals may question their own *desire* for the relationship (i.e., Do I really want to pursue this relationship? How committed am I to this relationship?) and/or their partner's desire for the relationship (i.e., How much does this person like me? Does this person want a romantic relationship with me or do they just want to be friends?). In the opening scenario of this chapter, it is clear that Carmen is questioning her own desire to continue the relationship with Cesar. People might also be insecure about their own *evaluations* or assessments of the relationship (i.e., How do I view this relationship? How important is this relationship to me?) and/or their partner's evaluation of the relationship (i.e., Does my partner want to maintain this relationship?). Carmen also seems to be questioning the "goodness" or quality of her relationship, noting that she and Cesar have relational problems that are only likely to worsen if they are no longer geographically proximal. Those in close relationships might also question their own *goals* for the relationship (i.e., Do I want to stay in a relationship with my partner?) and/or their partner's goals for the relationship (i.e., Does my partner want this relationship to work out in the long run? Does my partner want this relationship to last?). It is clear that Carmen is also suffering from doubts about the future of her relationship with Cesar, as she notes that their future paths seem to be taking them in different directions.

In addition to self and partner uncertainties, relational uncertainty is comprised of a concept called **relationship uncertainty**, which is characterized by a lack of confidence about perceptions of the dyad or something about the relationship itself as its own entity. As such, relationship uncertainty is conceptualized at a higher level of abstraction than self- and partner uncertainties. It has four subdimensions about which relationship questions might arise: behavioral norms, mutuality of feelings, definition/ state of the relationship, and the future of the relationship. *Behavioral norms* entail standards for appropriate and normative behavior in the context of a particular relationship (i.e., What can I say to/how should I behave around my partner? What are the boundaries for appropriate and/or inappropriate behavior in this relationship?). *Mutuality of feelings* has to do with whether you perceive that you and your partner are on the same page about your feelings for each other and how you see the relationship (i.e., Do my partner and I feel the same way about each other? Does my partner like me as much as I like them?). *Definition of the relationship* deals with how you would describe, define, and generally categorize the relationship (i.e., Is this a platonic or a romantic relationship? What is the definition or the state of this relationship? Are we monogamous or is it okay to see other people?). Finally, *future of the relationship* includes your judgments of whether the relationship will continue (i.e., Will my partner and I stay together? Where is this relationship going?).

Even if self and partner uncertainties are low, relationship uncertainty may be high due to certain qualities of the relationship (i.e., my partner and I both want the relationship, evaluate it positively, and want a future together, yet the relationship may be untenable due to insurmountable religious differences, family members' disapproval of and lack of support for the relationship, the inability to find work in the same city, etc.). Research has shown that the three sources of relational uncertainty tend to co-occur, yet they are posited as conceptually—if not empirically—distinct from each other (Goodboy et al., 2021; Knobloch, 2007a). Research has also shown that not all relational uncertainties are created equally. In the context of married couples, generally speaking, relational uncertainty (and especially self-uncertainty) has been negatively related to relational quality. But the particular sources of relational uncertainty are relevant, as spousal uncertainties related to communication (e.g., misunderstandings, quality of communication) and sex (e.g., frequency of sexual activity, quality of sex life) in marriage have emerged as the strongest predictors of relationship quality indicators such as satisfaction and commitment (Knobloch, 2008b).

FLIPPING THE SCRIPT

Is Uncertainty Always Negative or Is Ignorance Sometimes Bliss?

Uncertainty has a long history of dark side implications, beginning with Berger and Calabrese's (1975) articulation of uncertainty reduction theory (URT). In brief, URT posited that a primary motivating force in the communication between individuals involved in initial interactions is the reduction of uncertainty, as uncertainty is an uncomfortable state for most individuals who instead prefer the ability to reliably explain and predict another's behavior. While research exists to support the claim that uncertainty is undesirable as compared to information that allows us to more accurately interpret and more effectively respond to another person, the notion that uncertainty is always negative has been challenged by various programs of related research (Afifi & Morse, 2009; Brashers, 2001). Perhaps most relevant to the context of close relationships is research on dialectical tensions—specifically the dialectic of certainty's internal manifestation of novelty-predictability (Baxter, 2006). This dialectic emphasizes the tension partners face while balancing the need to maintain some sense of order, routine, and stability (predictability) with keeping things exciting, interesting, and new (novelty). Related research has shown how too much predictability or certainty can be harmful to romantic relationships, as boredom is a key reason for the deterioration and dissolution of courtships (Hill et al., 1976). Therefore, one bright side of uncertainty is that it can keep relationships interesting. In addition, uncertainty may actually be preferred to certainty under specific conditions, such as when we suspect the information we will discover in the process of reducing our uncertainty will be negative in nature (Afifi & Burgoon, 1998; Afifi & Reichert, 1996; Baxter & Wilmot, 1985). Clearly, another bright side of uncertainty is that it prevents (or at least postpones) some negative and unwanted relational experiences.

Predictors of Relational Uncertainty

The majority of research on relational uncertainty has been conducted in the context of dating relationships, and this research has revealed several conditions, qualities, predilections, or external factors that tend to correspond with elevated relational uncertainty perceptions. These are discussed as individual, relationship, and external predictors.

Individual Predictors

Some enduring behavioral tendencies, preferences, or personality variables have been linked to the experience of uncertainty in close relationships, including one's general **tolerance of ambiguity**. First conceptualized as a personality characteristic, tolerance of ambiguity has also been studied as an aspect of the general work-related values of national cultures (Frenkel-Brunswick, 1948, 1949; Hofstede, 1980). Ambiguity tolerance refers to the way a person (or group) perceives, interprets, and responds to information or circumstances that are unclear or uncertain (Furnham & Marks, 2013). Individuals with a high tolerance for ambiguity are quite comfortable with—and in fact may actively prefer—ambiguous situations or information, often perceiving such circumstances as more stimulating and/or challenging. Conversely, those with a low tolerance for ambiguity find uncertain situations inherently threatening and stressful and strive to avoid them whenever possible. As such, those who are predisposed to be intolerant of ambiguity should be more sensitive to relational uncertainty, and should experience more stress, anxiety, and discomfort with its presence in close relationships.

An individual's **attachment** style has also been associated with the experience of relational uncertainty. Individuals who are insecurely attached are prone to experiencing more relational uncertainty than those who are securely attached. Preoccupieds and fearful avoidants (i.e., those who have high levels of attachment anxiety and negative internal working models of themselves) are especially likely to report increased relational uncertainty (Fox & Warber, 2014).

Theory in Practice

Attachment Styles in Close Relationships

Attachment theory explains how the bonds that are formed with important others through interactions with them, beginning from birth and our experiences with primary caregivers, impact how we relate to others (Bowlby, 1969, 1973). Our attachment experiences lead us to develop internal working models of ourselves, others, and relationships that influence the types of relationships we are drawn to as well as the decisions we make and the ways in which we behave in those relationships. In short, if we have had positive attachment experiences with close others who have encouraged us to form the perception that important others will be available, attentive, and responsive to our needs, we should have positive feelings about ourselves and about others that lead us to develop a secure attachment style. Conversely, if we have had negative attachment experiences that have led to the idea that close others will not be available to us when we need them or that they will not be attentive/responsive to our needs, we should have negative feelings about ourselves and/or about others that will lead us to become insecurely attached. According to Bowlby (1977; Ainsworth, 1989), our attachment style is formed early in life, during infancy and toddlerhood, and has the potential to impact close attachments with others throughout our lives.

Other perspectives on attachment styles have emerged, important among them a focus on attachment styles in adulthood, as empirical evidence suggests that the attachment style formed in childhood may indeed change as a function of our experiences in close relationships as adults. Four adult attachment styles have been identified (Bartholomew, 1990; Bartholomew & Horowitz, 1991). These are distinguished by one's internal working models (positive or negative of self and others), and they can be considered according to the degrees of attachment anxiety (the fear that important others will not be available and responsive) and attachment avoidance (the desire to avoid closeness with others) experienced by an individual (Guerrero, 2015).

Securely attached individuals have a positive view of self and others and low attachment anxiety and avoidance. These people are comfortable depending on others in close relationships, but they are also comfortable on their own, and generally have the greatest capacity for successful and satisfying close relationships. *Preoccupied individuals* have a negative view of self but a positive view of others and high attachment anxiety but low attachment avoidance. Preoccupieds strongly desire relationships with others, becoming overly dependent on them, feeling unworthy without them, and going to great lengths to attempt to maintain them. Yet, they experience a great deal of anxiety in terms of their close relationships with others and in their desperation to hang onto these relationships, and this may lead to relational behaviors that are negatively evaluated (e.g., self-centeredness, poor communication, emotionality, sensitivity, and perhaps even controlling, aggressive behaviors; Bartholomew & Horowitz, 1991; Guerrero & Jones, 2003; Guerrero et al., 2009). *Dismissive avoidant individuals* have a positive view of self but a negative view of others, and low attachment anxiety but high attachment avoidance. Dismissives do not prioritize relationships and are uncomfortable with intimacy, hence they tend to avoid becoming involved with others due to a preference for maintaining autonomy and independence. Finally, *fearful avoidant individuals* have negative views of themselves and others and high attachment anxiety and avoidance. Fearful avoidants shun relationships because they are afraid of being rejected and perceive that it is highly likely they will be. Fearful avoidants would like to be able to get close to others and form functional relationships, but they are afraid to trust others due to past negative relationship experiences.

Research with adult attachment styles has compellingly demonstrated the strong impact that these styles can and do have on our close relationships with others, including our communication in those relationships and how satisfying those relationships are. As you will see throughout this book, attachment styles are predictors of or are otherwise correlated with various dark side relational behaviors, including relational uncertainty.

Depression as an aspect of individuals' mental health is also predictive of relational uncertainty perceptions (Theiss, 2018). Several studies have shown direct relationships between symptoms of depression and elevated levels of relational uncertainty (e.g., Knobloch & Knobloch-Fedders, 2010; Knobloch et al., 2011). Depression may have an especially robust impact on increased perceptions of partner uncertainty, as those with depressive symptoms evince a need for excessive reassurances from their partner and also experience increased perceptions of interpersonal rejection from the partner (Knobloch et al., 2011; Starr & Davila, 2008). As women are almost twice as likely as men to be diagnosed with depression, women may be particularly prone to experience elevated relational uncertainty levels.

Relationship Predictors

In addition to individual difference predictors, certain elements of the romantic partner's relationship have been shown to increase perceptions of relational uncertainty. The quality most often studied in this regard is the degree or stage of **intimacy** (i.e., psychological closeness, emotional connection) between the partners. In some of the earliest work linking relational uncertainty perceptions to intimacy in close relationships, Berger and Calabrese's (1975) uncertainty reduction theory posited that uncertainty should be highest at the beginning stages of relationships, when intimacy is low. Further, Berger and colleagues have argued that low levels of intimacy should correspond with doubts at the individual level, while relationship or dyadic level doubts likely creep in a bit later, once the budding acquaintanceship becomes a relationship (Berger & Bradac, 1982). In other words, self- and partner uncertainties should be especially high when intimacy is low. Almost by definition, early relationship stages are a time in which individuals have the least amount of basic knowledge about each other.

It seems inevitable that doubts and questions will arise not only about a partner's desire, evaluation, and goals for the fledgling relationship, but about one's own desire, evaluation, and goals for that relationship. This uncertainty should organically decline over time, as partners progress from acquaintances to a close, intimate connection.

Although some research supports the notion that relational uncertainty will be highest when intimacy levels are lowest (e.g., Parks & Adelman, 1983), other perspectives have focused on changes in intimacy—as opposed to absolute degrees of intimacy—as instigators of heightened relational uncertainty. Originally, the relational turbulence model posited a curvilinear relationship between uncertainty and intimacy, such that moderate levels of intimacy should result in particularly high amounts of relational uncertainty (Solomon & Knobloch, 2004). Specifically, relational uncertainty was expected to peak when romantic partners transition from casually dating, where individuals are still largely independent, to seriously dating, where partners become mutually interdependent and committed. The escalating change in intimacy that is a hallmark of these middle stages of romantic relationships precipitates a loss of stability that should naturally cause individuals to experience increased doubt about that relationship. Yet, evidence in support of this pattern has been inconsistent, instead suggesting that relational uncertainty is high even in casual, nonintimate acquaintanceships. This uncertainty tends to reduce slowly as individuals become closer and more intimate, finally declining most drastically as partners become extremely close/intimate (Solomon, 2016).

Because evidence in support of this curvilinear relationship between intimacy and relational uncertainty has been inconsistent, the relational turbulence model (now, relational turbulence theory) was revised to move the focus from changes in intimacy, specifically, to any event or situation that causes relational uncertainty and turbulence (Solomon et al., 2010, 2016; Solomon & Theiss, 2008; Theiss & Solomon, 2006a). Any transition within the romantic relationship (including but not limited to changes in intimacy level or relationship stage), whether positive or negative in nature, may possibly prompt relational uncertainty, although at this point only a limited number of studies provide evidence for that claim. **Transitions** are conceptualized broadly as changes in identities, roles, routines, or circumstances that may occur at the individual, dyadic, or situational level, which then necessitate modifications to the ways in which the partners relate to one another (Solomon, 2016; Solomon et al., 2016; Theiss, 2018). In the vignette at the start of this chapter, Carmen is anticipating a transition in her relationship that will minimally involve changes in her relational routines and circumstances. The move from a geographically close to a long-distance relationship is a change in external circumstances that may result in decreased interdependence with Cesar, as the need to coordinate day-to-day activities and interactions will be reduced. These changes may also bring about a change in the roles that Carmen and Cesar perform for each other. In a proximal relationship, romantic partners typically play the role of primary companion (among other roles), but distance such as the one that faces Carmen and Cesar may lead to both of them turning to others such as friends or family members for everyday companionship.

External Predictors

Circumstances, situations, or even others outside the romantic relationship may affect perceptions of relational uncertainty within that relationship. Research has long pointed to ways in which members of romantic partners' social networks can serve to facilitate or hinder the development of a stable, satisfying relationship between the partners (Parks, 2011; Sprecher et al., 2002). Social network members such as friends can help facilitate relationships by aiding in romantic partners' management of relational uncertainty (Vallade et al., 2016). On the other hand, social network members can interfere with romantic relationships by engaging in behaviors (or being perceived to engage in behaviors) that increase relational uncertainty. An investigation of **perceived network involvement**, or a person's perceptions of the behaviors that close others (such as family members and close friends) direct toward their romantic relationship, revealed that when close others behave in ways that demonstrate support for the romantic association, relationship uncertainty is diminished (Knobloch & Donovan-Kicken, 2006). Conversely, when close others behave in ways that demonstrate a lack of support for the romantic association, relationship uncertainty is increased.

Outcomes of Relational Uncertainty

In addition to what is known about antecedents of relational uncertainty, extant research has also identified various personal and relationship consequences of relational uncertainty. The outcomes of relational uncertainty are perhaps most indicative of its dark nature, as negative or unpleasant consequences have been identified at cognitive, affective, physiological, and communicative levels. These are discussed next.

Individual Outcomes

Cognitive reactions. One especially common cognitive consequence of relational uncertainty is its tendency to "heighten people's reactivity to dyadic circumstances," which results in more extreme, and more biased, judgments (Knobloch, 2007a, p. 44). In other words, individuals who perceive high levels of relational uncertainty tend to overreact and blow things out of proportion in the context of their relationship. Numerous studies have demonstrated that the perception of irritating partner behavior is exacerbated under conditions of relational uncertainty. Specifically, individuals find their partner's annoying behaviors and habits more severe and threatening to the relationship when they are experiencing relationship doubts (Solomon & Knobloch, 2004; Theiss & Solomon, 2006a; Theiss & Knobloch, 2009). Another common cognitive outcome of relational uncertainty is its tendency to correspond with elevated perceptions of **relational turbulence**. That is, heightened relational uncertainty tends to encourage partners to see their relationship as less stable, more chaotic, and basically in turmoil (Knobloch, 2007b; Knobloch & Theiss, 2010). Relational uncertainty has also been linked to the perception that discussing sensitive topics will be threatening to one's own face and/or to the relationship (Knobloch & Carpenter-Theune, 2004). Such sensitive topics include the state of the relationship, relationship norms, past romantic relationships, topics expected to cause conflict, and relationships/activities with third parties, including social network members and potential romantic rivals.

Affective reactions. The experience of relational uncertainty has been associated with a host of negative emotions, which may be intense at times. Jealousy is an especially common reaction to increased relational uncertainty, which can aggravate the perceived threat of rival third parties (Afifi & Reichert, 1996; Knobloch et al., 2001; Theiss & Solomon, 2006b). Other emotions such as anger, sadness, and fear have also been associated with elevated relational uncertainty, as has the affective experience of hurt (Knobloch et al., 2007; Knobloch & Theiss, 2010; McLaren et al., 2011). A longitudinal study demonstrated relational uncertainty's positive associations with perceptions of the intensity of hurt, intentionality of hurt, and relational harm sustained by the hurt (Theiss et al., 2009).

Physiological reactions. Although research in this capacity is still in its very early stages, studies have revealed an increase in salivary cortisol, a stress hormone, during stressful interactions where relational uncertainty is implicated. For example, during interactions where the romantic partner was behaving in a hurtful manner, partner uncertainty was associated with higher cortisol reactivity (Priem & Solomon, 2011). In addition, a romantic partner's helpful messages of support appear to be less effective in miti-gating stress levels (as assessed via salivary cortisol) under conditions of high partner uncertainty (Priem & Solomon, 2011). Another study revealed that relational uncertainty is indirectly related to elevated cortisol levels through the conflict management behaviors of marital partners (King & Theiss, 2016). More specifically, increased relational uncertainty corre-sponded with attempts to avoid conflict, and attempts to avoid conflict led to elevated amounts of salivary cortisol. In addition, relational uncertainty in the wake of a severe transgression in the context of dating couples has been associated with decreased testosterone, which in turn is associated with less disclosure (Crowley et al., 2018).

Relationship Outcomes

Taken together, the preponderance of evidence suggests that individuals prefer indirect and/or reduced communication when they are experiencing high relational uncertainty. As noted previously, one cognitive consequence of relational uncertainty is the perception that discussing sensitive or charged topics with the romantic partner will be risky. This perception clearly influences behavior, as topic avoidance has been established as a consistent outcome of relational uncertainty across various relationship types in order to avoid awkward, embarrassing, or contentious interactions (Afifi & Burgoon, 1998; Afifi & Schrodt, 2003; Knobloch & Carpenter-Theune, 2004). In the scenario that opened this chapter, Carmen's relational uncer-tainties about the future of her relationship with Cesar are affecting her communication with him, as research evidence would suggest they should. Rather than engaging him directly about where their relationship is going or the upcoming events that will separate them, she would rather avoid discussion of those topics because she anticipates they will cause conflict in the relationship.

Because individuals with high relational uncertainty typically wish to avoid directly talking about sensitive, face-threatening topics like the state of the relationship, more indirect strategies may be used to glean pertinent information about the definition, status, or nature of the relationship (Baxter & Wilmot, 1985). Some of these indirect, covert strategies were termed **secret tests**, which basically represent ways to reduce uncertainty about a partner's commitment to the relationship without directly asking them (Baxter & Wilmot, 1984). The secret tests were discovered by asking college students to describe how they get information about various relationship types: romantic, platonic cross-sex friendships, and cross-sex friendships with romantic potential. From these interviews, six types of secret tests emerged, in addition to a direct strategy, when entailed candidly and openly asking the other about uncertainties in a straightforward manner rather than secretly maneuvering to gain information. Far, far more of the information acquisition strategies reported by the college students in this study were indirect (as opposed to direct) in nature. Further, most of these strategies seem to be used during early stages of developing relationships, a point when relational uncertainty is especially high and communicating directly about those uncertainties feels particularly precarious (Bell & Buerkel-Rothfuss, 1990).

Triangle tests were a very commonly reported secret test in this study, particularly by those who were discussing information acquisition strategies in the context of romantic relationships. Women were also substantially more likely than men to report the use of triangle tests, which entail the creation of three-person triangles to ascertain your partner's feelings about you or their commitment to the relationship. There are two types of triangle tests, which require the presence of some third-party rival—one who is romantically interested in you (a *jealousy test* to see if your partner reacts to this threat by expressing their love for you) or one who is romantically interested in your partner (a *fidelity check*, to see if your partner remains faithful to you when tempted by a rival). Note that these third-party rivals may actually exist (suddenly your ex-partner begins texting you, expressing a desire to get back together, and you tell this to your partner to see if they express jealousy), or a situation may be fabricated to make it appear as though a third-party rival exists (you have a friend of yours—who is unknown to your partner—flirt with your partner at a party to see if they take the bait or stay faithful to you).

Endurance tests were also described quite frequently in the original Baxter and Wilmot (1984) study, again, particularly in the context of romantic relationships. These behaviors entail increasing the partner's relationship costs and/or reducing their relationship rewards, basically to see how much they will put up with from you. The idea here is that if your partner really cares about you and is truly committed to the relationship, they will tolerate such trying behaviors. These endurance tests took three specific forms in this study: behaving negatively toward the partner, making inconvenient requests, and putting oneself down excessively to the point of aggravating the partner. Returning to the vignette that opened this chapter, Cesar could begin making demands of Carmen related to her upcoming move in an endurance test of her love and commitment to him. He might ask her to give up her plans to attend graduate school in Seattle and instead remain with him in Chicago. If she declines, Cesar may see this as an indicator of her lack of commitment to the future of the relationship.

Separation tests were a secret test that was reported often in the context of cross-sex friends with romantic potential. Women were significantly more likely than men to report using this strategy, which involves creating or using distance to gauge the other's depth of feeling for you. On the one hand, the idea is that if the other really cares, then they should have no trouble surviving a temporary physical separation. On the other hand, this strategy might entail placing the onus for initiating contact on the other. For example, you might stop being in touch with or seeing the other for a few days to see how long it takes them to reach out to you.

Also commonly reported in the context of cross-sex friends with romantic potential was the use of *indirect suggestion* tests, which entail using jokes or hints or even nonverbal immediacy behaviors such as touch to imply one's own feelings about/commitment to the relationship, and to assess the partner's reaction to the information that is revealed. Indirect suggestions are a face-saving way to reveal one's own level of interest and commitment, and they allow an opportunity for the partner to communicate their feelings too, all without directly broaching the issue. For instance, you might joke about getting married (e.g., "We've been together so long, we're like an old married couple!"), which gives you an opportunity to see how your partner responds. But because you are ostensibly just joking about it, it is less face threatening than bringing up the issue more directly because it affords you some deniability.

Public presentation tests are secret tests that are more likely to be used in developing relationship stages, as they involve labeling the relationship in front of third parties while the partner is also present. For example, introducing the other as "my boyfriend/girlfriend" for the first time without prior discussion of the label, to see how your partner reacts to your use of the label, constitutes a typical public presentation test. Certain behaviors that communicate to outsiders that the two of you have an intimate relationship (e.g., **tie signs** such as putting your arm around the other's waist, kissing) might also be used in front of outsiders to see how the partner reacts to this obvious public statement about the nature of the relationship.

Perhaps the least manipulative secret test that was discovered is the *third-party* test, in which members of the other person's social network (e.g., your partner's friends) are tapped for information about their interest in you or commitment to the relationship. While this strategy is indirect, it does not have the same element of game playing that can be problematic with other secret tests.

In a follow-up study to Baxter and Wilmot's (1984) original research, an additional secret test was identified in a sample of college students in romantic relationships: *spying* on the partner's oral and written communications in order to gather information about the relationship's definition and status (Bell & Buerkel-Rothfuss, 1990). Interestingly, the differences between women and men that were reported in the initial study on triangle tests were not replicated in this subsequent study. Further, while some support emerged in this study for the notion that people use secret tests when they have a pretty good idea that their partner will respond in ways that make clear their positive feelings about and commitment to the relationship, other research suggests that some secret tests are used when desire for relationship termination is high (Chory-Assad & Booth-Butterfield, 2001).

General Uncertainty Reduction Strategies

Of course, strategies for acquiring information and reducing uncertainty other than secret tests have been articulated, and in fact may be more widely used across relationship types and stages. As part of his research and writings on uncertainty reduction theory, Berger (1979, 1987) identified three general methods of reducing uncertainty.

Passive uncertainty reduction strategies involve noninteractively, unobtrusively observing the target of your uncertainty. Passive information-seeking strategies can be as simple as noticing that a classmate whom you do not know well, but would like to know better, often wears t-shirts that feature the name of your favorite baseball team. The fact that your classmate wears this paraphernalia often probably lets you know—without asking or otherwise intruding upon the person—that they are a fan of the same baseball team that you are. You may use this information at some point to strike up a conversation with this person on the basis of your shared interest. Note that, by definition, passive strategies are unobtrusive in nature. If your observation of another goes too far (i.e., if it becomes noticeable and bothersome or even scary for the target), then this behavior could be characterized as obsessive relational intrusion or even stalking.

Active information acquisition strategies require interaction not with the actual target of your uncertainty, but instead with some third party. Active strategies can take two forms, the first of which looks a lot like the triangle tests that were identified as one type of secret test. In other words, you can manipulate the social environment (i.e., introduce a third-party rival) and see how your partner responds. Alternatively, and perhaps more appropriately, you could simply (and directly) ask some third party—usually, a member of your target's social network—about the target. This strategy corresponds with the third-party strategy that has been labeled a secret test, although as noted previously, this strategy exemplifies some key differences from the other secret tests (e.g., it is not necessarily used in an effort to manipulate or play games).

Interactive uncertainty reduction strategies include direct contact with the target of your uncertainty, undertaken in an effort to gather information that reduces that uncertainty. The simplest way to do this is to ask questions of the target, but the same effect could be accomplished by self-disclosure given the norm of reciprocity, which encourages us to respond to others in kind (Gouldner, 1960). In other words, especially in early relationship stages, others are likely to respond to our self-disclosures with self-disclosures of their own, usually about the same topic and at the same level of intimacy or superficiality (Altman & Taylor, 1973; Berger, 1979). Interactive uncertainty reduction attempts will be enhanced if you create a comfortable (and, if necessary, private) environment for the target and if you demonstrate interest in the target during interactive information seeking attempts.

In recognition of the frequency with which individuals now attempt to acquire information in computer-mediated contexts, **extractive** information-seeking strategies were identified later (Ramirez et al., 2002). Extractive strategies are noninteractive and can be performed without the target's knowledge—as is true of passive strategies. Extractive strategies entail using the information that is available to you online in the form of archived information that is maintained over time (e.g., conducting a Google search and then availing yourself of the information you find, such as social media profiles).

Uncertainty in Mediated Contexts
Acquiring Information Online

While the advent of computer-mediated technologies has changed much about the ways in which people can and do communicate with each other, generally, available research suggests that it has not changed much about the basic ways that individuals attempt to reduce their uncertainty or otherwise acquire information. For example, across several studies investigating communication on social networking sites, the same uncertainty reduction strategies that were identified by Berger are still used across various relational stages, such as getting acquainted and after romantic relationship termination (Antheunis et al., 2010; Tong, 2013). Of course, however, the specific *ways* in which these passive, active, and interactive strategies are carried out has evolved along with technology. As a social networking site, Facebook provides numerous opportunities for passive, active, and interactive information seeking, as well as for information acquisition through extractive methods. Participants in Fox and Anderegg's (2014) study of uncertainty reduction using Facebook across relational stages demonstrated that passive strategies such as looking through the partner's pictures, scrolling through timeline posts, and repeatedly checking their page were commonly used across relationship stages, ranging from before they even met to dating exclusively. In addition, interactive strategies such as liking the partner's status and chatting online were prominent across relational stages. Active strategies such as friending the partner's friends and family members were less commonly used in early relationship stages, unsurprisingly, but increased once the relationship became established. Although evidence related to the extractive strategy is presently quite limited, some research suggests it is used (although less frequently than passive, active, or interactive strategies) in the context of online dating (Gibbs et al., 2011).

Conclusion

As you have learned throughout this chapter, relational uncertainty is a topic that lends itself quite naturally to examination through a dark side lens, due to the primarily negative consequences it has for individuals and their relationships. With that said, it is also clear that too much certainty can be boring for partners and their relationship—and sometimes, ignorance is indeed bliss. You have learned about the various individual, relationship, and external factors that tend to increase the experience of relational uncertainty, as well as its cognitive, affective, physiological, and communicative consequences. As this research makes quite clear, relational uncertainty can have destructive implications and may manifest in the use of manipulative, furtive methods of garnering desired information about one's partner and the romantic relationship. As you have seen, there are other ways of obtaining relationally relevant information that—even if they are more face threatening—may be worth using in the long run for the sake of efficiency, accuracy, and forthrightness. After reading this chapter, you should have a better understanding of what relational uncertainty is; why and when it occurs; the effects it can have on you, your partner, and/or your relationship; and how to (and how not to) communicate under conditions of relational uncertainty.

Discussion Questions

1. In your opinion, are all the sources of relational uncertainty equally troubling, or is there one (or more) types that is/ are especially problematic in terms of negative relational consequences? Explain your thinking.

2. Discuss the various predictors of relational uncertainty. Based on your experience, are any key predictors missing from this list? What are they?

3. Discuss the consequences of relational uncertainty, both positive and negative. Do you think the pros of uncertainty typically outweigh the cons, or vice versa? Explain your thinking.

4. Develop your own examples for each of the seven secret tests (triangle, endurance, separation, indirect suggestion, public presentation, third party, and spying). In your opinion, which one of these secret tests is the "worst" to use in the context of a romantic relationship? Why?

5. Discuss the pros and cons of using each of the four general strategies for reducing uncertainty. Which do you tend to use the most, and why?

Chapter 3

Topic Avoidance and Secrets

Recall the scenario about Carmen and Cesar that opened Chapter 2. Carmen and Cesar have been involved in a serious romantic relationship for about 2 years, but after graduation, their paths appear to be taking them in different directions. Carmen is experiencing a lot of self- and relationship uncertainty, specifically. These doubts cause Carmen to start withdrawing from Cesar. Rather than openly discuss sensitive topics, she tries to avoid discussions that she knows will cause conflict or upset feelings—such as her move to Seattle for graduate school while Cesar begins a job working for his family in Chicago. Further, she starts keeping things from Cesar, such as her desire to move to Seattle early, at least a month before her graduate program begins, rather than spend the entire summer in Chicago with Cesar. The uncertainties that Carmen is experiencing about her own commitment to the relationship and the relationship's viability are influencing her communication with Cesar in the forms of topic avoidance and secret keeping.

Just as relational uncertainties are commonly experienced across various relationship stages, so too can topic avoidance and secrecy permeate interpersonal relationships. Virtually every close relationship is marked by some level of topic avoidance, and even those in healthy relationships often harbor secrets. For example, in this scenario, Carmen's communication with Cesar is diminished as she prefers to avoid the discussion of difficult topics and goes so far as to keep some things secret from him. In this chapter, we begin with a brief discussion of privacy and the dominant theoretical perspective on privacy management processes. Then, we will position topic avoidance and secret keeping as special cases of privacy management, identify some of the more frequently avoided topics and kept secrets, consider some general reasons people say they avoid talking about certain things and keep certain information confidential, discuss some typical consequences of these information management strategy choices, and close with a brief introduction of some criteria for revealing secrets. Although the dark side of topic avoidance and secret keeping is the focus of this chapter, as you will see, these relational behaviors can have positive outcomes—or at least, may not always result in negative consequences.

Information control strategies that take the form of reduced communication have been vilified in part because of the **ideology of openness** that has dominated both laypersons' and scholars' perspective that open communication (i.e., personal disclosures) leads to healthy and happy close relationships (Parks, 1982). The ideology of openness should be especially salient and impactful for individuals who were socialized in low-context, individualistic cultures that value direct, explicit communication, such as the United States (Hall, 1976). Studies conducted with participants in the United States often bear this out. The benefits of openness in close relationships have long been touted in media representations and empirical research, and the concomitant drawbacks associated with information management choices that favor a more circumscribed approach to the sharing of personal information have been made clear (Pennebaker, 1995). Yet, people often prefer to maintain some degree of privacy, and deliberately restricting or withholding information via topic avoidance and secret keeping has both positive and negative consequences. As such, the ideology of openness seems to be an oversimplified approach to the study of information control in close relationships. As many other scholars have argued previously, a more complete picture of these processes recognizes the pros and cons that are associated with both openness and with more restricted information exchange.

Privacy Management

Topic avoidance and secret keeping have been identified as special cases of privacy management (T.D. Afifi, 2007), and a brief discussion of the relationship of these concepts to more general notions of privacy is relevant here. Although self-disclosure is central to the development and maintenance of close relationships, individuals have varying privacy needs that help dictate if and the extent to which information is shared or discussed with others (Altman & Taylor, 1973). Communication privacy management (CPM) theory provides the most comprehensive explanation for the ways in which people establish and preserve control over their privacy boundaries, and the complications that can ensue when these privacy boundaries are breached and preferences regarding the disclosure of private information are disrupted (Petronio, 1991, 2000, 2002).

CPM theory (originally named communication boundary management theory) holds that individuals create symbolic boundaries around information that is considered sensitive or private. Such privacy boundaries protect us when it comes to whether and how private information is concealed from or revealed to another, as they provide a means by which the risks related to self-disclosure can be controlled or managed. Petronio (2016) identifies three basic "operating principles" of CPM theory: private information ownership, private information control, and private information turbulence. **Private information ownership** deals with assumptions about who owns private information. In general, people tend to think that their own private information is theirs to share or not, as they deem appropriate and to whom they deem appropriate. Interestingly, even when people choose to share their personal information with others (called information co-owners in the language of CPM theory), they still believe that decisions about sharing that information more widely should be theirs alone. In other words, just because someone has shared private information with you does not give you the right to share it with anyone else. Only the original owner of the private information should be able to make those choices.

Private information control highlights how individuals create and employ privacy rules in order to regulate the dissemination of their personal information. Privacy rules are guidelines developed between people that regulate what information is shared and how it is disclosed. Numerous factors can influence the development of privacy rules, such as relevant cultural guidelines and idiosyncratic personal preferences regarding more or less openness. Privacy rules are often learned from the norms surrounding the management of private information in one's family of origin. In addition, characteristics of the relationship in question (e.g., closeness, commitment, attraction, liking, trust, relationship type, power differentials), biological sex (e.g., research has established a slight tendency for females to be more disclosive than males, particularly when it comes to more intimate topics), and personal goals/motivations (e.g., to get closer to a romantic partner, to protect oneself from vulnerability) also impact the formation of privacy rules (Petronio et al., 1996). Although privacy rules often become rather routinized, they can be adapted to reflect changes in people's preferences, relational status, and/or situational features. As part of the privacy management process, these privacy rules and collective privacy boundaries must be coordinated and negotiated between or among co-owners of private information.

Finally, **private information turbulence** reflects the difficulties and disruptions that sometimes arise when attempting to coordinate privacy boundaries and information regulation between two or more people. Privacy rules are not always effective in achieving preferred levels of privacy management, and thus they may need to be changed and renegotiated. New life events can sometimes be the cause of this turbulence, such as Carmen and Cesar's change from a geographically close couple to a long distance one in the vignette that opened this chapter. Topics that once might have been open for discussion such as the relationship's future now seem to be forbidden. Turbulence can also be caused by overt breaches (e.g., when a co-owner violates the established privacy rules by revealing the original owner's private information to other parties in a way that is not sanctioned by the original owner) and by privacy violations such as snooping.

Privacy Violations via Mediated Contexts
Snooping

Intrusive behavior can be covert, when it is done without the other's knowledge or permission, or overt, when one pries into or meddles in another's personal business (Petronio, 1994; Vinkers et al., 2011). **Snooping** is a covert intrusive act wherein a person examines another's private communications (e.g., text messages, email) secretly and without permission (Derby et al., 2012). Although snooping does not have to occur via mediated contexts such as your partner looking at your Instagram account when you accidentally leave the app open on your phone, it often does occur in these ways. Newly married couples report never or rarely engaging in intrusive acts (and perceive that their partner never/rarely does either), and only report doing so when they have low levels of trust in their husband/wife and when they perceive a low level of disclosure from the partner (Vinkers et al., 2011). Snooping in the family context (i.e., parental snooping on their adolescents/teens) also appears to be infrequent, according to available empirical research (Rote & Smetana, 2018). Yet, research shows that two thirds of college daters report engaging in snooping behaviors—usually when their partner is taking a shower (Derby et al., 2012; Rote & Smetana, 2018). The college student daters' snooping behaviors primarily entailed going through the partner's text messages, accessing their cell phone more generally, viewing the partner's internet history, or accessing their email. These snooping behaviors were typically motivated by general curiosity in addition to the specific suspicion that their partner was cheating on them. The college student daters agreed that snooping was not okay in early relationship stages, but when in an established monogamous relationship, one fourth agreed that snooping was acceptable. Further, college student daters felt that snooping was justified by the suspicion of a partner's bad behavior, but otherwise agreed that the snooper should feel guilty for this privacy violation. Those who have been cheated on in the past, who feel increased jealousy, who are slightly older, and who are female were more likely to report having snooped on a romantic partner. Research on snooping as a parental monitoring strategy suggests that parents report using it less often than they use other strategies, such as directly asking questions of their adolescent children (Hawk et al., 2015). In this study, snooping appeared to be more of a last resort, used when parents perceive problems in the adolescent child's behavior, the relationship they have with their child, and their ability to effectively parent their child. Snooping has been associated with more negative interactions between parents and teens, and with teens' increased depressive symptoms over time (Rote & Smetana, 2018).

Violations such as snooping are not just problematic from a privacy management perspective. Indeed, such intrusive behaviors may be used in order to gain a form of psychological control over another person, and research has suggested that snooping and more overt intrusive acts (e.g., looking at private information on a computer/phone without permission, monitoring whereabouts, monitoring interactions/friendships) constitute potential forms of digital dating abuse/aggression, as these sorts of privacy invasions provide a way of keeping tabs on a partner (Leff & Vaughn, 1985; Reed et al., 2016). Further, Rote and Smetana (2018) concluded that parental snooping is especially harmful for teens, as it can lead to perceptions of a coercive family environment. As these studies reveal, in addition to the privacy violations that are caused by this behavior, snooping may have a darker purpose: to establish and/or maintain some type of control of another person.

As CPM theory makes clear, privacy—or at least the right to privacy—is highly valued, and the management of privacy is a key consideration even in close relationships where information is more freely shared, comparatively speaking. Although privacy needs differ from person to person, some of the ways in which people attempt to maintain their privacy boundaries and control information are consistent. Topic avoidance and secret keeping are common information control strategies that aid us in regulating information that may be considered private, or even information that is known to others but that is considered too sensitive or difficult for open discussion.

Topic Avoidance and Secret Keeping

Topic avoidance is an intentional act that occurs when people actively, intentionally evade discussion of a particular topic (W.A. Afifi & Guerrero, 1998, 2000). Unlike the related notion of secret keeping, both parties may be aware of the information that is being avoided, but despite this potential awareness, the information is "off the table" in terms of discussion. For example, in the vignette that opened this chapter, both Carmen and Cesar know that Carmen will be moving to Seattle at some point, but she chooses to avoid the topic despite Cesar's awareness of it. While topic avoidance can be used at any time, research suggests that in romantic relationships, topic avoidance is at its highest when intimacy levels are moderate (Knobloch & Carpenter-Theune, 2004).

Secret keeping entails the intentional concealment of information from another, often because it is perceived that revealing the information would be especially risky (T.D. Afifi et al., 2007; Caughlin & Petronio, 2004). For instance, in the vignette that opened this chapter, Carmen is keeping her plan to move to Seattle earlier than expected a secret from Cesar because she anticipates that revealing that information will cause problems in the relationship such as conflict and hurt feelings on the part of her partner. Unlike private information, which other people do not have a right to, secrets may involve information that another person(s) is entitled to know, yet the secret keeper chooses or is otherwise obligated to withhold (Bellman, 1981).

Both topic avoidance and secret keeping appear to be quite prevalent across various ages and relationship types. Studies have established certain topics that are typically avoided or kept secret in close relationships. Guerrero and W.A. Afifi's synthesis of extant work on topic avoidance across close relationship contexts revealed the following frequently evaded topics: current relationship issues (i.e., discussion of relational norms, the status of the relationship, and negative relational behavior), negative life experiences (i.e., past negative personal experiences and failures), dating experiences (i.e., past/present dates, romantic partners, or romantic relationship experiences), sexual experiences (i.e., past/present sexual behavior and preferences), friendships (i.e., current friendships with others, feelings about those friends), and dangerous behaviors (i.e., irresponsible or dangerous behaviors such as drinking, smoking, or skipping school) (W.A. Afifi & Guerrero, 1998; Guerrero & W.A. Afifi, 1995a, 1995b).

Similar topics are sometimes kept secret, but additional secret topics have been reported in past research. Past dating and/or sexual history, sexual affairs, differences of opinion or personality conflicts, romantic interests, expectation of relational termination, mental health issues, physical/psychological/sexual abuse, someone else's secret, pleasant surprises, illegal activities, and drinking/partying have all emerged as information that is kept secret in the contexts of friendships and romantic relationships (Caughlin et al., 2005). Further, secrets are often studied in the family context, and three general types of family secrets have been identified: **taboo secrets**, which involve information or activities that are stigmatized or generally frowned upon by society (e.g., drug or alcohol addiction); **rule violations**, which break the family's rules for acceptable behavior (e.g., abortion, premarital pregnancy); and **conventional secrets**, which include information that is not generally deemed suitable or socially appropriate for discussion (e.g., politics, death, religion, money/finances) (Vangelisti, 1994a; Vangelisti & Caughlin, 1997).

FLIPPING THE SCRIPT

When Secrets Aren't Really Secret

Recently, scholars have begun to research secrets that are only *ostensibly* secret. Called **putative secrets**, these secrets have actually already been discovered by the person the secret is being kept from, but the secret keeper still thinks the information is secret (Caughlin et al., 2009). In other words, if a friend is keeping a secret from you and you find out about it, but you allow the friend to continue to believe that the secret is unknown to you, then the secret has become putative in nature. In the vignette that opened this chapter, if Cesar found out that Carmen was planning to move to Seattle 1 month earlier than expected, yet he did not let her know that he had found out, then that secret would be a putative one (i.e., the secret keeper still believes that the information is secret when it is not).

Initial studies on putative secrets reveals that they are relatively common across various relationship types (e.g., friendships, families, romantic relationships). Typical putative secret topics include past dating/sexual history, infidelity, surprises, physical health issues, substance abuse, drinking/partying, family problems, personality conflicts, and confidence betrayals. Unsurprisingly, research shows that more negatively valenced putative secret topics (e.g., infidelity, confidence betrayals, personality conflicts) result in more hurt and relational distancing than positively valenced putative secret topics (e.g., surprises). In addition, currently managing a putative secret being kept by a romantic partner leads to more conflict with that partner, particularly if the person from whom the secret is being kept is also dissatisfied with the romantic relationship (Aldeis & T.D. Afifi, 2015). How the secret keeper is keeping the putative secret matters as well, with forms of avoidance (i.e., topic avoidance and physical avoidance of the person the secret is being kept from) and overt deception resulting in negative outcomes.

Finally, why the secret keeper is keeping the putative secret matters. When putative secret keepers are thought to be keeping the secret to protect themselves, or just because they tend to be a secretive person in general, the person the secret is being kept from feels more hurt by the putative secret and wants more distance from the secret keeper. This finding is in keeping with available research that identifies these as more selfish motivations for information control, which characteristically have negative relational implications (Bradbury & Fincham, 1990). Yet, when putative secret keepers are thought to be keeping the secret to protect the relationship with the person the secret is being kept from, the same negative associations emerged. This is surprising, as research has consistently shown that information control for relationship protective reasons is generally seen as a prosocial motivation for topic avoidance, and more unselfish motivations are typically associated with more positive relational implications (Caughlin & T.D. Afifi, 2004).

Caughlin et al. (2009) interpret this finding in light of a key difference between topic avoidance and secret keeping. With topic avoidance, the information being avoided is often known to both parties; with secret keeping, only one person is aware of the information. Becoming aware that a close other is keeping a secret from you, as with putative secrets, and perceiving that this is being done in order to protect the relationship, may be taken as an indicator of a weak relationship. Let's return to the example that opened this chapter to illustrate this point. If Cesar finds out that Carmen is keeping the news that she plans to move to Seattle earlier than expected secret from him and he perceives that she is keeping this information secret in order to protect their relationship, then that could be a relatively clear indicator to him that their relationship is on shaky ground if the two of them cannot withstand and work through issues of that nature openly and honestly together.

Consequences of Withholding Information

Revealing secret information to another person and/or engaging in open communication about information that is already known by both parties has been shown to improve people's physical and psychological health (Pennebaker, 1995). Disclosing or otherwise talking about issues can assist in garnering social support from others (sometimes called **support marshaling**), which is especially advantageous when dealing with information that is particularly stressful, upsetting, or difficult to cope with (Crowley, 2015; Derlega et al., 1993). Although concealing information may have positive effects as well, such as increased cohesion among those who are "in on" the secret (e.g., family members), numerous destructive consequences for individuals and their relationships have been associated with withholding information (Vangelisti, 1994a). Hence, topic avoidance and secrecy can be characterized as dark in nature. With that said, recall that both topic avoidance and secrecy are commonly reported even in healthy, happy relationships, which leads to the conclusion that withholding information can be beneficial—or at least may not be overtly harmful.

Personal Consequences

One particularly relevant consequence of secrecy has to do with the **thought suppression** that accompanies keeping a secret (Wegner et al.,

1987). Generally speaking, when we are keeping a secret, we try hard to keep from thinking about that secret (and from perhaps accidentally revealing any information about it). Yet, research has shown that efforts to suppress our thoughts often lead to the opposite effect of **hyperaccessibility**, wherein we actually think *more* about the secret, paradoxically, which may increase the chance that we will leak it (Abramowitz et al., 2001; Wegner, 1989). These ruminative thoughts can become intrusive in nature and may lead us to become fixated on the secret. When actively avoiding a topic, a similar process occurs whereby our thoughts about the topic become invasive and bothersome (Bouman, 2003). Such thought suppression has been shown to result in negative effects for both physical health and psychological well-being, such as a decrease in the secret keeper's self-esteem (Petrie et al., 1998; W.A. Afifi & Caughlin, 2006).

Theory in Practice

Does Thought Suppression Increase the Likelihood of Secret Revelation?

The available research on the negative outcomes of withholding information has largely focused on the thought suppression that accompanies secret keeping. Two theoretical perspectives are especially relevant here: the cognitive preoccupation model of secrecy (Lane & Wegner, 1995) and the fever model (Stiles, 1987). The cognitive preoccupation model holds that secrecy leads to thought suppression in order to prevent accidentally leaking the secret information. But unfortunately, this thought suppression actually increases the number of intrusive thoughts the secret keeper has about the secret information. In turn, these intrusive thoughts lead to increased thought suppression efforts. In this way, the cycle of thought suppression–intrusive thoughts is self-perpetuating and results in cognitive preoccupation with the secret information. The model makes no claims regarding to what degree (if at all) this preoccupation encourages or discourages secret revelation, however. That's where the fever model may be useful.

The fever model claims that withholding information produces intrusive thoughts in the form of **rumination** about that information. Such rumination is uncomfortable and distressing for people; Stiles equates the negative cognitions and affect that accompany this ruminative process to a fever, like the kind that gets higher and higher when you have a physical infection. To stop the ruminative thoughts and the resulting psychological discomfort (i.e., the fever), people want to disclose the secret information as a form of catharsis, to get it out of their system. In other words, the fever model holds that the intensity of distress associated with concealing secret information is associated with increased revelation of that information, and once the secret information is revealed, the distress is relieved.

Taken together, these models illustrate the bothersome nature of ruminative thoughts, and the fever model in particular suggests that when they become distressing enough, the withheld information will be disclosed. Yet, research does not always bear this out. Other scholars have shown that rumination works in combination with identity concerns, such that the identity relevance of the secret can reverse the emboldening effects of rumination on revelation. Secrets that are tied to our identity encourage us to ruminate more, but if we can resist the negative effects of rumination, the same identity-relevant concerns (i.e., the extent to which the secret constitutes an essential component of who we are, how we see ourselves, and how we want others to see us) actually serve to constrain our willingness to share the secret information (W.A. Afifi & Caughlin, 2006).

Relational Consequences

Despite criticisms of the ideology of openness, which was discussed earlier in this chapter, research across various relationship types (e.g., courtship, marriage, parent–child, adolescent/young adults–stepparents) suggests that disclosure is associated with increased relational satisfaction—and conversely, that topic avoidance is associated with decreased relational satisfaction. The same relationship emerges with regard to secrecy, wherein intentionally concealing unknown information from a close other (e.g., a family member) decreases relational satisfaction (see T.D. Afifi et al., 2007).

Notwithstanding the negative outcomes that have been identified for topic avoidance and secret keeping, repressing information is common even in healthy, satisfying relationships. Often the parties involved in a relationship perceive the presence of certain **taboo topics**, which are recognized as off limits for discussion because such conversation would lead to adverse consequences (Baxter & Wilmot, 1985; Rawlins, 1983). Across platonic friendships, friendships with romantic potential, and romantic relationships, commonly identified taboo topics include relationship status, extra-relationship activity (activities and relationships with others outside of the primary relationship), explicit discussion of relational norms, previous relationships with members of the opposite sex, conflict-causing topics, and negative self-disclosures (Baxter & Wilmot, 1985). Taboo topics can be negotiated implicitly, which appears to render them less problematic in close relationships. Put another way, people in relationships do not have to explicitly state that "this topic is off the table," and it may be best not to do so if it can be negotiated more implicitly or communicated more indirectly. In a study of college student dating relationships, explicit negotiation of taboo topics led to decreased relational satisfaction if daters were not highly committed to their romantic relationship (Roloff & Ifert, 1998).

The typicality of topic avoidance and secret keeping, combined with their at times inconsistent relationship with various outcomes, suggests that other considerations are relevant in determining whether information control in the forms of topic avoidance and secret keeping will have detrimental effects. Some of those considerations are discussed below.

Issues That Impact the Consequences of Withholding Information

A key element that should determine how topic avoidance and secrecy affect individuals and their relationships is the degree to which the people involved value open communication and see it as a marker of a good relationship. The general takeaway from the **standards for openness hypothesis** is that evading discussion of some topics is only harmful to the extent that doing so is seen by one or both partners as an indicator that the relationship is not healthy (T.D. Afifi & Joseph, 2009). Women often have higher standards for openness than men. Related to such standards for communication are the rules that people have regarding the appropriateness of certain topics for discussion. While these privacy rules are flexible and have the potential to change, as discussed previously, they tend to become routine and they strongly impact the outcomes of withholding information (Petronio, 2002, 2016). For example, if one of your privacy rules is that the topic of money is not appropriate for discussion, then you won't be troubled by avoidance of that topic. In other relationships where the people involved have different privacy rules, however, avoiding a topic as central as the couple's finances may seem like a red flag. As such, it is important to bear in mind individual differences like these when considering the consequences of topic avoidance and secret keeping.

Sometimes it is the *perception* of how much information is withheld in a relationship that is problematic, as opposed to the actual degree to which topics are being avoided or secrets are being kept. In the context of romantic and parent–adult child dyads, research has shown that the perception of another's topic avoidance has a stronger correlation with dissatisfaction than does either person's actual avoidance (Caughlin & Golish, 2002). In terms of secret keeping, scholars have found that perceived concealment of information by a close other is associated with decreased relational well-being and increased conflict in the context of marriages, and with inferior parenting in the context of adolescent–parent dyads (Finkenauer et al., 2005, 2009). Results like these suggest the possibility that the problem is not with actual, objective levels of topic avoidance and/or secret keeping, but with individuals' perceptions of such information control strategies.

Finally, individuals' underlying motivations for avoiding topics and/or keeping secrets can influence the outcomes of such information regulation attempts. More specifically, the extent to which topic avoidance and/or secret keeping are seen as legitimate, fair, justifiable choices likely depends—at least in part—on why these choices were made in the first place. Several overarching reasons for suppressing or concealing information have been identified in empirical research.

Reasons for Withholding Information

Generally speaking, individuals usually cite a protective desire as their fundamental impetus for withholding information from a close other. The various motivations for topic avoidance and secret keeping have been synthesized according to the extent to which these reasons serve to protect oneself, to protect a close other (e.g., a romantic partner, friend, or family member), or to protect the relationship that one has with the close other (T.D. Afifi et al., 2005; T.D. Afifi & Steuber, 2009). Conversely, sometimes information exchange becomes circumscribed in close relationships not because one wishes to protect the relationship, but because of the desire to end the relationship (Knapp, 1978). Finally, people may choose to avoid topics or keep secrets because of the nature of the information itself, and due to people's inherent desire for information/communication that is of high quality (W.A. Afifi & Guerrero, 2000).

Individual-based motivations. Protecting oneself is one of the most common reasons for keeping secrets, particularly for U.S. residents. The two primary reasons that exemplify this category are the need to maintain a positive identity or face, and the need to protect one's privacy (Guerrero & W.A. Afifi, 1995a; W.A. Afifi & Guerrero, 2000). These are characterized as individual-based motivations because the concern here is primarily—if not solely—about protecting oneself. **Identity management** concerns deal with the need to protect one's identity or face, and entail the desire to avoid being embarrassed, criticized, or judged by another. Identity management concerns are invoked when we wish to avoid the vulnerability that can accompany discussions of sensitive or private information. Across numerous studies and various relationship types (i.e., families and friendships), identity management has emerged as the most important motivator of topic avoidance (W.A. Afifi & Guerrero, 1998; Guerrero & W.A. Afifi, 1995a). **Privacy management** concerns deal with the need for independence and autonomy and the desire to keep private information from others by controlling the extent to which it is discussed/shared. This motivation for topic avoidance is often seen in the family context, where teenagers with higher privacy needs tend to avoid discussing certain topic with their parents (W.A. Afifi & Guerrero, 2000).

Relationship-based motivations. Relationship-focused concerns are often reported to underlie information control decisions, particularly the desire to protect one's relationship (Baxter & Wilmot, 1985; W.A. Afifi & Guerrero, 2000). **Relationship protection** is the stimulus for information control decisions when we wish to safeguard the relationship from harm, and potentially when we wish to enhance the relationship. This desire has been found to be a particularly strong reason for topic avoidance across relationship types (i.e., romantic relationships, friendships, and family relationships), and results in the avoidance of difficult topics that could potentially induce relational conflict. Some research has shown that this motivation works as intended: people who engage in topic avoidance for relationship protective reasons generally do not suffer negative consequences (Caughlin & T.D. Afifi, 2004).

Conversely, and somewhat paradoxically, the same information control strategies can be used to achieve the de-escalation or demise of a close relationship (W.A. Afifi & Guerrero, 2000). **Relationship de-escalation**, then, motivates information control due to the underlying desire to prevent a relationship from becoming closer in nature, or perhaps even to encourage the demise of the relationship altogether. When this motivation is operative, negative topics may still be avoided (e.g., what is the point of discussing difficult, conflict-inducing topics when you anticipate that the relationship will soon end?), but even more positively valenced topics that could augment feelings of closeness are also eluded.

Information-based motivations. In addition to individual- and relation-ship-focused reasons for the use of information control strategies, scholars have also identified information-based motivations for topic avoidance (W.A. Afifi & Guerrero, 2000). Information-based concerns deal with people's desire for high-quality communication and interactions with others. It stands to reason that if communication about an issue is expected to be inferior or frustrating, then it is unlikely that such communication will ensue. More specifically, these information-based motivations include concerns about partner unresponsiveness, futility of discussion, and communication efficacy. Information is withheld due to concerns about **partner unrespon-siveness** when we are worried that the close other will be unhelpful, perhaps because they will think the issue is minor and inconsequential, or because they do not have the knowledge or skills necessary to discuss the issue productively. We might also avoid discussion of a topic due to perceptions of the **futility of discussion**. When we have learned that conversations about a topic with a particular other will be pointless, a waste of time, or uninteresting, we may avoid such conversations due to the overall feeling that talking about it would be fruitless and ineffectual. For example, when two people disagree on an issue that is important to them (e.g., politics), and both are deeply entrenched in their respective positions (e.g., conser-vative versus liberal), attempting to have a constructive discussion about the issue can be like banging your head against a brick wall.

More recently, scholars have identified and begun to research how perceptions of one's own **communication efficacy** are related to decisions to avoid topics or keep secrets (T.D. Afifi & Steuber, 2009). A long history of research on *self-efficacy*—a person's certainty that they can successfully perform the behaviors required to produce a particular outcome—suggests that people are less likely to attempt any behavior or activity about which they do not feel efficacious (Bandura, 1977). Communication efficacy, then, is a specific type of self-efficacy that encompasses one's judgments about their own communication skills and whether they feel able to successfully broach a topic or reveal secret information (W.A. Afifi & Weiner, 2004).

With regard to the example that opened this chapter, it is possible that Carmen is withholding information from Cesar for any number of protec-tive reasons. Keeping information secret that Cesar would find upsetting and does not want to hear protects him—at least in the short term—from facing an unpleasant reality. It also temporarily protects the relationship from premature de-escalation and from any conflict that might ensue when Cesar learns of Carmen's altered plans. Finally, it likely protects Carmen herself from any undesirable consequences, such as a negative evaluation from Cesar. On the other hand, it is also possible that Carmen is keeping her early move to Seattle secret from Cesar because she perceives that the discussion would be futile, or because she lacks the communication efficacy to broach such a difficult topic effectively, or perhaps even in an attempt to de-escalate the relationship (which she already has doubts about, as established in Chapter 2) and hasten its demise. These examples illustrate an important but hitherto undiscussed point about the motivations for withholding information: most decisions to avoid topics and/or keep secrets are likely spurred by multiple, potentially interrelated motivations (Knobloch & Carpenter-Theune, 2004). Put another way, the motivations for topic avoidance and secret keeping are not necessarily mutually exclusive.

Criteria for Revealing Secrets

In addition to the consequences of withholding information, available research has exhibited a focus on understanding individuals' criteria for secret revelation. In the context of family relationships, several criteria for revealing secrets have been identified (Vangelisti et al., 2001). These include considerations of the secret keeper, such as when the secret jeopardizes the secret keeper's welfare or when the revelation will be somehow rewarding for the secret keeper (e.g., approval from the target of the disclosure). They also include considerations of others, such as the target to whom the secret will be disclosed (i.e., anticipating a positive response from the target, trusting the target enough to reveal the information) and the person(s) from whom they require permission in order to tell the secret. They also entail situational considerations, such as when a good opening arises in the conversation, in the interests of disclosure reciprocity, when there is an important (possibly urgent) reason for sharing the secret, or when the secret would likely be exposed anyway.

Informed by this research, the revelation risk model (T.D. Afifi & Steuber, 2009) argues that there are three primary criteria for secret revelation that cut across relationship types (i.e., that are not specific to the disclosure of family secrets). These are catharsis, the target's need or right to know the information, and whether the secret keeper was asked by others or by the target specifically to reveal the information. Together, individuals' criteria for revealing secrets along with their reasons for keeping secrets or withholding information should combine to illuminate various aspects of the secret keeping/revelation process (i.e., when and in what ways the secret will be revealed).

Theory in Practice

The Role of Goals in Disclosure Management Choices

If secret keeping is an intentional, purposeful act (Bok, 1983), then it stands to reason that keeping secrets must allow individuals to achieve some sort of goal—or likely, more than one goal simultaneously. As such, several theoretical perspectives on disclosure management decisions have taken a goals approach, or otherwise consider goals an intrinsic component of disclosure decisions. Various theories exist that can be housed under a multiple goals framework, and they all share a set of basic assumptions about communication, namely that communication is purposeful, that individuals are often in pursuit of several goals at the same time, and that these goals may be in conflict with each other (Caughlin, 2010).

Informed by a multiple-goals perspective, Caughlin and Vangelisti (2009) derived several propositions that are expected to shed light on decisions to conceal or reveal information. In general, they posit that individuals' reasons for keeping secrets (i.e., their goals) and their criteria for revealing secrets should predict various aspects of the secret revelation process, including how they keep their secret, when they will choose to reveal their secret, and how they will reveal their secret. Further, these authors hold that certain ways of concealing secrets and certain ways of revealing secrets should be more successful than other ways in achieving multiple concurrent goals. These authors further predict that the perceived reasons that other people (e.g., romantic partners) keep secrets from us and the criteria that these people use in deciding to reveal secrets to us will be related to our perceptions of relational quality.

Up to this point, extant research on secrets has largely focused on identifying the consequences of keeping secrets and understanding why people choose to reveal their secrets. These areas of inquiry have been focal points of the study of topic avoidance as well, as suggested by the information covered in this chapter. Caughlin and Vangelisti (2009) argue that a multiple goals perspective on secret keeping provides an integrated way of studying both reasons for and consequences of disclosure management choices.

Conclusion

In this chapter, you have learned about the ideology of intimacy, the importance of privacy and privacy management, and the information control strategies of topic avoidance and secret keeping that are used in the service of privacy management. We have discussed some of the consequences of topic avoidance and secret keeping, noting that—while positive outcomes are not unheard of—negative consequences at the individual and relational levels generally result from the use of these strategies. Whether or not negative outcomes obtain, however, often depends on other factors, such as the individuals' standards for openness and the withholder's reasons for topic avoidance and/or secret keeping. After reading this chapter, you should have a better understanding of the differences and similarities between topic avoidance and secret keeping; the types of information that are generally avoided or concealed; the implications of such information control strategies for you and for your close relationships; the elements that may exacerbate or attenuate these effects; and some of the recognized criteria for revealing secret information.

Discussion Questions

1. Compare and contrast topic avoidance and secret keeping. What do they have in common? How are they distinct?

2. Discuss the effects of topic avoidance and secret keeping.

3. What is your take on the ideology of openness? Do you believe that the cornerstone of high-quality, healthy relationships (and generally, any communication with others) is open, intimate disclosure? Why or why not?

4. Identify and discuss the various motivations for information control strategies such as topic avoidance and secret keeping. Which two motivations are most commonly reported?

5. Explain the cognitive preoccupation model of secrecy and the fever model and how they might work together to predict when a secret will be revealed.

Chapter 4

Relationship Transgressions

Sometimes romantic relationships are damaged or even come to an end through no particular fault of the partners involved. Couples may grow apart, fall out of love, or find that life is taking them in different directions, as with Carmen and Cesar in the previous chapters. Sometimes, however, romantic partners knowingly or even unknowingly misbehave and break important relational rules. Imagine if Cesar repeatedly made intentionally hurtful comments to Carmen, or if Cesar displayed a lot of unwarranted jealousy toward Carmen, or if Carmen frequently lied to Cesar about important matters, or if Carmen had cheated on Cesar. These are commonly identified relational transgressions, and although they vary in perceptions of severity, they typically have important—sometimes drastic—implications for the romantic partners, their relationship, and sometimes even those outside of the romantic relationship.

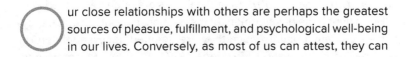

ur close relationships with others are perhaps the greatest sources of pleasure, fulfillment, and psychological well-being in our lives. Conversely, as most of us can attest, they can also entail any number of undesirable and challenging experiences that lead to negative affect, stress, and general dissatisfaction. Close others are often those who have the power to inflict the most harm on us, and it is virtually inevitable that they will do so at some point (Fincham, 2000; Rusbult et al., 1991). Even if close others such as relational partners never engage in severe bad behaviors such as abuse, stalking, or infidelity, arguably minor bad behaviors are a commonplace source of tension, negative emotion, and conflict.

The focus of this chapter is on relationship transgressions, a term that covers a variety of offenses that are often committed by close others (i.e., romantic partners, friends, and family members). In this chapter, we will consider the conceptualization of relationship transgressions and identify commonly committed transgressions in different types of relationships. We will also discuss the various factors that come into play when evaluating different transgressions and how these evaluations impact the personal and relational consequences of transgressions. Finally, we will close with a discussion of extradyadic considerations that become relevant when transgressions occur.

Transgressions in Interpersonal Relationships

People in close relationships often commit **relationship transgressions**, or violations of implicit or explicit rules for appropriate behavior within the context of the relationship in question (Metts, 1994). Generally speaking, rules stipulate expected and preferred relational behavior, while at the same time prohibit inappropriate or unacceptable behavior. Relational rules of conduct are often implicitly inferred or assumed rather than directly or explicitly stated, but they may also be openly named and negotiated. More implicit rules may stem from larger societal and cultural standards of suitable relational behavior (e.g., in the United States, romantic relationships are usually expected to be monogamous and infidelity is disdained as abhorrent; Betzig, 1989), while more explicit rules tend to emerge as unique to the relationship at hand (e.g., Carmen and Cesar appear to have mutually agreed that the topic of her move to Seattle is off limits for discussion; Metts & Cupach, 2007). Relational rules are often negotiated and established during the development of the relationship, but of course they may emerge at any point in which they are deemed necessary in order to better navigate the relationship (Metts, 1994). Although transgressions are sometimes defined in other ways (e.g., as any behavior that hurts, devalues, or victimizes the target, or simply as synonymous with infidelity), the rule-based conceptualization is preferred due to its inclusivity and its application to various relational types (Metts & Cupach, 2007).

Because *transgression* is a broad term that covers a variety of offenses, it may be tempting to characterize anything your partner does that you do not like or that you disagree with as a relational transgression. However, Metts (1994) argues that transgressions constitute relational disturbances because they have three major features: (a) salience, (b) focus, and (c) consequence. Transgressions are *salient* because they have implications for the individuals who have experienced the offense and for their relationship. Transgressions have *focus* because they violate specific standards of acceptable relational behavior that can be identified by the affected parties in the relationship. Finally, transgressions have *consequence* in that they require some kind of redress attempt in order to assuage their negative impact.

If you recall what you learned from Chapter 1 of this textbook, it may seem to you that the concept of relational transgressions has some conceptual overlap with **aversive interpersonal behaviors**. You will remember that aversive interpersonal behaviors deprive people of positive outcomes or rewards and/or serve to inflict negative outcomes or costs on the target (Kowalski, 1997). Transgressions, too, could be said to constrain rewards and impose costs on the target, and the concept has much in common with aversive interpersonal behaviors. Yet, the term *aversive interpersonal behaviors* has been used a bit more broadly to describe irritations and annoyances (e.g., nagging your partner, behaving arrogantly) that, while certainly not preferred, perhaps do not rise to the level of breaching a relational rule for appropriate behavior. That said, both terms cover various negative behaviors and events, but the term *transgression* is used most often in the communication discipline with regard to more serious offenses (e.g., infidelity).

Frequently Committed Transgressions

Transgressions are common occurrences, as indicated previously, with adults reporting that they have been the victim of a betrayal of some sort in nearly half of their relationships with others (i.e., romantic, family, friends, coworkers; Jones & Burdette, 1994). Transgressions are most often examined within heterosexual romantic relationships, including marriage, although clearly they are not restricted to that context. Sexual infidelity is the prototypical relational transgression, and it is often identified as the worst and most damaging transgression—especially when extradyadic sexual activity is coupled with emotional infidelity (Bachman & Guerrero, 2006; Hall & Fincham, 2006; Thompson, 1983). After sexual intercourse with some third party, college students identify wanting to date others or actually dating others, deception about some important issue, and flirting/kissing/making out with some third party as behaviors they consider transgressions in the context of a romantic relationship (Metts, 1994).

Other transgressions noted by college students include privacy violations, such as betraying another's confidence or keeping important information secret; disregarding the primary relationship in some way, such as forgetting/changing plans or special occasions, breaking promises, not being there when needed, and failing to reciprocate expressions of love and commitment; displaying unwarranted jealousy; perpetrating physical violence/abuse; using unfair or inappropriate conflict behaviors (e.g., kitchen-sinking, or throwing all of your past mistakes back in your face even if the conflict does not have anything to do with those past mistakes); making negative comparisons to others; lacking sensitivity or consideration; and terminating the relationship without warning or explanation (Metts, 1994; Metts & Cupach, 2007).

Across various relationship types (i.e., married partners, dating couples, same-sex friends, opposite-sex friends, coworkers, and family members), noncollege student adults reported many of the same transgressions in their relationships, including affairs, deception, having a confidence betrayed, lack of support, being ignored or avoided or excluded, being criticized, and being gossiped about (Jones & Burdette, 1994). Other transgressions have been identified as well, such as violating another's desired intimacy level, neglecting a close other, substance abuse, deviant (sexual) behavior, and verbal aggression (Cameron et al., 2002; Emmers-Sommer, 2003).

Consequences of Transgressions

Transgressions are disruptive, especially when we are the victim of them as opposed to when we are the perpetrator (Cameron et al., 2002). They negatively impact the quality and durability of the relationship, and they can precipitate relationship dissolution and other negative relational consequences (Dillow, 2016). Some research has found that severe transgressions (i.e., infidelity, physical aggression, and deception about important issues) lead to the termination of romantic relationships (Baxter, 1986; Cupach &

Metts, 1986). Yet, other work reveals that relationships often persist despite major relational transgressions, although the quality and closeness of the relationship is usually compromised (Jones & Burdette, 1994; Jones et al., 1999). Perhaps surprisingly, some research even suggests that marriages and courtships are at times not appreciably impacted by, and in fact may even improve after, transgressions have occurred—even serious transgressions such as sexual infidelity (Charny & Parnass, 1995).

The unanticipated positive outcomes that have been reported after the disclosure of an extramarital affair are both personal and relational, and include becoming more assertive, taking better care of and improving oneself, growing closer to each other, prioritizing the family unit, and realizing the importance of good relational communication (Olson et al., 2002). Of course, these examples make clear that it really is not the transgression itself that improves the relationship (i.e., an extramarital affair does not necessarily or naturally lead to increased closeness between spouses). Instead, it seems likely that some sort of pro-relationship transformative processes occur between the partners following the relationship transgression in these cases. Rusbult and her colleagues posit that the ways in which a person responds to their partner's relational transgressions may be one of the critical components of relationship quality and stability, noting that our usual response to bad behavior within a close relationship is to react negatively or destructively (particularly for distressed couples). However, in certain instances, we can modify our natural tendencies toward responding to negativity in kind and instead react constructively to bad behavior. This is **accommodation**, and it represents one way that "damage control" can be enacted in a relationship (Rusbult et al., 1991). The results from Rusbult et al.'s (1991) work indicate that decisions to accommodate or not are affected by a person's level of commitment to the relationship. Specifically, personal commitment (i.e., attraction to the partner, attraction to the relationship, and relationship identity) affects an individual's willingness to accommodate, such that more committed individuals are more likely to engage in accommodation.

The target of the transgression's perceptions of the offense and the person who committed it (e.g., attributions of responsibility, perceived motives for commission) and post-transgression factors (e.g., accommodative processes, the degree of conflict caused by the transgression, whether forgiveness is sought and granted, improved communication between the couple, the decision to recommit to the relationship) tend to dictate the degree to which transgressions are relationally destructive (Buunk, 1987; Dillow, 2019; Spring, 1996).

Although any transgression typically causes increased stress and negative emotions, even if only temporarily, transgressions are distinguishable often from even a very young age on the basis of how severe they are and how personally responsible the perpetrator is for the transgression (Fehr & Baldwin, 1996; Fitness, 2001; Slomkowski & Killen, 1992). The personal and relational outcomes of transgressions vary based on these considerations, in addition to others such as the motivation for committing the transgression and qualities of the relationship before the offense was committed.

Severity of the Transgression
Partner and relationship consequences of sexual infidelity and other transgressions are impacted by the transgressed-against partner's perception of the severity of the rule violation, and transgressions vary in the extent to which they are typically evaluated as more or less severe. The nature of the behavior itself is certainly a factor here (e.g., accidentally hurting another's feelings is generally seen as less severe than inflicting physical harm on another), as are other issues including whether the transgression is known to members of the social network (Vaughan, 1986). When transgressions are known to others outside the primary relationship, they can be particularly embarrassing and are thereby usually considered more severe in nature (Metts, 1994).

In addition, perceptions of severity are potentially tied to the extent to which the rule that was violated has been established explicitly (versus implicitly) and whether the transgression has occurred previously. Breaking explicitly stated rules, especially more than once, carries with it the presumption of intent on the part of the transgressor, and transgressions that are perceived by the offended person to have been intentionally committed are typically evaluated as more severe in nature (Metts, 1994).

Responsibility Attributions for the Transgression
The outcomes of transgressions are also influenced by the offended person's responsibility attributions for the offense. Attributions of responsibility are adaptive; identifying who harmed us and why may help us avoid additional harm in future (Fincham, 2000). Attributions of responsibility are also quite common, particularly for negative events and behaviors, as people have a natural motivation to try to understand why such things happen.

Theory in Practice

Attribution Theory and Relationship Transgressions

Attribution theory (Heider, 1958) deals with the ways in which people make sense of their own and others' behavior. We make **attributions**, or develop explanations for, the causes of behaviors (both our own and other people's) and events that happen in our lives. In other words, when a romantic partner commits a relational transgression, we make efforts to determine why they did and how personally responsible they are for the bad behavior. In general, attributions allow us to determine whether a behavior like a transgression was committed due to internal or external causes. We determine this via three considerations about the behavior: its locus of control, its stability, and its controllability (Weiner, 1985). Locus of control has to do with whether we perceive that the behavior was committed due to something internal to our partner (e.g., some personal trait or predisposition, such as high promiscuity or sensation seeking) or due to some external factors outside of our partner (e.g., some circumstance or situational feature, such as being under the influence of alcohol/drugs). Stability concerns our perception of whether the behavior is relegated to a one-time occurrence or if it can be expected to occur repeatedly, over time. Controllability has to do with our perception of whether the behavior was caused by something under our partner's control (e.g., skill, self-control) or by something out of their control (e.g., luck, fate, actions of another).

Internal attributions result when we determine that a behavior stemmed from an internal locus of control, is stable and therefore likely to be repeated in future, and was under the perpetrator's control. **External attributions** result when we conclude that a behavior stemmed from an external locus of control, is temporary and therefore unlikely to occur again, and is not controllable by the perpetrator. While external attributions may lead us to evaluate our partner as less blameworthy, perhaps because we think the behavior was not intentionally committed, internal attributions generally lead to evaluations of more partner blameworthiness for the behavior (Harvey, 1987). Further, internal attributions about a romantic partner's behavior negatively impact relational quality indicators such as satisfaction, communication, and the desire to continue the romantic relationship (Karney et al., 1994; Mongeau & Schulz; Pearce & Halford, 2008). Thus, attributions of responsibility play a crucial role in making sense of a romantic partner's relationship transgression, deciding who to blame for the transgression, and how we will ultimately react to the transgression.

Our attributions are influenced by characteristics of the primary relationship (e.g., how satisfied we are with our romantic partner, how well we know and much we trust our romantic partner) and our knowledge of the situation (Fincham & Bradbury, 1989; Holmes & Rempel, 1989). Yet, generally speaking, we have an intrinsic tendency to attribute our own transgressions more positively/externally but attribute our partner's transgressions more negatively/internally; this is called the **fundamental attribution error** (Jones & Burdette, 1994). If the offended partner makes internal and stable attributions for a severe transgression such as intimate partner violence (e.g., my romantic partner shoved me because they are a violent and abusive person) instead of attributing the bad behavior to external, temporary causes (e.g., my romantic partner shoved me because they lost their temper in the heat of the moment and lost control), then the transgression is difficult to forgive and is likely to result in especially negative outcomes.

Pre-Transgression Relationship Qualities

The consequences of transgressions are also affected by the quality of the romantic relationship before the transgression was committed. Research on **positive illusions** suggests that we have a tendency to see our partner through rose-colored glasses, exaggerating their positive attributes while also downplaying the importance of their faults and mistakes (Murray et al., 2003). In other words, our need to be absolutely sure that we are with the "right" person leads us to idealize our romantic partner. The body of research on positive illusions confirms its self-fulfilling nature, suggesting that transgressions—especially more minor ones—may be evaluated as less severe and therefore less relationally damaging when we have positive illusions about our romantic partner.

The influence of other pre-transgression relationship qualities on the consequences of relationship transgressions has been examined as well. A number of investment model features have been studied in the context of relational transgressions (Rusbult, 1980). The investment model identifies three characteristics of relationships (particularly romantic relationships) that serve to increase one's commitment to that relationship. Commitment, in turn, impacts a number of outcomes, including but not limited to responses to relational transgressions.

Theory in Practice

The Investment Model and Relationship Transgressions

Arguably, the investment model provides one of the most well-evidenced explanations for why romantic relationships persist over time, and it has been shown to successfully account for a variety of relational decisions and behaviors (such as those that are implicated in the aftermath of a romantic partner's relational transgression). As conceptualized by Rusbult (1980, 1983), the investment model is comprised of four major components: satisfaction, investment, quality of alternatives, and commitment. Rusbult (1980) defined satisfaction as "positivity of affect or attraction to one's relationship" (p. 102). In addition, investments in a relationship are thought of as those resources that we devote to a relationship that we cannot get back if the relationship ends. Investments are further categorized in two ways: extrinsic (tangible resources, such as places of residence, vehicles, and other material possessions) and intrinsic (intangible resources, such as emotional energy and time). Furthermore, quality of relational alternatives is conceptualized as "the perceived desirability of the best available alternative to a relationship" (Rusbult et al., 1998, p. 359). Relational alternatives are typically thought of as other potential relational partners, but note that a viable and attractive alternative to the current relationship may be simply choosing not to be involved in any romantic entanglements. These three components—satisfaction, investment, and quality of alternatives—combine to predict commitment, which is thought of as "the tendency to maintain a relationship and to feel psychologically attached to one's relationship" (Rusbult, 1980, p. 102). More specifically, increased satisfaction and investment, along with decreased perceptions of quality of relational alternatives, combine to predict increased commitment to a relationship. Decades of research exists to support the workings of the investment model in explaining reactions to transgressions, decisions to maintain romantic involvements, and stay-or-leave relationship decisions.

In an initial investigation establishing the relationships among the investment model variables, Rusbult (1983) discovered that when satisfaction and investment levels are high, and the perceived quality of alternatives is low, an individual's commitment to a romantic relationship is increased. This increased commitment level then leads to a greater likelihood of long-term continuance of the romantic relationship. In a similar investigation, Drigotas and Rusbult (1992) also found that commitment carried the most weight with individuals when deciding whether to terminate or maintain romantic relationships. These results have been replicated in samples of varying demographics, including African American dating couples (Davis & Strube, 1993), married and dating partners, couples with differing educational and income levels (Rusbult et al., 1986b), and friends as well as romantic partners (although the relationship between satisfaction and commitment was stronger for romantic partners than for friends; Lin & Rusbult, 1995).

The investment model not only impacts decisions to dissolve or to continue romantic involvements, as noted previously, but also the ways in which transgressions are handled within romantic relationships. In a series of studies, Rusbult and her colleagues demonstrated that increased levels of commitment to a relationship result in the likelihood that an individual will accommodate (rather than retaliate) when a romantic partner commits a relational transgression (Rusbult et al., 1998, 1991). Other related research also supports the assertion that the pre-transgression relational qualities identified by the investment model impact individuals' post-transgression responses and decisions in romantic relationships in meaningful ways.

Increased investment in the romantic relationship and commitment to our romantic partner encourage more positive responses to their transgressions (e.g., attempts to repair the relationship) and discourage more negative responses (e.g., ruminating about the relationship's future; Roloff et al., 2001). Increased investment and satisfaction also lead to other positive responses, such as more integrative communication (i.e., positive, productive communication with the goal of resolving the issue; may entail questions and explanations, sharing of affective states, and negotiating ways to prevent the issue in future); and decreased perceptions of quality alternatives are associated with increased post-transgression relationship repair efforts (Guerrero & Bachman, 2008). While not components of the investment model, love and affection also represent pre-transgression relationship characteristics that have also been linked to the decision to remain with a partner after a transgression involving violence (Strube & Barbour, 1984).

Transgressions and Social Networks

When it comes to relationship transgressions or relational distress, it is not enough to consider what transpires between the romantic partners who are directly involved. Parks (2011) said it best when he noted that "what happens in a relationship often does not stay in that relationship" (p. 362). Indeed, relationships impact and are impacted by social network members such as close friends and family, whose behaviors and communication may serve to facilitate, hinder, or even overtly damage romantic relationships (Driscoll et al., 1982; Parks & Adelman, 1983; Sprecher et al., 2002). Some research suggests that we may wish to hide relational difficulties (such as a partner's relationship transgression) from extradyadic sources in order to garner and/or preserve our social network members' approval of and support for our romantic relationship (Crowley, 2012). Other research suggests that relational problems are a common topic of discussion with social network members such as close and trusted friends, and that we engage in such **extradyadic communication** about relational difficulties for a variety of reasons, such as to marshal social support and to assist in coping with relationship challenges (Burleson & MacGeorge, 2002; Goldsmith, 2004; Julien & Markman, 1991).

FLIPPING THE SCRIPT

Does Talking to Others About Our Partner's Bad Behavior Really Make Us Feel Better?

When we experience something negative, such as a romantic partner's relational transgression, we often turn to social network members to help us cope with the negative relational event and generally to feel better about what has happened. Such **support marshaling** efforts entail a person's attempts to garner more desired support from social network members, while at the same time reducing the amount/type of undesired support that is received (Crowley, 2016; Crowley & Faw, 2014). But to what extent does talking to social network members about relational difficulties actually help us receive desirable social support and feel better about the problem?

An expanding area of scholarly inquiry has recently emerged, focusing specifically on **support gaps** that are experienced when communicating with social network members in the wake of transgressions. Research has found that, after conversations with social network members about a romantic partner's relationship transgression, victims report a **support deficit**, or receiving less social support than they desired (Pederson et al., 2020). This is unfortunate, because receiving adequate or even greater than desired levels of high-quality social support (i.e., a **support surplus**) from a social network member can result in less negative affect for the victim of the offense (i.e., feeling less dejected, stressed, angry, and hurt; Pederson et al., 2020; Pederson & McLaren, 2017).

Further, interactions with social network members can influence the offended person's post-transgression behavior toward the transgressor. When the transgressed-against person receives emotional support and validation from social network members, they are less likely to forgive the transgressor (Eaton & Sanders, 2012). Conversely, other research has shown that those who receive high levels of emotional support expressed less motivation to avoid the transgressor (Pederson et al., 2020). Moreover, when social network members validate the transgressed-against person's experience (i.e., communicate that the offended person's perspective is correct and that they have a right to be angry), the transgressed-against person's desire for revenge against the transgressor is increased (Eaton, 2013). Although these findings are clearly somewhat mixed in nature, they reveal the important impact that social network members can have—often through their provision of social support during difficult times—on post-transgression relational behaviors and decisions.

In an exploratory investigation, numerous motives for extradyadic communication about negative relational events were identified, both from the romantic partner's and the social network member's (i.e., in this case, a friend's) perspective (Vallade et al., 2016). Romantic partners report discussing negative relational events that they have experienced with their friends for reasons such as garnering social support or advice, venting negative feelings or talking through the issue, reducing uncertainty, seeking validation or perspective, wanting to feel better, or simply because it can be entertaining.

During conversations about the transgressed-against partner's relational difficulties, friends in the confidant role report somewhat conflicting motivations. On the one hand, they want to comfort, distract, or appease the person who is experiencing the relational problem, often attempting to spare their feelings and protect the friendship from harm. Yet, during focus group discussions, friends in the confidant role often exhibited frustration with discussions of their friend's relationship problems, especially when negative relational events and subsequent conversations about them occurred often and when the transgressed-against partner did not really listen to or take the friend's advice or perspective into account. These confidant friends were especially likely to report saying what they thought the other person wanted to hear about the negative relational event. On the other hand, friends are sometimes motivated to provide an honest perspective about the romantic relationship and the negative relational event, even when that honesty might compromise the quality or closeness of the friendship (Zhang & Merolla, 2006).

FLIPPING THE SCRIPT

The Unintended Consequences of Discussing a Partner's Transgression With Social Network Members

During times of relational distress, such as when a romantic partner commits a relationship transgression, it is not uncommon that we would share the information with members of our social network for any number of reasons (e.g., for catharsis, to repair our image, to garner social support). Yet, such disclosures may have unintended consequences, particularly if the romantic relationship persists despite the transgression. A large body of research has demonstrated the importance of social network members' (i.e., family and friends') support for dating and (especially) married relationships, as such support affects the relationship's quality and continuance (Bryant & Conger, 1999; Greeff, 2000; Parks, 2011; Parks & Adelman, 1983; Parks et al., 1983; Sprecher & Felmlee, 1992, 2000). However, social network members are not automatically or necessarily supportive of such relationships and can in fact be critical of them despite the expectation of their support (Leslie et al., 1986). Further, some research has shown that close friends are even less forgiving than the victims of the transgression themselves, especially if the transgressor does not apologize or otherwise make amends for their bad behavior (Green et al., 2008; Pederson & Faw, 2019).

As such, the (perhaps natural) tendency to blame our partner and speak more negatively of them when discussing a severe transgression that they have committed with our friends or family members is likely to result in more negative perceptions of the partner and less support for the romantic relationship from social network members going forward (Gray & Silver, 1990; Zhang & Merolla, 2006). Another unintended consequence of discussing a partner's severe transgression with social network members is the negative effect that such knowledge can have, even for those outside the romantic relationship. Some social network members themselves feel a need for social support in the wake of learning of a transgression experienced by a close other due to the negative emotional outcomes they personally experience, despite being "only" indirectly affected by the transgression (Faw & Pederson, 2018). Further, when social network members share the coping experience with the victim, approaching the problem of the transgression and its aftermath as something to be handled together (i.e., **communal coping**; Lyons et al., 1998), the social network members report perceiving the transgression as more intentional and feeling more angry and hurt toward the transgressor (Pederson & Faw, 2019). Although romantic partners often naturally rely on their network of family and friends in the wake of experiencing a transgression, it is clear that such reliance has unintended consequences for all parties involved, and for their relationships with each other.

Beyond whether and why romantic partners discuss relational troubles such as transgressions with others outside the primary relationship, the way in which they discuss these issues is both affected by and affects qualities of the romantic relationship. Generally speaking, when our romantic partner commits a transgression, we can discuss that transgression with others outside the relationship in **transgression-minimizing** or **transgression-maximizing** ways (Vallade & Dillow, 2014). Transgression-minimizing communication attempts to downplay or maybe even justify our partner's transgression, perhaps absolving our partner of responsibility for their behavior and generally minimizing the overall offensiveness of the act and/or our partner's role in its commission. Transgression-maximizing communication, on the other hand, plays up the culpability and offensiveness of our partner's transgression, often by openly accusing, blaming, and criticizing our partner. Transgression-maximizing messages are more likely when the romantic relationship is in distress, and when the partner's transgression is perceived as more severe by the victim (Gray & Silver, 1990; Vallade & Dillow, 2014).

Yet, when transgressions are committed in relatively high-quality relationships (i.e., where victims report being more invested, satisfied, and committed, and perceiving fewer quality alternatives to the relationship prior to the transgression), the transgressed-against partner is less likely to engage in transgression-maximizing communication with social network members (i.e., friends and family)—although it must be noted that these positive relational qualities did not go so far as to encourage victims to use transgression-minimizing communication (Vallade & Dillow, 2014). When transgressed-against partners do use transgression-maximizing extradyadic communication, not surprisingly, this leads to subsequent decreases in their relational quality over time (i.e., decreases in the offended person's investment, satisfaction, and commitment, and increases in perceived quality of relational alternatives).

Conclusion

As you have learned in this chapter, relationship transgressions are violations of implicitly or explicitly stated relationally relevant rules that usually have negative or destructive implications for intimate partners and their relationships (and even potentially for their relationships with social network members outside of the relationship). Although transgressions encompass a number of different types of rule violations, the prototypical transgression is sexual infidelity, which is identified as the top transgression in college student dating relationships. You have learned here that the magnitude of the transgression's impact is based on factors such as the severity of the transgression, the offended partner's responsibility attributions for the transgression, and certain characteristics of the relationship before the transgression occurred (e.g., investment, satisfaction, quality of alternatives, and commitment). Severe offenses, those for which negative attributions are made by the offended partner, and those that occur in relationships that are generally less satisfying and committed typically have more destructive consequences. The knowledge that you take away from this chapter should help you understand how you evaluate transgressions in your own relationships and why you make those judgments. If you wish to maintain your relationship despite experiencing a transgression, some of what you learned in this chapter should help you see how this is possible.

Discussion Questions

1. Discuss relationship transgressions by thoroughly defining the concept and distinguishing it from related concepts. What are the top transgressions identified in the context of romantic relationships? What is considered the prototypical relationship transgression?

2. Discuss the three major factors that impact the consequences of relational transgressions in romantic relationships. How do you think these factors might work together to determine transgression consequences? Do you see any areas of contradiction among the factors?

3. Explain attribution theory, making sure to delineate how the attributions influence judgments of and responses to relational transgressions.

4. Explain the investment model, making sure to discuss how the various components work together (i.e., how they impact each other) and how they impact post-transgression relational decisions and behaviors.

5. Discuss the motivations for conversations about transgressions between victims and social network members from the perspective of both parties. What kind of dilemmas do social network members (i.e., friends) report experiencing in these types of conversations? Discuss the advantages and drawbacks of victims choosing to talk about their partner's relational transgressions with social network members, from both the victim's and the social network member's perspectives.

Chapter 5

Hurtful Communication

Mara and Cate have been in a romantic relationship for 2 years, and they recently decided to move in together. Shortly thereafter, Mara began an intensive graduate program in addition to maintaining her full-time work schedule. Naturally, this limited the amount of time that Mara has available to spend with Cate. One day, when Mara calls Cate to tell her that she will be working late and won't be home for dinner again, Cate responds by saying, "We never spend time together lately because you're always too busy with work and school. You don't act like I'm important to you anymore. You don't treat me like I'm a priority in your life. If you don't start making time for me and our relationship, I'm going to end things." Mara is surprised, as she did not realize how upset Cate was about the new schedule. Mara is also disheartened because she perceives that there's very little she can do to correct the problems Cate has identified, other than drop out of school (which she does not want to do) or cut back on her work hours (which isn't feasible, given her financial situation and the fact that she now has to pay for her graduate education in addition to her other expenses). Yet, Mara is happy in her relationship with Cate and does not want it to end. She responds to Cate by saying "You're right. I have to make time for you and our relationship if I expect this relationship to work. I'm sorry I haven't made you a priority lately. You are the most important thing in my life, and I want to make sure you know that."

As discussed in the previous chapter on relational transgressions, even in the closest of relationships, it is unavoidable that partners will at times engage in behaviors that are harmful to each other. These negative behaviors are typically termed *relationship transgressions*, which were defined in Chapter 4 as violations of rules that stipulate acceptable and unacceptable behavior within the context of the relationship (Metts, 1994). Transgressions are most often examined within romantic relationships, although of course they are not limited to that context. In developing close relationships, romantic partners and friends negotiate these rules for appropriate behavior implicitly and/or explicitly, and these rules serve as important guidelines throughout the relationship. It follows that violations of such rules are disruptive, as they negatively impact the quality and longevity of the relationship. Violations of these relationally relevant rules can lead to destructive relational consequences, including relational termination. Perhaps counterintuitively, they also may indirectly lead to more prosocial relational outcomes.

Many relational transgressions will be considered throughout the remainder of this textbook, some of them quite serious in nature (i.e., sexual and emotional infidelity, aggression and violence, obsessive relational intrusion and stalking, bullying, and cyberbullying, and destructive conflict). In this chapter, we turn our attention to the relational transgression of hurtful communication and the related affective experience of hurt, more generally. We will discuss various types of hurtful communication, numerous considerations that influence the degree of hurt feelings experienced as a result of a hurtful message or event, the connection between physical pain and social or symbolic pain (such as that caused by another's hurtful communication or behaviors), and we will close with an overview of common responses to hurtful messages.

The Experience of Hurt

The feeling of **hurt** is experienced when people perceive themselves to be emotionally wounded by the communication and/or actions of another, or by their perception of another's failure to do or say something that was desired or expected (Feeney, 2004; Leary et al., 1998; Vangelisti, 2007). Some scholars have argued that the distinguishing feature of hurt is actual or perceived **devaluation** of oneself or one's relationship with another (Leary et al., 1998). When a close other says or does something that leads us to believe they feel we are not very important or valued, and/or that we are easily replaceable, then devaluation has occurred. The experience of hurt is negative in nature, and it typically co-occurs with a number of specific emotions, including anger, sadness, guilt, shame, and fear. Hurt has been conceptualized as a relationship transgression in its own right (e.g., when you hurt a close other intentionally) and as the product of a transgression (e.g., a romantic partner's sexual infidelity) that usually entails relational devaluation and leads to feelings of vulnerability (Feeney, 2005; Folkes, 1982; Vangelisti, 2001; Vangelisti et al., 2005).

Although scholars have different perspectives on how hurt is induced, Vangelisti (2015) identifies three elements that are shared by most extant conceptualizations of hurt. In the first place, hurt is clearly an interpersonal experience in that we feel hurt as a result of someone else's behavior (or their failure to behave as expected/desired) toward us in the context of our interactions/relationship with that person. Secondly, hurt entails some form of symbolic, affective, psychological wounding at the hands of someone else, often a close other as opposed to a stranger or acquaintance (Leary et al., 1998). And finally, hurt occasions the attendant feeling of vulnerability, as we often experience hurt at the hands of a close other (implicitly or explicitly, purposefully or accidentally), perhaps as a result of a relationship transgression, and there is always the possibility that our loved one may hurt us again in future.

Hurtful Communication

Now that we have an understanding of the affective experience of hurt, we turn our attention to the focus of this chapter: hurtful communication. **Hurtful communication** (originally termed hurtful messages) is defined as something someone else said or did (or failed to say or do) that causes emotional injury and engenders psychological pain (Feeney, 2005; Leary et al., 1998; Vangelisti, 2015). The emotional wounds that accompany hurtful communication are not negligible; words can, indeed, hold great destructive power and typically violate implicit rules (or worse) in close relationships. In that way, hurtful communication can function as a relational transgression.

Types of Hurtful Communication and Hurtful Events

In an initial elucidation of messages that hurt, Vangelisti (1994) asked two groups of undergraduate college students to recall and report on a time when someone said something to them that hurt their feelings. Examination of these open-ended responses revealed a typology of 10 forms of hurtful message speech acts, identified in Table 5.1.

TABLE 5.1   Initial Typology of Hurtful Messages

Speech Act	Definition	Example
Informative statements	Disclosure of factual information that is undesired and cannot be refuted or redressed	"I don't love you anymore."
Evaluations	Negative description of value, quality, or worth	"You are the worst romantic partner I've ever had."
Accusations	Allegations of offenses or faults	"You're such a hypocrite."
Express desires	Statements of preference that are undesired	"I never want to see you again."
Directives	Orders or commands that are unwanted	"Don't ever contact me again."
Advise	Suggesting a course of action	"Break up with her so you can have some fun."
Threat	Expressions of intent to inflict punishment	"I'll break up with you if you ever hang out with him again."
Joke	Statements or behaviors (e.g., pranks) intended to be funny	"I see your girlfriend wears the pants in this relationship so you must wear the skirt!"
Lie	Deceptive statements	"The worst part was that he lied about seeing his ex over winter break."
Question	Inquiries or interrogations	"Why aren't you over your break-up yet?"

Adapted from: Vangelisti (1994)

Note that these hurtful messages are roughly in order from most frequently occurring to least frequently occurring. That is, the most commonly reported hurtful messages include (a) disclosures of factual information that cannot be disputed (e.g., "I want you to move out") or that concern things that cannot be changed (e.g., "I'm attracted to someone else"); (b) depictions of another's inferior quality or worth (e.g., "You aren't good enough for me"); and (c) accusatory charges of fault or wrongdoing (e.g., "You're a liar"; Vangelisti, 1994). In the vignette that opened this chapter, many of Cate's hurtful messages to Mara are probably most accurately classified as accusations, although other hurtful communicative acts (e.g., threats to end the relationship) are involved, and both informative statements and negative evaluations also seem to be clearly implied.

This raises the important point that these types of hurtful communication are not necessarily mutually exclusive. For instance, it is easy to see how a statement from your best friend ("Since you started dating Pat, you don't treat me like I'm a priority in your life") can be informative, evaluative, and accusatory at the same time. One element that can help distinguish informative statements from related types of hurtful communication is that these types of messages cannot be adequately disputed or refuted. If your romantic partner tells you they are leaving you for someone else or that they are sexually attracted to another person, there is really nothing you can say to argue against those statements. On the other hand, evaluations (e.g., "Our relationship is so dysfunctional") and accusations (e.g., "You're selfish and spoiled") can at least be reasonably disputed, if not refuted entirely.

Scholars outside the field of communication advanced Vangelisti's (1994) original typology of hurtful messages to the broader consideration of hurtful events, noting that hurtful communication need not be verbal in nature (i.e., it may also take nonverbal forms) and, in fact, that the absence of messages or actions may also be hurtful. Leary and his colleagues found the presence of six categories of hurtful events in the retrospective accounts of their study participants across various relationship types. These categories include (a) *criticism*, (b) *betrayal*, (c) *active disassociation* (i.e., overt rejection, ostracism, or abandonment), (d) *passive disassociation* (i.e., covert or implied rejection, such as being ignored), (e) *teasing*, and (f) *devaluation*, or feeling used or taken for granted (Leary et al., 1998). Note that the last two forms of hurtful events (i.e., teasing and evaluation) were reported by a minimal number of persons. Participants in this study rated these hurtful events with regard to both degree of hurt and judgments of rejection. According to these study findings, acts of disassociation (both active and passive) and betrayal were seen as more severe than criticisms.

Although Vangelisti's (1994) typology of hurtful messages and Leary et al.'s (1998) general typology of hurtful events are both broadly applicable across different types of relationships (e.g., dating, friendships, family relationships), Feeney (2004) argued that the nature of hurtful events is likely to differ somewhat according to relationship type. Using the Leary et al. typology as a starting point, Feeney conducted a study in which she asked undergraduate college students to report on a clearly recalled instance in which a romantic partner said or did something that hurt their feelings. Five categories of hurtful events specific to romantic relationships emerged: (a) *active disassociation* (i.e., behaviors that signal a lack of interest in the partner, including denial of feelings of love and commitment or even relationship termination), (b) *passive disassociation* (i.e., being ignored or excluded from the partner's disclosures or activities), (c) *criticism* (i.e., negative verbal comments about one's appearance, behavior, or personal characteristics), (d) *sexual infidelity* (i.e., violation of the sexual exclusivity norms of the relationship), and (e) *deceptive acts* (i.e., overtly lying, breaking promises, betraying confidences/revealing secrets).

Feeney's findings are in large part a replication of Leary et al.'s research, although some strategies (i.e., teasing) did not emerge in the specific context of romantic relationships, while others (i.e., sexual infidelity) are obviously unique to this particular context. As seen in previous studies, criticisms—although still distressing for recipients—were seen as less severe than instances of sexual infidelity, which is often judged as the worst type of betrayal.

Degree of Hurtfulness

The extent to which an individual experiences hurt as a result of hurtful messages or behaviors like those described previously in this chapter depends on several factors, including whether the recipient is able to challenge or argue against the hurtful message, whether the recipient has control over that which is implied by the hurtful message, whether the hurtful message was delivered deliberately, the extent to which the recipient anticipates being hurt by the initiator, how the experience of hurt is interpreted and made sense of by the recipient, personal qualities and characteristics of the recipient, and the overall quality of the relationship with the hurtful communicator. All these factors (and a few others) will be discussed in more detail.

Inability to refute the message. Scholars have argued that the level of hurt experienced by an individual as the result of another's hurtful communication is greater when the individual is unable to contest or refute those types of informative statements, or when they do not have control over what is implied by the informative statement (Vangelisti, 2007). Conversely, negative accusations and evaluations may be disputed and/or relevant behaviors may be changed, and as a result are perceived as less hurtful. In the vignette that opened this chapter, Mara may perceive that

Cate's statements are refutable, but that ultimately they will be difficult to do anything about. Put another way, Mara's graduate program and work schedule are demanding, and if she needs or wishes to continue both (as it seems she does), it appears it will be hard to remedy the issues Cate expresses regarding their relationship.

Perceived intent of hurtful communication. Scholars have also linked the perceived intentionality of hurtful communication to the degree of hurt that is experienced, as well as to the degree of relational harm that is caused. Generally, hurtful messages that are perceived as more intentional are also judged as more painful, and recipients of intentional hurtful communication feel less close to/more psychologically distant from the person who hurt them and less satisfied with their relationship with that person (McLaren & Solomon, 2008; Vangelisti & Young, 2000). Intent has been positively associated with negative relational consequences (e.g., psychological distancing) when these negative relational outcomes serve as an indirect assessment of the experience of hurt. When the experience of hurt is assessed directly, however, intent is sometimes associated with the experience of hurt in important ways while at other times the connection between the two has not been significant. Further, even messages and behaviors that are perceived to be unintentional can be hurtful. For example, Feeney (2004) found that passive disassociation was evaluated as less intentionally hurtful, yet it still had negative, enduring effects on the recipients' self-confidence.

Frequency of hurtful communication. The inconsistencies in the association between intent and relational outcomes (such as psychological distancing and relationship dissatisfaction) that have been revealed in available research may be due to the moderating effect of the frequency with which hurtful communication is delivered by a particular source. When the initiator of the hurtful communication repeatedly causes the recipient to feel hurt, then the positive association between intentionality and degree of hurt experienced is diminished, seemingly because the recipient becomes accustomed to the initiator's hurtful messages and behavior (Vangelisti & Young, 2000). This tendency to become habituated to another's hurtful communication suggests that some people may start to anticipate being hurt at the hands of a close other, and when that expectation is formed, those people may be less likely to experience intense feelings of hurt as a result of the close other's hurtful communication and behaviors. Note that those with higher self-esteem seem less likely to succumb to such expectations, however, as they often report being surprised by a close other's hurtful behavior (Vangelisti et al., 2005). Perhaps those with higher self-esteem are less vulnerable to hurtful events more broadly, given their inherent confidence and positive self-perceptions.

Of course, it is sometimes the case that one can feel a great degree of social pain, even when expecting to be hurt at the hands of someone who is often hurtful (Vangelisti et al., 2007). Such a pattern may be observed when an individual's expectations about another's behavior do not align with the way they desire the other person to behave, such as when one's mother is the source of repeated hurtful communication and behaviors (Burgoon et al., 1995). Put another way, even though a close other such as one's mother may often be hurtful (thus establishing the expectation of hurt for the recipient), this behavior never becomes preferred by the child. Thus, in this case, the desire for less hurtful behaviors from the perpetrator is stronger than the expectation of being hurt, and it is this desire rather than the established expectation that is linked to the experience of hurt for the recipient.

How the experience of hurt is explained by the recipient. Of course, it is not only aspects of the perpetrator's message such as intent and frequency that matter when understanding behavior that is more or less hurtful. The way the recipient interprets, explains, and otherwise makes sense of the hurtful communication or behavior also impacts how much hurt they feel. In general, when recipients believe that the hurtful message disparages or depreciates the relationship they have with the hurtful communicator (perhaps because the message was interpreted as communicating dislike or disregard for the recipient or communicating that the relationship is not important), recipients are likely to experience a greater degree of hurt (McLaren et al., 2012; Vangelisti et al., 2005). Further, Vangelisti et al. (2005) found that recipients with lower self-esteem are more likely to perceive relational denigration in the content of a close other's hurtful communication, suggesting that intrapersonal qualities impact how recipients make sense of and interpret hurtful communication.

Personal characteristics of the recipient. Some other relatively stable aspects of the recipient have been linked to the experience of hurt. For example, some studies have shown that women generally experience more hurt as a result of hurtful communication or events than men (e.g., Feeney & Hill, 2006; Miller & Roloff, 2005). In addition, recipients with an **avoidant attachment orientation**—those who have developed negative mental models of others as untrustworthy and unreliable, and therefore are reluctant or unwilling to develop intimate relationships with others—felt less hurt and distress when recounting hurtful events (Feeney, 2005). Avoidantly attached individuals are characterized by their unwillingness to get close with or open up to others, a strategy that serves to disallow them from becoming intimate with (and thereby, vulnerable to) close others. In addition, research has suggested that avoidantly attached individuals experience less distress in response to hurtful behaviors because they have learned coping mechanisms that allow them to direct their attention to other things that are less upsetting (Fraley & Shaver, 1997).

Conversely, recipients of hurtful communication who have an **anxious attachment orientation**—those who have developed positive mental models of others (but have negative views of themselves) and very much desire close relationships with others, but tend to experience a lot of anxiety in those relationships about whether or not the close other will abandon them—tend to feel more distress and greater hurt when recalling hurtful events (Feeney, 2005). Anxiously attached individuals are perhaps the most vulnerable in close relationships as they are so dependent on them, thus it is not surprising that hurtful events trigger heightened anxiety about the continuance of the relationship and are experienced as especially threatening and hurtful.

Qualities of the relationship with the hurtful communicator. Beyond personal qualities such as self-esteem and attachment orientation, some relational qualities appear to buffer the potential negative impact of hurtful communication. Satisfaction with the relationship that the recipient has with the hurtful communicator has been most often studied in this regard, and scholars have identified a number of benefits that are associated with satisfying relationships in the context of hurtful communication (Vangelisti & Young, 2000). These benefits include experiencing less hurt, a higher likelihood of perceiving the hurtful behavior as unintentional, and feeling less psychologically distant from the hurtful communicator. To return to the vignette that opened this chapter, the findings from these studies suggest that Mara would not have experienced especially intense hurt feelings as a reaction to Cate's hurtful messages in the vignette that opened this chapter, as she expressed general satisfaction with the relationship that the two of them share.

Some relational qualities do not serve to buffer the negative effects of hurtful communication, but instead appear to exacerbate them. The recipient's increased commitment to the relationship with the hurtful communicator may actually aggravate the negative impact of hurtful events that devalue the relationship and/or disregard the recipient, as commitment to a relationship is a form of dependence that intensifies vulnerability (Lemay et al., 2012). Other research with the relational turbulence model (Solomon & Knobloch, 2004) has identified the disordered relational state of turbulence as one that impacts the experience of hurt in meaningful ways.

Theory in Practice

The Roles of Uncertainty and Partner Interference in the Experience of Hurt

Much research has focused on identifying and better understanding the factors that provoke hurt feelings. One such study applied the relational turbulence model (Solomon & Knobloch, 2004) to better understand some of the precursors of hurt feelings in romantic relationships. The relational turbulence model deals primarily with the experience of three indicators of relational uncertainty (self, partner, and relationship, discussed in Chapter 2) and partner influence in the forms of both facilitation and interference (the former entails assisting with one's goal-directed behavior and the latter involves behaving in ways that hinder such goal-directed behavior) in achieving our everyday goals during **transitions** (i.e., times during which romantic partners are adjusting to shifting identities, roles, and/or relational circumstances; Solomon et al., 2016). Evaluations of relational uncertainty and partner influence inform perceptions of **relational turbulence**, or the feeling that the relationship is tumultuous, chaotic, and tenuous (Solomon et al., 2016). When a relationship is experienced as turbulent, those involved tend to be overly sensitive and reactive to even mundane relational events. In essence, the model posits that when we feel uncertain about our relationship, or when we perceive that our partner is uncertain about our relationship, or when we are uncertain about the viability of the relationship itself, and when we perceive that our partner interferes with (rather than helps facilitate) our goal-directed behavior, then we are apt to feel that our relationship is in a turbulent state. When we experience such turbulence, our cognitions, emotions, and communication within the relationship become more extreme or polarized in nature.

Recently, the relational turbulence model was elaborated by specifying the causal mechanisms that connect relational uncertainty and partner influence with cognitive, affective, and communicative reactivity, and it is now known as relational turbulence theory (Solomon et al., 2016). A long program of research with the model has consistently shown that increased relational uncertainty (in particular, partner uncertainty or relationship uncertainty) and/or perceived interference from a romantic partner are linked with a host of indicators of relational turbulence, including (but not limited to) increased negative emotions, including jealousy; more severe and relationally threatening appraisals of irritating behaviors in the relationship; elevated depressive symptoms; increased relational tumult and upheaval; increased topic avoidance; and heightened relationship dissatisfaction (Afifi & Reichert, 1996; Goodboy et al., 2020; Knobloch, 2007b, 2008a; Knobloch et al., 2007; Solomon & Knobloch, 2004).

With regard to the experience of hurt, specifically, Theiss et al. (2009) longitudinally examined the relational turbulence model in the context of hurt feelings in college student dating relationships, finding that elevated self-, partner, and relationship uncertainty—as well as increased partner interference—were all associated with heightened intensity of hurt feelings, greater perceived intentionality of the hurtful communication/behaviors experienced during hurtful episodes, and perceptions of more relational damage as a result of hurtful episodes that had occurred throughout the 6-week study. Related research by McLaren and Solomon (2014) revealed that relational turbulence was associated with the intensity of women's (but not men's) hurt. Further, in a separate study, McLaren et al. (2011) found that, under conditions of relational turbulence, college students in romantic relationships experienced more intense hurt and judged messages as more intentionally hurtful. On the other hand, those who were high in self-uncertainty (i.e., they doubted their own commitment to and desire to be involved in their romantic relationship) appear to be less threatened by a partner's hurtful messages, as they experience fewer negative emotions and less hurt. These findings demonstrate the impact of a number of personal, partner, and relational qualities on the experience of hurt in romantic associations.

The type of relationship under consideration may also impact the degree of hurt experienced (Vangelisti & Crumley, 1998). Scholars have compared hurt feelings across different relationship types (i.e., romantic relationships, family relationships, and nonfamily/nonromantic relationships), finding that hurt was especially intense in the context of family relationships. However, people who were hurt by family members did not report more relational distancing than the romantic or nonfamily/nonromantic groups, perhaps because family relationships are nonvoluntary (i.e., we are not able to choose our biological family) and it may be perceived as difficult—if not impossible in some cases—to maintain distance from family members.

Other factors that may influence degree of hurt. In addition to these factors, a few other considerations may also impact the degree of hurt experienced in response to a hurtful communication or hurtful event. Early research with hurtful messages suggested that those that were focused on relational issues (e.g., "You're not a good friend to me") are more hurtful than messages that implicate personality traits (e.g., "You're selfish and spoiled;" Vangelisti, 1994). The manner in which hurtful messages such as informative statements are delivered also appears to matter. **Message intensity**, or the forcefulness with which a sender communicates their "attitudinal position" toward something, impacts the degree of hurt experienced by the recipient of the message (McEwen & Greenberg, 1970, p. 340). Specifically, hurtful messages that are communicated in a harsh way (as opposed to a more neutral/less forceful way) or that include extreme language are interpreted as more negative (Young, 2004).

Further, feelings of hurt are likely to persist over time for those who have a tendency to take conflict personally and those who tend to **ruminate** about hurtful events (Miller & Roloff, 2014). Taking conflict personally and rumination are related processes, in that those who are more apt to personalize conflict are also more likely to ruminate about it (e.g., thinking persistent and intrusive thoughts about what was said and done and how much it hurt). Essentially, rumination encourages reliving the hurtful event and the resultant hurtful emotions over and over again for a period of time.

Finally, if you wish to soften the blow of your hurtful message, you might try a joking strategy. At least one study has found that humorously phrased hurtful messages (i.e., when a close other was trying to be funny but instead it resulted in hurting your feelings) are perceived as less intentionally hurtful and judged as causing less hurt than hurtful messages that are not humorously phrased or interpreted as an attempt at humor (Young & Bippus, 2001). With that said, some scholars would consider joking hurtful messages as attempts at teasing, which is discussed later in Chapter 12.

Hurtful Communication in Mediated Contexts
Do Hurtful Messages Hurt Less When They Are Not Delivered Face-to-Face?

The proliferation of computer-mediated technologies now allows us to communicate with each other in a variety of different ways. Because computer-mediated communication may be impersonal, interpersonal, or **hyperpersonal** (i.e., even closer/more intimate than if the people involved were face-to-face, as they often are when communicating interpersonally; Walther, 1996) in nature and content, one might wonder whether face-to-face hurtful messages cause more hurt than mediated hurtful messages, given that the latter may constitute a more impersonal format. At this time, virtually no scholarship has explored this question. Perhaps unsurprisingly, one study that has examined mediated hurtful messages in a college student sample revealed that hurtful text messaging between close friends is relatively common. Further, hurtful communication from a close friend delivered via a text message was evaluated as more hurtful if it was perceived to have been sent with the intent to hurt. In addition, these individuals reported feeling that their relationship with the friend was more distant as a result of the hurtful communication if they perceived the hurtful communication to be intentional (Jin, 2013). These outcomes (feeling more hurt and more relationally distant) were especially likely for those whose friendships were not very satisfying. In addition, in line with some previous research on hurtful communication, women (as compared to men) felt more hurt and reported more distancing as a result of a close friend's hurtful texting. Although the study of hurtful communication expressed via mediated channels is clearly in its infancy, these results suggest that we might expect more similarities than differences when it comes to how people perceive and react to hurtful communication, regardless of the delivery modality.

Social Pain's Connection to Physical Pain

Relatively recently, scholars within and outside of the communication discipline have undertaken research that has demonstrated the interconnections between the ways in which physical pain (e.g., stubbing your toe) and **social pain** (e.g., an actual or perceived separation from social relationships with others, and the vulnerability that accompanies such a separation) are experienced (Vangelisti, 2015; Vangelisti & Brody, 2021). Given the obvious similarities between hurt and social pain, evidence for a connection between social and physical pain is elucidated here. For example, research by neuroscientists has identified commonalities in the neural pathways that are implicated in the experience of both types of pain (see Sturgeon & Zautra, 2016). A program of research by Eisenberger et al. (2003) found that the region of the brain known to be activated under conditions of physical pain is similarly activated when individuals feel socially excluded (and presumably, when they feel hurt due to that behavior).

In addition, this program of research has shown that taking an over-the-counter pain reliever commonly used to reduce physical pain is also associated with a decrease in individuals' self-reported social pain (DeWall et al., 2010). From the communication discipline, research by Vangelisti et al. (2014) also investigated the effect of an over-the-counter pain reducer on reports of social pain following an experience of social exclusion and after reliving a hurtful experience. The results from this study show that the medication for physical pain reduced social pain for women, but not for men, as compared with those individuals who took a placebo. Although in its early stages, research on the interconnections between physical and social pain has implications for the study of hurt and hurtful communication/behaviors and may provide an explanatory mechanism for some individuals' resilience in the face of hurtful communication and events.

Responses to Hurtful Communication

When hurt by another, individuals may react in one of three general ways: actively and verbally, acquiescently, or invulnerably (Vangelisti & Crumley, 1998). **Active verbal responses** entail constructive (e.g., asking for an explanation in order to better understand) or destructive (e.g., attacking the partner or using sarcasm) confrontation with the partner regarding the hurtful communication. This response to hurtful communication is most commonly employed and is especially likely to be used by individuals who are more satisfied in their relationships, perhaps as a way to contain and/or repair the damage of hurtful communication and to keep their already satisfying relationship on track. One study has shown that women are more likely than men to say that they would engage in active verbal responses to hurtful messages, even though—or perhaps because—they are also more likely to report especially intense hurt feelings as compared to men (Miller & Roloff, 2005).

Individuals who have been hurt by a close other may instead react with **acquiescent responses**, including yielding to the initiator of the hurtful communication and their ability to emotionally wound. Acquiescent responses may entail apologizing or conceding/giving in to the perpetrator. In the vignette that opened this chapter, Mara engaged in both of these behaviors (i.e., apologizing and conceding) when she responded to Cate's hurtful message by acknowledging the validity of Cate's complaints, apologizing for her behavior, and agreeing that she needs to change her behavior in order for the relationship to be successful. Individuals report using the acquiescent strategy when feeling particularly hurt by a partner's hurtful communication, perhaps as a means of putting an immediate end to the feeling of hurt that is experienced.

Finally, evasive reactions such as **invulnerable responses** include efforts to pretend that the hurtful communication was not in fact hurtful (e.g., laughing off or ignoring the message). These invulnerable responses are more common when individuals perceive that the hurtful message and/or the hurt itself do not greatly affect their relationship, and when they are feeling less hurt. Alternatively, this passive response to hurtful communication or behaviors may be used when recipients of hurtful messages are too emotionally overwhelmed to productively discuss their feelings. Of course, an invulnerable response may be used in the immediate aftermath of receiving a hurtful message or experiencing a hurtful behavior, but that does not preclude the possibility that the recipient could later choose to more fully engage the hurtful event with an acquiescent or active verbal response.

Conclusion

As you have learned from this chapter, hurtful events or hurtful communication occur when another person says or does (or fails to say or do) something that causes emotional and psychological injury and results in the feeling of hurt. The feeling of hurt may be engendered by any relational transgression (e.g., a friend's unwarranted jealousy, a romantic partner's emotional infidelity, a family member's deception). Alternatively, hurting a close other may itself be considered a transgression, as such behavior typically violates implicit or explicit rules for appropriate relational behavior. Although we can experience hurtful events or communication at the hands of anyone, research has shown that our close others (e.g., romantic partners, family members) are common perpetrators (Leary et al., 1998). All hurtful events or communication are not equal, however.

As you have seen in this chapter, many different factors combine to determine how much hurt will be incited by a particular hurtful event, including the perceived intent of the communication, the frequency of the communication, the content and delivery of the communication, personal characteristics of the recipient, qualities of the recipient's relationship with the hurtful communicator, and the way in which the recipient makes sense of the hurtful event. You have seen some early evidence for the link between the experience of physical pain and the experience of social pain, a relatively recent area of inquiry that has the potential for exciting future discoveries. Finally, you have learned three typical ways that people respond to hurtful communication and some considerations that induce them to respond in these ways. The knowledge you have now should help you better understand the harm hurtful communication can do and under what conditions it is most likely to cause such harm. You should also have an understanding of better (and worse) ways to respond to hurtful events in your own life.

Discussion Questions

1. Various typologies of hurtful messages or events were introduced in this chapter. Discuss the typology that you perceive to be most valid and applicable and provide an argument for your choice.

2. Discuss and distinguish among the three most frequently reported hurtful messages as identified by Vangelisti's (1994) work, generating your own examples of these types of hurtful messages. Do you agree that informative statements are most hurtful? Why or why not?

3. Quite a large number of factors that impact the degree to which hurtful events incite feelings of hurt were overviewed in this chapter. Identify, define, and discuss the five most important, in your opinion. Justify your choices.

4. Define and distinguish among the three responses to hurtful communication that were identified in this chapter, providing an example of each one. Then, discuss what is known about them from a research perspective (e.g., when people are more likely to use a particular response, etc.).

Chapter 6

Jealousy

> *Tiana and Trey have been dating for a few months. Recently, Trey recon-*
> *nected with his former romantic partner, Gia. Trey and Gia were together*
> *for several years before they broke up about a year ago, and they did*
> *not remain friends after their breakup. Tiana did not realize they were*
> *in contact at all until recently, when one of her friends told her she saw*
> *Trey and Gia having drinks at a local bar. Tiana sees Gia as a rival for*
> *Trey's affections, and she feels threatened by Trey's reconnection with*
> *his ex-partner (especially since Trey has not told her anything about*
> *it). Tiana wonders why Trey and Gia have chosen to reconnect now.*
> *Why wouldn't Trey tell her about it? Is this really something to worry*
> *about, or is it innocent? Tiana feels scared that she might lose her*
> *relationship with Trey to Gia, and she feels angry at the idea that Gia*
> *might be actively pursuing Trey and that Trey would have drinks with*
> *his ex without telling her.*

As was undoubtedly evident to you as you read the opening
vignette, Tiana is experiencing jealousy in the context of her
romantic relationship with Trey. Jealousy was mentioned as

a possible relationship transgression in Chapter 4 (although note that jealousy expression and experience are not always considered violations of relational rules for appropriate behavior—more on that later). In this chapter, we will discuss what jealousy is and when it might be considered reasonable as opposed to transgressive in nature. We will identify various types of jealousy before turning our attention to romantic, reactive jealousy for the majority of the chapter. Both the experience of jealousy (i.e., its cognitive and emotional components) and the expression of jealousy (i.e., how jealousy is behaviorally expressed or communicated in close relationships) will be elucidated, as will several communication theories related to these processes. We close with information regarding the consequences or outcomes of jealousy expression for individuals, their romantic partners, and their relationships.

Jealousy in the Context of Close Relationships

Although not as ubiquitous as some other bad behaviors discussed throughout this textbook, there may be times when "the green-eyed monster" rears its (potentially) ugly head in the context of your close relationships. If and when it does, it can be problematic for you, the close other, and the relationship the two of you share. **Jealousy** is defined as an interactive, interpersonal experience made up of cognitive, affective, and communicative elements; it entails the need to protect and defend a valued relationship from the threat of a perceived or actual third-party rival (Bevan, 2013). Across various close relationship types, jealousy occurs when exclusivity norms are violated by a rival who is threatening the relationship. Think of jealousy as a three-person triangle comprised of you, someone close to you (e.g., a romantic partner), and a rival third person who is (or who you think is) trying to interfere in your relationship by diverting your partner's desire for a relationship with you to a relationship with the rival.

Closely related to jealousy are other experiences such as rivalry and envy. In fact, the term *jealous* is often used colloquially when really the experience being described is envy, not jealousy (Dunn, 1983; Salovey & Rodin, 1989). For example, most people's response to hearing that someone they know won the lottery would be "I'm so jealous!" but the feeling in this case is envy. As noted previously, jealousy requires three people whereas both rivalry and envy can occur between two people. Perhaps the best way to distinguish among these three concepts is to consider who currently possesses the thing of value in question: you, the other person, or neither of you (Guerrero & Andersen, 1998a). In cases of jealousy, you possess something of value that another person (i.e., the third-party rival) wants. The term *rivalry* is used when at least two people compete for some reward that neither of them currently possess (e.g., competing with a stranger for a job, an award, a scholarship, etc.), or that both of them have in some measure but are competing against each other to get more of/hold on to. If you have siblings, undoubtedly you have experienced at least a few instances of sibling rivalry wherein you compete with each other for your parents' approval and love (despite the fact that love is not a limited resource and therefore no competition is necessary!). *Envy* occurs when you wish you had some positive quality or commodity that another person possesses. Envy is often experienced in conjunction with jealousy if a rival is indeed trying to interfere in your romantic relationship and you perceive that this person has positive characteristics (e.g., physical or social attractiveness, intelligence, money, power, etc.) that you do not feel you have. In the vignette that opened this chapter, Tiana would be experiencing both jealousy and envy if she felt that Gia, Trey's ex-partner, was more attractive or funnier or more confident than she is and she wished she had those qualities.

Depending on the circumstances, the experience and expression of jealousy are sometimes perceived as reasonable and deserved. However, when jealousy is experienced and expressed, yet it is not warranted or justified (e.g., if Trey has done nothing to violate the monogamy rules of his relationship with Tiana and therefore she has no right to feel jealous), then it can be considered a relationship transgression, or a violation of rules for appropriate and acceptable behavior in the relationship (Metts, 1994). Yet, some would argue that Tiana's jealousy experience is perfectly warranted or justified in this particular example—that, in fact, Trey has committed relational transgressions by violating important relational rules that then quite naturally results in Tiana feeling jealous because her relationship with him appears to be legitimately threatened by some rival third party. Determining whether jealousy is a transgression will clearly vary depending on who you are asking.

Types of Jealousy

The preceding discussion and examples focused specifically on one type of jealousy—**romantic jealousy**—which occurs when the rival third party is interfering with the continuation or quality of your romantic relationship. *Sexual jealousy* may also be a factor in the context of romantic relationships, and it occurs when you think the rival third party is having or would like to have sex with your romantic partner. Although romantic jealousy has most often been the focus of scholarly inquiry, jealousy can and does occur outside of romantic entanglements and other types of jealousy have been identified (Bevan & Samter, 2004). *Intimacy jealousy* (i.e., concerns that your partner/close friend has more intimate and personal communication with someone besides you), *activity jealousy* (i.e., concerns that the outside activities of your partner/friend are coming between the two of you), and *power jealousy* (i.e., concerns that another person has more influence over your partner/friend than you do) are also sometimes problematic in close relationships. Further, *friend jealousy* occurs when you are concerned that a friend's relationships with other friends will interfere with your relationship with them (e.g., when a rival third party is trying to become your best friend's new best friend) and *family jealousy* occurs when you are worried about a close other's relationship with their family members superseding their relationship with you (e.g., you are afraid that your friend/romantic partner is closer to their siblings than to you). As it has been the focus of most research, the focus of this chapter is romantic jealousy.

Jealousy has also been distinguished according to degree of jealousy experienced, an approach that discriminates between reactive and pathological jealousy (e.g., Cobb, 1979; Mullen, 1991; Tarrier et al., 1990). **Reactive jealousy**, sometimes known as "normal" jealousy, is a more reasoned experience that entails several characteristics, including an actual (versus an imagined) threat to the relationship, a mild to moderate (versus extreme) degree of emotional distress, and the undertaking of behaviors that are intended to protect the relationship from the threat of the rival. Reactive jealousy should last only as long as the current jealousy situation lasts (e.g., if Trey stops communicating with his ex-partner Gia, then Tiana should stop feeling jealous because the problematic behavior—the relational rule violation—has ceased). Reactive jealousy is justified by the partner's relational rule violations and is therefore not considered a relationship transgression.

Pathological jealousy, on the other hand, is intense, irrational, and unwarranted; it is jealousy blown far out of proportion. Also known as delusional jealousy, morbid jealousy, or suspicious jealousy, pathological jealousy may be sparked by an imagined (versus an actual) threat to the relationship, an extreme and powerful (versus more moderate) degree of emotional upset, and the use of possibly obsessive detection and protection behaviors targeted toward the partner and the rival. Some of these detection behaviors include confirmatory strategies, wherein the jealous person goes to great lengths to confirm their suspicions (e.g., constant questioning of the partner, accusing the partner of bad behavior, and initiating conflict about the jealousy situation). Numerous negative outcomes may accompany pathological jealousy, including obsessive preoccupation with the jealousy experience (e.g., intrusive thoughts and suspicions), aggressive or even violent reactions to the jealousy situation, and intense negative affect (possibly even suicidal thoughts, in especially severe cases). Pathological jealousy may extend past the current jealousy situation, and it will almost certainly be interpreted as a relationship transgression (or worse!).

FLIPPING THE SCRIPT

Does Feeling Jealous Mean I'm Crazy?

Jealousy has negative connotations for many people, in part because it is often portrayed in the media in its most extreme and dramatic forms. In such portrayals, jealousy usually leads to possessive, even obsessive, behaviors like stalking, extraordinary revenge attempts, or violence. Pines (1992) recounts a story in which a middle-aged woman kidnapped her rival (a younger woman for whom her husband had left her) at gunpoint, shaving her head and removing her clothes before finally tarring and feathering her and then leaving her at the local garbage dump. Jealousy has gotten a bad reputation in part because of such dramatic portrayals, and as a result, individuals who express their jealous feelings in romantic relationships may run the risk of being accused of or made to feel that they're acting "crazy." This may be particularly true for women, as many of these media portrayals feature females in the vein of the adage "hell hath no fury like a woman scorned." However, this kind of extreme jealousy-induced behavior is not the norm, as it reflects a situation in which a person has lost control over themselves. People who have lost control of themselves in this way sometimes do, in fact, describe feeling crazy as a result of their jealousy. In reality, though, the expression of jealousy is most often not pathological in nature but is indeed considered "normal" (even reasonable and defensible) depending on what form the jealousy takes. In cases of "normal" or reactive jealousy, the romantic partner's bad behavior (e.g., their relational transgression)—not your experience or expression of jealousy—is the problem. The expression of "normal" or reactive jealousy can have positive or negative outcomes in romantic relationships (Pfeiffer & Wong, 1989). In cases of pathological or suspicious jealousy, your experience and expression of jealousy—not the romantic partner's behavior—is the problem. The expression of patho-logical jealousy leads to negative personal and relational outcomes that can be extreme. Realizing that "normal" or reactive jealousy is okay and recognizing when your jealousy experience and expression are starting to become pathological and out of control are first steps in more effectively coping with the green-eyed monster in your own romantic relationships.

Although pathological jealousy is worse than "normal" jealousy in virtually every respect, including more destructive personal, partner, and relational outcomes, most research in the communication discipline has focused on "normal" experiences of jealousy. Accordingly, this chapter considers the experience and expression of reactive romantic jealousy.

The Experience of Jealousy

As indicated previously, jealousy is conceptualized as having interrelated cognitive, affective, and behavioral components (White, 1981a; Pfeiffer & Wong, 1989). The cognitions and emotions that accompany the experience of jealousy can be sparked by behaviors in which the close other is engaging (e.g., communicating with past romantic partners, as in the vignette that opened this chapter, or demonstrating obvious romantic/sexual interest in rivals), or your own perceptions and relationship preferences (e.g., your feelings of inadequacy, low self-esteem, or your desire for an exclusive relationship; Salovey & Rodin, 1985; White, 1981b). Recently, scholars have been interested in the effects of social media (especially social network-ing sites) on the experience of jealousy in romantic relationships with an eye toward the ways in which partners' social media use can exacerbate this experience.

Jealousy in Mediated Contexts
Social Networking Sites

Research suggests that romantic partners' use of social networking sites (and other forms of social media) may be especially likely to trigger and/or aggravate feelings of jealousy. In a study of college students, Muise et al. (2009) found that increased Facebook use leads to increased experiences of Facebook jealousy (i.e., jealousy related specifically to your romantic partner's use of Facebook, such as friending an attractive person who is unknown to you). Some of these individuals noted that the elevated accessibility of information as well as the lack of context available to help guide the interpretation of that information on Facebook are two factors that especially intensify feelings of jealousy. In other words, because Facebook allows you to have access to so much information about your partner's relationships with others, and because Facebook communication can be ambiguous or unclear in the absence of contextual cues, people are especially likely to become jealous about these types of interactions. For instance, say Tiana (from the opening vignette) becomes aware that Trey has been leaving comments on Gia's Facebook wall. What does that mean? Does it mean anything at all? What are Trey's intentions? Is Gia posting on his wall in return? What's the nature of the communication between them? Communicating with an ex can be perfectly innocent on the part of both parties and may merely reflect a desire to maintain a casual, platonic friendship. On the other hand, communicating with an ex may signal something more threatening for your current romantic relationship with your partner.

Further, some people feel unable to restrict the amount of time they spend on their partner's Facebook page or on Facebook, generally, and Facebook intrusiveness (i.e., an excessive connection to Facebook that obstructs daily activities and relationship functioning) has been associated with jealous thoughts, increased monitoring or surveillance of the partner, and relationship dissatisfaction (Elphinston, & Noller, 2011). Taken together, these findings point to the potential existence of a negative "feedback loop" between Facebook use and jealousy (Muise et al., 2009). Access to potentially threatening information on your partner's Facebook page or other social networking sites may motivate you to keep an even closer eye on your partner's activities on such social networking sites and to spend even more time on their social networking sites (especially if you are also strongly attached to using those types of sites and already spend a lot of time doing so). If this happens, your feelings of jealousy will probably escalate. Some research leads to the conclusion that this pattern of increased electronic surveillance may be particularly common for individuals with a preoccupied or a fearful-avoidant attachment style (Fox & Warber, 2014). (Revisit Chapter 2 for a refresher on the four adult attachment styles.)

Carpenter and Spottswood (2021a, 2021b) account for the tendency for online environments such as social networking sites to exacerbate the experience of jealousy under particular conditions. They developed the hyperperception model to explain when an observer's perceptions of the intimacy or psychological closeness of online interactions between two other people (a sender and a receiver) will be elevated in a way that does not match the reality of the situation. In other words, when observers (in the context of romantic jealousy, this is the person experiencing jealousy) in online environments such as social networking sites are privy to the online interactions of two other people (in the context of jealousy, this is the jealous person's romantic partner and some third-party rival), they have a tendency to see those interactions as much more personal, intimate, and close in nature than they really are—and certainly as more intimate than the two people involved in the interaction (i.e., the romantic partner and the rival) would report the relationship to be. This is thought to occur due to the positivity norms that are operative on social networking sites such as Facebook, which encourage people to post information and to interact with each other in ways that make oneself and others appear as socially attractive as possible. Certain factors serve to increase this hyperperception, such as seeing the two people (i.e., the romantic partner and the rival) interact online only and not in any face-to-face settings, and observing the sender's (i.e., the romantic partner's) interactions with the rival only (and not with any other people on the social networking site). Early research with this model (Carpenter & Spottswood, 2021b) has shown that observing the partner with the rival in online environments only led to the experience of more jealousy, increased motivation to use social networking sites to monitor their partner's online activities, and the use of more signs of possession (described later in this chapter as one type of communicative response to jealousy) in an attempt to discourage possible rivals.

Other forms of social media use have been compared to Facebook use, as the latter's popularity appears to be waning, and early research suggests that a partner's use of Snapchat to communicate with another provokes even more jealousy, possibly because Snapchat reflects your partner's choice to communicate more privately with a third-party rival (Utz et al., 2015). Conversely, when it comes to partners *receiving* messages from unknown rivals, Facebook elicited stronger feelings of jealousy than Snapchat, maybe because of Facebook's public nature and thus the increased possibility of a possible rival being made widely known to social networks. Limited research has also delved into the use of emoticons on Facebook, finding that the presence of a winking emoticon (versus no emoticon) leads to more jealousy (especially for males in one study) while a smiling emoticon does not (Fleuriet et al., 2014; Hudson et al., 2015).

> Although the study of jealousy and social media is still in its early stages, results like these highlight the potential drawbacks of social media use in the form of its capacity to escalate and intensify experiences of romantic jealousy.

Cognitive jealousy includes negative thoughts such as suspicions and anxieties about the threat of a rival third party. Jealous cognitions or thoughts typically occur in the form of primary and secondary appraisals or evaluations of the jealousy situation that occur once we become suspicious about the presence of a rival, and they influence (and are likely influenced by) our affective states regarding the jealousy experience (White & Mullen, 1989).

Primary appraisals are more general, and essentially involve your assessment of whether there is any kind of relationship between your partner and the rival, and if there is, what the nature of that relationship might be. In the vignette that opened this chapter, Tiana has learned that her romantic partner met his ex for a drink, and she is now sensitive to the possibility of a rival threat to her romantic relationship. During the primary appraisal process, Tiana might wonder how often Trey and Gia have gotten together and if they plan to get together again, and she might consider the factors that could have led to the desire for this reconnection. Essentially, primary appraisals encompass your judgments about the potential for a rival relationship, the existence of a rival relationship, and the level of threat posed by a rival relationship.

If Tiana's primary appraisals suggest that there is indeed a credible threat from Trey's ex as a rival third party, she will proceed to *secondary appraisals*, which are more specific than primary appraisals. Kelley (1983) proposed four types of secondary appraisal: (a) an assessment of the romantic partner's motives, (b) social comparison of oneself to the rival, (c) an assessment of one's own alternatives to the romantic relationship, and (d) an assessment of what would be lost if the romantic relationship ended due to the jealousy situation. During the secondary appraisal process, Tiana will try to determine why Trey wants to reconnect with Gia and if his motives are platonic or more ominous. Is it because Trey is still in love with Gia? Or is it because Gia has gotten engaged to someone else and merely wanted to share the news with Trey, as an old friend? If Trey's motives are innocent, then that may put an end to her experience of jealousy. If the motive is not perceived to be so innocent, then Tiana will continue with the appraisal process.

Tiana may compare herself to the rival third party as part of the second-ary appraisal process; as discussed previously, this can elicit feelings of envy. Does Gia have positive qualities that Tiana does not think she has? Tiana may also begin considering her own potential relational alternatives, on the chance that the rival threat is serious and she perceives the loss of her romantic relationship as probable. If Trey leaves Tiana for his ex, are there other people who Tiana might be interested in dating? Is Tiana a person who is comfortable being without a romantic partner? Tiana will also give some thought to the degree of ultimate loss that she perceives if, indeed, her romantic relationship ends due to this rival threat. If she has high-quality alternatives to Trey, or even if she does not perceive good alternatives but she is just as happy being on her own as she is being in a relationship, she may not assess her ultimate loss as unduly devastating, and thus her emotional reaction to the jealousy situation may be milder. If Tiana does anticipate that the loss of her partner and the romantic rela-tionship would be devastating and she also thinks that loss is imminent, then her emotional response to the jealousy situation is likely to be more negative and intense.

The preceding examples highlight the centrality of relational uncertainty in the jealousy experience, as was discussed in Chapter 2. A jealousy sit-uation typically raises many doubts and questions for individuals, causing them to question their partner's feelings about them as well as their part-ner's happiness with and commitment to the romantic relationship (Afifi & Reichert, 1996). If that uncertainty is threatening, it will lead to negative emotional responses.

Emotional jealousy deals with the affective states that often accom-pany the jealousy experience, such as fear, anger, and sadness. In line with Lazarus's (1982) argument about the relationship between cognition and emotion, sequential models of the jealousy experience generally hold that jealous cognitions invariably precede jealous feelings (White, 1981a), while others believe that jealous emotions usually but not always follow jealous cognitions (Pfeiffer & Wong, 1989) with less emphasis on the order of the two experiences in favor of highlighting the reciprocal relationship between them (Guerrero & Andersen, 1998a). Regardless of the order of occurrence, jealous cognitions and emotions affect each other, and they combine to influence how people respond to the jealousy situation.

Jealous emotions are often, although not always, negative in nature. Anger and fear are the two emotions most commonly experienced in a jealousy situation (Guerrero & Andersen, 1998a). You may be angry at your romantic partner for betraying you by showing romantic interest in someone else and/or you may be angry at the third-party rival for attempting to divert your partner's attentions, especially if the rival is someone known to you (e.g., Guerrero et al., 2005). If the rival is a friend of yours, they are committing a relational transgression in the context of your friendship if they are actively pursuing your partner or otherwise overtly indicating their romantic or sexual interest in your partner. Some research shows that you are more likely to be angry at your partner as compared to the rival, however, which makes sense if your partner is committing a relational transgression by demonstrating romantic interest in another and the rival is someone unknown to you (Paul et al., 1993). You may also be fearful of losing your romantic partner and the romantic relationship that the two of you share to the third-party rival (White & Mullen, 1989). Fears of being abandoned and of losing the relationship as well as uncertainty about the state and future of the relationship underlie this emotional response (Bringle, 1991; White & Mullen, 1989).

Other negative emotions or affective experiences have been associated with the jealousy experience, including sadness, hurt, insecurity, envy, and even guilt (Guerrero & Andersen, 1998a; Stearns, 1989; White & Mullen, 1989). Following anger and fear, sadness is the third emotion most central to the experience of jealousy (although sadness appears to be even more central to experiences of envy as compared to experiences of jealousy). Sadness may occur due to the possible loss of the romantic partner and your relationship and the aftermath of such a loss. As identified previously, you may feel envious of the third-party rival if you see in them positive characteristics that you feel you do not have but wish you did have, and hurt feelings accompany almost any experience of betrayal. Feelings of guilt may be experienced if you worry that something you did (or failed to do) resulted in your partner's romantic interest in the rival third party. Women may be more likely than men to blame themselves for the jealousy situation, which may lead them to experience guilt more often than men in this context (Becker et al., 2004).

To a lesser degree, positive affective responses have also been associated with the experience of jealousy. These more positive feelings include elevated sexual arousal/passion, love, appreciation, and even pride (Guerrero & Andersen, 1998a; Guerrero et al., 2005; Pines, 1992; White & Mullen, 1989). Sometimes things get a little stale and partners begin to take each other for granted, especially in long-term relationships, and a rival's interest may reinvigorate feelings of sexual interest, gratitude, and love for your partner. You may even feel proud that your romantic partner is attractive enough to attract the attention of others.

Behavioral jealousy entails the detection and/or prevention behaviors that we use when a third-party rival is perceived (Pfeiffer & Wong, 1989). Cognitive appraisals and affective responses to the experience of jealousy lead to these types of coping behaviors, in that we will choose different expressions of behavioral jealousy based on our jealous thoughts and emotions. Detection behaviors include anything you might do to uncover evidence related to the presence of a rival third party in order to confirm your suspicions, such as snooping through your partner's phone or other belongings while they are in the shower or monitoring their online activities. The goal of protection behaviors is to intervene to ensure that your partner and the rival do not establish or escalate a relationship. You might call your partner away from interactions with the rival, point out negative characteristics of the rival in front of your partner, or warn the rival (or your partner) to cease the problematic behavior. Other coping behaviors have been identified as well, but very little research has investigated how they function in the jealousy experience (Bevan, 2013; Buunk, 1982).

Limited research has examined the links among these three dimensions of jealousy and various relational outcomes, but we know that marital satisfaction is decreased when a person is experiencing cognitive, emotional, or behavioral jealousy (Guerrero & Eloy, 1992). Further, some research suggests that cognitive jealousy has especially deleterious effects on relationship outcomes such as adjustment, satisfaction, and overall relational quality, particularly when partners are ruminating on their jealous thoughts (Barelds & Barelds-Dijkstra, 2007; Elphinston et al., 2013). If jealousy triggers positive emotional responses, it may encourage you to stop taking your partner for granted, increase your efforts to maintain the relationship, and possibly redouble your commitment to your partner (Pines, 1992). Sometimes romantic partners will intentionally try to instigate feelings of jealousy in their partner (called jealousy induction or jealousy evocation) as a means of social control in order to obtain these positive benefits (White, 1980). Not surprisingly, however, this strategy can backfire and have negative outcomes for the health and satisfaction of the relationship that are quite the opposite of what was intended (Guerrero & Andersen, 1998a). As with conflict, covered in Chapter 13, how jealousy is expressed or communicated may be the deciding factor with regard to how the jealousy experience ultimately impacts the quality and continuation of the romantic relationship, and thus a more extended discussion of jealousy expression is warranted.

The Expression of Jealousy

Prior to the 1990s, the vast majority of research was concerned with the experience rather than the expression of jealousy (Duck, 1992). As noted previously, some early work focused on coping strategies used when experiencing jealousy and distinguished between behavioral responses to jealousy based on their intent to detect evidence related to a rival threat or to keep a rival threat from developing, escalating, or otherwise damaging the primary relationship. Jealousy expression behaviors were also investigated in several other dichotomous ways, including confrontational/ partner-attacking/negative behaviors as compared with nonconfrontational/ partner-enhancing/positive behaviors (see Bevan, 2013). As research on jealousy expression began to proliferate, an expanded conceptualization of jealousy expression emerged, which can entail behaviors and messages between you and your romantic partner or between you and the rival third party (Guerrero, 1998a). In keeping with this conceptualization, Guerrero and her colleagues have been responsible for the development of a broader and more comprehensive approach to the expression of jealousy, termed *communicative responses to jealousy* (Guerrero & Andersen, 1998b; Guerrero et al, 1995, 2011).

Communicative Responses to Jealousy

Communicative responses to jealousy (CRJs) are defined as behavioral responses to the experience of jealousy that carry communicative value and that have the potential to help an individual fulfill individual and/or relational goals (Guerrero et al., 1995). The most recent research reveals the presence of 11 specific CRJ strategies/behaviors that cluster together into four primary types of general CRJs: constructive communication, destructive communication, avoidant communication, and rival-focused communication (Guerrero et al., 2011). Use of these strategies differs according to jealous thoughts, jealous emotions, and consequences for the individuals involved and their relationship(s).

   Constructive responses. Two responses are identified as constructive because using them to express jealousy typically results in positive outcomes for the people involved and for their romantic relationship. **Integrative communication** entails a productive, nonaggressive discussion of the jealousy experience with your partner that is focused on solving the problem at hand (Guerrero, 2012). Integrative communication may involve questioning your partner about their motives, feelings, and actions; asking for explanations for your partner's actions; sharing your emotions regarding the jealousy situation with your partner and explaining why you feel the way you do; and discussing the actions that can be taken moving forward in order to prevent similar jealousy situations from occurring. Note that the expression of emotion is thought to be a critical part of the success of such discussions in order to elicit your partner's empathy and thereby to help your partner better understand how you feel (Andersen et al., 1995). It is crucial to display the appropriate tone, attitude, and demeanor during these discussions, being careful to remain calm and keep from losing your composure (or your temper). Trying to engage in integrative communication when you are experiencing jealousy-related anger will probably be unsuccessful (Guerrero et al., 2005), as intense anger will prevent you from being able to approach integrative communication with the proper attitude. In addition, rumination about the feelings of jealousy leads to more use of all other CRJs *except* integrative communication (Carson & Cupach, 2000), suggesting that intrusive thoughts about the jealousy will also prevent you from being able to profitably discuss the jealousy situation. These findings suggest a need to hold off on using integrative communication until you are experiencing fewer intrusive, repetitive, negative thoughts about the jealousy and until you are composed enough to have a fruitful discussion. Integrative communication should be supportive and constructive, and if conducted appropriately, it is the best way to communicate your jealousy experience to your partner.

Compensatory restoration involves behaviors that are directed toward improving yourself (e.g., trying to be a better romantic partner, attempting to enhance your physical appearance) or the relationship (e.g., spending more time together as a couple, using relational maintenance behaviors, giving gifts to your partner). Compensatory restoration does not directly address the jealousy itself or its underlying issues, and it tends to be used when an individual considers their romantic relationship with the partner indispensable to their happiness, and thus they fear losing the relationship to the rival (Carson & Cupach, 2000). Too much compensatory restoration can have unintended negative effects if your partner perceives these behaviors as desperate attempts to do anything you can to hold on to them and the relationship, as they can reveal that you are overly dependent on your relationship and your partner (Guerrero & Afifi, 1998a). But some compensatory restoration is appropriate and appreciated; after all, you are making an effort to better yourself and the relationship you have with your romantic partner, and in the process, to show them that your current relationship is more attractive than other options (such as developing a relationship with the rival). But do not take it too far—use compensatory restoration in moderation along with integrative communication for best results.

Destructive responses. As their name indicates, destructive CRJs usually lead to negative individual and relational consequences. These three strategies are aggressive or passive aggressive and manipulative in nature; they are used with the intent to control and/or punish the romantic partner (Guerrero, 2012). **Violent communication** entails not just physical violence toward the partner such as hitting or throwing things, but also threats of physical harm to the partner. Research suggests that people choose to express their jealousy via violence very infrequently; instead, they most often use one of the other CRJs to express their jealousy. With that said, when partners do become violent, they often indicate that jealousy is a cause (Guerrero & Andersen, 1998a; Pines, 1992). Obviously, violent communication is never an appropriate or effective way to express jealousy or to deal with any relational difficulty.

Negative communication is basically the opposite of integrative communication and includes a wide range of behaviors that are damaging and destructive, but that stop short of violence or threats. Negative communication with your partner can be direct or indirect in nature, and can involve arguing, yelling, or otherwise behaving in a hostile manner, giving your partner the silent treatment, withholding affection from your partner, showing scorn for your partner by rolling your eyes or mocking them, giving your partner dirty looks, and being sarcastic. These behaviors do nothing to help address or resolve the issue at hand and only serve to worsen the jealousy situation.

Counter-jealousy induction involves purposeful attempts to make your romantic partner jealous because they first made you feel jealous. As discussed previously, jealousy induction may be used because you want to continue the romantic relationship and you are trying to get your partner to appreciate you more or show more love to you. If your partner does become jealous as a result of you flirting with an attractive third party, for example, you may take their jealousy response as an indicator of their feelings for you. If your partner does not become jealous, you may infer that their feelings for you are not that strong. Jealousy evocation may also be used for revenge motivations, as a way to get back at your partner for their role in the initial jealousy situation (Fleischmann et al., 2005). Although jealousy induction may in fact serve its intended purpose (to elicit more positive behavior from your partner toward you or to get revenge against your partner for making you jealous to begin with), it can obviously go very wrong and in rare cases may even lead to violence. Even if violence is not elicited by jealousy induction, many (if not most) people are unlikely to want to continue a romantic relationship with a person who uses this type of game playing and manipulation.

   Avoidant communication. Compared to constructive and destructive CRJs, avoidant responses are less active and more passive. The two CRJs that fall into this category are used when the goal is to avoid communication about the jealousy experience. **Denial** occurs when you do not admit how you are feeling and instead pretend like you are not actually experiencing jealousy. You may deny that you are feeling jealous if your primary concern is to maintain your self-esteem and your positive face (i.e., to keep from looking bad or being perceived in ways that you do not like). **Silence** is being quiet, decreasing communication, and not talking about your experience of jealousy. Note that this type of silence and giving your partner the silent treatment (which was identified previously as a form of the negative communication CRJ) are differently motivated. Purposely giving the silent treatment is an attempt to show your scorn for and punish your partner by eliminating the benefits of communication with you. It may also be an effort to try to alter your partner's behavior by punishing them with the silent treatment until they comply. Silence, on the other hand, is not motivated by the desire to punish, control, or otherwise manipulate your partner. Instead, becoming silent in response to jealousy is more about protecting your own needs. Silence indicates a lack of desire to talk about the jealousy situation now, but it does not preclude the possibility that—after you feel ready—you can initiate a productive discussion about the jealousy experience.

   Rival-focused responses. Remember that jealousy involves three people: you, your romantic partner, and the third-party rival. Although all the jealousy expression strategies discussed thus far only deal with communication or interaction between you and your partner, the final category of CRJs focuses on the rival. **Signs of possession** are public displays used to communicate to rivals that your romantic partner is "taken." Public displays of affection or tie signs can signal the nature of your relationship with your partner to others. You might kiss your partner or refer to him as "my boyfriend" in front of the rival in order to make clear that your partner is already romantically involved. **Rival derogation** occurs when you attempt to put down or denigrate the rival in an effort to make them seem less attractive to your partner. You might, for example, casually mention to your partner that rumor has it the girl you saw him flirting with has slept with a lot of people. **Surveillance** involves overt or covert activities intended to find out more about the rival relationship, and therefore to reduce your uncertainty about the jealousy experience. Surveillance can include spying on your partner, questioning the partner, or trying to interfere in your partner's relationship with the rival. You might check your partner's phone or social media for information about the rival relationship or call your partner frequently to check up on them, especially if you think the partner is with the rival. **Rival contact** includes direct contact with the rival, potentially for information-seeking purposes to reduce your uncertainty about the rival's intentions. Rival contact can also include confrontation of the rival in an effort to warn them directly to stay away from your partner.

Relational Correlates of Jealousy Expression

Your choice of CRJ to express jealousy naturally has personal, partner, and relational consequences. Considerable research reveals the benefits of using constructive responses (especially integrative communication), and they are the most frequently reported responses to experiencing jealousy (Bevan, 2013). Research has shown that partners tend to respond most positively to the use of constructive CRJs (Yoshimura, 2004a). People tend to use both integrative communication and compensatory restoration when they are highly invested in and committed to their romantic relationship and want to maintain it, and increased investment is also associated with more compensatory restoration (Bevan, 2008; Guerrero & Afifi, 1998a). Integrative communication is also a good way to alleviate uncertainties about your partner and the relationship that may have been spurred by the jealousy situation.

On the other hand, people who are not very happy in their romantic relationship are more likely to use destructive CRJs, especially negative communication, and destructive CRJs are so named because they generally have negative individual and relational consequences (Guerrero et al., 2011). People tend to use destructive CRJs when they are very angry about the jealousy situation and sometimes when they want to get revenge against the romantic partner. Women appear to be particularly sensitive to and bothered by their partner's use of destructive CRJs (Guerrero, 2014). Violence is the least frequently reported CRJ, but all the destructive CRJs should be avoided if you hope to handle the jealousy situation in ways that are conducive to the continued existence of your romantic relationship.

Avoidant communication does not appear to be a very direct or effective way to express jealousy, and at least one study indicates that the use of these strategies is linked to dissatisfaction with the romantic relationship (Andersen et al., 1995). Other research has uncovered no relationship at all between the use of avoidant CRJs and relationship satisfaction, however (Guerrero et al., 2011). Passive strategies such as avoidant communication may have their place, but it seems that they are best used only as a temporary response to jealousy. If you see your partner conversing with an attractive person at a party, you may feel a little jealous but not be willing to admit to that jealousy or otherwise talk about it until you determine if there is really anything to worry about. Or, perhaps you think you already have evidence to suggest a credible threat from a rival, such as in Tiana's case in the opening vignette of this chapter, but you feel that your emotions are too out of control to talk with the partner about it right now. In these cases, a little avoidant communication while you continue to appraise the situation and/or calm down is probably not harmful, and it may even be beneficial. However, if there is indeed a credible threat to your relationship from a rival third party, then avoidant CRJs will not help you address and correct the jealousy situation and get your romantic relationship back on track.

Behind the two constructive responses to jealousy, signs of possession are the next most frequently reported jealousy expression (Bevan, 2013). Signs of possession may actually work to keep rivals away from your partner, and these behaviors may make your partner feel loved and valued. Women, in particular, tend to be more relationally satisfied when their partner uses signs of possession (Guerrero, 2014). But it is easy to see how signs of possession can be taken too far and how that can reveal your insecurities to others. People are more likely to use surveillance and rival contact when they are experiencing a high level of negative, intrusive, ruminative thoughts about jealous feelings (Carson & Cupach, 2000). Surveillance is used more often by people who really want to hang on to their romantic relationship, but paradoxically the use of less surveillance (and rival contact) is reported in more satisfying romantic relationships (Bevan, 2008; Guerrero & Afifi, 1998a). Rival derogation has a good chance of backfiring; rather than making the rival look bad, you may just be making yourself look petty and insecure. Rather than making your partner realize that the rival really is not such an appealing alternative, you run the risk of making your partner more aware of some of your own less attractive qualities. While surveillance or even rival contact may help you feel better depending on the nature of what you find out from your efforts, if your partner becomes aware of your surveillance behaviors then you have created another problem in your relationship by communicating to your partner that you do not trust them and revealing the lengths you are willing to go to in order to find "dirt" on them. In short, although the use of some rival-focused responses here and there may be helpful when experiencing jealousy given that some of these strategies can serve to reduce your uncertainty about the jealousy situation, using too much of them is inadvisable. Further, there are other, more effective ways of reducing uncertainty, such as integrative communication.

Sex Differences in Jealousy Expression

The differences between men and women with regard to the expression of jealousy are generally small in magnitude, but a few consistent findings have emerged that warrant discussion here (Buss, 1988; Guerrero & Reiter, 1998). Some scholars have concluded that men tend to use rival contact more often than women, although this association is inconsistent. On the other hand, research fairly reliably reveals that women are more likely to use both constructive CRJs, integrative communication and compensatory restoration. Women appear to be especially effective in expressing emotion in the ways that are required by effective integrative communication. The ways in which women use compensatory restoration tend to differ from men's use of this strategy. Specifically, women are more likely to focus on increasing their physical attractiveness as a form of compensatory restoration. Finally, women are more likely than men to use counter-jealousy induction as a means of control.

Theory in Practice

Profiles of Jealousy Expression

Various theoretical models have been employed in an attempt to better understand how jealousy is expressed, such as Guerrero and Andersen's (1998b) componential model of jealousy. This model highlights certain precursors (e.g., personality characteristics, such as low self-esteem; relationship characteristics, such as decreased commitment; situational characteristics, such as the nature of the jealousy threat; strategic elements, including goals such as counter-jealousy induction) that can impact an individual's perception of the threat of jealousy. Once a rival threat is perceived, individuals experience a number of interrelated emotions (e.g., anger, sadness) and cognitions (e.g., suspicion, worry). These jealousy-related cognitions then prompt the identification of any goals (e.g., relationship continuation, information seeking) that the individual wishes to achieve through their choice of jealousy expression strategy. These goals—along with the jealousy-related emotions that are experienced—combine to predict the communicative response to jealousy that is selected, and these CRJs have differing consequences for the primary relationship, as has been discussed elsewhere in this chapter.

The most comprehensive theoretical approach to jealousy expression is found in Bevan's (2013) jealousy expression profile theory (see Figure 6.1). Her analysis and synthesis of available research revealed numerous characteristics that are associated with a jealous individual's selection of CRJs, finding that certain characteristics (e.g., cognitive, emotional, personal, relational) influence how people typically choose to express their jealousy. She concluded that people tend to choose constructive CRJs (i.e., integrative communication, compensatory restoration) when they are female, experiencing emotional jealousy, fearful, invested in and satisfied with the primary relationship, and when their goal is to continue the primary relationship. Conversely, individuals generally choose destructive CRJs (i.e., negative communication, violent communication, counter-jealousy induction) when they are experiencing cognitive

Constructive Jealousy Expression is more likely if jealous individuals:

- Are female
- Are satisfied with their relationships
- Are invested in their relationships
- Have the goal of maintaining their relationship
- Are experiencing emotional jealousy
- Are experiencing fear

Avoidant Jealousy Expression is more likely if jealous individuals:

- Are in an early relationship stage (e.g., dating)
- Are experiencing congnitive jealousy
- Are ruminating about their jealousy
- Are experiencing emotional jealousy

Destructive Jealousy Expression is more likely if jealous individuals:

- Are dissatisfied with their relationships
- Have the goal of restoring equity via retaliation
- Are experiencing cognitive jealousy
- Are ruminating about their jealousy
- Are experiencing emotional jealousy
- Are experiencing anger, hostility, or disgust

Rival-focused Jealousy Expression is more likely if jealous individuals:

- Are experiencing cognitive jealousy
- Are ruminating about their jealousy
- Are experiencing emotional jealousy
- Are experiencing anger, hostility, or disgust

FIGURE 6.1   Jealousy Expression Profile Theory

Adapted from: Jennifer L. Bevan, *The Communication of Jealousy*, p. 156. Copyright © 2013 by Peter Lang Publishing Group.

and emotional jealousy, ruminating, angry, hostile, disgusted, dissatisfied with the primary relationship, and when their goal is to retaliate against their partner. Those who tend to select avoidant CRJs (i.e., denial, silence) are experiencing cognitive and emotional jealousy, ruminating, and are typically in early stages of the relationship (e.g., they are less committed to their partner). Finally, those who often choose rival-focused CRJs (i.e., signs of possession, rival derogation, surveillance, rival contact) are experiencing cognitive and emotional jealousy and are ruminating, angry, hostile, or disgusted.

While the componential model of jealousy and jealousy expression profile theory both focus on the experience and expression of jealousy from the jealous person's point of view, other models have taken a different approach. Bevan's (2006, 2011) consequence model of jealousy expression deals with the reactions of the jealousy target after the jealous person has expressed their jealousy. Targets of another person's jealousy expression are expected to experience relational uncertainty (as discussed in Chapter 2)—specifically, partner uncertainty, then self-uncertainty, which combine to influence relationship uncertainty—when another's jealousy is expressed to them. The jealousy target's relationship uncertainty is then posited to incite rumination about the other person's expression of jealousy. This rumination engenders feelings of upset and guilt/fear, and these affective responses are associated with attack and aggressive responses. Although this model does not account for the possibility of positive reactions to another person's jealousy expression, it has shown utility across a variety of relational contexts, including romantic/dating, sibling, and cross-sex friend relationships.

Conclusion

As you have learned in this chapter, different types of jealousy occur in different types of relationships, and jealousy is usually "normal" as compared to pathological. Further, jealousy is an interactive experience with several interrelated components—cognitions, emotions, and communication/behaviors—that each have individual and relational implications. Although jealous thoughts and jealous feelings can lead to relational dissatisfaction, jealousy is also experienced in the context of satisfying and happy relationships. The difference between the positive or negative outcomes of the jealousy experience is largely a result of how jealousy is expressed;

as such, communication plays a particularly vital role in the jealousy situation. Communicating about jealousy in constructive ways leads to the most consistently positive personal and relational outcomes. Importantly, you have learned about responses to jealousy that are more constructive and about responses to jealousy that are more destructive in nature. The knowledge gleaned from this chapter should help you recognize that some forms of jealousy are normative, it should give you a better understanding of the various components of jealousy with which people struggle, and it should help you decide what to do (and what not to do) the next time you experience romantic jealousy.

Discussion Questions

1. Discuss the difference between reactive and pathological jealousy. Provide an example of each type of jealousy. Which one of these types would be considered a relational transgression, and why?

2. Define cognitive jealousy and explain the primary and secondary appraisal process whereby people attempt to interpret and make sense of their jealousy experience.

3. Define emotional jealousy and discuss the various affective responses (both positive and negative) that may be felt as part of the jealousy experience. Why or under what conditions might these various emotions be experienced during a jealousy situation?

4. Identify and define/explain the 11 communicative responses to jealousy (CRJs) that were covered in this chapter. Which of these appear to be the most, and the least, commonly used?

5. Discuss the relational correlates of jealousy expression that you have learned about in this chapter. In other words, what are the conditions or factors that impact which communicative response to jealousy is selected? What do we know about the consequences or outcomes of using these CRJs?

Chapter 7

Deception

Recall the scenario about Tiana, Trey, and Gia that opened Chapter 6. Tiana's boyfriend Trey had recently reconnected with his former romantic partner Gia without telling Tiana about it. Tiana only realized this was going on when a friend told her they had been seen having a drink together. Although Tiana feels threatened by Gia as a potential rival for Trey's affections, she decides to wait it out and see what happens without confronting Trey. As time goes by, Trey never mentions Gia, yet Tiana finds evidence to suggest that the two of them are getting together pretty frequently. When Tiana asks him where he has been after a night out with Gia, he is vague and noncommittal, saying he has been "out with friends." If the relationship between Trey and Gia really is innocent, Tiana does not understand why Trey will not be honest with her and come clean about it.

This scenario not only demonstrates that Tiana is experiencing jealousy (as discussed in Chapter 6), but it also shows that her experience of jealousy is based on what appear to be some relationship transgressions on the part of her partner, Trey. Specifically, it is clear from this vignette that Trey has not been honest with Tiana about his involvement with his former romantic partner. The expectation that others—especially close others like romantic partners and friends—will be honest with us is fundamental to close relationships. Yet, anecdotal and scholarly evidence has traditionally suggested that some types of deception may be a relatively common component of everyday life. In this chapter, we will discuss deception as a relationship transgression, or a violation of explicit or implicit rules for appropriate and inappropriate relational behavior. In the first half of the chapter, basic information such as the definition of deception, basic principles of deception, types of deception, and general motives for deception in the context of close relationships will be overviewed. In the second half of the chapter, we move to a discussion of deception detection, including accuracy, more and less reliable cues to deception, the truth-default and trigger events that may prompt its abandonment, as well as a recent perspective on how deception judgments are made (and how they might be improved).

Deception in the Context of Close Relationships

From an academic standpoint, **deception** is defined as intentionally transmitting (or strategically failing to transmit) information to create a belief in the target that the sender knows or believes to be false (Zuckerman et al., 1981). This definition of deception is fairly broad, yet it excludes instances such as mistakenly relaying incorrect information (as long as you believe it to be true at the time you communicate it); this is merely an error, not an attempt to knowingly deceive. Further, a message cannot be considered deceptive if you did not actually intend the target to believe it or take it literally (e.g., joking, sarcasm, or idiomatic expressions such as "I'm as blind as a bat"). Finally, according to this definition, it is not possible to deceive yourself (e.g., Burgoon et al., 1996).

Yet, as with most definitions, not all deception scholars agree on this conceptualization and its implications. For example, Trivers (2011) believes self-deception is possible and points to an evolutionary advantage of self-deception, arguing that believing our own falsehoods actually improves our ability to deceive others (i.e., believing our own untruths makes it more likely that others will believe them too). In addition, other scholars have debated intentionality as a prerequisite of deception, as we do not (and cannot) always know another's intent—and further, deception may be spontaneous and off-the-cuff as opposed to purposefully planned in advance.

To account for these considerations, other scholars acknowledge the role that perception plays in communicative processes, defining deception more inclusively as "a speaker who knowingly and intentionally misleads another person as well as the perception of a message's purpose as intentionally deceptive" (Levine & Knapp, 2018, p. 330). Put another way, some deception scholars recognize that the mere perception of another person's intent to mislead is sufficient for the target of a message to feel deceived.

As a strategic method for controlling information, deception takes many forms, generally ranging from low-stakes lies to high-stakes lies (DePaulo et al., 1980; Ekman, 1985). **Low-stakes lies** are colloquially known as white lies; they are often told in the interest of politeness and the consequences of getting caught in this type of lie are relatively minor (e.g., feeling embarrassed). For example, if your friend asks if you like her new super-short haircut and you say you do (even though you really do not), this type of low-stakes lie is told so that you do not hurt your friend's feelings. If your romantic partner makes dinner for you and you think it is terrible, but you say you thought it was delicious, this low-stakes lie keeps your partner from feeling badly after they did a nice thing for you.

High-stakes lies, on the other hand, can carry serious personal and legal penalties if discovered and are most often told for selfish reasons. Crimes of deception such as perjury (i.e., making false statements while under oath) or identity theft/fraud (i.e., presenting yourself as someone else using that person's wrongfully obtained personal information for economic gain) can result in the loss of your personal freedom as a result of imprisonment and/or the expense of paying large fines. High-stakes lies do not have to be in the form of crimes, however; lying to a friend in order to hide a drug addiction or lying to a romantic partner in order to hide a long-term affair, as examples, could result in the end of those relationships if your lie is revealed. Serious lies typically cover up some type of bad behavior and/or entail an attempt to claim an identity that is not one's own, but they may also be more altruistic in nature (e.g., to conceal a loved one's serious illness; DePaulo et al., 2004). Typically, lies are considered high stakes if the discovery of them could lead to the loss of something you value very highly, such as your freedom, your job, your standing as a student at a particular institution, and/or your close relationship with another person.

Of course, lots of deceptive acts are not easily categorized as either low- or high-stakes lies, and instead would fall somewhere between the two extremes. The consequences of medium-stakes lies are more serious than the embarrassment, guilt, or hurt feelings that accompany the discovery of low-stakes lies, but less serious than the loss of one's freedom and/or a valued relationship that accompany high-stakes lies. For example, say you lied to your boss to get a promotion. After a few weeks in your new role, your employer uncovers your deception and demotes you back to the position you were in before you got the promotion. That consequence is assuredly worse than merely being embarrassed, but not as bad as being fired from your job.

You might think that a difference in the type of lie that is told (i.e., low- or high-stakes) would impact how well people are able to lie, or the likelihood that they will get away with their deception. People should be especially motivated to get away with high-stakes lies due to the severe consequences of being discovered, and therefore they should be more successful in their high-stakes deceptive attempts because of this heightened motivation to succeed. However, in the context of deception, increased motivation seems to harm rather than heighten our chances for success. The **motivational impairment effect** holds that the increased motivation that accompanies the telling of high-stakes lies comes with a concomitant increase in the amount of anxiety and nervous arousal we feel when lying (DePaulo & Kirkendol, 1989). We work hard to conceal and control any outward expression of this anxiety, knowing that appearing visibly nervous may give us away. Often, though, we go too far in our attempts to control our nervousness, and as a result we come across as atypically rigid and generally unnatural. In these instances, it is our overly controlled demeanor that ultimately reveals our deception. Counterintuitively, then, the increased motivation behind high-stakes lies ends up impeding our ability to successfully deceive others.

Basic Principles of Deception

Decades of interdisciplinary deception scholarship has provided a wealth of empirically-based information about deception in interpersonal relationships. From available scholarly literature, two simple principles regarding the reasons for and general frequency of deceptive acts can be distilled.

Deception is functional. The simplest explanation for why people lie is because it is sometimes functional, just as telling the truth is sometimes functional. When it seems that a lie will serve a function or help us achieve a goal more successfully than the truth will, we might choose to deceive. Deception can help us achieve a variety of goals that allow us to maximize our psychological and material rewards, such as acquiring resources, managing our image, negotiating interactions, navigating relationships, and avoiding punishment (Buller & Burgoon, 1994; Camden et al., 1984;

Zuckerman et al., 1981). Perhaps the most common goal that deception helps us achieve is that of basic politeness and social appropriateness. In the interest of not being rude or hurting another's feelings, we often pretend to like things that we really do not care for or to have the same opinions as others about topics that are not terribly important to us. In this way, Vrij (2007) has characterized deception (particularly in the form of low-stakes lies) as a social lubricant that essentially enhances our ability to get along with each other by reducing conflict among us. Imagine a person who insisted on telling the absolute truth all the time, with no exception; that person would likely have a difficult time initiating and maintaining relationships with others due to their perceived lack of social skills.

Deception is common (or is it?). To return to an idea that was introduced at the beginning of this chapter, we typically expect others (especially close others) to be honest with us. Yet historically, empirical evidence has suggested that we should abandon this expectation because most people dissemble fairly often. Numerous diary studies in which people (e.g., college students and adults who were not attending college) were asked to record their lies daily indicated that most people report lying between one to two times per day, on average, and people confess to lying in about 25% of their face-to-face and mediated interactions (e.g., DePaulo et al., 1996; DePaulo & Kashy, 1998; George & Robb, 2008; Kashy & DePaulo, 1996). Although some research has found that deception is more common in face-to-face contexts as opposed to mediated contexts (e.g., Lewis & George, 2008), other research suggests that deception may be especially common in mediated interactions, especially in the context of online dating websites.

Deception in Mediated Contexts
Online Dating Websites

Both anecdotal experience and research evidence indicate that deception in online dating contexts is rampant. About one out of five of people admit to deception in their own online dating profile and expect that almost all other online daters (nine out of 10) are lying about their profile as well. Men on dating websites tend to lie about their income, education, height, age, and sometimes even their marital status (at least one out of 10 men with online dating profiles are thought to be married). Women on dating websites tend to lie about their age and aspects of their physical appearance such as weight (weight is downplayed by only about 5 pounds by a woman in her 20s, but that amount can increase to almost 20 pounds for an online dater in her 40s). Women have also been shown to exaggerate their height by about 1 inch, just as men have (Epstein, 2007). In terms of the photographs that are presented in online dating profiles, at least one out of three have been judged to be inaccurate representations of the person's actual appearance, with women more likely than men to post inaccurate pictures of themselves (e.g., outdated or retouched pictures; Hancock & Toma, 2009).

Rather than relying solely on self-reports of deception in one's online dating profile, some research operates from a more objective "ground truth" approach where the information in a person's profile is verified directly by assessing observable information about the person, such as weighing the person to see how much they actually weigh (versus the weight this person indicated in their profile), measuring the person's height to assess how tall they really are (versus how tall this person claims to be in their profile), and examining the person's driver's license to see how old they actually are (versus how old this person claims to be in their profile). These ground truth studies conclude that deception in online dating profiles is quite common indeed, with eight out of 10 participants lying about at least one aspect of their profile (women most commonly lie about their weight; men most commonly lie about their height). Yet, these researchers conclude that the magnitude of most of these deceptions is rather small in nature—in other words, in the majority of cases the lies are subtle. Most of the time, they do not deviate appreciably from the truth, such that you probably would not be able to detect them even when you are able to see the person in a face-to-face meeting (Toma et al., 2008).

Deception in order to make oneself look better has historically been a very common motivation, even offline, but research clearly reveals the likelihood of being deceived by online daters. Yet, despite the quantity of lies, perhaps it is comforting to know that research from the ground truth approach suggests that those deceptions may not matter in meaningful ways when all is said and done.

Across various studies, people report lying most often about what they like, how they feel, and what they think. They also report lying about what they have done, where they are/were, what they plan to do, what they have accomplished, and their personal failures. Although people sometimes lie to avoid punishment or to gain material rewards, DePaulo et al. (2003) concluded that deceivers are usually more interested in psychological rewards—for example, the creation of an impression that is more favorable to others. Most of the lies told are of the lower stakes variety; people view these lies as relatively unremarkable in nature and do not report feeling badly about telling them. The results of these studies (and others) have led to the conclusion that people are frequent liars and that deception is a common occurrence. Note that more recent research, however, paints a different picture whereby these elevated estimates of deception frequency may not be representative of the behavior of most people; instead, these estimates appear to be driven by a small percentage of the population who are especially copious liars (see Serota et al., 2010).

FLIPPING THE SCRIPT

Are Most People Frequent Liars?

As you will recall, earlier deception studies (particularly work by DePaulo and her colleagues) suggested that the prevalence of deception in every-day life is quite high, as these scholars concluded from the data they had that people report being deceptive in roughly one out of every four interactions they have (and that college students are especially likely to lie to their mothers). However, more recent research calls into question the frequency with which most people deceive, and instead reveals an intriguing pattern whereby the vast majority of lies are told by a small group of especially prolific liars.

In a large-scale study with a representative sample of 1,000 Americans who were asked to report on the lies they had told within the last 24 hours, on average, people reported telling one to two lies during the previous day, a finding that seemingly replicates previous research by DePaulo and colleagues (Serota et al., 2010). Yet, a closer look at the *distribution* of responses (rather than the mean or average of the responses) revealed that the majority of people in the sample (60%) reported no deception at all the prior day, and most strikingly, almost half of all lies reported in the sample were told by the top 5% most active or prolific liars (Serota et al., 2010). In other words, it appears to be the outliers in this sample—those extremely prolific liars—who, when lumped with everyone else, are driving up the average rates of deception in a way that is not representative of what is actually happening. If those outliers are considered independently from the rest of the sample (i.e., if we do not attempt to look at the mean or average score across people, including these outliers), then it becomes obvious that we are dealing with two different groups of people: one group who does not report a high prevalence of deception (the majority of people) and another group who does report a very high prevalence of deception (the much smaller group of prolific liars).

In addition to collecting data from a new sample, Serota et al. re-analyzed data from three of the earlier deception studies (including the diary data from the DePaulo et al. 1996 study) by looking at the distributions of deception frequency (again, as opposed to the mean or average of deception, which is the marker that DePaulo et al. attended to). This re-analysis of some of the original scholarship that led to the initial conclusion that lying is very prevalent supported the more recent assertion that a small percentage of really productive liars is perpetrating the most deception, while the majority of people report little to no deception on a daily basis. To further evidence this conclusion, a follow-up study with nearly 3,000 people from the United Kingdom confirmed this pattern of a few prolific deceivers (Serota & Levine, 2015). The especially prolific liars in this Serota et al. study tended to be younger males with higher occupational status who espoused the view that some lies are acceptable, they reported lying to close others and to supervisors in the workplace, and said they had experienced negative consequences of their deception.

Taken together, emerging findings (based on newly collected samples that are quite large, from both the United States and outside of it, as well as re-analysis of the original data that led to initial claims about deception's prevalence) demonstrate the necessity of distinguishing between everyday and high-volume deceivers. In contrast to what we thought we knew for years about the frequency of lying, it now seems as if the more accurate pattern is that most people tell few (or no) lies on any given day whereas most lies are told by a small percentage of prolific liars.

Types of Deception

There are many means by which we can deceive others. Several primary deceptive strategies have been identified, and in accordance with the inclusive definition of deception presented earlier in this chapter, these acts range from outright lies to over- or understating the truth to omitting consequential details in order to produce an inaccurate or incomplete impression in another.

Falsifications. Also known as fabrications or simply as lying, **falsification** is communicating information you know or believe to be false to another as if it were true (Ekman, 1985). If you miss the final exam in one of your classes because you overslept, but you make up a story about how you were in a car accident just before class to tell your professor in the hopes of being able to make up the exam, the made-up story is an example of falsification. It is the complete opposite of—or at least very different from—the truth of the matter. In that way, falsifications have very little, if any, truth to them. Some research with U.S. samples has shown that these types of outright lies are the most commonly reported form of deceptive act (Guthrie & Kunkel, 2013; Metts, 1989).

Equivocations. Also known as evasion, **equivocation** occurs when we make indirect or ambiguous statements that seem to have communicated a message they really did not convey (Bavelas et al., 1990). When your friend asks if you like her new haircut and you really do not but do not want to hurt her feelings, you might say something like "It's really unique!" or "That's a really popular cut right now." Because "unique" is an ambiguous term that could be positive or negative in nature and because the latter statement is indirect (i.e., it does not directly answer the question you were asked about whether you like the haircut; it merely states a related fact), your friend will likely interpret your message positively, as if you really do like her new haircut—especially if you deliver these statements with the right tone and facial expressions. Equivocations are certainly not outright lies, but they are deceptive because they intentionally mislead others by creating an impression that is not accurate or honest.

Overstatements and understatements. **Overstatements** (more commonly known as exaggerations) and **understatements** (also known as minimizing) are opposite strategies: the former involves embellishing or stretching the truth and the latter involves toning down or diminishing the truth (Turner et al., 1975). People often exaggerate to make themselves look better and/or to make a story more interesting, and some research with a U.S. sample has shown that exaggerations are the second most common form of deception in romantic relationships (Guthrie & Kunkel, 2013). For instance, exaggerations are common during job interviews, wherein candidates might truthfully report their job duties but overstate their experience, knowledge, and/or skill with regard to particular tasks. People often minimize when they want to distance themselves from something. For example, even when accused individuals confess to crimes, they often downplay or minimize their role and/or their culpability for the event. They might admit to discharging their weapon during the commission of a robbery but not to actually shooting anyone directly. They might admit to being at the scene, but not to helping plan the crime in advance. Overstatements and understatements have some truth to them, but they are deceptive because they purposely misrepresent the truth in order to create a false impression in another person.

Omissions. Also known as concealment, **omission** entails leaving out information that you know is meaningful or relevant in order to leave another with an incorrect impression of events (Ekman, 1985; Turner et al., 1975). If you go out tonight with some of your friends and run into an ex-romantic partner, but when your current romantic partner asks about your night you merely tell them you were with friends (and fail to explicitly state that your ex was there), that is an omission of consequential information that leaves your partner with a false impression of your evening. Omissions have some truth to them in that typically what is communicated verbally is true (i.e., in the preceding example, you were indeed out with friends), but they are deceptive because you are intentionally leaving out important information that you know would change the other person's view of the situation if they knew it. In the vignette that opened this chapter, Trey's failure to tell Tiana that he has reconnected with his ex and that they are in contact with each other and get together fairly frequently is a lie of omission. When Trey says he is "out with friends," there is (arguably) some truth to that—Gia could perhaps be considered an old friend. But strategically failing to mention that the friend in this case is a former romantic partner functions to intentionally keep Tiana in the dark about the true, complete picture of what Trey is doing. Thus, such omissions are deceptive in nature. If you have trouble seeing omissions as a form of deception, imagine yourself as the receiver instead of as the sender. If your romantic partner acted as Trey did in the scenario, wouldn't you feel deceived?

As these strategies make clear, deception is more than telling bald-faced lies. It includes any purposeful attempt (or any attempt that is perceived as purposeful) to conceal or distort the truth or to mislead or delude others. In addition, deceptive strategies may be crafted and executed at the dyadic level rather than at the individual level. In other words, two or more people may collude by cooperating and collaborating in order to mutually construct stories and otherwise carry out the various deceptive acts together (Knapp & Comadena, 1979). Although some research indicates that most people typically do not feel too badly about most of their lies, in the context of romantic relationships, other research has demonstrated increases in the deceiver's feelings of guilt and shame across various types of deception to the extent that the deceiver is more satisfied with and committed to their relationship (Horan & Dillow, 2009). In other words, when people who are in satisfying and committed romantic relationships deceive their partner, they report feeling guilty and ashamed about having done so.

Motives for Deception

As noted previously, lying serves many functions and can help people achieve any number of goals (just as telling the truth can be functional and help you achieve goals). Numerous motives for deception have been identified, and no single typology of motivations is dominant in the deception research (e.g., Hample, 1980; Seiter et al., 2002). In the context of close relationships, research has revealed three general motives for deception: partner-focused, self-focused, and relationship-focused motives (Metts, 1989). Broadly speaking, deception motives are typically distinguished and evaluated according to their perceived degree of altruism or selfishness.

Partner-focused motives. Lies that are told for **partner-focused motives** are told for the sake of the other person (i.e., for the sake of the person to whom you are lying). These motives broadly entail helping the other maintain their preferred self-image or protecting the other from hurt, worry, or psychological harm. We may also tell lies that have a partner-focused motive when we are trying to protect the other's relationship with some third party (e.g., you might lie to your parents about one of your sibling's behavior to try to prevent problems in their relationship). Unlike self-focused motives, partner-focused motives are usually viewed as more altruistic and less selfish in nature, and telling these types of lies may have positive outcomes (Seiter et al., 2002). For example, telling your romantic partner that he "always looks attractive to you" despite that he has put on some weight recently and does not feel at his best is an effort to be kind and avoid hurting the partner's feelings. Deception for the sake of someone other than yourself tends to be viewed as more acceptable. But of course, this is a bit of a gray area. In the vignette that opened this chapter, Trey may have felt that his lies of omission—especially very early on, when he first reconnected with his ex Gia and things were innocent—served to protect Tiana from feeling threatened about something that (at that point, anyway) did not warrant a threat. However, if Tiana was asked whether she felt this deception was enacted primarily in order to protect *her*, she would likely feel that Trey's lies of omission served to protect himself far more than anyone else.

Self-focused motives. Lies that are told for **self-focused motives** are told for the benefit of ourselves and are therefore viewed as more selfish and less altruistic. These motives include achieving any number of personal goals, including maintaining or improving one's own image, protecting one's own resources (including the romantic partner and the relationship the two of you share), gaining power/control in a relationship (e.g., pretending like you care about your partner less than you really do), or avoiding negative outcomes for oneself such as resentment, anger, shame, embarrassment, or criticism. For instance, lying to your romantic partner to cover up an act of sexual infidelity so that you do not lose the partner/relationship is a lie that primarily benefits you. In the vignette that opened this chapter, most people would agree that Trey's lies of omission primarily benefitted him, allowing him to continue his extradyadic relationship with Gia while his current girlfriend Tiana was none the wiser. Lies that are self-motivated are typically viewed as more deplorable than partner-motivated lies, and although most people do not seem to experience much regret following deception, self-motivated lies can result in increased feelings of shame and guilt (Seiter & Bruschke, 2007; Seiter et al., 2002).

Relationship-focused motives. Lies that are told for **relationship-focused motives** are supposedly told for the good of the relationship. These types of lies are motivated by dyadic-level concerns, such as avoiding any type of unpleasant interaction with the other (such as conflict) and generally avoiding potential damage to the relationship the two of you share. For example, assume you saw your ex-romantic partner for coffee last week. The meeting was entirely platonic; neither you nor your ex is interested in being anything but friends. Yet, you choose to deceive your partner about this meeting in order to avoid the conflict that would likely follow its revelation. If your primary motivation is to preserve the relationship from harm, then this lie is primarily relationship motivated. This motive should be perceived as less altruistic than partner-focused motives but more altruistic than self-focused motives, and research reveals moderate acceptability ratings of the avoiding conflict motive in the context of close relationships (i.e., marriage, friendship, and family; Seiter et al., 2002).

Relationship-motivated lies appear to have differing outcomes in that sometimes they are beneficial for the relationship (as they are intended to be), but at other times they make the situation worse. Continuing with our meet-an-ex-for-coffee example, assume your current romantic partner believes your lie at first but later finds out the truth. At this point, your current partner probably will not believe that the meeting between you and your ex was innocent, in part because you initially felt the need to lie about it. After all, if there was really nothing to it, why wouldn't you have come clean in the first place? Often, relationship-motivated lies start with good intentions but may end up making things worse in the long run if your deception is discovered (Metts, 1994).

It is important to note that these deception motives are not mutually exclusive, meaning that a lie can be motivated by one, two, or all three of these reasons. In the vignette that opened this chapter, Trey's deception probably had different degrees of self, partner, and relationship motivations, assuming that he would like his romantic relationship with Tiana to continue despite his transgressions with Gia. In determining the motivation behind a lie, it is important to consider which of these (your partner, you, or the relationship) is of utmost or primary concern. The motives underlying deception appear to be the best predictor of others' acceptability ratings of and emotional reactions to that deception, even cross-culturally, with less altruistic lies evaluated as more unacceptable and resulting in more negative emotional responses for the person who was lied to.

Relational Effects of Deception

Although deception is not universally negative and people are even able to recognize certain circumstances in which it is necessary to deceive a romantic partner, weighty deceptions about important relational issues violate relational rules for appropriate behavior and are classified as relationship transgressions (Boon & McLeod, 2001; Metts, 1994). When these types of deceptions are revealed, the partner who was lied to typically reacts with negative affect such as distress and anger (McCornack & Levine, 1990a). The partner who was lied to may also experience hurt feelings, a decrease in self-esteem, and a desire to seek revenge against the person who lied to them (O'Hair & Cody, 1994). Further, realizing that a partner has been untruthful leads one to feel less satisfied with and less committed to their romantic relationship and can result in increased conflict and suspicion (Cole, 2001; O'Hair & Cody, 1994). Cases of serious deception are very difficult to forgive, and the result may be relationship termination (Hayashi et al., 2010; McCornack & Levine, 1990a).

Deception Detection

In part because deception is somewhat common in that most people deceive from time to time, you may be tempted to think that most people are fairly good at accurately detecting deception when someone lies to them. After all, it seems natural that we tend to get better at things we have more practice with—the more we are lied to, the better we should become at detecting others' lies. However, quite a large body of research suggests that this is not the case. Deception detection accuracy rates as reported in empirical studies have historically been unimpressive, suggesting that people are only slightly better than chance at **deception detection**, or correctly differentiating between truths and lies. Past research reveals that people can correctly discern when they are being lied to between 45% and 60% of the time, with an average accuracy rate of approximately 54% and with the highest rates topping out around 67% (Bond & DePaulo, 2006). These slightly better than chance findings have obtained under various conditions (e.g., in interactive and noninteractive contexts, with motivated and nonmotivated lies, with planned and off-the-cuff deception, and in mediated and nonmediated contexts) and with differing samples (e.g., college students, noncollege student adults, and even experienced experts such as professional investigators). One exception may be a group referred to as **wizards**; this is a small proportion of experts in the criminal justice system who defy statistical odds by accurately distinguishing lies (typically high-stakes lies) from truths in better than 80% of cases (O'Sullivan & Ekman, 2004). Only recently has research begun to reveal a pattern of improved deception detection accuracy rates among laypeople and some explanations for those improvements (see Levine, 2015).

FLIPPING THE SCRIPT

Are We Really That Bad at Detecting Deception?

Decades of research on the topic of deception detection accuracy has led to the conclusion that, under normal circumstances, most people are only slightly better than chance at correctly distinguishing truthful statements from deceptive ones. This body of evidence suggests that you would be almost as accurate in detecting another's deception if you simply flipped a coin to determine whether a person is lying to you rather than if you tried to discover their deception by relying on nonverbal leakage cues that were thought to be indicative of lying (Ekman & Friesen, 1969). More recent research shows evidence of an uptick in these accuracy rates, however, finding (and replicating) accuracy rates in the 60% range, the 70% range, and even the 90% range (Levine, 2015). The improvements in accurate lie–truth distinctions seem to be a function of whether the detector is skilled in persuading the would-be deceiver to confess (Levine et al., 2014); whether the detector is able to craft questions that elicit answers that reveal information that is helpful in distinguishing between truth and lie tellers (Levine, Blair, & Clare, 2014); and the extent to which the detector is in possession of informational, situational, and/or behavioral familiarity and knowledge related to the deceiver's claims, motives, and typical behavioral patterns (Blair et al., 2010; Bond et al., 2013;

Burgoon et al., 2010; Reinhard et al., 2013). Two particular approaches to improving deception detection accuracy highlight the importance of paying attention to the deceiver's story and comparing that to evidence that either confirms or disconfirms what they say is true.

The CiC (content in context) approach suggests that, rather than focusing on leakage cues to identify deception, you will have more success if you rely on the content of the communication surrounding the deception, listening closely to the person's statements and comparing them to other related evidence that you have (or can get access to later) or to what is usual in the context at hand, keeping your ears open for any contradictions (Blair et al., 2010). Asking questions that have **diagnostic utility** can improve your deception detection accuracy, but do not ask questions like "Why should I believe you?" as Levine et al.'s (2014) research has demonstrated that this question has negative utility (i.e., it makes an innocent truth teller look guilty and deceptive because the truth teller knows you are suspicious of them and they may not be able to prove that they are telling the truth). When truth tellers become aware that their listener is suspicious and does not trust what they are saying, they tend to get defensive, which comes across as (i.e., looks a lot like) how we think someone who is being deceptive would behave (e.g., they get visibly flustered, their pitch goes up).

The SUE (strategic use of evidence) approach suggests that, if you do have evidence that potentially controverts the lie teller's story, you should withhold that information to see whether the deceiver's story contradicts what you know to be true in order to catch lie teller in the act of lying (e.g., Hartwig et al., 2005). These types of diagnostic information are so important in accurately detecting deception that without them even trained experts such as police detectives are usually no better at accurately detecting deception than are laypeople (Bond & DePaulo, 2006).

Deception detection is a complicated process, made all the more difficult because most people enter most interactions with a truth bias. The term **truth bias** initially referred to the tendency to believe romantic partners, specifically, but has evolved to a more general inclination to believe what other people tell us, unless we have some reason not to believe it (McCornack & Levine, 1990b; McCornack & Parks, 1986). In close relationships, this may be a natural outcome of the trust between relational partners (Miller & Stiff, 1993). However, the propensity to believe that others are being honest with us is operative even when we do not know the other person well. The double standard in evaluating deception may help account for this phenomenon (Bond & DePaulo, 2006).

The **double-standard perspective** claims we have two sets of rules by which we tend to evaluate our own deception versus the way we tend to judge others' deception. Unsurprisingly, we consider our own deceptive communication as relatively benign distortions that are rationalized because they are warranted in the service of everyday social interactions. Therefore, we see our own deception as fairly unremarkable—certainly not as an indicator that we could or should be labeled as a liar. Conversely, we tend to evaluate others' deception as morally wrong, label others who deceive as liars, stereotype liars as anguished and guilty as a result of their lies, and conclude that those who exhibit behaviors associated with this stereotype are most likely deceptive. As such, because most people can deceive without "looking like" this stereotypical notion of a liar, our tendency to believe even those we are not close to is reinforced.

Yet, attending to such nonverbal cues and relying on them as indicative of deception (or not) is problematic, as research has shown quite convincingly that most behavioral cues once thought to be corollaries of deception (e.g., lack of eye contact) are not reliable indicators of lying (DePaulo et al., 2003). One reason for this is because deceivers realize the importance of controlling their behaviors in order eliminate or reduce those cues that might make them appear deceptive (Zuckerman et al., 1981). Thus, it makes sense that if we are looking for deceivers to behave as we *think* liars should behave in order to detect deception, we will be thrown off the trail (and thus, tend to believe what we are being told rather than question the veracity of it) more often than not.

This explanation leads organically to a second important reason why accurate deception detection is difficult: people have a tendency to look for the wrong so-called cues to deception and to rely heavily on those misleading cues to draw conclusions regarding another's truthfulness or dishonesty (Ekman & Friesen, 1969). This tendency is strong and persistent, and it has translated to significant efforts on the part of deception scholars to empirically determine which cues (if any) are consistently and robustly associated with deception. By and large, these efforts have revealed that only a few behaviors have any reliable association with deception at all, and even these behaviors can be idiosyncratic in nature. These findings are supported by an evolutionary perspective on deception, which suggests that any patently apparent cues to deception would have been identified by people long ago, effectively allowing us to evolve as proficient deception detectors (see Bond et al., 1985). To succeed in deceptive endeavors, deceivers must instead be adaptable. Some of the following behaviors are more or less consistently associated with deception, but of course, none of them is always present every time a liar lies; furthermore, even when present, these cues may be indicative of something other than deception.

Relatively Reliable Cues to Deception

Vocal pitch. One nonverbal cue that has evinced perhaps the most valid and consistent link to deception is vocal **pitch**. Quite a bit of research shows that pitch, how low or high a person's voice is, often increases (i.e., becomes higher) during deceptive communication (Bauchner et al., 1980; DePaulo et al., 2003; Ekman, 1988; Sporer & Schwandt, 2006). This increase in vocal pitch during deception is thought to be an indicator of the underlying affective states or encoding and decoding demands that most people experience when they lie. Lying looks effortless for roughly 5% of the population who are considered seamless or natural liars (later renamed natural performers; Ekman, 1992), and still others seem to enjoy deception and feel downright gleeful about their ability to fool others (a phenomenon called duping delight; Ekman, 1981). Further, some scholars have positioned deception as so "routine" as to leave deceivers emotionally unfazed (DePaulo et al., 2003). Yet, deceivers may feel tense and anxious when trying to deceive another—particularly when the stakes are high. Vocal pitch tends to rise along with the feelings of nervousness (and in the case of duping delight, the feelings of excitement) that organically accompany deception (Villar et al., 2013). In addition to being one of the few reliable nonverbal indicators of deception, increased vocal pitch is also one of the more objective, as deceivers are typically not conscious of it and therefore do not try to control it in the way they do other, more obvious cues that have been thought to indicate deception.

Pupil dilation. **Pupil dilation**, or expanding in diameter, has also been shown to be reliably associated with lying (DePaulo et al., 2003; Webb et al., 2009). DePaulo et al. suggested that pupil dilation's relationship with deception may be a function of the affect associated with deception or perhaps due to the contextual demands of information processing, possibilities that are borne out by available research. A large body of research shows that pupils dilate under conditions of negative arousal such as stress and pain (Oka et al., 2000) as well as under conditions of positive arousal (Andersen et al., 1980). Further, pupil dilation has long been associated with cognitive load (Beatty, 1982). Pupil dilation is perhaps the most objective nonverbal indicator of deception, as it is not controllable merely by will alone.

Blinking. In addition to pupil dilation, other eye behaviors such as blinking have been studied as potential correlates of deception. Blinking may be expected to decrease due to the cognitive effort that is required of some lies, such as making up a story (Holland & Tarlow, 1972, 1975). Blinking could also increase during deceptive communication, as blinking is a relatively subtle way of expending the excess energy experienced under the conditions of stress and anxiety that can accompany deception (Harrigan & O'Connell, 1996). Some studies have shown that blinking does increase during deception (DePaulo et al., 1985).

Speech errors. A relatively wide range of **speech errors** (i.e., grammatical errors, stuttering, false starts, sentence fragments, and dysfluencies that disrupt smooth speech delivery, such as filled pauses, extra-long pauses, and extended response latencies) have long been thought to be made more often under deceptive conditions (Sporer & Schwandt, 2006; Vrij et al., 2000; Zuckerman et al., 1981). Some evidence suggests that deceivers may exhibit increased repetition and longer response latencies during unplanned lies (DePaulo et al., 2003; see also Davis et al., 2005). These speech errors are thought to be induced by the guilt, anxiety, and worry that most people feel when attempting to deceive others.

An important point about these relatively more reliable indicators of deception was made earlier, but bears repeating—higher vocal pitch, pupil dilation, blinking, increased repetition of words and/or phrases, and taking longer to respond are not *always* signs that you are being deceived. Obviously, pitch increases, pupils dilate, people naturally have to blink, and speech dysfluencies occur for many reasons that do not have anything to do with deception. As a result, interpreting these cues is a complex undertaking during everyday interactions. With regard to vocal pitch and speech errors in particular, interpretation is more accurate when you have some level of **behavioral familiarity**—when you are familiar enough with the other person's baseline behavior (e.g., their normal pitch, how fluent their speech usually is) to render deviations from normal behavior meaningful in potentially deceptive interactions (Burgoon et al., 2010).

Inconsistent and Unreliable Cues to Deception

Smiling. Contradictory evidence exists regarding the association between smiling and deception. For some time, scholars were concerned with the question of whether deceivers smile more or less often than truth tellers, and research exists to support either claim. Other evidence demonstrates no association between smiling and lying. Taken together, most research suggests that it is not how often one smiles that distinguishes deceivers from truth tellers; instead, it is the type of smile in question. That is, deceivers are more likely to display false smiles during deception as opposed to genuine smiles, also known as Duchenne smiles. Duchenne smiles are characterized by a raising of the cheeks that causes crow's feet wrinkles in the skin at the sides of the eyes, whereas deceptive smiles (which only raise the corners of the mouth) do not cause this pattern of wrinkling. People exhibit fake smiles fairly frequently, often to disguise negative affective states such as anxiety and sadness, and generally to appear more pleasant to others (Ekman et al., 1988).

Body movements. Various body movements have been examined in conjunction with deception. Adaptors are behaviors that help meet physical (e.g., scratching an itch) and psychological needs (e.g., biting one's nails when bored or anxious), and may be displayed due to the underlying negative feelings induced by some situations, especially situations that make us feel nervous. Although three types of adaptors are recognized, two types—**self-adaptors** (self-touching such as twirling one's hair, scratching, or biting one's nails) and **object adaptors** (manipulating objects such as clicking a pen, playing with a fidget spinner, or jangling keys)—are most relevant to deception. Some studies have demonstrated that these types of adaptive behaviors are exhibited more often during deception (Caso et al., 2006; DePaulo et al., 1985), although other research does not report such increases. Other body movements have also been investigated, and most studies have found that deceivers exhibit fewer illustrators (gestures used for emphasis) and display reduced hand, foot, and leg movements as compared to truth tellers (Caso et al., 2006; DePaulo et al., 2003; Sporer & Schwandt, 2007). Over-controlling body movements may be an attempt by deceivers to avoid seeming nervous during deceptive encounters.

Eye contact. Common wisdom tells us that deceivers give themselves away because they are not able to look us in the eye while lying to us. However, the results of most research studies refute this old adage, finding no statistically significant relationship between eye contact and deceptive behavior (DePaulo et al., 1985, 2003). In fact, Hartwig and Bond (2011) concluded from their meta-analytic work that eye contact is more weakly related to deception than most other nonverbal cues that have been studied, and gaze aversion is more weakly related than nearly half of other nonverbal cues that have been studied. One reason this supposed cue to deception is not reliable may be because so many people recognize eye contact as a cultural stereotype of lying. If you know that most people believe deceivers do not look their targets in the eye while lying, you realize that maintaining good eye contact is something you need to do if you do not want to look like a liar. Cues such as eye contact are under our direct control when deceiving, and it is fairly easy to make sure to maintain good eye contact under these circumstances.

Considering Patterns of Cues as Opposed to Cues in Isolation

While studies of cues to deception in isolation have led to the conclusion that nonverbal indicators of deception are too inconsistent and weak to effectively distinguish deceivers from truth tellers, emerging research on patterns of such cues points to the utility of considering constellations of such cues (Hartwig & Bond, 2014). Although very little research currently examines such patterns, early studies suggest that deceivers' patterns of behavior are simpler (exhibiting fewer unique body movements such as illustrators, adaptors, and head movements such as nodding), shorter, and more repetitive than truth tellers' patterns of behavior (Burgoon et al., 2014, 2015).

Focusing on Verbal Rather Than Nonverbal Cues

Although some cues are more or less reliably linked with deception, when faced with a potential deceiver, you should not focus on nonverbal cues to the exclusion of what the person is actually saying. Contrary to long-held beliefs about certain nonverbal cues as giveaways of deception, inconsistent information—what is said during potentially deceptive encounters—is likely the best indicator of deception. Research has discovered that the vast majority of lies (98%) are discovered in other ways besides observation of the potential deceiver's demeanor during the deceptive encounter (Park et al., 2002). Deceivers sometimes cannot keep their stories straight, or they (or some third party) may provide information that contradicts other facts that we know (or later discover) to be true, which is one reason deceivers may be less likely to provide verifiable references (Park et al., 2002). Deceivers provide significantly fewer details, generally spend less talk time responding to questions during deceptive interactions (DePaulo et al., 2003; deTurck & Miller, 1985), and sometimes actively block access to information (Hartwig & Bond, 2011). Further, deceivers' stories are less plausible and logically structured and they express more uncertainty and internal discrepancies (DePaulo et al., 2003; Hartwig & Bond, 2011).

Much like behavioral familiarity is often necessary when attempting to identify deception from another's nonverbal cues, **informational familiarity**—when you are familiar enough with the other person's life to be privy to certain information about them—is often necessary when attempting to evaluate whether information is consistent or inconsistent (Burgoon et al., 2010). For example, students can often successfully deceive professors because professors have very little informational familiarity about students' lives. If you deceive us by saying you had to miss the final exam because of a death in your family when really no such death occurred, we do not usually have any access to personal knowledge that would contradict or support that. You would have a more difficult time telling that lie to a person who knows you better.

Other Factors That Might Influence Deception Detection Accuracy

The preceding review suggests that relying on cues to deception will not aid you in detecting deception more accurately. You may wonder if there are any other qualities that might enhance your detection abilities, such as your relationship (or lack thereof) with the deceiver. Given concepts such as behavioral familiarity, it seems intuitive that we would have more success in accurately detecting a close other's deception because we know that person better. Some research has shown that we are better at detecting friends' and spouses' deception as compared to strangers' deception, but accuracy rates were highest for friends (Comadena, 1982). Other research suggests higher accuracy rates for strangers, perhaps because the truth bias is stronger for people we know and like (Burgoon et al., 2009), and many studies report the same accuracy rates for romantic partners as for strangers (e.g., Levine & McCornack, 1992). Other factors such as the interactivity of the context and whether you are trying to detect deception when the deceiver is someone of your own culture (versus someone of another culture) also do not seem to markedly improve deception detection accuracy (Bond & Atoum, 2000; Burgoon et al., 2001). Taken together, findings such as these reinforce the emerging notion that cues to deception are unreliable and should be forsaken in favor of attending to information that is conveyed verbally by the deceiver, such as changes in the deceiver's original story or statements that contradict facts you know to be true.

Theory in Practice

Rethinking Deception Detection

As you have learned throughout this chapter, what we think we know about the frequency of deception and how to more accurately detect another's deception is beginning to change based largely on a program of research by Levine and his colleagues. This program of research has culminated in the development of truth-default theory (TDT), a theory about deception and deception detection that pivots from the former reliance on nonverbal cues as indicators of deception to a focus on contextualized communication content (Levine, 2014, 2020). TDT is a broadly pitched modular theory that is anchored by the notion of the **truth default**, which is the idea that most people's default position is to believe another person and to judge their communication as honest. In contrast to other perspectives on deception detection, Levine has argued that the truth default—the presumption of honesty—is an adaptive one from an evolutionary perspective, helping to make our communication with others more efficient (i.e., because we are not continually suspicious and closely monitoring cues to deception) as well as accurate, in most cases (i.e., because most people are indeed honest most of the time). As you have learned elsewhere in this chapter, recent research suggests that only a few people in the population (i.e., prolific liars) are responsible for telling the majority of lies that have been reported in empirical research.

According to TDT, when people do choose to lie, most have a reason for it (with the exception of compulsive or pathological liars). When targets (i.e., the person being lied to) are aware of these motivations or reasons to lie, they may become suspicious and more likely to judge a message as deceptive. For instance, in the vignette that opened this chapter, Tiana is aware that Trey has a reason to lie about what he is doing and who he is with when he gets together with his former romantic partner, Gia. Because Tiana is aware of his underlying motivation, she is more apt to be suspicious and to consider Trey's responses as potentially deceptive.

Although the truth-default state is the cognitive baseline from which we operate, TDT argues that we can abandon the presumption of honesty if certain "triggers" to deception are present. These triggers include (a) the potential deceiver's projected motive (i.e., do you think a lie would help the other person achieve their goals more effectively than the truth would?), (b) the potential deceiver's behavioral displays (i.e., do you think the person has a dishonest demeanor?), (c) a lack of message coherence (i.e., is the person contradicting themselves?), (d) if you have outside knowledge or evidence that some of the things the person is telling you are false, and/or (e) if some third party told you of the person's deception (i.e., as you may recall from the previous chapter, Tiana's friend was the first person to warn her that Trey had reconnected with Gia, clueing Tiana in that Trey may be lying about his activities). The presence of one or more of these triggers can encourage us to become suspicious of another and to abandon the truth default—at least temporarily. When that happens, we start to pay close attention to the potential deceiver's communication and the information they are giving us.

At this point, TDT holds that if enough evidence is not available to make a judgment of truth or deception, then we may remain suspicious for a while or simply revert to the truth-default state. If enough evidence is available to suggest the person is being honest, then a judgment of truth is made. But if enough evidence emerges to suggest that the person is lying (e.g., they cannot keep their story straight, a third party gives us evidence that directly contradicts their story, etc.), then we are likely to conclude that a message was, in fact, deceptive. Note that TDT makes clear that all these processes need not occur—and in fact, usually will not occur—within the constraints of one particular interaction. Instead, they typically unfold over time, and successful deception detection may not occur until sometime after the deceptive message was first received.

TDT encourages us to discard our overreliance on the potential deceiver's behavioral cues, instead claiming that deception is most accurately detected by comparing the information provided by the deceiver to what you know—or what you can find out—about their story (or when the deceiver confesses their lie.) Levine argues that questioning the potential deceiver with diagnostic utility, or prompting the potential deceiver to provide useful information while at the same time avoiding or ignoring behaviors that may be misleading (e.g., eye contact) and useless information, is critical when interacting with a potential deceiver in order to obtain information that will allow you to make a more accurate judgment of deception. Put another way, diagnostically useful information is the degree to which you can use some information to make an accurate inference about the truthful or deceptive nature of someone's communication (Levine, 2014). Levine (2020) concludes TDT's propositions with this: "Expertise in deception detection rests on knowing how to prompt diagnostically useful information, rather than on skill in the passive observation of sender behavior" (p. 100). In the relatively brief period since its inception, TDT has shaken up decades of scholarly thought on the processes of deception detection, and it appears to be on track to continue to shape future deception scholarship in substantial ways.

Conclusion

As you have learned in this chapter, deception takes many forms, can be motivated by differing concerns, and is functional—often even appropriate. However, serious lies are perceived as relationship transgressions and can have negative consequences for partners involved in close relationships. Although deception was once thought to be remarkably commonplace, recent research challenges this long-held notion by demonstrating that the elevated average rates of deception may have been driven by a smaller percentage of people who are especially prolific liars. You have also learned in this chapter that deception has been historically difficult to accurately detect, and relying on cues to identify deception is likely to be unsuccessful. As part of this discussion, some common myths about reliable cues to deception were debunked by scholarly research, and a new theoretical approach to deception detection processes was introduced. From this, you have learned the importance of attending to a potential deceiver's verbal cues, allowing the deceiver to tell their story and considering that story in the context of the evidence you have, without revealing what you already know to be true of the situation, and asking diagnostic questions (while avoiding questions with low or negative diagnostic utility). Now that you are in possession of this knowledge, it may be easier for you to understand how and why deception occurs, the effect it can have on close relationships, and how you can improve your deception detection accuracy in the future.

Discussion Questions

1. Based on the information presented throughout this chapter, do you agree or disagree with the assertion that deception is something that most people do a lot of the time? Why or why not? Justify your response with what you have learned from this chapter.

2. Identify and discuss the types of deception that were presented here. Provide an example of each.

3. Identify and discuss the various motives for deception that were identified in this chapter, with the goal of distinguishing among them. Provide examples of lies told for each of these three major reasons. Are these motives mutually exclusive? Why or why not?

4. According to what you have learned here, are most people generally pretty good deception detectors? Why or why not?

5. Based on what you have learned from this chapter, what advice would you give to someone who wants to improve their ability to successfully detect a close other's deception? As part of this discussion, identify some of the more reliable cues that have consistently been associated with deception as well as some of the more unreliable cues that are less consistently associated with deception.

Chapter 8

Infidelity

Recall the scenario about Tiana, Trey, and Gia that opened Chapters 6 and 7. Tiana's boyfriend Trey has been in touch with his former romantic partner, Gia, for several months now, attempting to deceive Tiana by not revealing that he has reconnected with his ex. As months pass, Tiana suspects that Trey and Gia are seeing each other more and more often. She finds evidence that the two of them are frequently in contact via text messaging and social media, and Trey is spending more and more of his time "out with friends." Finally, Tiana confronts Trey with what she suspects: Trey has been cheating on her with Gia. Trey denies that anything sexual is going on with Gia, but he admits that they have been in touch for months and have been getting together more and more often. He apologizes for deceiving Tiana about this, saying that it began as a totally innocent thing—he just wanted to establish a platonic friendship with Gia—but that it escalated and he thinks he is in love with her again.

Unfortunately, this scenario is not unusual in college student courtships. Despite the abhorrence with which most individuals in the United States who have been surveyed view infidelity, the prevalence rates for this particular relationship transgression are quite high. In addition to implicit and explicit relational rules for trust and honest communication that have been discussed in previous chapters, rules regarding monogamy and sexual/emotional exclusivity are very typical in heterosexual dating and married relationships (whereas **polyamory** has historically been less common in the United States, although recent research suggests that these types of relationships are on the rise). For heterosexual romantic relationships that abide by monogamy rules—which will be the primary focus of this chapter, as very little empirical research exists at this point regarding infidelity in LGBTQIAP relationships or regarding the various types of polyamorous relationships and because sexual exclusivity norms may look somewhat different in these relationships—one partner's commission of infidelity is often devastating, but it does not necessarily signal the end of the relationship. In this chapter, we will discuss infidelity in the context of close, monogamous, heterosexual relationships. We will identify and explain various types of infidelity, including sexual and emotional infidelity, and discuss their prevalence, predictors, and consequences. Further, we will delve into how and why consequences for and evaluations of sexual versus emotional infidelity may be different for men versus women, and we will discuss various theoretical perspectives that purport to explain (or explain away) these differences.

Infidelity in the Context of Close Relationships

One of the most fundamental expectations of people involved in monogamous relationships is that romantic partners will be faithful, both sexually and emotionally. Not only is **infidelity** a clear violation of implicit (if not explicit) relational rules for partner behavior in terms of appropriate extradyadic interaction and exclusivity, it is an activity that is widely reviled by most people in the United States and around the world (Betzig, 1989). Yet, despite the strong negative feelings of most individuals toward this typically severe relational transgression, infidelity is quite common in courtships and marriages.

Types of Infidelity
Three forms of infidelity have been identified, the first two of which vary according to the type of exclusivity rule that was breached and the type of partner resources being shared with third parties. **Sexual infidelity** occurs

when an individual devotes sexual resources to someone other than their romantic partner, and has been defined rather broadly as extradyadic "sexual activity" (Shackelford & Buss, 1997, p. 1035). Such sexual activity violates monogamy rules and includes, but is not limited to, sexual intercourse with a third party, but a more specific definition has thus far eluded infidelity scholars. Which sexual activities and behaviors "count" as infidelity? Research has shown that those activities differ according to various factors, including individual perceptions, preferences, and values; relationship-specific rules and expectations; the definition or status of the relationship; cultural norms; religiosity and religious beliefs; and the transgressor's motives for the sexual activity (Tafoya & Spitzberg, 2007). Some research has shown that college students hold relatively broad conceptualizations of what counts as infidelity. When asked to identify activities that represent unfaithfulness, for example, "dating/spending time with another" was the most frequently listed, followed by sexual intercourse with another and other sexual behaviors such as "flirting, kissing, and necking" (Roscoe et al., 1988).

Emotional infidelity occurs when a person invests emotional resources such as attention, social support, psychological intimacy, time, and feelings of affection in someone other than their romantic partner (Shackelford & Buss, 1997). Falling in love with a viable rival is probably the prototypical example of emotional infidelity (although this type of infidelity can occur in the absence of feelings of romantic love for the third party). Emotional infidelity violates rules for emotional and psychological exclusivity.

Communicative infidelity occurs when an individual strategically commits sexual infidelity in order to send a message to their romantic partner (Tafoya & Spitzberg, 2007). Essentially, the type of resources being allocated extra-dyadically and the exclusivity rules that are broken in cases of communicative infidelity are the same as sexual infidelity. In many, if not most cases, the transgressor does not want their romantic partner to discover their sexual infidelity. However, in cases of communicative infidelity, sexual infidelity is committed for the express purpose of communicating a message to the transgressed-against partner. Behaviorally, communicative and sexual infidelity look the same; to conclude whether an act of sexual infidelity qualifies as communicative infidelity, you must know the transgressor's motive and what they hope to accomplish by committing the infidelity.

Each of these types of infidelity will be discussed in more detail throughout the remainder of this chapter, with a particular focus on sexual infidelity as the most frequently studied form of infidelity.

Sexual Infidelity

As indicated previously, the vast majority of American people who have been surveyed feel that sexual infidelity in the context of marriage is always wrong (Laumann et al., 1994)—although those who have committed infidelity themselves are more approving of the act (Tafoya & Spitzberg, 2007). Marital sexual infidelity is widely disdained in most other countries that have been studied as well, with a few exceptions (i.e., Bulgaria, the Czech Republic, and Russia; Widmer et al., 1998). This purported condemnation notwithstanding, available evidence suggests that sexual infidelity is a frequent occurrence with relatively well-established predictors and generally negative personal and relational outcomes.

Prevalence of Sexual Infidelity

Estimates of the prevalence of sexual infidelity range considerably, with estimates on the higher end suggesting that as many as 70% of dating relationships and as many as 40% of marriages have experienced at least once instance of infidelity (Tsapelas et al., 2011). Sexual infidelity is especially prevalent in dating relationships as compared to marriages. A study of 18–24-year-old college students indicated that 49% of males and 31% of females reported engaging in extradyadic sexual intercourse while involved in a serious romantic relationship (Wiederman & Hurd, 1999). When arguably "milder" forms of sexual infidelity such as romantic kissing were considered, those numbers jumped to 68% of males and 61% of females. An examination of several large-scale studies indicates that infidelity occurs in less than 25% of married, heterosexual relationships, and other studies suggest that infidelity may be even less common in marriages (i.e., 12%; Blow & Hartnett, 2005; Wiederman, 1997).

Although the precise percentages may vary, the picture they paint is that sexual infidelity seems to occur less frequently in marriages, and some research suggests that being married is a deterrent when it comes to the commission of sexual infidelity (Blow & Hartnett, 2005). A synthesis of relevant research over a 60-plus-year period with more than 90,000 individuals of various ages and from various countries across married, cohabiting, and dating relationships put the rate of infidelity perpetration at close to 30% (Tafoya & Spitzberg, 2007). Because estimates of sexual infidelity are likely to be underreported for various reasons (e.g., social desirability concerns, differing notions of what "counts" as infidelity), any statistics related to rates of sexual infidelity should be interpreted with caution. With that said, the evidence certainly suggests that sexual infidelity is a relatively common experience in various types of serious romantic relationships.

Predictors of Sexual Infidelity

Although numerous antecedents of extradyadic sexual activity have been identified through extensive research on this topic, several primary predictors are often highlighted: biological sex of the transgressor, aspects of the primary romantic relationship, opportunity factors, and relatively stable individual differences or traits.

Sex. Although some research reveals no or minimal sex differences in terms of who is more likely to commit sexual infidelity (e.g., Wiederman, 1997), a number of studies across various types of relationships suggest that men are more likely to commit sexual infidelity than women (e.g., Allen & Baucom, 2004). As compared to women, men tend to view sexual infidelity as more acceptable, they have a stronger desire to engage in sexual infidelity, they have more extradyadic sexual partners, and they report more instances of sexual infidelity (Brand et al., 2007; Lieberman, 1988; Prins et al., 1993; Spanier & Margolis, 1983). This appears to be true outside of the context of heterosexual relationships as well, as gay men have more extradyadic partners than lesbians or heterosexual men, and sexual nonmonogamy is more common and conventional (Blumstein & Schwartz, 1983; Buss, 2000; McWhirter & Mattison, 1984). Other scholars argue that the prevalence of sexual infidelity in developed countries is becoming more equivalent between men and women, particularly with regard to younger individuals (i.e., under the age of 40; Atkins et al., 2001; Wiederman, 1997). These trends suggest that the historically seen sex differences in the commission of sexual infidelity may be evaporating.

Aspects of the primary romantic relationship. Dissatisfaction with the primary romantic relationship has been shown to increase the urge to commit sexual infidelity (Prins et al., 1993), and several studies have demonstrated a link between relational dissatisfaction and the actual commission of sexual infidelity (Atkins et al., 2001). Nearly 75% of married individuals who engage in sexual infidelity claim marital difficulties as the reason why they did so (Spanier & Margolis, 1983). The link between relational dissatisfaction and infidelity (both sexual and emotional) appears to be especially strong for women, as women who engage in extradyadic sexual activity are significantly more unhappy with their primary relationship than are men (Glass & Wright, 1985; Prins et al., 1993). Unfaithful men, on the other hand, tend to report higher levels of premarital dissatisfaction than women

(Allen et al., 2008). Dissatisfaction with a reduction in the amount of sexual activity in the relationship has also been discovered as a reason for the commission of sexual infidelity for married men in particular (Liu, 2000). Boredom, low-quality communication, and a lack of emotional support in the primary romantic relationship have also been linked to extradyadic sexual activity (Allen et al., 2005). For college student courtships in particular, being less invested in the romantic relationship leads to more sexual (and emotional) infidelity (Drigotas et al., 1999).

Workplace opportunities. When the opportunity to cheat presents itself, particularly in the form of available and attractive alternative partners in the workplace, sometimes even individuals who are happy with their primary romantic relationship will take advantage of it (Atkins et al., 2001). For example, people who have extradyadic sex with coworkers are not always dissatisfied with their primary relationship; instead, they are simply capitalizing on an option that is easily available to them (Wiggins & Lederer, 1984). This may be true especially for men (Liu, 2000). Other research has shown that potential sexual partners in the workplace increase the likelihood of committing infidelity (Treas & Giesen, 2000), and a large majority of people report meeting their extradyadic sex partner in their place of work (Glass, 2003; Wiggins & Lederer, 1984). Opportunities in the form of perceiving increased relational alternatives outside of the workplace (e.g., residing in a heavily populated area), however, do not seem to consistently or consequentially encourage the commission of sexual infidelity (Wiederman, 1997).

Enduring personal qualities. The transgressor's attachment style has been linked to the commission of sexual infidelity, as men with dismissive avoidant and women with anxious or insecure (e.g., preoccupied) attachment styles are more likely to cheat (Allen & Baucom, 2004; Bogaert & Sadava, 2002). (See Chapter 2 of this textbook for an extended discussion of attachment theory.) Conversely, individuals who are securely attached are less likely to engage in sexual infidelity (Miller & Fishkin, 1997).

Personality traits have also been examined in relation to sexual infidelity, and this research reveals some consistencies across various cultures and areas of the world outside of the United States. Specifically, people who are higher in **extroversion** (i.e., sociable, outgoing people who prefer high levels of external stimulation in the form of interacting with lots of other people), **openness to new experiences** (i.e., people who are willing to try new things and to think outside the box), and **neuroticism** (i.e., people who are biased to experience negative emotions such as anxiety) are more likely to cheat (Orzeck & Lung, 2005; Whisman et al., 2007). Additionally, people who are lower in **agreeableness** (i.e., those who are less warm, sympathetic, and sensitive to others' needs) and **conscientiousness** (i.e., those who are unconcerned with following the rules and doing the right thing by behaving in socially acceptable ways) are more likely to engage in sexual infidelity (Costa & McCrae, 1992; Whisman et al., 2007).

Psychological disorders have also been associated with sexual infidelity, in that those who have elevated levels of **psychopathy** (i.e., people who behave in manipulative, controlling, antisocial ways, with disregard for others' rights and feelings) and **narcissism** (i.e., people who have an inflated sense of self, who have fragile egos, and who need excessive admiration from others) are more likely to cheat (Buss & Shackelford, 1997; Hurlbert et al., 1994; Neubeck & Schletzer, 1969). Both narcissism and psychopathy (along with **Machiavellianism**) have been identified as part of a trio of particularly malevolent subclinical personality traits called the **dark triad** (and more recently, a fourth trait—**sadism**—has been added to create the dark tetrad) that is potentially related to infidelity. Elements of the dark triad/tetrad have been associated with the general preference for sexual relationships that are casual and free of commitment, and with a somewhat exploitative approach to sex. More specifically, narcissists prefer friends with benefits and one-night stands, while psychopathy has been associated with a preference for booty calls, and both traits were associated with the proclivity toward less committed relationships (Jonason et al., 2012). More closely connected to our discussion of sexual infidelity, the dark triad has also been associated with **mate-poaching** behaviors, in that those with dark triad traits are more likely to attempt to poach other people's partners and are more likely to be poached themselves (Jonason et al., 2010). Mate poaching is the deliberate attempt to "steal" someone else's romantic partner away from their established, monogamous relationship.

Dissatisfaction with the primary relationship appears to be the chief cause of sexual infidelity, followed by workplace opportunities (or some combination of the two). But as noted previously, numerous other predictors have been identified. Experiencing parental divorce or having been divorced oneself often leads to an increased likelihood of committing sexual infidelity (Amato & Rogers, 1997; Wiederman, 1997). A woman may be more likely to cheat if her education level exceeds that of her partner's (Forste & Tanfer, 1996). Higher income seems related to increased likelihood of infidelity through its impact on other predictors such as increased education and opportunity (Atkins et al., 2001). Starting a relationship at a younger age (i.e., 16 years or younger) and maintaining longer relationships have both been associated with infidelity (the latter for women in particular; Amato &

Rogers, 1997; Forste & Tanfer, 1996). There are also certain times in relationships, such as during pregnancy or in the months following the birth of
a child, when men are especially likely to cheat (Whisman et al., 2007). In
addition, although evidence is mixed and other variables likely influence
the process, attending religious services may decrease the likelihood of
sexual infidelity for some groups of people (i.e., African Americans and
Hispanic Americans; Atkins et al., 2001; Treas & Giesen, 2000).

Consequences of Sexual Infidelity

Although the outcomes of sexual infidelity are not exclusively negative
(some couples report post-infidelity increases in relational satisfaction and
other unintended relationship improvements; Hansen, 1987; Olson et al.,
2002), infidelity is an especially threatening transgression that brings a rival
third party into the relationship (Metts & Cupach, 2007). It is a particularly
hurtful, harmful relational transgression that typically has serious negative
consequences and is difficult to forgive, in part due to the violation of exclusivity norms that are such central elements of the romantic attachments
of people who were socialized in the United States (Bachman & Guerrero,
2006; Feeney, 2005).

As compared with other negative events such as criticism, deception,
or behaviors that exclude or otherwise signal disinterest in one's partner
or the romantic relationship, sexual infidelity is seen as the worst of these
behaviors. Specifically, it is perceived as most hurtful and destructive, as
most closely associated with the offended partner's feelings of power-
lessness, and as the hurtful behavior that has the most negative long-term
effects for both the offended partner and the relationship (Feeney, 2005).
Related research supports the claim that sexual infidelity is the most hurtful
transgression when compared with other partner bad behaviors or relational difficulties such as physical distance between the partners, keeping
secrets, a lack of emotional support from the partner, temporary termination
of the relationship by the partner, deception, jealousy, conflict, betrayals
of trust, inequitable relationships, and relational uncertainty (Malachowski
& Frisby, 2015).

In addition to being an especially hurtful transgression, research suggests that sexual infidelity (along with relationship termination) is evaluated
as the most unforgivable hurtful event as compared with one's partner
dating or flirting with a third party, lying, communicating various types of
hurtful messages (e.g., messages that devalue you, make unfair accusations, or state negative desires/preferences), making threats of harm, or

violating confidences (Bachman & Guerrero, 2006). The way in which the infidelity is discovered or revealed has implications for the transgression's forgivability, however, with those who catch their partner "red handed" in the act of infidelity or learn of their partner's infidelity through some third party reporting the least likelihood of forgiveness and the most relational damage. On the other hand, when partners confess their infidelity without having been prompted or questioned about it, the offended partner is more likely to forgive the transgression (Afifi et al., 2001).

Other negative outcomes for the partner who was transgressed against include increased negative affect, such as hurt, resentment, jealousy, fear of abandonment, sadness, and shame (Charny & Parnass, 1995; Metts & Cupach, 2007). The offended partner is also likely to experience a decrease in self-esteem as well as reduced personal and sexual confidence (Charny & Parnass, 1995). Along with other partner behaviors like criticism and deception, sexual infidelity incites the offended partner's anger and leads to less trust in the transgressor (Charny & Parnass, 1995; Feeney, 2005). Sexual infidelity also begets other transgressions such as deception in an attempt to cover up the infidelity (Feeney, 2005). Emotional infidelity may operate similarly, as we saw in the vignette that opened this chapter, wherein Trey's emotional infidelity with Gia necessitated deceiving his partner Tiana. Negative outcomes for the relationship include increased conflict and likelihood of relationship termination, although relationships that are marred by even a transgression of this magnitude do not always terminate (Buunk, 1987; Metts & Cupach, 2007). For instance, if forgiveness occurs, it should transform the negative affect that attends the discovery or revelation of a partner's infidelity, increasing the likelihood of relational continuance. Relationships are more likely to terminate when sexual and emotional infidelity co-occur.

The outcomes of sexual infidelity are impact by many factors, as discussed previously, including characteristics of the relationship and perceptions of the romantic partner before the transgression occurred. Specifically, numerous studies indicate that higher pre-transgression relationship satisfaction and commitment encourage the transgressed against person to make less negative responsibility attributions for their partner's bad behavior and to forgive their partner for committing sexual infidelity (Allemand et al., 2007; Guerrero & Bachman, 2010; McCullough et al., 1998). In addition, perceiving that the partner is a unique commodity who cannot easily be replaced encourages transgressed against individuals to respond with more constructive communication and decreased desire to end the relationship (Dillow et al., 2012). Conversely, transgressed against people who are not highly invested in their romantic relationship and who perceive a great many high-quality alternatives to that relationship are more likely to communicate destructively, terminate the primary romantic relationship, or just let it fall apart on its own after learning of their partner's sexual infidelity (Rusbult et al., 1982).

Up to this point, most of the sexual infidelity research that has been conducted and discussed throughout this chapter has dealt with "actual" or offline infidelity (as opposed to online or cyber infidelity), different-sex infidelity (as opposed to same-sex infidelity, when a heterosexual-identified person cheats with a person of the same sex), and infidelity that occurs in the context of heterosexual relationships. Research is just beginning to help us get a better understanding of how romantic partners react to online infidelity and same-sex infidelity.

Infidelity via Mediated Contexts
Is Online Sexual Infidelity as Bad as "Actual" Sexual Infidelity?

The advent and proliferation of technology have opened new venues through which infidelity can be committed. Online or cyber infidelity is broadly defined; it may include sexual (engaging in cybersex with someone online) and/or emotional (developing a close emotional connection to someone online) elements (Guadagno & Sagarin, 2010), and it is becoming a more frequent cause for divorce (Atwood, 2005). With regard to sexual infidelity in particular, questions have arisen regarding the degree to which online sexual infidelity or cybersex is viewed in the same way as "actual" or offline sexual infidelity (which includes physical contact) and whether romantic partners will react in similar ways to online versus conventional sexual infidelities.

A program of research by Whitty suggests some commonalities in perceptions of online and offline sexual infidelity, in that online infidelity is often perceived as counting as an "actual" act of sexual infidelity and one that women (as compared to men) tend to respond particularly negatively to (Dijkstra et al., 2013; Whitty, 2003, 2005). Women tend to more strongly endorse certain behaviors (e.g., cybersex, phone sex) as cheating when compared to males (Guadagno & Sagarin, 2010). Yet, overall, it appears that people generally tend to experience less negative emotional reactions to online infidelity as compared with offline infidelity. Further, both online and offline infidelity have been found to elicit similar jealous reactions from offended partners (Groothof et al., 2009; Guadagno & Sagarin, 2010). That is, the same differences that are usually seen in the ways that heterosexual men and women react to sexual versus emotional infidelity when it is offline (i.e., heterosexual men tend to become more jealous and upset about their female partner's sexual infidelity, while heterosexual women tend to become more jealous and upset about their male partner's emotional infidelity) are sometimes replicated in the context of online infidelity (but see Henline et al., 2007 for an exception).

Although most online affairs do not transcend the online context or otherwise move offline, a small portion of them do (Rotunda et al., 2003). Even if they do not, transgressed against partners (particularly women) seem to be reacting to this type of online behavior in ways that are more similar to than different from their reactions to offline or "actual" infidelity.

FLIPPING THE SCRIPT

Is Same-Sex Infidelity as Bad as Different-Sex Infidelity?

A long history of research reveals that, in heterosexual relationships, a romantic partner's sexual infidelity with an opposite-sex third party often causes the transgressed against person to react with high levels of romantic jealousy. In other words, when a heterosexual romantic partner cheats with someone of a different sex, it is well established that the person who got cheated on will feel hurt and will worry that their relationship with their romantic partner is being threatened by the partner's interest in a third-party rival. More recently, scholars have wondered if the same level of hurt and relational threat will be incited by a heterosexual romantic partner's same-sex infidelity, or sexual activity with a person of the same sex as the extradyadic partner. Same-sex sexual activity is becoming more frequent among men and women who identify primarily as heterosexual, and this increasing sexual fluidity seems to be especially prominent for college-aged individuals. Thus, even heterosexual-identified individuals may engage in or be the victim of a partner's same-sex infidelity at some point.

Evolutionary approaches have often been used to frame investigations of differences in heterosexual men's versus women's reactions to different-sex infidelity, as discussed elsewhere in this chapter, arguing that differing reproductive concerns are the reason heterosexual men are more upset by their female partner's different-sex sexual infidelity while heterosexual women are more upset by their male partner's different-sex emotional infidelity. That is, men are thought to be more upset by their female partner's sexual infidelity with another man due to concerns about paternity, while women are thought to be more upset by their male partner's emotional infidelity with another woman due to concerns about the willingness of the male partner to invest in the couple's offspring (versus invest in offspring from an extradyadic affair). Because reproductive concerns or threats are irrelevant in cases of same-sex infidelity, however, such sex differences may not emerge.

Supporting this logic, some research (most of it making use of hypothetical scenarios wherein individuals are asked to imagine their heterosexual partner's same-sex infidelity) has shown that both men and women report feeling less negative emotion in response to same-sex (as opposed to different-sex) infidelity (Denes et al., 2015; Sagarin et al., 2003). In fact, men sometimes report positive feelings of sexual arousal in response to their female partner's same-sex infidelity (Denes et al., 2015). Other research suggests that women react more negatively than men to same-sex infidelity. Women have been found to be more emotionally upset and more likely to contemplate terminating the relationship than men when they imagine their partner's same-sex infidelity (Weiderman & LaMar, 1998), whereas men are less upset by their female partner's same-sex infidelity (Confer & Cloud, 2011; Denes et al., 2015). Further, 65% of women in one sample reported preferring that their male partner cheat with another woman as opposed to a man, while men were four times more likely than women to report preferring that their female partner cheat with a woman (Apostolou, 2019). Yet, more recent research reveals that the motivation underlying the partner's commission of same-sex infidelity matters, at least for women. When a male partner's same-sex infidelity was thought to be motivated by the desire for sexual experimentation, women reported feeling more benevolent toward the partner and being more willing to continue the relationship (Denes et al., 2020). It should also be noted that some individuals in this study did not consider same-sex infidelity to be cheating, due to its same-sex nature.

Although research on same-sex infidelity is still in its early stages as compared to research on different-sex infidelity, preliminary work suggests that heterosexual-identified women may be particularly sensitive to their male partner's same-sex infidelity as compared to his different-sex infidelity. Further, the findings from this line of research thus far call into question the long-standing **evolutionary explanations regarding infidelity,** with regard to the supposed differences between heterosexual men's and women's responses to sexual versus emotional infidelity that are discussed elsewhere in this chapter.

Emotional Infidelity

Emotional infidelity is most often studied concurrently along with sexual infidelity (whereas sexual infidelity is often studied as a standalone topic), and most of that research has been devoted to the examination of differences between heterosexual men and women with regard to which type of infidelity they find most upsetting and jealousy provoking. More specifically, evolutionary psychology perspectives have largely influenced how differences between men's and women's evaluations of infidelity have been studied, and consequently what we believe to be true based on results from this research. Findings from this program of research provide some evidence for the evolutionary-based claim that heterosexual men will find their female partner's sexual infidelity more upsetting and jealousy inducing, whereas heterosexual women will find their male partner's emotional infidelity more upsetting and jealousy inducing. In brief, evolutionary psychology perspectives explain these findings according to the different biological imperatives related to reproduction that men versus women have.

Theory in Practice

Evolutionary Psychology Perspectives on Reactions to Sexual Versus Emotional Infidelity

Evolutionary psychology perspectives posit that heterosexual men and women should have different concerns related to reproduction that are biologically based, and these concerns will dictate which type of infidelity is most troublesome for which sex (Buss, 1989, 1994; Buss et al., 1992). Men's concerns regarding reproduction have to do with the uncertain paternity of any potential offspring (women are confident that the child they are carrying is theirs, whereas men may have had some uncertainties in this regard throughout history and the extended period of human evolution). Genetic testing is possible today in order to definitively determine paternity, but an evolutionary perspective holds that these reactions are inherent in our biological makeup. If a male's partner does not give birth to his offspring, then his genes cannot be passed on, and thus it was adaptive for a male to attempt to prevent other men from having sex with his female partner. On the other hand, a woman has no doubts that her genes will be passed on via her offspring, making a male partner's extradyadic sexual activity less relevant. Instead, women's reproductive concerns have to do with securing the resources of the male partner in order to help ensure their offspring's survival. Thus, it was adaptive for women to attempt to prevent their male partner from forming emotional attachments to other women and potentially diverting resources from the primary relationship.

Based on this evolutionary perspective, heterosexual men and women are expected to evaluate sexual and emotional infidelity differently. Specifically, men evaluate their female partner's sexual infidelity as most upsetting and jealousy producing due to the doubt regarding the paternity of any potential offspring that is generated by a female partner's sexual infidelity. On the other hand, women's concerns regarding reproduction are not related to maternity, but instead have to do with the male partner's ability and willingness to invest his resources into the child and the primary romantic relationship to improve the likelihood of surviving and thriving. As such, the evolutionary perspective indicates that heterosexual women evaluate their male partner's emotional infidelity as most upsetting and jealousy evoking because the male's investment in the primary romantic relationship and related offspring is threatened by his extradyadic emotional attachments.

A good bit of research supports or can otherwise be explained by such evolutionary psychology perspectives, as discussed elsewhere in this chapter, although some caveats (e.g., methodological considerations) and other potential explanations (e.g., the double-shot hypothesis) and perspectives (e.g., the social-cognitive theory of jealousy) should be kept in mind. More recently, scholarship that operates from perspectives other than evolutionary psychology suggests that, perhaps unsurprisingly, women and men typically find both major types of infidelity to be upsetting, threatening, and jealousy provoking.

The majority of available research that tests evolutionary-based hypotheses documents the expected differences between heterosexual men and women when a forced-choice research paradigm is employed. In other words, when heterosexual men and women are forced to choose *either* their partner's hypothetical sexual infidelity (e.g., having a one-night stand) or their partner's hypothetical emotional infidelity (e.g., falling in love with someone else) as most upsetting, men typically choose sexual infidelity as most upsetting while women usually select emotional infidelity as most distressing.

In addition to this forced choice paradigm, however, reactions to sexual and emotional infidelity have been assessed via continuous measures (i.e., instead of forcing individuals to choose which type of infidelity is worse, continuous measures allow individuals to rate both types of infidelity as highly upsetting) and physiological measures (i.e., assessments of the body's objective physiological reactions to different types of infidelity, such as heart rate and electrodermal activity). Even when these other assessments of degree of upset are used, the preponderance of scholarly evidence indicates that heterosexual men respond more negatively to their female partner's sexual infidelity while heterosexual women respond more negatively to their male partner's emotional infidelity (Buss et al., 1992; Sagarin et al., 2003). With that said, be aware that most of this research employs hypothetical scenarios where infidelity is only possible in the future (not actual infidelity in the present or past). Some research has shown that this pattern of sex differences is not replicated when men and women are queried about suspected past infidelities (Wiederman & Allgeier, 1993).

Despite the consistency of these sex difference findings, the evolutionary perspective's positioning of the differences as biologically based has been challenged or otherwise called into question. Other scholars have argued that no sex differences should be apparent with regard to sexual versus emotional infidelity because such differences should not have evolved to be adaptive for the species. The **social-cognitive theory of jealousy** holds that differential mechanisms for reacting to emotional versus sexual infidelity would not have been adaptive for human beings (Harris, 2003). As one potential challenge, sexual and emotional cues to infidelity can overlap (e.g., increasing contact with and/or focusing more attention on a rival third party; Shackelford & Buss, 1997), which would instigate confusion and uncertainty regarding which type of infidelity is occurring and whether any protective action is necessary. Further, if men focus on cues to their partner's sexual infidelity to the exclusion of cues that might indicate her emotional infidelity, then the male may have missed his window of opportunity to thwart the infidelity by the time sexual cues are apparent. As such, in Harris's view, it would not have been adaptive to evolve content-specific mechanisms for detecting infidelity; instead, general mechanisms for detecting any type of infidelity would have been more adaptive for the species. In other words, the general motivation to appraise and react to relational threats (of any form) could have evolved in similar ways for men and women.

Another critique of the evolutionary perspective comes not in the form of questions about whether the sex differences between men and women in terms of their reactions to sexual versus emotional infidelity really exist. Instead, this critique offers a different explanation for the pattern of sex differences that has long been reported in research from an evolutionary perspective. The **double-shot hypothesis** holds that people are most distressed anytime they believe that both types of infidelity (sexual and emotional) are co-occurring (DeSteno & Salovey, 1996). Further, because of typical stereotypes about differences in the sexes, it is likely that men infer that a female partner who is having sex with someone else is also emotionally involved with that person (because of cultural stereotypes that have historically held that women only become sexually involved with men with whom they are in love). Thus, for men, a female partner's sexual infidelity is most upsetting not due to evolutionary factors, but because it implies a strong likelihood that emotional infidelity is also taking place. Conversely, it is likely that women infer that a male partner who is emotionally attached to someone else is also having sex with that person (because of cultural stereotypes that have historically held that men do not require emotional connection to engage in sexual relations, and if they do form a deep connection with someone else, they are probably also having sex with that person). Therefore, for women, a male partner's emotional infidelity is most upsetting not for evolutionary reasons, but because it implies a strong likelihood that sexual infidelity is probably also a factor.

So which perspective is correct? Recent research comparing these explanations suggests that the answer is in the eye of the beholder, to some degree. A large-scale review of the available literature on all three perspectives (i.e., evolutionary, social-cognitive, and double-shot) using both forced-choice and continuous assessments suggests that the sex differences posited by an evolutionary perspective are strongest for heterosexual male college students in the United States, who do indeed appear to rate sexual infidelity as most distressing (Carpenter, 2012). However, men from other countries and men who are not college students tend to find emotional infidelity most upsetting. In fact, a more general pattern that emerged from this large-scale review suggested that most women and men tend to select emotional infidelity as most upsetting, leading the author to conclude that men and women are more similar than different in their responses to sexual and emotional infidelity.

In general, the conclusions from this large-scale review were more consistent with Harris's (2003) social-cognitive theory that men and women should react similarly to sexual and emotional infidelity, perhaps because humans evolved a more general mechanism for responding to relational threats from a rival third party. Some results were also consistent with the double-shot hypothesis, especially results related to gay men and lesbian women. Specifically, for everyone whose partner is female (i.e., lesbian women and heterosexual men), believing the partner is involved sexually with someone else implies a concomitant emotional involvement. On the other hand, for everyone whose partner is male (i.e., gay men and heterosexual women), believing the partner is emotionally involved with someone else implies a concurrent sexual involvement. When two types of infidelity are implied, then an affair is implicated, and it is easy to see how this situation would elicit elevated perceptions of threat and accompanying emotional distress.

Predictors of Emotional Infidelity

Because emotional infidelity is not often studied as a standalone behavior, as noted previously, we know less about the reasons some individuals commit emotional infidelity. However, we do know that just as dissatisfaction with the primary romantic relationship predicts sexual infidelity, so too does it predict emotional infidelity (Glass & Wright, 1985). It also seems that women (as compared with men) are more likely to engage in emotional and sexual infidelity concurrently, and emotional infidelity generally lasts longer than sexual infidelity (which may be a one-time occurrence, such as a one-night stand).

Consequences of Emotional Infidelity

Scholars have identified differential consequences of sexual and emotional infidelity for the transgressed against partner, whereby emotional infidelity typically results in inward, self-focused reactions such as depression, self-blame, helplessness, and insecurity. Conversely, sexual infidelity leads to revulsion, astonishment, humiliation, hostility, vengefulness, and even sexual arousal, suicidal, or murderous feelings (Metts & Cupach, 2007). In addition, while sexual infidelity tends to engender attributions of blame and feelings of anger across both men and women of varying age ranges, emotional infidelity leads to more feelings of hurt and increased worry that the transgressor will terminate the relationship (Sabini & Green, 2004).

As noted throughout this chapter, most available research has focused on infidelity that occurs in the context of heterosexual relationships. More recently, scholarship has started to emerge regarding infidelity in gay, lesbian, and bisexual relationships, but findings are somewhat mixed. Generally speaking, heterosexual men and women tend to become more upset (including feelings of anger, betrayal, and threat) in response to sexual infidelity as compared with gay men and lesbian women. Gay men report less jealousy than heterosexual men, while lesbian women report less jealousy than heterosexual women (Dijkstra et al., 2013). Although there may be a difference between heterosexual males and females in terms of their negative reactions (i.e., upset) to sexual versus emotional infidelity, some research has shown that neither bisexual men and women nor gay men and lesbian women significantly differ from each other in the degree to which sexual versus emotional infidelity upsets them (Frederick & Fales, 2016). Conversely, other studies find that lesbian women (as compared to gay men) are most upset by their partner's sexual infidelity, while gay men (as compared to lesbian women) are more upset by their partner's emotional infidelity (Dijkstra et al., 2001). In addition, gay men have been found to respond with less jealousy to suspected partner infidelity, possibly because gay male relationships are often more nonmonogamous, as gay males may have more permissive attitudes toward extradyadic sexual activity and a higher desire for variety in this capacity (Barelds & Dijkstra, 2006).

Communicative Infidelity

As the last and least studied form of infidelity, communicative infidelity is behaviorally equivalent to sexual infidelity, with the former defined as any extradyadic sexual activity that is used in part to send a romantic partner a message (Spitzberg & Chou, 2005; Spitzberg & Tafoya, 2005; Tafoya & Spitzberg, 2007). In other words, this type of infidelity points to the potentially communicative function of sexual infidelity as an activity that carries relational messages. Communicative infidelity is used intentionally and strategically in order to achieve personal (e.g., to get more attention from the partner) or relational (e.g., to encourage the partner to end the relationship) goals.

Spitzberg and colleagues have identified three primary motives underlying the commission of communicative infidelity: jealousy, sex drive, and revenge. These motives differ in the extent to which they are perceived as acceptable and justifiable from the perspective of the person who cheated, and men may be more approving of their own (potential) communicative infidelity than are women (Spitzberg & Tafoya, 2005; Tafoya & Spitzberg, 2007). Perhaps not surprisingly, however, transgressed against partners do not perceive that any of the following motives for committing communicative infidelity are acceptable (Dillow et al., 2011).

As discussed in Chapter 6, **jealousy** is comprised of cognitive, emotional, and behavioral components (see Pfeiffer & Wong, 1989). Cognitive jealousy entails suspicious thoughts, worries, and anxieties related to a romantic partner's faithfulness. Emotional jealousy has to do with the negative affective reactions (e.g., fear, hurt, anger) that tend to accompany doubts about a partner's fidelity. Behavioral jealousy includes any actions that expose one's jealous cognitions and emotions (e.g., protective or detective actions such as telling the rival the partner is "taken" or surveilling the partner). The experience of jealousy in the context of a romantic relationship can motivate communicative infidelity, and behavioral jealousy in particular is associated with approval of communicative infidelity from the point of view of the transgressor.

Sex drive as a motive for the commission of communicative infidelity has numerous elements, including sociosexuality and sexual adjustment. Sociosexuality deals with the degree to which one is comfortable engaging in casual sex, or sex outside of a committed relationship (see Simpson & Gangestad, 1991). It can be thought of as a continuum in which individuals who are comfortable with sex with no strings attached have a more unrestricted sociosexual orientation (anchoring one end of the sociosexuality continuum), while those who confine sex to relationships characterized by commitment and closeness have a more restricted sociosexual orientation (anchoring the other end of the sociosexuality continuum). Having a more unrestricted sociosexual orientation can motivate communicative infidelity, and it is also related to approval of communicative infidelity from the perspective of the offender.

Sexual adjustment, an indicator of sexual quality and sexual identity, is three-dimensional, comprising sexual depression, sexual self-esteem, and sexual preoccupation (see Snell & Papini, 1989). Sexual depression refers to a person's general sense of unhappiness and dissatisfaction with their sex life and sexuality. Relatedly, sexual self-esteem deals with a person's confidence and positive evaluations of their own sexual prowess and sexuality. Finally, sexual preoccupation is a proclivity to be consumed by thoughts of sex to the point of obsession, finding it difficult to think of anything else. One or more of these dimensions of sexual adjustment may serve as the reason for communicative infidelity, and sexual preoccupation has been associated with approval of communication infidelity from the transgressor's viewpoint, perhaps because it is seen as a natural product of obsessive sexual thoughts.

Revenge is thought to be a common motive for the act of communicative infidelity, as prior research has revealed it as a motive for sexual infidelity (Glass & Wright, 1992; Mongeau et al., 1994; Roscoe et al., 1988). As discussed later in Chapter 9, revenge entails retaliation or getting back at a person who has done you wrong, and it may be perceived as a way to reestablish a sense of equity in the relationship. Revenge is often triggered by anger, which commonly accompanies the discovery of a partner's sexual infidelity (Feeney, 2005). Perhaps not surprisingly, revenge as a motive is associated with approval of communicative infidelity by the perpetrator.

Research on communicative infidelity is still in its infancy, and very little is currently known about sexual infidelity as a strategic communicative act. As noted by Tafoya and Spitzberg (2007), communicative infidelity may be particularly hard to forgive and may result in especially negative outcomes due to its intentional (and potentially vengeful) nature (Spitzberg & Tafoya, 2005). Further, other motives for communicative infidelity may exist, as a recent series of studies uncovered additional motives for same-sex infidelity, including attraction and the desire to experiment sexually with someone of the same sex (Denes et al., 2020). These motives may be specific to same-sex infidelity, of course, especially in the case of experimentation.

Conclusion

As you have learned in this chapter, infidelity can be only sexual in nature, only emotional in nature, or both sexual and emotional in nature. In addition, sexual infidelity may be used strategically to send the romantic partner a message, in the case of communicative infidelity. You have learned about online infidelity (as compared to traditional offline infidelity) and same-sex infidelity in heterosexual relationships (as compared to the more commonly studied different-sex infidelity). Various predictors of infidelity were discussed, and dissatisfaction with the romantic relationship was revealed as the primary reason for both sexual and emotional infidelity. With the exception of heterosexual male college students in the United States, most individuals find emotional infidelity more upsetting and jealousy provoking than sexual infidelity, possibly because it elicits more concern about the transgressor's commitment to the primary relationship. Although infidelity does not have exclusively negative outcomes, its consequences are most often destructive for both the transgressed against partner and the primary romantic relationship. The information you have learned in this chapter should help you understand why infidelity occurs, identify conditions under which infidelity may become a problem in your own romantic relationships, understand the effect that infidelity can have on your romantic relationships, and recognize what to do (and what not to do) if you wish to continue your romantic relationship after an infidelity transgression.

Discussion Questions

1. Compare and contrast the three major types of infidelity that were identified in this chapter. Identify and discuss some of the more severe consequences of sexual and emotional infidelity.

2. Identify and discuss the various predictors of sexual and emotional infidelity that were overviewed in this chapter. Which do you think is most likely to encourage the commission of sexual infidelity, and why?

3. According to what you learned in this chapter, how does offline infidelity compare to online or cyber infidelity?

4. Based on the information discussed in this chapter, how does different-sex infidelity (which has traditionally been studied most often) compare to same-sex infidelity?

5. Explain what the evolutionary psychology perspective, the double-shot hypothesis, and the social-cognitive theory have to say about differences in the ways in which women and men perceive and evaluate sexual versus emotional infidelity.

Chapter 9

Responses to Relationship Transgressions

The last several chapters of this textbook have dealt with relationship transgressions such as hurtful communication, jealousy, deception, and infidelity. This chapter focuses on what happens after a relational partner commits a transgression—particularly a major transgression such as infidelity. In the vignette that opened Chapter 8, Tiana suspects that her boyfriend Trey has been cheating on her with his ex-girlfriend, Gia. When a severe transgression such as sexual infidelity is discovered or suspected in a romantic relationship, the person who was transgressed against obviously may respond in any number of potential ways. These responses fall into two general categories: pro-relationship (i.e., reactions that facilitate the continuance of the relationship, despite the transgression) or anti-relationship (i.e., reactions that contribute to the dissolution of the relationship in the wake of the transgression). For instance, when Tiana suspects Trey's infidelity, she may respond by trying to get back at Trey by cheating on him with her own ex-romantic partner—a retaliatory response that amplifies the damage to her relationship with Trey. On the other hand, Tiana may respond by forgiving Trey for the infidelity, despite the pain it caused, as long as he promises never to see or be in contact with Gia again.

D ealing with the aftermath of a relationship transgression is one of the most painful and difficult issues that couples face, and how partners react in the wake of transgressions—especially serious ones—sets the stage for the future of that relationship. In the most general sense, partners can respond constructively or destructively to relational transgressions. In this chapter, the term *constructively* is used to represent a manner that enables the continuance of the romantic relationship, while the term *destructively* is used in reference to a manner that contributes to the demise of the romantic relationship. With that said, it is recognized that so-called constructive responses are not always preferred or healthy, in the traditional sense. Put another way, constructive responses that enable relationship continuation are not always appropriate responses to major, severe relational transgressions.

In this chapter, we will examine conflicting bright and dark side responses to relational transgressions: revenge (an anti-relationship response that is typically characterized as dark in nature) and forgiveness (a pro-relationship response that is typically characterized as bright in nature). We will discuss the related predictors of these responses, and we will focus on the specific ways in which revenge and forgiveness are typically communicated in close relationships. Be aware that most of the available research on these topics—and therefore, the evidence discussed in this chapter—has been conducted in the context of romantic relationships in the United States.

General Reactions to Transgressions

The previous chapters of this textbook have been devoted to an exploration of some of the various ways close others can and often do harm each other in the context of romantic relationships. As has been made clear in these chapters, "all partners in close relationships eventually behave badly" (Rusbult et al., 1991, p. 53). Frank Fincham (2000), a psychologist known for his program of research on forgiveness processes, discusses the inevitable yet somewhat paradoxical truism that the ones we love most are most likely to hurt us. Of course, this does not mean that romantic partners are bound to commit major transgressions like sexual or emotional infidelity, given enough time. It simply means that, in order to have a close relationship with another, we must make ourselves vulnerable to that person, and it is precisely this vulnerability that paves the way for inflicting and incurring harm.

Although individuals are prone to behaving badly in their closest relationships and the unavoidability of being hurt by a relational partner is evident, close relationships can and often do survive negative relational events. While the type and magnitude of harm that was caused obviously has implications for partners and their relationship, perhaps even more important is what couples do—how they communicate and otherwise behave—after the harm has occurred. In other words, even major transgressions such as a long-term affair may not signal the death knell for romantic relationships. At least initially, the immediate outcomes of the relational transgression largely depend on whether the injured partner responds in more destructive, anti-relationship ways (i.e., revenge) or if the injured party is willing and able to react in more constructive, pro-relationship ways (i.e., forgiveness). These dark and bright side reactions, respectively, are two fundamental responses to negative relational events or partner bad behaviors that constitute critical components of relationship continuance, stability, and overall quality.

Revenge: A Darker Response

As with many concepts discussed throughout this textbook, various conceptualizations of **revenge** have been forwarded. All of these begin with some injury or wrongdoing (perceived or actual) that has been inflicted upon a target by an offender and include the target's resultant acts intended to cause harm to the offender in return, as punishment for their initial offense (e.g., Stuckless & Goranson, 1992). McCullough et al. (2001) hold that vengefulness entails beliefs about the moral nature of using vengeful behaviors for the purpose of achieving goals, including teaching the offender a lesson, saving face, and restoring the moral balance. Moving away from the notion of revenge as "merely" a behavior or an act, Yoshimura and Boon (2018) position revenge as a type of message that is initiated by a perceived offense and that communicates that the offender's behavior is unacceptable by some standard. Further, this message is intended to create a particular outcome and/or change in future interactions by influencing how one or both parties subsequently think, feel, or act. Importantly, this sense of first being wronged by another as the motivation and moral justification for one's own bad behavior makes revenge conceptually distinct from aggressive behaviors, which also intend harm but without a necessary initial moral violation as provocation.

Revenge is frequently identified as a leading motivator for the reactions and responses that people engage in after discovering a partner's relationship transgression (McCullough et al., 1998). Revenge is ubiquitous, pervasive, and universal, having been documented across virtually every culture and society (Brown, 1991; Daly & Wilson, 1988). Although revenge appears to be as inevitable as behaving badly in close relationships is, some specific explanations for and predictors of revenge have been identified in extant literature.

Explanations and Reasons for Revenge

Evolution. Available research supports the idea that enacting revenge may have evolved as an adaptive mechanism for policing the processes of exchange that occur in social interactions. For instance, if a member of a social group is unfairly allocating resources needed for your continued existence and propagation, retaliation could serve to urge the offender to allocate resources more fairly and generally to behave more collaboratively, and it may also serve to discourage bad behavior in future (Daly & Wilson, 1988; McCullough et al., 2013). From an evolutionary perspective, retributive messages—if successful—should right the initial wrong of the unfair allocation of resources, help ensure future cooperative behavior, and possibly prevent future harm by communicating to any potential offenders that you will not tolerate being wronged without imposing some consequences on the wrongdoer. These outcomes should then enhance your likelihood of survival and procreation.

Culture. Although revenge is prevalent across numerous cultures, culture has a differential impact on the conditions under which retaliation is attempted and the form that revenge takes. The types of revenge that have been discussed thus far typically occur in institutionalized cultures, where retribution is used to punish and deter unfair behavior and foster cooperation and collaboration (Sommers, 2009). Revenge is also common in honor cultures, where retaliation is an obligatory response to disrespect or resource threats in order to protect one's reputation, social status, and resources. Retaliation in such cultures is intended to discourage future acts of disrespect and resource encroachment. Although both men and women are likely to seek retribution in response to feeling wronged by another, they appear to do so in different ways. Men are thought to engage in more overt forms of retaliation (e.g., attacks, threats) while females use more indirect and covert forms of revenge (e.g., reputation defamation; Bjoerkqvist et al., 1994).

Personality characteristics. Several personality traits have been linked to the proclivity to seek revenge, including low agreeableness (i.e., people who are lacking in warmth, sympathy, and who are insensitive to others' needs) and high neuroticism (i.e., people who are negatively biased to experience the world as distressing and anxiety inducing). In fact, one study indicated that these two personality characteristics account for 30% of the desire to exact revenge (McCullough et al., 2001). In addition, recent meta-analytic work indicates that high levels of narcissism (i.e., people who have a fragile ego and an overly inflated sense of self and what one deserves) are associated with revenge across numerous samples (Rasmussen, 2016). Individuals who are high in **narcissistic entitlement** (i.e., people who believe they are so special or superior that they deserve special treatment and/or more rewards than others) tend to be less forgiving, and forgiveness is antithetical to revenge (if you have truly forgiven someone, then you have no desire to seek revenge; if you are seeking revenge, then you have not truly forgiven the offender). Narcissists tend to demand that offenders pay for the harm they have caused before they will consider forgiveness (Exline et al., 2004). Those with a Type A personality (i.e., people who tend to be hostile, competitive, and who display a strong sense of time urgency) have also reported more acts of aggressive revenge in the workplace context (Baron et al., 1999).

Cognitions. Revenge is enacted in order to achieve goals, some of which were discussed previously as part of the conceptualization of revenge (e.g., to cause a change in the offender, to restore justice, to feel better about the offense, to save face; Boon et al., 2009). More specifically, five conflict goals have been found to be relevant to retaliating against an offender. These are *justice goals*, which are intended to elicit respect from the offender; *power-hostility goals*, which are intended to establish power and dominance over the offender; *identity goals*, which are intended to restore one's own face; *relationship goals*, which are intended to continue a relationship with the offender; and *economic resource goals*, which are intended to acquire concrete recompense from the offender (Yoshimura, 2007).

Cognitive appraisals and attributions of blame and causality for events are central to the motivation to enact revenge. If an offender is personally acknowledged as the cause of the wrongdoing (as opposed to situational or contextual reasons that might have contributed to the offense, for example), and further, if the offender is judged to have committed the wrongdoing intentionally, the offended person is more likely to seek retribution—particularly if the wrongdoing was especially damaging and/or the offended party is ruminating about the offense (Bradfield & Aquino, 1999; Bies & Tripp, 2005). Other research has also established **rumination** (i.e., repetitive, intrusive thoughts, typically about a negative event) as a correlate of a penchant for revenge and of vengeful behavior (McCullough et al., 2001). Of course, our cognitive appraisals and attributions may be biased in this regard, as people have an established tendency to assign blame for others' bad behavior to something internal, dispositional, and stable about the offender, as opposed to something external, circumstantial, and temporary (Ross, 1977).

Emotions. Although revenge is calculated, goal directed, and planned, it is not without relevant and impactful affective components. In fact, in investigating the central prototypical characteristics of vengeance across a series of studies, Elshout et al. (2015) found that participants identified vengeance as an intensely emotional experience. More specifically, anger, humiliation, envy, and vindictiveness emerged as emotions that are central to the revenge experience. Further, other emotions such as sadness, shame, disappointment, and fear were identified as being peripherally related to vengeance. In addition, vengeance was seen as both satisfying (i.e., with satisfactory and sweet feelings) and dissatisfying (i.e., with feelings of remorse and regret).

Communicating Revenge

Situating revenge as a communicative message requires a closer look at the ways in which messages of revenge are communicated to offenders, including the content of such messages. Although research on revenge enactment is sparse, relatively speaking, and has been conducted mainly in the context of dating or workplace relationships, revenge acts take place across various relationship types. In perhaps the first broad study of specific revenge acts in romantic relationships, Yoshimura's (2004b) participants provided as many as 10 examples of things that they had done (or things that someone they knew had done) to get revenge against or get even with romantic partners. The prompt was designed specifically to elicit revenge acts committed by both males and females. Using content analysis, the examples provided by study participants were categorized into 15 overarching types of revenge activities (see Table 9.1 for a complete description).

As the opening vignette of this chapter illustrated, and studies show, the most frequently reported act of revenge for both males and females was to begin a new romantic or sexual relationship with someone else in order to get even with a current or former romantic partner (a finding that was later replicated by Boon et al., 2009). This might be with someone the romantic partner knows and/or is close with in some way (e.g., a friend, family member, former romantic partner, or even an enemy) or someone with no particular connection to the romantic partner. In fact, participants in Yoshimura's study were more likely to report beginning a new relationship

TABLE 9.1 Types of Revenge Behaviors

Revenge Act	Examples
Initiate new romantic/sexual relationship	• Dated/had sex with my partner's friends or siblings • Dated/had sex with other people my partner doesn't know • Dated/had sex with my partner's enemies or rivals
Active distancing	• Ceased all communication with my partner • Avoided or excluded my partner • Broke up with my partner
Resource damage	• Vandalized my partner's property (e.g., car, home) • Disposed of my partner's property (e.g., clothes, personal documents)
Manipulation attempts	• Flirted with others and made the partner aware of it • Flaunted new partners • Pretended to forget about partner • Stood the partner up on a date • Threatened to sleep with someone else • Kidnapped children or pets • Said I am pregnant or actually got pregnant
Harassment	• Made verbally abusive comments to partner • Made harassing phone calls to partner • Followed/spied on partner • Sent hate mail to partner • Called partner names
Reputation defamation	• Made comments about how small partner's sexual attributes are or how bad their sexual performance is • Betrayed partner's secrets to others • Spread rumors that made partner look bad
Sabotage/disrupt social connections	• Turned partner's family/friends against them • Told partner's new love interest bad things about them • Told partner's parents about their bad behavior
Resource withdrawal	• Stole partner's belongings • Spent partner's money • Took back gifts I had given the partner
Threats/attacks against romantic rival	• Physically attacked partner's new romantic interest • Was rude to partner's new romantic interest • Threatened to beat up partner's new romantic interest
Relationship invalidation	• Destroyed memorabilia from the relationship • Said the relationship meant less than it did • Left partner's property outside • Destroyed mutual belongings

(continued)

TABLE 9.1 Types of Revenge Behaviors *(continued)*

Revenge Act	Examples
Physical threats and assault against romantic partner	• Physically harmed partner • Threw things at partner • Poisoned partner • Had another person harm the partner
Intimacy withdrawal	• Withheld affection/sex from partner
Self-harm	• Used excessive alcohol or drugs • Spent time with bad influences • Tried to commit suicide
Financial damage	• Sued partner • Got partner fired • Demanded repayment of loans from partner
Change/alter appearance	• Dressed sexier • Changed my physical appearance

Adapted from: Yoshimura (2004b)

with a friend or family member (i.e., sibling) of the romantic partner, a move that is effectively a two-pronged act of revenge as it also serves to compromise the partner's relationship with someone else with whom they are close. Further, the selection of this revenge act may be a direct reaction to the initial offense that was committed against the avenger, as some research has shown that the nature of the initial offense is an important predictor of the nature of the revenge behavior (e.g., Boon et al., 2009). As illustrated by the opening vignette of this chapter, tit-for-tat revenge (you cheated on me, so the best way to get even is to cheat on you in return) is common.

The second most frequently reported revenge behavior was to overtly distance oneself from the partner emotionally and/or physically, often by avoiding communication with them or terminating the relationship. The third most frequently reported means of revenge was to damage or destroy the romantic partner's belongings (e.g., vehicle, home, clothing, etc.).

Eliminating those revenge behaviors that were infrequently reported and using factor analysis, the original 15 categories were later reduced to six: *destructive exit* (acts that imply actual or symbolic relationship termination, such as initiating romantic or sexual relationships with others and destroying shared belongings or mementos of the relationship), *truculent deprecation* (embarrassing and offensive acts of reputation defamation, such as revealing nude pictures of the person to others and insulting the person), *distancing* (avoiding the person physically and withholding affection/sex), *provocation* (acts undertaken to provoke the person, including accusations of infidelity, withholding financial resources, and even throwing objects at the person), *relational weaponization* (using third-party relationships to hurt the person, such as flirting with or dating the person's friends or family members), and *emotional manipulation* (acts that hurt the person's feelings or make them feel disrespected or guilty; Yoshimura et al., 2013; Yoshimura & Boon, 2018). Although an individual's choice of revenge behavior is based on numerous considerations, generally speaking, avengers prefer to maximize the effect of the act while also minimizing their own personal risk as well as the personal consequences of performing the behavior.

FLIPPING THE SCRIPT

Is Revenge Really Sweet?

Forgiveness is generally considered a virtue while revenge is considered a vice, which has overwhelmingly negative connotations and is largely disavowed. Depending on how it is communicated, it can be perceived as immature, passive aggressive, and used by individuals who suffer from low emotional control. However, research suggests that revenge is a universally common, rational, goal-directed, strategic activity that has (or at least has the potential to have) some bright side elements (Frijda, 1994). For example, although considering past vengeful actions is associated primarily with negative emotions, some (slight) positive affective responses have also been reported (Yoshimura, 2007). Some people report that retaliating against a wrongdoer not only helps the offended party restore their face, along with a sense of justice and equity, but in fact it helps the offended person feel better about the offense (Boon et al., 2009).

Indeed, numerous studies reveal some positive aspects of revenge in the form positive emotions and rewards, including satisfaction. One particularly interesting (and convincing) study used Positron Emission Tomography data to show that the reward centers of the brain were stimulated in individuals who were pondering an act of revenge in the form of punishing a wrongdoer, even under conditions when punishing this person would not benefit them personally (i.e., even if the punishment served to change the wrongdoer's future behavior, this had no benefit for the offended person as they would not be interacting with the wrongdoer again; de Quervain et al., 2004). Some preliminary research suggests that revenge can indeed be sweet if it is clear that the offender understands the offended party's reasons for retaliating (Funk et al., 2014). Yoshimura and Boon (2018) posit that revenge could garner positive outcomes if it works to restore the offended person's face and self-esteem, rectifies a power imbalance in their relationship with the offender, and diminishes "pain from either the initial offense or relative to what the offender experiences as a result of the vengeful act" (p. 87).

On the other hand, these revenge experts also recognize the difficulty (if not the impossibility) of undoing the damage that was caused by the initial offense, even if the offended party's revenge attempt is considered successful. Supporting this claim are numerous studies that demonstrate the experience of positive affect on the offended party's part when *thinking about* retaliation, but conversely, actually enacting revenge is associated with various negative outcomes (e.g., increased hostility and anger; Bushman et al., 2001). Further, revenge seems to be most satisfying immediately following the vengeful act, but this feeling tends to fade over time (Crombag et al., 2003). Although more evidence is necessary, the state of current research on revenge suggests that it is, at best, bittersweet.

Forgiveness: A Brighter Response

The previous discussion of revenge makes clear the tendency for people to respond to slights or other negativity in kind, by perpetrating aversive or destructive behavior in return for the destructive behavior that was first visited upon them—a tendency that is especially strong for members of distressed couples (Rusbult et al., 1991). However, in certain instances, people can modify their natural tendencies toward responding to negativity in a tit-for-tat manner and instead react constructively, in more pro-relationship ways, to bad behavior. This is known as **accommodation**, and it represents one way that "damage control" can be enacted in a relationship following a negative relational event. Typically, individuals are more likely to choose accommodation over retaliation when the quality of their romantic relationship (e.g., satisfaction, investment, commitment) prior to the negative relational event was higher (and their perception of quality alternatives to the primary relationship was lower). Accommodation processes can pave the way for forgiveness, which requires—among other things—a transformation of negative to positive affect toward the transgressor and a decreased motivation to retaliate against the transgressor.

Like many concepts discussed throughout this textbook, forgiveness has a number of different conceptualizations in the literature. Common among them, however, is the idea of **forgiveness** as an intrapersonal, transformative process of related prosocial changes from negative to positive psychological states with regard to the offender, despite the recognition that the offender has not earned and has no right to expect such mercy (Baumeister et al., 1998; Fincham, 2000; McCullough et al., 2000; Waldron & Kelley, 2008). Forgiveness is multifaceted and complex, and there is general consensus among forgiveness scholars across disciplines that positive changes in emotions, cognitions, behavioral inclinations, and/or actual behavior toward the offender are necessary to say forgiveness has occurred. As implied by this conceptualization, forgiveness has interpersonal as well as intrapersonal components, in that a positive transformation of affect, cognitions, or inclinations toward the offender should ultimately be evident in the form of the offended partner's treatment of and communication with the offender (Fincham, 2000).

McCullough et al. (2003) define forgiveness as a set of three motivational changes experienced in response to a transgression, including decreased motivation to attempt to enact revenge against the transgressor, decreased motivation to avoid the transgressor, and increased conciliatory motivations and feelings of benevolence toward the transgressor, despite their commission of the offense. These **transgression-related interpersonal motivations**, or TRIMs, serve as the dimensions of forgiveness according to these scholars; thus, forgiveness following a relational transgression is assessed as a low level of revenge and avoidance and a high level of goodwill toward the offender.

These motivations likely change over time, such that in the immediate wake of a serious transgression such as sexual infidelity, revenge and avoidance motivations are probably high while benevolence motivations are probably low. According to McCullough et al.'s operationalization, this pattern of motivations indicates little or no forgiveness. But forgiveness is a process, and with the passage of time and transformation of the negative affect that follows the discovery of major transgressions, these motivations may change and a higher degree of forgiveness may be seen. With that said, it may be the case that forgiveness does not lead to a reconciled relationship (and of course, a relationship can be reconciled even in the absence of forgiveness), but true forgiveness certainly helps pave the way for a relationship that has been damaged by a partner's transgression to be reconciled (Waldron & Kelley, 2008).

As these conceptualizations indicate, forgiveness and revenge should not be able to comfortably coexist, as the transformative process of forgiveness stipulates that the offended party no longer desires retaliation against the offender (Boon & Sulsky, 1997). In this way, revenge and forgiveness might be fruitfully illustrated as anchoring two extremes of a "responses to transgressions" continuum, as one appears to preclude the other. Although relatively recent, the empirical study of forgiveness (which began in earnest in the mid 1980s) is often carried out in the context of responses to relationship transgressions. As with revenge, some reliable predictors of forgiveness have emerged.

Explanations and Reasons for Forgiveness

McCullough et al. (1998) argued the presence of four primary determinants of forgiveness granting: the quality of the primary relationship prior to the offense, the enduring personality characteristics of the offended party, social-cognitive considerations, and elements related to the offense and the person who committed it. Each of these predictors will be discussed in more detail.

Primary relationship characteristics. The quality of the primary romantic relationship prior to experiencing a partner's bad behavior has long been identified as a predictor of destructive or constructive responses to transgressions (e.g., Rusbult, 1983). Across multiple studies, pre-transgression relationship qualities such as satisfaction, investment, and commitment have been associated with whether forgiveness is granted. Unsurprisingly, offended parties in higher quality relationships (i.e., those that are marked by higher levels of satisfaction, investment, and commitment) are more likely to forgive a partner's relational transgression, sometimes even when that transgression is severe (Finkel et al., 2002; Guerrero & Bachman, 2010; Kachadourian et al., 2004).

Personality characteristics. Two of the big five personality characteristics seem to share a close relationship with forgiveness, especially high levels of agreeableness but also low levels of neuroticism (McCullough et al., 2007). In addition, those high in narcissistic entitlement and narcissism are generally less forgiving (Exline et al., 2004). As you will recall from our discussion of revenge earlier in this chapter, these same personality characteristics have been relatively reliably associated with the choice to take revenge instead of to forgive, but in opposite ways (e.g., high levels of agreeableness are associated with forgiveness, whereas low levels of agreeableness are associated with revenge).

Social-cognitive. Attributions regarding the offense, empathy for the offender, and rumination appear to be critical predictors of forgiveness granting. Attributions of intentionality, responsibility, avoidability, and blameworthiness clearly impact whether forgiveness is granted (as well as the extent to which the offended party feels empathy for the offender), and forgiveness is less likely in cases of intentional, avoidable offenses for which the offender is clearly to blame (Boon & Sulsky, 1997; Weiner, 1995). Numerous studies have demonstrated that increased **empathy** (the willingness and ability of the offended party to put themself in the offender's shoes in an attempt to really understand and share how they feel) is associated with increased likelihood of forgiveness (Fehr et al., 2010). As noted previously, rumination has been linked to an increased tendency to retaliate, and related research has demonstrated an association between increased ruminative thoughts about an offense and a decreased likelihood of forgiving the person who committed that offense (Berry et al., 2005).

Offense related. The severity of the offense is a factor in determining whether forgiveness will be granted, and unsurprisingly, more negative/severe transgressions are less likely to be forgiven (Guerrero & Bachman, 2010; Kelley & Waldron, 2005). Further, the offender's behavior in the aftermath of the transgression affects the offended person's forgiveness-granting decisions, as offenders who display remorse, apologize, and actively engage in **forgiveness seeking** are more likely to earn the offended partner's empathy and subsequently be forgiven (McCullough et al., 1997; Merolla & Zhang, 2011). The importance of the offender's apology cannot be overstated (Fife et al., 2013). Effective apologies entail taking responsibility for one's actions, expressing sincere regret, promising not to engage in the problematic behavior in future, pledging to do the work required to repair the relationship with the offended party, and directly asking for the offended person's forgiveness.

Communicating Forgiveness

Forgiveness granting, or communicating forgiveness to an offender, is a crucial aspect of the interpersonal forgiveness process that has not yet received much research attention. In a qualitative study across various relationship types, Kelley (1998) identified three general ways people report communicating forgiveness to a wrongdoer: *directly* (explicitly forgiving the offender), *indirectly* (downplaying the offense), and *conditionally* (forgiving only if certain conditions are met, such as Tiana's forgiveness of Trey with a caveat in the vignette that opened this chapter). Participants in Kelley's study reported the use of direct forgiveness far more often than the other two forgiveness-granting strategies.

Waldron and Kelley (2005) extended this typology with the identification of five types of forgiving communication, three of which correspond with those from the original forgiveness-granting strategies: *explicit forgiveness* (which corresponds with the original conceptualization of directly forgiving), *minimizing* (previously known as indirectly forgiving), and *conditional forgiveness* (which corresponds with the original conceptualization of conditionally forgiving another). Two additional strategies were identified, including *nonverbal displays* (an indirect means of signaling forgiveness to another by body language and nonverbal cues such as hugs or smiles) and *forgiveness by discussion* (talking about the offense, which may set the stage for forgiveness to occur/be granted but in and of itself does not constitute forgiveness according to the conceptualizations of most forgiveness scholars).

The type of partner bad behavior has been shown to impact the choice of forgiveness-granting strategy, as conditional forgiveness is more likely to be selected (and indirect forgiveness/minimizing is less likely to be selected) in the case of more severe transgressions (Waldron & Kelley, 2005). Further, the selection of forgiveness-granting strategies has implications for the relationship. Explicit or direct forgiveness granting and nonverbal displays have been associated with improved relational outcomes such as reduced damage to the relationship and increased relational satisfaction. Conversely, conditional forgiveness has been associated with deleterious relational outcomes, including the offended partner's feelings of continued negativity and decreased relational satisfaction (Merolla, 2008; Merolla & Zhang, 2011; Waldron & Kelley, 2005). Conditional forgiveness is likely to be face threatening for the offender and may even be perceived as controlling and manipulative, which does not align with scholarly conceptualizations of forgiveness (Merolla, 2017).

Whether anything short of complete and total forgiveness counts as "true" forgiveness is a point of contention among forgiveness scholars (Fincham, 2000). Supporting the notion that perhaps conditional forgiveness is not really forgiveness at all, the bulk of the research suggests that conditional forms of forgiveness weaken the relationship, perhaps because conditional forgiveness implies that some level of negative affect and distrust of the partner remains, which is at odds with most scholars' conception of forgiveness as a positive transformation of negative affect. With that said, the question of whether all negative affect toward the transgressor must be eradicated to say that forgiveness has occurred is another area of debate in the forgiveness literature (Metts & Cupach, 2007).

Is Forgiveness Always Virtuous?

While revenge is widely condemned and reviled, forgiveness enjoys a reputation of virtuousness, with forgiveness generally being perceived as "what's best" for both the forgiveness granter and the forgiveness seeker. But is forgiveness always desirable? By and large, empirical research has focused on the positive aspects of forgiveness (but not without recognizing that forgiveness is not universally or solely positive). Are some acts unforgivable, like severe transgressions such as infidelity or violence? Are some offenders unforgivable, perhaps because they are unremorseful and unapologetic? Does forgiveness of an offense encourage the commission of future offenses?

Some argue that forgiveness is virtually always best, even under conditions of a severe offense committed by an unrepentant offender (Garrard & McNaughton, 2010; Govier, 1999). Further, some scholars argue that forgiveness does not sanction the bad behavior, and most conceptualizations of forgiveness recognize that you are extending "undeserved mercy" to the offender (Waldron & Kelley, 2008). Given that forgiveness entails a transformation of negative emotions, thoughts, and/or behaviors to positive ones, you might consider the extent to which forgiveness benefits you as the forgiveness granter and offended party, as much as—if not more than—the forgiveness-seeking offender. Although these are philosophical questions that obviously have no right or wrong answer, consideration of them is warranted given that how you feel about these questions undoubtedly influences your tendency to seek revenge or to grant forgiveness in the wake of a partner's relationship transgression. Further, research has revealed a potential dark side of forgiveness for the forgiveness granter, suggesting that while forgiveness may be virtuous, it may come at a cost for the offended person.

The dark side of forgiveness-granting. Although forgiveness enjoys an almost untarnished reputation with a variety of documented benefits, it is not a magic bullet for all relational difficulties. There is a dark side of forgiveness wherein costs are sometimes entailed, including **exploitation risk** of continued partner offenses for the forgiveness granter (Burnette et al., 2012). The offender's post-transgression behavior in the form of apologizing and making amends for the offense can influence the offended person's perceptions of exploitation risk, as better quality apologies lead to perceptions of decreased exploitation risk and increased relationship value in the future for the transgressed against partner. As granting forgiveness for transgressions can leave the forgiver vulnerable to being reoffended in future, increased distress is experienced after forgiving exploitative partners if forgiveness is granted for the sake of the relationship (e.g., to continue a dysfunctional codependent relationship) versus for the sake of one's self (e.g., because the offender feels that forgiving is the right thing to do, that they will reap positive benefits from doing so; Gabriels & Strelan, 2018; Strelan et al., 2017). Other potential drawbacks for the forgiver have been identified that are dependent on specific personality traits of the offender. For example, the tendency to forgive less agreeable spouses has been associated with negative changes in self-respect over time (Luchies et al., 2010), a result that may have been obtained because the partner continued to reoffend.

Recent research has linked forgiveness to the likelihood that a transgressor will reoffend, possibly because forgiveness removes undesired outcomes for the offender (e.g., the offended partner's anger or other negative emotions; McNulty, 2010). Across several different types of studies (i.e., survey, experimental, longitudinal, diary), forgiving a partner for a transgression has been shown to encourage that partner to reoffend, if they are lower in agreeableness (McNulty & Russell, 2016). These findings have not encouraged scholars to claim that forgiveness is detrimental, but its effects are clearly nuanced (Overall & McNulty, 2017). Forgiveness—particularly for severe transgressions—may need to be supplemented with **partner regulation behaviors** (i.e., communicative strategies that explicitly express opposition to the partner's objectionable behavior, such as requiring change and blaming the partner); otherwise the offender may feel free to continue their hurtful behavior unimpeded (Russell et al., 2018).

Other negative consequences for the forgiveness granter have emerged in available research. When the partner is a frequent offender, the tendency to forgive has been associated with declines in relationship satisfaction for the forgiver (McNulty, 2008). Forgiveness that is unwarranted (e.g., because of the severity and/or frequency of the partner's offenses) may protract a dysfunctional relationship, and it can also negatively impact the forgiveness granter's mental health (Luchies et al., 2010). Difficulties with forgiveness in the context of abusive relationships have been identified, in that dominant abusers who are able to provoke empathy from their female targets are more likely to be forgiven, which suggests a destructive cycle wherein empathy elicits forgiveness, which is then associated with continued patterns of abuse (Tsang & Stanford, 2007).

Forgiveness can have negative implications for social network members as well, given that it may influence the forgiver's relationship with third parties. Some research has shown that close friends or family members of the offended person are less willing to forgive offenders even after the transgressed against partner has granted forgiveness. Offended partners seem more likely to forgive offending partners because they are strongly committed to the relationship (which of course third parties are not) and because of a tendency to make more benevolent attributions for the offenders' behavior (a tendency that third parties do not share; Green et al., 2008). In this way, forgiveness of a partner for a major transgression can have complications for the forgiver's extradyadic relationships with friends and family members who may not be supportive of, and may openly oppose, the decision to forgive.

Whether or not social network members are supportive of the decision to forgive a romantic partner's offense may be related to the ways in which the offended person reveals and discusses these offenses with them. **Transgression-minimizing communication** intentionally diminishes the severity of the partner's offense, perhaps by providing situational explanations for the behavior or claiming that the behavior really was not that bad (Vallade & Dillow, 2014). **Transgression-maximizing communication**, on the other hand, exacerbates the severity of the partner's offense, possibly by overtly blaming the partner and talking about the negative consequences that have been suffered due to their transgression. Transgression-minimizing messages may serve to shore up social network members' support for the relationship, despite the transgression, and thus they may be less likely to oppose forgiveness of the partner's transgression. Conversely, transgression-maximizing messages should result in decreased support for the relationship from social network members, and therefore opposition to forgiving the partner for their offense may be openly expressed.

Other Responses to Relational Transgressions

Of course, revenge and forgiveness are not the only two possible responses to relational transgressions. Rusbult et al. (1982) presented a general typology of constructive and destructive responses to dissatisfaction in close relationships, regardless of the source of that dissatisfaction. **Voice** (engaging in problem-solving discussions with the partner, seeking help outside of the relationship, changing oneself for the better) and **loyalty** (waiting the problem out, hoping it will improve, standing by the partner) are two pro-relationship responses to a partner's bad behavior and the dissatisfaction that comes along with it. **Neglect** (treating the partner poorly, psychologically distancing oneself from the relationship, refusing to discuss problems or otherwise work on the relationship, letting the relationship fall apart) and **exit** (separating, breaking up, or divorcing) are two anti-relationship responses to relational dissatisfaction.

Across a series of studies, Rusbult and colleagues identified a number of factors that are correlated with the use of these responses, including qualities of the relationship prior to the emergence of relational difficulties (e.g., satisfaction, investment, and the perception of quality relational alternatives; Rusbult et al., 1982), the severity of the relational difficulties (Rusbult et al., 1986), and qualities of the individuals involved in that relationship (e.g., self-esteem and sex-role orientation; Rusbult et al., 1986, 1987). Perhaps unsurprisingly, greater pre-transgression satisfaction and investment in the primary relationship has been associated with increased pro-relationship responses (i.e., voice and loyalty) to negative relational events. Conversely, perceiving high-quality alternatives to the relationship appears to prompt more exit (and fewer loyalty) responses. More severe negative relational events lead to more voice and exit (and fewer loyalty) reactions. Those with higher self-esteem are more likely to exit the relationship (and less likely to react with neglect). Further, this program of research has shown that the pro-relationship responses of voice and loyalty result in more positive consequences, both in the short and long term (e.g., increased relational satisfaction and commitment).

Conclusion

Although revenge was treated as a dark side issue in this chapter, and forgiveness was characterized as a bright side concept, such a distinction is overly simplistic. As with other concepts that have been discussed in this textbook, revenge can have positive elements and outcomes (e.g., it may actually serve to restore equity and prevent similar behaviors from happening in future), and forgiveness is not universally positive (e.g., it may entail an exploitation risk for the forgiveness granter). In addition, these two concepts were treated as mutually exclusive in this chapter, a treatment that is also overly simplistic. While revenge may be our first instinct after experiencing a romantic partner's relational transgression, over time the prosocial transformations required by forgiveness may occur (Rusbult et al., 2001). As you have learned in this chapter, revenge is a common reaction to offenses such as relationship transgressions, and this reaction is particularly likely under certain circumstances. Forgiveness is not quite as instinctual as retaliation for most individuals, but it is more likely depending on certain characteristics of the offended, the offender, and the offense. As you have also learned in this chapter, revenge and forgiveness are communicated in specific ways, and the selection of these strategies influences the future of the relationship between the offended and the offender. The knowledge gleaned from this chapter should help you recognize that it is normal to feel vengeful after a relational partner's transgression, but that—if you value the relationship enough to want to continue it—perhaps revenge is not the best choice. And, although forgiveness may not immediately seem possible, you have learned that forgiveness is a process that takes time.

Discussion Questions

1. Discuss the pros and cons of retaliating against a close other (i.e., romantic partner, close friend, or family member) after they knowingly commit a relational transgression or intentionally harm you in some way. Based on what you have learned, is revenge really sweet or are there better ways to handle partner bad behavior? Explain your thinking.

2. The typologies of revenge behaviors provided in this chapter are specific to romantic relationships. In your opinion, are any of these relevant to retaliation in other types of close relationships (e.g., with a best friend or sibling)? In your experience, are there any revenge behaviors that are missing from these typologies, if we consider revenge activities in other close relationship contexts?

3. Do you agree that "true" forgiveness requires letting go of all negative affect toward the person who harmed you? Why or why not?

4. Do you believe it is accurate to position revenge and forgiveness as anchoring two opposite ends of a continuum? Can revenge and forgiveness coexist? Why or why not? Illustrate your points with relevant examples.

5. Identify and discuss the various predictors that cut across both revenge and forgiveness (e.g., agreeableness as a personality trait has been shown to predict both revenge and forgiveness, but in opposite ways). Use this information to develop a profile of a person who is less likely to seek revenge and more likely to forgive a close other for an offense.

Chapter 10

Aggression and Intimate Partner Violence

In the late 1970s came a turning point for what was then more commonly known as domestic violence. This turning point was instigated by the experiences and actions of Francine Hughes, a Michigan woman who suffered more than a decade of violent physical, sexual, and psychological abuse at the hands of her husband, Mickey Hughes. Francine dropped out of high school as a sophomore to marry Mickey, himself a high school dropout, and the physical violence began just weeks into their marriage. Mickey's ongoing pattern of controlling behaviors also began early in the marriage. He was extremely possessive, jealous, and quick to anger. He told Francine what she could wear, where she could go, and with whom she could interact, effectively isolating her from others outside their relationship. After 7 years (and four children) together, Francine sought a divorce. Despite this, Mickey's abuse did not stop, yet after he was gravely injured in a car accident, Francine agreed to let him move back in with her and the children. On the last day of his life, Mickey was again violently beating Francine. He refused to let her give the children dinner. He destroyed class materials for the nursing course she was taking and insisted that she drop out of school. Francine called the police, but when they arrived they claimed they could do nothing because they had not witnessed the violence firsthand. When they left, *the abuse resumed. Mickey threatened Francine with a knife in front of the children. He raped her. Later that night after Mickey was asleep, Francine poured gasoline around the bed he was sleeping in and set it on fire. She then took her children to the police station, where she confessed her crime. Mickey died of smoke inhalation, and although Francine was charged with first-degree murder, she was found not guilty by reason of temporary insanity. The story of Francine and Mickey was widely reported in the media at the time, spurring a book and a made-for-television movie (both entitled* The Burning Bed*). The story inspired law enforcement and social service agencies to implement more proactive and effective policies to help put a stop to domestic violence.* (Grimes, 2017)

Aggression in all its forms is by definition harmful to those who are on the receiving end of it. Aggression can be usefully considered as a sort of umbrella term that encompasses a host of other destructive behaviors, including intimate partner violence (which itself can include sexual violence, as you will see). The common thread among these behaviors is that they are all aggressive because they all intend some form of damage to another. In this chapter, we will discuss the conceptualization of aggression and its various types, including physical, sexual, verbal, and social aggression. After a basic understanding of these distinctions, we will move to a discussion of various aspects of intimate partner violence, encompassing the types, prevalence, predictors/antecedent conditions for perpetration, risk factors for victimization, and consequences. Note that the information covered in this chapter primarily reflects and is applicable to heterosexual relationships, as little empirical work is currently available on lesbian, gay, bisexual, transgender, queer, intersex, asexual, and pansexual (LGBTQIAP) relationships.

Types of Aggression

Before commencing a discussion of intimate partner violence, which will be the primary focus of this chapter, a brief overview of aggression is necessary. **Human aggression** is itself a broad term that has defied singular conceptualization but can be defined as any behavior that intends any form of harm to a target, and the target is motivated to avoid the behavior/harm (Anderson & Bushman, 2002). It may entail proactive or reactive behaviors, overt or covert actions, and has been defined in a number of different ways, ranging from relatively minor behaviors (e.g., teasing) to more serious ones (e.g., sexual violence), and from symbolic behaviors (e.g., verbal aggression that results in emotional and/or psychological harm) to more tangible ones (e.g., physical abuse). Given the inclusivity of general definitions of the term, aggression is often broken down by type. These types include (but are not limited to) physical, sexual, verbal, and social. **Physical aggression** entails behaviors that cause bodily harm to another, such as hitting, pushing, kicking, and beating up (Straus & Gelles, 1986). Physical aggression is often conceptualized synonymously with **violence** (although the conceptualization of violence itself is hotly debated), which has been defined as any action or behavior intended to cause physical harm (Sugarman & Hotaling, 1989)—but it should be noted here that others define violence more narrowly, as the intent to inflict *extreme* harm, such as death (Anderson & Bushman, 2002). All instances of physical and sexual violence are aggressive in nature, but of course, not all acts of aggression qualify as violence since aggression may be symbolic.

Sexual aggression could be considered a specialized form of physical aggression (and in fact is often referred to as sexual violence), as it too includes behaviors that cause physical harm to another. The distinguishing characteristic of sexual aggression/violence is that the bodily harm in question is sexual and nonconsensual in nature (e.g., sexual assault, molestation; Carr & VanDeusen, 2004). When sexual violence occurs within the context of an intimate relationship, it is often considered part of intimate partner violence, discussed later. **Sexual harassment** and gender harassment can be considered under the rubric of sexual aggression as well. The former can include unwelcome sexual advances, requests for sexual favors, or a wide range of other verbal (e.g., making sexual comments or jokes), nonverbal (e.g., making sexual gestures, displaying sexual images), or physical contact (e.g., touching or grabbing someone) that is sexual in nature (U.S. Department of Education, 2010). **Gender harassment** includes calling someone gay or lesbian in a malicious way that is explicitly intended as an insult or using any derogatory term for homosexuality (Gruber & Fineran, 2007). Gender harassment may also be considered a specialized form of verbal aggression, discussed next.

Relatively (and arguably) "milder" forms of aggression are symbolic rather than physical in nature. **Verbal aggression** includes messages that are intended to psychologically/emotionally harm the target (Infante & Rancer, 1996). Verbally aggressive messages can be infrequent and situationally incited, but when they occur often across contexts and targets such behavior is representative of trait verbal aggressiveness: the enduring tendency to attack others' self-concepts with the intent to symbolically hurt them. Unlike verbal aggression, **social aggression** may not be communicated directly to the intended target and may instead be expressed to third parties in an effort to harm the target. It is a circuitous, roundabout, sometimes covert and indirect form of aggression that is intended to harm another's social standing and/or self-esteem (Galen & Underwood, 1997). It may manifest in the form of social rejection or exclusion, snubbing, gossiping, mocking, or spreading rumors. (When social aggression takes the form of verbal messages, it can be viewed as a specialized type of verbal aggression.) This type of aggression is seen in children as young as 3 years old, and research has suggested that adolescent girls are more likely than adolescent boys to perpetrate it, whereas boys are more likely to initiate direct forms of aggression, such as physical and verbal aggression (Card et al., 2008; Salmivalli et al., 2000).

Up to this point in the chapter, the general forms of aggression that have been introduced are not specific to any particular type of relationship. Put another way, the previously discussed varieties of aggression could be perpetrated in various relationship types, including family, romantic, friendship, or acquaintance, or even by strangers. The remainder of this chapter will focus on a frequently studied type of violence that occurs specifically in the context of close, intimate relationships.

Intimate Partner Violence

Intimate partner violence is a form of aggressive behavior that is a subset of violence and has been defined most simply as physical harm that is committed within the context of an intimate (typically romantic) or otherwise close relationship (e.g., Kelly & Johnson, 2008). Admittedly, this is an oversimplified notion of the various types of violent behaviors—and the motives that underlie those behaviors—that often occur between romantic partners, and such a general approach is not terribly informative. To remedy such an overgeneralized view, three primary types of specific intimate partner violence have been identified by scholars: situational couple violence, intimate terrorism, and violent resistance (Johnson, 2011). Michael P. Johnson (2008), the originator of this typology, argues that the three types of intimate partner violence vary dramatically in almost every respect.

Types of Intimate Partner Violence

Situational couple violence (also called common couple violence) occurs when conflict situations—which are typically somewhat frequent, rather ordinary occurrences in close relationships—escalate too far, arguments become aggressive, partners "blow up," and violence ensues (Johnson, 1995). Situational couple violence is the most commonly reported type of intimate partner violence, and about 40% of surveyed individuals indicate that they have experienced only one fairly minor incidence of this type of violence. Unlike intimate terrorism (discussed next), this type of violence is spontaneous and typically not part of a pattern of coercive control, although some cases are indeed chronic and/or severe—potentially even life-threatening—in nature (Johnson, 2011). Unlike intimate terrorism and violent resistance, discussed later, situational couple violence is equally likely to be perpetrated by both men and women (i.e., the initiation of this type of violence is **gender symmetric**), it usually entails comparatively less severe forms of violence (e.g., grabbing, pushing, throwing things), and it is often reciprocal in nature (i.e., when one partner initiates violence during a conflict situation, the other partner responds in kind; Johnson, 1995). Because this type of violence is spontaneous and instigated by factors specific to the particular situation or conflict at hand, it is difficult to isolate reliable predictors of situational couple violence.

Intimate terrorism (also called coercive controlling violence) is synonymous with what most people think of as domestic violence and is illustrated particularly well by Mickey Hughes's behavior in the vignette that opened this chapter. Intimate terrorism is a strategic, manipulative, repeated pattern of attempts to exert control over a romantic partner by using violence (Johnson & Ferraro, 2000; Johnson & Leone, 2005; Kelly & Johnson, 2008). The violence can be physical and/or sexual in nature, and it is accompanied by a number of coercive tactics such as threats, intimidation, continual surveillance, withholding of resources (e.g., money), **gaslighting**, blaming the victim, use of the children to achieve desired outcomes (i.e., using children as a bargaining chip to get what one wants), psychological/emotional/verbal abuse, isolating the victim, and so on. (See Figure 10.1 for more examples of strategies used by intimate terrorists to exert power and control over their victims.)

All the tactics of physical and/or sexual violence depicted Figure 10.1 are designed to keep a partner under constant control by an intimate terrorist, and the violence that accompanies these tactics occurs frequently—roughly once per week, which is significantly more often than situational couple violence occurs (Johnson, 1995). Intimate terrorism usually escalates over

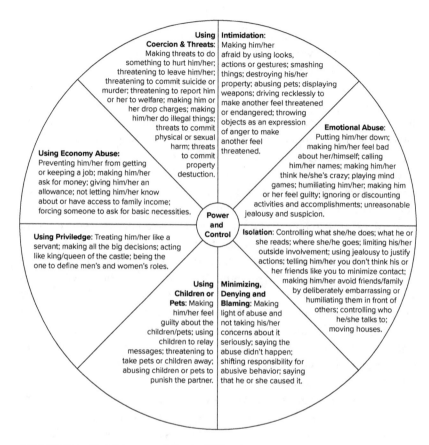

FIGURE 10.1 The Power and Control Wheel

Adapted from: Copyright © by moggs oceanlane (CC by 2.0) at https://commons.wikimedia.org/wiki/File:(2)_Cycle_of_abuse,_power_%26_control_issues_in_domestic_abuse_situations.gif.

time, occurring more often and becoming more severe as intimate terrorists become even more coercive and controlling (Johnson & Ferraro, 2000). This was certainly the case for Francine Hughes in the vignette that opened this chapter, who referred to herself as "a beaten-down, scared animal" when she was being victimized. Although heterosexual males are more likely to perpetrate intimate terrorism, according to available evidence, use of this strategy has also emerged with heterosexual wives and lesbian couples (Hines & Douglas, 2010; Johnson, 2008; Renzetti, 1992). All things considered, gender is not the best predictor of who will perpetrate intimate terrorism. In addition to the desire to control one's partner, two reliable predictors of the perpetration of intimate terrorism include **gender traditionalism** (i.e., the belief in traditional, stereotypical ideals concerning binary biological gender, including the types of roles that should be played by males versus females—for example, the belief that women should take care of the home while men are the family breadwinners)—and **misogyny** (i.e., strong negative feelings/beliefs toward women, including dislike, hatred, prejudice, and contempt; Sugarman & Frankel, 1996). Misogynistic individuals, and those who ascribe to gender traditionalism (whether they be women or men), are more likely to enact intimate terrorism.

Victims of intimate terrorism may respond passively—or at least non-violently—to their partners' violent control attempts. Conversely, some may respond with **violent resistance** of their own. This may occur the first time these individuals are terrorized by their partner, or it may not occur until long into the pattern of abuse, when it seems that only a reciprocal violent response (e.g., typically physical violence of some sort, perhaps even homicide) will bring an end to the intimate terrorism perpetrated by their partner. To return again to the vignette that began this chapter, Francine Hughes's murder of her husband Mickey by immolation in response to the years of intimate terrorism she experienced at his hands exemplifies violent resistance. Although this type of offender is violent, unlike intimate terrorists, they do not exhibit a pattern of controlling and coercive behaviors. Violent resistance might be seen as an extreme form of self-defense, but as a means of putting an end to a partner's intimate terrorism it is often ineffective and may in fact serve to escalate the perpetrator's intimate terrorism even more (Johnson, 2011).

Now that we have a grasp of the basic types of intimate partner violence, we will move to a discussion of the prevalence of this form of violence in romantic relationships, predictors of intimate partner violence perpetration, risk factors for victimization, and consequences of this type of violence.

Prevalence of Intimate Partner Violence

Before embarking on a discussion of the rates at which intimate partner violence is experienced and/or perpetrated, a note about discrepancies is warranted. It is important to be aware that not everyone agrees on what constitutes violence to begin with; there is considerable difference in conceptualizations of the term in empirical research, and further, laypeople often differ in the behaviors they consider to be violent. Such differences may be cultural in nature (i.e., a result of socialization), but they sometimes differ depending on whose perspective is privileged. Perpetrators (whether male or female) tend to think their own use of violence is more acceptable (Gracia et al., 2015), and such perceptions may lead to underreporting of the perpetration of violence. In short, often times what "counts" as intimate partner violence depends on how it is defined, who you are asking, and how honest those individuals are willing to be about those behaviors when they participate in our research studies. Keep that caveat in mind during the following discussion of the prevalence of intimate partner violence.

When considering the experience of intimate partner violence in society as a whole, data from the Centers for Disease Control's National Intimate Partner and Sexual Violence Survey (NIPSVS) is informative (Walters et al., 2019). This is a nationally representative survey that collects data regarding sexual violence, stalking, and intimate partner violence from U.S. adults. In terms of sexual violence experienced at the hands of an intimate partner, the results of this survey show that one in five women has experienced completed or attempted rape in her lifetime, while one in 14 men was forced to penetrate (completed or attempted) someone else against his will. Not quite half of all women (43.6%) and a quarter of all men (24.8%) who were surveyed reported experiencing some form of sexual violence during their lifetime (e.g., rape, being forced to penetrate another, **sexual coercion**, or unwanted sexual contact such as being groped or kissed). The majority of sexual assaults—about 73%—are perpetrated by someone the victim knows, including intimate partners but also acquaintances, and sexual assault is one of the violent crimes that people are least likely to report to authorities (Truman & Langton, 2015). According to the Youth Risk Behavior Surveillance study, adolescents and young adults—particularly adolescent girls of color—are especially susceptible to sexual assault, including rape (Kann et al., 2014).

In terms of intimate partner violence (i.e., physical violence excluding sexual violence), the NIPSVS reveals that one in four women and one in 10 men reported some form of intimate partner violence-related impact during their lifetime (Walters et al., 2013). More specifically, nearly one third of women (30.6%) and men (31%) experienced intimate partner violence (i.e., slapping, pushing, shoving) during their lifetime. Further, 21.4% of women and 14.9% of men experienced intimate partner violence that is categorized as severe (i.e., hit with a fist or something hard, kicked, hair pulled, slammed against something, choked, suffocated, beaten, burned, or use of a knife or a gun) during their lifetime. Less is known about the experience of intimate partner violence in same-sex relationships, although the limited research that is available suggests that intimate partner violence occurs at a similar rate (or perhaps even at a higher rate) as in heterosexual relationships (Stanley et al., 2006).

FLIPPING THE SCRIPT

Intimate Partner Violence and Sexual Assault in LGBTQIAP Relationships

Most of the research covered in this chapter deals with aggression and intimate partner violence in the context of heterosexual relationships. Unfortunately, lesbian, gay, bisexual, transgender, queer, intersex, asexual, and pansexual individuals and their romantic relationships have been relatively overlooked by researchers, perhaps because of the ways in which U.S. society has historically responded to these relationships. The same is true when sexual assault is the particular form of violence under consideration, as some early definitions positioned rape as something only females could experience (i.e., in 1927, the FBI defined rape as "carnal knowledge of a female"—and did not revise this definition to include males until 2012). Scholars have only just begun empirically investigating intimate partner violence and sexual assault in LGBTQIAP contexts (Pérez & Hussey, 2014), and the study of males who are sexual assault victims is still in its infancy (Donne et al., 2018). The early research that is available suggests that LGBTQIAP romantic relationships experience just as much—if not more—violence than heterosexual couples (Dank et al., 2014), and the risk of sexual assault for members of this community is alarmingly high (e.g., Walters et al., 2013). Those who identify as men and who are also members of sexual orientation minority communities are at an especially high risk for experiencing sexual violence; and further, these men are less likely to seek the support that they need and deserve following such experiences (Donne et al., 2018). In addition, within the LGBTQIAP community, those who identify as female, Black/African American, and male-to-female transgender young adults are at a higher risk of intimate partner violence victimization relative to those who identify as male, members of other-than Black/African American racial/ethnic groups, and female-to-male transgender young adults (Reuter et al., 2017). In terms of consequences for those in the LGBTQIAP community who have been victims of intimate partner violence, research has shown that they are more likely to engage in sexual risk-taking behaviors and are also more likely to experience adverse mental health outcomes (Reuter et al., 2017). The study of intimate partner violence and sexual violence in LGBTQIAP relationships is timely and consequential, and this area of inquiry is in need of additional empirical investigation.

Predictors of Aggression and Intimate Partner Violence Perpetration

Any number of factors may underlie the tendency to behave in an aggressive manner, more generally, and the perpetration of intimate partner violence (including sexual violence), more specifically. Certainly, the perpetration of intimate partner violence is the result of the interaction of many antecedent variables at the individual and social/community levels. As such, the following account of predictors is not exhaustive but does represent some of the key factors that have been reliably associated with the perpetration of aggression and violence in close relationships (and sometimes outside of those relationships). In the following, these antecedent conditions are broken down into comparatively more stable, enduring characteristics as well as more short-term, situation-specific predictors.

Relatively Stable Predictors

Certain traits or predispositions to respond in particular ways render some people more likely to be aggressive in a variety of contexts, romantic and otherwise. For example, as discussed previously, trait verbal aggression is an enduring tendency to attack other people's self-concepts (in addition to or instead of their positions on an issue). Narcissists, with their elevated yet unstable self-esteem, become quite angry and are especially prone to aggression and violence when their fragile egos are threatened or when they are otherwise provoked (Bushman & Baumeister, 1998; Kjaervik & Bushman, 2021). Hostility is also a contributing factor, both to general aggression and to intimate partner violence (Infante et al., 1989). Men who are hostile toward women, in particular, are especially likely to perpetrate intimate partner violence (Anderson & Anderson, 2008). Anger has also been shown to be moderately strongly (although somewhat inconsistently) associated with intimate partner violence (e.g., Birkley & Eckhardt, 2015; Norlander & Eckhardt, 2005). Several internalizing negative "emotions" such as anxiety and depression have been shown to be both predictors and consequences of intimate partner violence (Dutton & Karakanta, 2013; Swan et al., 2005).

Studies typically show that members of U.S. racial/ethnic minority groups (with the exception of Asian Americans) are more likely to perpetrate intimate partner violence, but note that these studies often aggregate data across racial/ethnic subgroups in too broad a manner, obscuring potentially important distinctions (Tjaden & Thoennes, 2000). Such studies also typically neglect to consider the potential ramifications of factors related to socioeconomic status, such as occupation and income. Research has shown that low occupational status and low annual household income are consistently related to an increased likelihood of perpetrating intimate partner violence (Cunradi et al., 2002). Cultural and/or religious values that demand retribution, usually in the form of violence, for insults to one's honor or one's family's honor—such as those that are present in some areas of the southern and western United States, in addition to some regions outside the United States—may also provoke violent behavior within and outside of close relationships (Cohen et al., 1996; Cohen & Nisbett, 1997).

Abuse in the family of origin may also play a role in the perpetration of intimate partner violence through the process of **intergenerational transmission**. Boys who grow up watching their fathers abuse their mothers are more likely to then perpetrate the same abuse with their own intimate partners, and girls who witness this behavior are more likely to fall victim to it themselves in their later romantic relationships (Murrell et al., 2007). (Although it is not mentioned in the vignette that opened this chapter, Francine Hughes witnessed violence in her family of origin; her father was abusive to her mother.) Bandura's (1978) social learning theory provides an empirically sound theoretical framework for the idea of intergenerational transmission of violence. Quite simply, this theory holds that children learn how to behave by modeling the behaviors of those around them. Parents are usually children's primary role models, making them prime targets for this modeling behavior. Yet, of course, witnessing violence in the family of origin does not guarantee that one will either perpetrate it or fall victim to it. Intergenerational transmission of intimate partner violence appears to be especially likely when boys internalize their fathers' patriarchal beliefs about heterosexual male dominance and the accompanying negative (e.g., sexist) attitudes about and devaluation of women, general likelihood of blaming the victim, and acceptable attitudes toward violence (O'Hearn & Margolin, 2000).

Biological sex may also play a role, as males have been shown to perpetrate more violence across contexts, including the commission of violent crimes (Anderson & Bushman, 2002), and most studies show that young men (ages 18–29 years old) are more likely to perpetrate intimate partner violence. Some research also shows that heterosexual males are more likely to perpetrate intimate partner violence, although this has been debated by scholars. This claim is likely true only for heterosexual males who hold traditional patriarchal attitudes toward women (e.g., believe that men are superior to women, believe that women are men's possessions, have a strong sense of personal entitlement) and who have positive attitudes toward violence against women (Bancroft et al., 2012). Considerable research indicates that men and women are motivated by different factors when they perpetrate intimate partner violence. Women are more likely to resort to intimate partner violence to protect themselves (e.g., in self-defense) or to get back at a partner who has perpetrated violence against them, but men are more likely to become violent when their partner defies their authority and/or when they perceive that they are losing control of the relationship (Dobash et al., 1998).

FLIPPING THE SCRIPT

Are Men Really More Likely to Perpetuate Intimate Partner Violence?

In popular culture, such as the movie *The Burning Bed* which was based on the true story that served as the basis for the opening vignette of this chapter, and in empirical research, heterosexual female victims are most often the focus of media portrayals and scholarship regarding intimate partner violence. Outside of the context of close relationships, males generally do seem to be more violent (e.g., they commit more violent crimes such as murder and aggravated assault; Anderson & Bushman, 2002). Yet, some of the earliest nationally representative surveys on violence between heterosexual married spouses showed that violence in these relationships is often reciprocal. More specifically, wives reported pushing and hitting their husbands as often as their husbands reported pushing and hitting them (Straus et al., 1980; Straus & Gelles, 1986). Further, wives reported initiating even more violent behaviors (e.g., kicking, beating up, threatening with a weapon) more often than husbands did (Straus & Gelles, 1986). A more recent review of large-scale research studies on violence in heterosexual relationships also suggested that women were as violent as men in intimate relationships (Archer, 2000). Clearly, men are victims of intimate partner violence and are deserving of increased scholarly attention, and research focused on men's experience of violence has been steadily increasing since the 1990s (Bates, 2020; Donne et al., 2018; Kimberg, 2008).

Yet, scholars who have controversially claimed that there is **gender symmetry** in domestic violence—that heterosexual women in close relationships are violent as often as men, or that heterosexual men are victims of violence in close relationships as often as women are—ignited a heated debate. Whether or not gender symmetry exists in intimate partner violence, empirically speaking, depends on what types of research studies (and what types of samples) are under consideration (Kimmel, 2002). *Family conflict studies* tend to show a pattern whereby intimate partner violence is perpetrated relatively equally by both men and women, providing some evidence for gender symmetry. These types of studies, which are often nationally representative yet on a smaller scale, ask only one partner of a couple who is living together about all the ways in which they express conflict in the family. In other words, this approach queries all the possible experiences of physical violence in the home, including those that are comparatively minor in nature (e.g., do not cause injury, are not reported or even considered a crime). Further, questions about sexual assault—a type of intimate partner violence if it occurs between cohabiting couples—are not asked. On the other hand, *crime victimization studies* suggest that intimate partner violence is more likely to be perpetrated by men. These types of studies have large sample sizes, but they only ask about events that individuals experience (or even report to authorities) as a crime, including sexual assault. Given these pertinent differences in what questions researchers are asking (i.e., about all violence experienced or about violence severe enough to have been interpreted as criminal), it is unsurprising that the family conflict studies tend to show a pattern of a lot of violence in the home, much of it being relatively more minor in nature, and the violence being approximately gender symmetric. (In Johnson's typology of intimate partner violence discussed earlier in this chapter, these instances of violence would represent situational couple violence.) On the other hand, the crime victimization studies suggest that intimate partner violence is perhaps infrequent, yet very severe when it does occur, it escalates over time, and it is primarily perpetrated by men. (In Johnson's typology, this would be indicative of intimate terrorism.)

These noteworthy methodological differences would seem to account for discrepancies in available research findings about whether women really are as violent as men in the context of close relationships, as the two types of studies are actually intended to better understand two different types of violent phenomena. Beyond this important methodological consideration, perhaps the focus of a debate about who is more likely to perpetrate/be victimized by intimate partner violence falls somewhat short of the mark. Put another way, perhaps there are more essential questions to ask. Although it certainly is necessary and important to better understand victims' experience with violence—all victims, including males as well as females, both in heterosexual and LGBTQIAP relationships—available evidence suggests that qualitative differences in intimate partner violence victimization are more striking and informative than any quantitative differences (or similarities) that might exist. That is, most research suggests that the consequences of intimate partner violence for women, both physically and psychologically, far outstrip the harm done to men as victims of intimate partner violence (Johnson & Ferraro, 2000).

Situational Predictors

Other antecedents of aggression and violence are not so stable or enduring, and instead are expected to vary across situations. **Interpersonal provocations** (e.g., being on the receiving end of another's physical or verbal aggression) are the most obvious—and possibly the most important—precursor to aggressive behavior both within and outside intimate relationships (Geen, 2001). Being frustrated in one's attempt to achieve a goal can elicit aggressive behaviors (Dill & Anderson, 1995). Even when the person responsible for goal frustration is not at hand, these aggressive behaviors may be displaced and directed toward whomever happens to be available at the time (Marcus-Newhall et al., 2000). Uncomfortable environmental or physically painful states (e.g., noisy environment, hot temperature, being in pain) can increase aggression, possibly by increasing one's level of negative affect (Berkowitz, 1993; Berkowitz et al., 1981). Men who are heavy users of alcohol are significantly more likely than men who do not drink or who drink in moderation to perpetrate intimate partner violence (O'Leary & Schumacher, 2003). The experience of state (i.e., temporary, context-based) negative affect such as anxiety, sadness, and anger typically precedes and increases the likelihood of aggression and intimate partner violence (Bell & Naugle, 2008; Shorey et al., 2015).

Theory in Practice

The Role of Communication Skills in the Perpetration of Violence

One reason that has been posited for the perpetration of verbal aggression and violence is a communication skills deficit on the part of the perpetrator (Infante, 1987). People who lack the skills and ability to argue or engage in conflict in appropriate, constructive, and effective ways (i.e., those who suffer from an argumentative skills deficiency) will likely resort to the use of verbal aggression, and in turn, verbal aggression exacerbates conflict and may set the stage for physical violence of some sort (Infante et al., 1989). More specifically, verbal aggression is thought to incite and catalyze any underlying hostility that might be present. This hostility is positioned as a necessary but perhaps not sufficient condition for the perpetration of violence. Therefore, incompetent communicators resort to verbal aggression, which engenders hostility, which may result in the perpetration of violence. Conversely, competent communicators avoid resorting to verbal aggression, hostility remains unprovoked, and violence should not ensue. In support of these relationships, early research with the argumentative skills deficiency model showed that spouses in marriages marked by intimate partner violence also reported higher levels of verbal aggression (Infante et al., 1989).

More recent research with this model has positioned cognitive ability (i.e., a person's ability to comprehend and to recall relevant aspects of the communication process) and emotional competence (i.e., a person's ability to convey their own emotional states effectively and to understand others' emotional states accurately) as specific indicators of better argumentative skills, as both are associated with improved communication during conflict (Aloia & Solomon, 2015). Results from this study of college student dating couples suggest that increased cognitive ability, in particular, is associated with decreased elements of verbal aggression (e.g., critical statements) during conflict. Indirectly, then, increased cognitive ability should be associated with the perpetration of less physical violence through the communicative factor of inhibited verbally aggressive statements. This research provides some evidence that improved communication skills— particularly during crucial times such as conflict discussions—can reduce aggressive, perhaps even violent, behaviors in intimate relationships.

Risk Factors for Intimate Partner Violence Victimization

Although anyone can become the victim of intimate partner violence and/ or sexual violence, some specific risk factors have been associated empirically with both forms of victimization throughout the years. As you have likely inferred from other information presented earlier in this chapter, simply being female is a risk factor for both sexual violence victimization and more extreme forms of intimate partner violence and control attempts (Breiding, 2014). Young women of color are at an especially high risk of suffering sexual violence, as are economically disadvantaged women (Rennison, 2002, 2018). Certain aspects of typical college life, including heavy alcohol consumption and sorority membership, significantly increase the risk of sexual assault victimization for women (so, too, does heavy alcohol use increase the likelihood of sexual assault perpetration; Franklin, 2016; Messman-Moore et al., 2009). Younger women (those 18–29 years old) appear to be most susceptible to intimate partner violence victimization.

Economically disadvantaged individuals with few financial resources and increased financial strain who live in economically disadvantaged areas are more likely to experience intimate partner violence (Raghavan et al., 2006; Rennison & Planty, 2003). Alaskan Natives and Native Americans—who have especially high rates of poverty as compared to other U.S. racial/ethnic groups—have consistently shown the highest rates of intimate partner violence victimization of any U.S. racial/ethnic group studied (Black et al., Merrick et al., 2011).

Having a severe mental illness (i.e., bipolar disorder, major depression, schizophrenia spectrum disorders) or other mental health condition (i.e., post-traumatic stress disorder) significantly increases the risk of experiencing intimate partner violence for both men and women (Goodman et al., 2001). Meta-analyses of studies of risk factors for intimate partner victimization reveal that the presence of other forms of violence and victimization in the relationship (e.g., sexual, emotional) is the strongest risk factor for intimate partner violence victimization for both men and women (Spencer et al., 2019).

Consequences of Intimate Partner Violence

Numerous outcomes of experiencing intimate partner violence and sexual violence have been identified in existing research, some of which have already been discussed in this chapter. Victims of sexual violence experience physical, psychological, and health damage (e.g., bodily injuries, gynecological problems including sexually transmitted infections, headaches, depression, anxiety, sleep disorders, post-traumatic stress disorder symptoms, substance use, suicidal ideation, etc.), both during/in the immediate aftermath of the assault and over the long term (Martin et al., 2011). Children and adolescent victims of sexual assault are likely to experience further sexual victimization as adults (Ullman & Najdowski, 2011).

Women are more likely than men to be physically injured by a romantic partner, those injuries are more likely to require medical treatment, and women are more likely to be killed by a romantic partner (Black et al., 2011; Hamby, 2018). Women also more often suffer from **polyvictimization**, or experiencing two or more forms of abuse (i.e., sexual, physical, psychological, or stalking). Those who are victims of intimate partner violence experience many of the same adverse psychological and health effects as those who are victims of sexual violence (perhaps not surprisingly, as sexual violence may in fact be characterized as intimate partner violence), including gynecological problems (e.g., miscarriage), depression, anxiety, post-traumatic stress disorder, substance use/abuse, and suicidal ideation (e.g., Black & Breiding, 2008).

When intimate partner violence is extreme and/or ongoing, economic disruptions may be experienced as well. In the case of *The Burning Bed* vignette that opened this chapter, Mickey Hughes—as part of a pattern of intimate terrorism—prevented Francine from continuing with her education, thereby preventing her from increasing her economic status (given the positive association that has been documented between education and economic status). Perpetrators of intimate partner violence may force victims to give up their jobs, or the perpetrator may find other ways to interfere with the victim's ability to successfully fulfill work responsibilities, resulting in job termination. Elimination of resources—financial and otherwise—is a common method by which intimate terrorists maintain control over their victims. Many women (often with children) who flee abusive relationships experience homelessness (Baker et al., 2003).

When women find themselves the victims of ongoing intimate partner violence and abuse, others often wonder why they do not just leave the abusive partner. Women perceive numerous barriers to exiting these types of relationships, such as being unable to provide for themselves and their children, lacking the necessary social support system, and the fear of increased violence if they leave (see Buel, 1999, for an extensive list of reasons). These fears are far from unfounded, as women have been shown to be in the most danger—even mortal danger—when attempting to leave or just after leaving an abusive partner (Dobash & Dobash, 2015). Yet, despite these obstacles, victims of severe intimate partner violence and intimate terrorism usually do leave their abusive partners (if the intimate terrorist does not self-destruct first), although it may take considerable time to shore up the resources necessary to do so, and it may require several attempts to successfully escape the abuser's web of entrapment (Johnson & Ferraro, 2000; Kirkwood, 1993).

Conclusion

In this chapter, you have learned about the umbrella concept of aggression and a few of its many subsets, including verbal aggression, sexual violence, and intimate partner violence. Because this book is focused on the context of close (romantic/intimate) relationships, the discussion in this chapter did not touch on other forms of violence, such as the psychological, sexual, and physical abuses that are directed toward children, people who are differently abled, and older adults. You have learned that not all intimate partner violence looks the same, and the type of intimate partner violence will determine prevalence estimates, antecedents of perpetration, relevant risk factors of victimization, and implications of experiencing intimate partner violence. The knowledge you have gained from this chapter should provide you with a deeper understanding of aggression and violence in close relationships, including why some people have a greater tendency to perpetrate violence and why some people are more likely to fall victim to it. Further, the discussion in this chapter should have left you with greater knowledge of the specific outcomes of intimate partner violence. Practically, you can apply some of what you learned from this reading to recognize precursors of violent behavior and strategies you can use to de-escalate potentially violent situations (e.g., improve cognitive abilities and communication skills, decrease anger and hostility, curb verbal aggression, etc.).

Discussion Questions

1. Discuss the prevalence of sexual violence and intimate partner violence in heterosexual relationships and same-sex relationships, including what is known about this form of violence in LGBTQIAP relationships.

2. Laypeople often assume that intimate partner violence is always about power and control. Would you agree with that statement? Evidence your response by discussing what you learned about these issues in this chapter.

3. It would be easy—yet an oversimplification—to assume that men are more likely than women to perpetrate intimate partner violence. Although some studies do show that trend, you have learned here about a number of factors that encourage males (and females) to perpetrate violence of various kinds. Discuss those factors.

4. Discuss some of the consequences of intimate partner violence for victims. Which ones do you think are most substantial, and why?

5. Although not a specific focus of this chapter, information about how to potentially avert violent situations can be gleaned from this reading. Discuss several ways intimate partner violence can be deterred based on what you have learned.

Chapter 11

Obsessive Relational Intrusion, Stalking, and Cyberstalking

> *Aliyah and Andre had been married for 5 years when Andre told her he wanted a divorce. It turns out that he had been having a long-term affair with Jayla, a coworker of his, and she was pregnant. When Aliyah found out about the affair and the pregnancy, she began harassing Jayla. For weeks, Aliyah called Jayla constantly, either hanging up or remaining silent until Jayla hung up. She sometimes did this repeatedly, up to 15 times an hour. Aliyah then intensified her harassment, leaving daily text, phone, email, and/or Instagram messages for Jayla, calling her names, cursing at her, and threatening to harm her and her unborn child if she didn't end her relationship with Andre. This went on for months. After telling Aliyah to stop the harassment or she would go to the police, Jayla changed her cell number and email address and blocked Aliyah on Instagram. But Aliyah escalated her behavior even further. She began showing up at Jayla's workplace, often following her home. Jayla frequently saw Aliyah outside her house, waiting and watching for hours. Aliyah's harassment of Jayla went on for nearly 2 years.*

nterpersonal aggression in any form can have a variety of destructive after effects, but perhaps no form of interpersonal aggression is as harrowing as unwanted, obsessive pursuit behaviors such as stalking. By its very nature, stalking is relentless, protracted, invasive, and fear inducing, as is illustrated by the situation that Jayla is enduring at the hands of Aliyah, her stalker. In this chapter, we will discuss three interrelated phenomena that all are characterized as forms of interpersonal aggression: obsessive relational intrusion, stalking, and cyberstalking. Research on these topics is in its early stages, comparatively speaking, and primarily focuses on stalking; thus, stalking will necessarily be the central focus of this chapter. We will distinguish among these forms of obsessive, unwanted pursuit; discuss factors that influence their identification; and identify general motives for such behavior. Further, we will discuss various prevalence estimates, theoretical perspectives, predictors, and consequences of stalking and cyberstalking.

Obsessive Relational Intrusion

Although the primary focus of this chapter is stalking, a related concept—**obsessive relational intrusion** (ORI)—also warrants discussion. ORI occurs when someone repeatedly pursues a close relationship with another person in ways that are unwanted, at least in part because they "invade one's sense of physical or symbolic privacy" (Cupach & Spitzberg, 1998, p. 234). In other words, ORI entails a pattern of repeatedly pursuing an intimate relationship with someone who does not want a close relationship with you.

Four general types of ORI have been identified: **pursuit** (e.g., driving by your home/work, calling you frequently, leaving notes or gifts, waiting outside your home/work, etc.), **hyperintimacy** (e.g., telling others the two of you were more intimate than you really are, joining you when you are interacting with others without being invited, making exaggerated claims about their affection for you, engaging in excessive self-disclosure, asking if you were seeing someone, claiming to still be in a relationship with you, etc.), **violation** (e.g., breaking into your home, recording conversations with you without your consent/knowledge, taking photos of you without your consent/knowledge, sending you offensive pictures, etc.), and **threat** (e.g., calling and arguing with you, cursing or using obscenities in reference to you, accusing you of sleeping around, warning that bad things might or will happen to you, physically harming you, damaging your property; Cupach & Spitzberg, 2000). ORI is commonly experienced by both males and females, particularly the less threatening forms of hyperintimacy and pursuit behaviors outlined previously. Narcissists, in particular, find the perpetration of these two particular forms of ORI acceptable when attempting to form a romantic relationship with another person (Asada et al., 2004).

ORI shares some commonalities with stalking, as you will see throughout this chapter. Generally speaking, both constitute forms of unwanted pursuit of a target, both are repeated over time, both can take many forms, both cause some degree of anxiety for the target, and both are victim defined (i.e., the victim decides whether the pursuit is repeated, unwanted, and frustrating or aggressive). In addition, both have been associated with various forms of sexual coercion, especially symbolic (e.g., manipulative/deceptive or psychological) sexual coercion (Spitzberg et al., 2001; Spitzberg & Rhea, 1999).

Despite their commonalities, ORI and stalking also have some key differences. For example, ORI victimization is related to experiencing more stress, whereas stalking is associated with the experience of fear (Spitzberg et al., 1998). ORI is unwanted pursuit that is carried out for reasons that are entirely relationship based, which is not always (but is often) the case with stalking. In other words, regardless of whether the pursuer is a stranger or is known to you in some capacity, the ultimate goal of their ORI is to establish a relationship with you (they just happen to be going about it overzealously in all the wrong ways). In this way, ORI is based on a fundamental mismatch of relationship goals: the pursuer wants to have a relationship with you, but you do not wish to have a relationship with them, or you do not wish to have the same kind of relationship that they desire.

Further, ORI tends to be a bit milder in nature, as it is usually "just" annoying, aggravating, and often exasperating, but not necessarily fear inducing or otherwise threatening (although it can be, as you saw from the four general types of ORI that were discussed previously). Yet, because the intrusiveness and recurrence of such unwanted pursuit behaviors are often perceived as hostile or menacing by targets, particularly if the target is female, ORI may "bleed over" into more extreme cases that would be considered stalking (e.g., violation and threat; Cupach & Spitzberg, 2000). Clearly, ORI behaviors vary in their severity and the degree to which they cause emotional distress for the target (Cupach & Spitzberg, 2000). Further, most instances of stalking also constitute ORI, in part because stalking too is often—but not always—motivated by relational desires (Spitzberg & Cupach, 2014). See Table 11.1 for some frequently reported ORI, stalking, and cyberstalking behaviors.

TABLE 11.1 Commonly Reported ORI, Stalking, and Cyberstalking Behaviors

ORI	Stalking	Cyberstalking
Calling and arguing with you	Unsolicited telephone calls/ texts/email that may be harassing, obscene, or threatening	Sending email
Asking if you are seeing someone	Watching, following, or lying in wait for you	Instant messaging
Calling and hanging up without speaking	Letters or gifts, often threatening or offensive in nature (e.g., sexual material)	Using spyware
Constantly asking for another chance	Damaging (or threatening to damage) personal property	Using recording devices
Watching you from a distance	Hurting you, your loved ones, or pets	Using listening devices
Making exaggerated claims about their affection for you	Violation of an order of protection	Contact via blogs
Refusing to take the hint that they aren't welcome		Using GPS trackers
Gossiping/bragging about your relationship to others		Using internet sites
Checking up on you through mutual friends		Contact via chat rooms
Driving by your house/ work		

Adapted from: Baum et al. (2009); Spitzberg and Cupach (2014)

Table 11.1 illustrates the overlap between ORI and stalking behaviors that are commonly reported by targets across numerous samples and studies. It also identifies the most common cyberstalking behaviors that have been reported and reveals how new media and other technologies have allowed for the emergence of previously impossible methods of stalking. It is probably clear from this chart that these ORI behaviors (given that they are comparatively less extreme) are quite similar to normative behaviors that are seen during typical relationship pursuit (i.e., pursuit that does not become unwanted or excessive in nature). Research has revealed the use of many comparable behaviors when attempting to initiate or escalate a romantic relationship with someone else. For example, attempting to increase contact with the object of your romantic interest is a common way to begin romantic relationships, as is increasing self-disclosure. Increasing affectionate expressions (e.g., saying "I love you" for the first time) are often the key to escalating romantic relationships. All these normative behaviors correspond with behaviors that have also been identified as ORI, such as making frequent contact with the target, making exaggerated claims about affection for the target, and engaging in excessive self-disclosure with the target (Cupach & Spitzberg, 1998).

Further, these behaviors correspond with some **affinity-seeking** strategies, which are used to get others to like us and are particularly important in initial interactions (Bell & Daly, 1984). Bell and Daly identified the existence of 25 affinity-seeking strategies, such as increasing nonverbal immediacy (smiling at or appropriately touching the other, behaving in a "warm" manner), openness, and self-inclusion. These strategies correspond with pursuit behaviors that have been identified as unwanted or excessive, such as exhibiting affection, engaging in self-disclosure, and putting oneself in contact with the ORI target through various means.

It is worth noting that similar behaviors are seen not just when pursuing a new romantic relationship, but also when attempting to reconcile a relationship with a former romantic partner (e.g., increasing contact and togetherness, Patterson & O'Hair, 1991; telling the former partner how you feel/why you wish to get back together, calling to set up contact; Bevan et al., 2003). Reconciliation attempts are likely to be particularly persistent when the couple has a history of breaking up and reconciling (called **on-again, off-again relationships**; Dailey et al., 2009). Rejection of another is not always direct, clear, and unequivocal, often for good reason (e.g., to save the face of the pursuer or the romantic partner with whom you are breaking up). Sometimes rejection is strategically ambiguous, perhaps because you recognize the possibility that you may wish to have a romantic relationship with the pursuer at some later date (e.g., at least one de-escalation disengagement strategy explicitly notes the possibility of getting back together in future, if it is meant to be; Cody, 1982). Even if rejection is unambiguous, having a history of breakups and reconciliations as in on-again, off-again relationships is likely to increase the pursuer's persistence.

Further, rejections based on internal attributions (e.g., my partner broke up with me because there is nothing appealing about me) versus external attributions (e.g., my partner broke up with me because school and work do not allow them to have time for a relationship right now) have been associated with stalking behaviors (e.g., surveillance, invasion, intimidation, harassment, threat, coercion, aggression, and violence) on the part of the rejected person. Research suggests this is especially true if the rejected person has high **rejection sensitivity** and their **self-regulation** abilities have been diminished (Sinclair et al., 2011). That is, rejected individuals who are hypervigilant regarding instances of rejection and tend to be particularly hurt by it, and who are generally unable to control their behavior in ways that facilitate (rather than obstruct) goal achievement, are more likely to engage in unwanted pursuit behaviors such as stalking a former romantic partner. Lack of self-regulation abilities is a key factor in both attachment theory and relational goal pursuit theory (both discussed later in this chapter) as explanations for persistent, unwanted pursuit.

The findings related to rejection sensitivity suggest the possibility that **unrequited love**—love that is not returned or reciprocated—may be a significant factor that motivates persistent pursuit efforts, especially when coupled with a lack of self-regulation abilities and increased rejection sensitivity. Unrequited love appears to be quite common in United States college student samples, with somewhere between 80% and 90% of undergraduates reporting having experienced unrequited love (Baumeister et al., 1993). In an unrequited love situation, the person has the option to keep their feelings for the other person a secret or to try to get the other person to feel the same way. If the latter is attempted unsuccessfully, research has shown that the person who rejects the unrequited lover actually feels more negative affect than the person who is left with their love unrequited. As such, perhaps only unrequited lovers with high rejection sensitivity feel "enough" negative emotion to motivate persistent pursuit efforts. Further, unrequited lovers with the ability to self-regulate likely understand that repeated attempts to initiate or continue a relationship with someone who does not feel the same way are probably going to be fruitless, rather than seeing such persistent pursuit as an effective way to achieve their goal.

Unwanted Pursuit in Mediated Contexts
Online Obsessive Relational Intrusion

Social networking sites such as Facebook certainly provide a venue for people to access information about, establish contact with, and even begin relationships with others. Unfortunately, various forms of social media deliver easy access to others, and this easy access often functions as another platform for the perpetration of unwanted pursuit behaviors. Indeed, although the study of **online obsessive relational intrusion** (o-ORI; also known as cyber obsessional pursuit) is in its infancy, one study revealed that former romantic partners most often reported behaviors such as looking at their ex's pictures (and pictures that others have posted that feature the former partner), sending their ex messages, posting on their ex's wall, reading their ex's wall conversations and mini feed, trying to add their ex as a friend, visiting the groups their ex has joined, checking out events their ex will be attending and friends they have recently added, and commenting on their ex's activity (e.g., posted photos). It is worth noting, however, that these behaviors would not "count" as o-ORI unless the target—the former romantic partner, in this case—was aware of them, they were unwanted, and they were perceived as bothersome. If those conditions are absent, these behaviors might be more accurately thought of as uncertainty reduction or information seeking attempts (see Chapter 2).

This study also revealed the most common unwanted pursuit behaviors that people (i.e., targets of o-ORI that is perpetrated by a former romantic partner) report experiencing: trying to add the target as a friend, sending the target messages, posting on the target's wall, looking at photos the target has posted (or that others have posted with the target in them), sending the target email, commenting on the target's content, joining the same networks as the target, sending the target invitations to groups or events, and posting on the walls of the target's friends/family/coworkers (Chaulk & Jones, 2011). The authors of this study concluded that social media sites such as Facebook facilitate o-ORI behaviors, offering would-be culprits a convenient, efficient way to pursue their target. Further, these kinds of o-ORI are not just irritating and frustrating for the target. Other research suggests that some types of o-ORI (e.g., surveilling an ex-partner's Instagram or their list of Facebook friends) also have negative consequences for the perpetrator, including more negative feelings toward the former romantic partner (e.g., increased anger, betrayal, confusion, sadness), elevated breakup distress, greater longing and sexual desire for the ex, as well as lower levels of personal growth moving forward (Marshall, 2012).

Victims of o-ORI have been shown to use a variety of strategies to cope or otherwise deal with the unwanted pursuit they are experiencing (Tokunaga, 2007). The most commonly used coping strategy is to ignore or avoid the pursuer and their attempts to communicate (e.g., avoid using the social media sites the pursuer uses to attempt contact). This strategy was reported in over 34% of o-ORI cases. The second most commonly used coping strategy—used in around 20% of o-ORI experiences—is technological active disassociation/disengagement, which is using technology to impede the pursuer. This strategy involves attempts to bar the pursuer from accessing the target's social media accounts (e.g., making social media content available only to verified friends). Finally, the third most commonly used coping strategy—used almost as frequently as techno-logical active disassociation/disengagement—is help seeking. This strategy entails seeking help from some third-party source (e.g., local authorities, web owners, internet service providers, or online support groups). Both technological active disassociation/disengagement and ignore/avoidance were perceived by targets to be successful in stopping o-ORI, as was one other strategy: technological privacy management/maintenance. Technological privacy management strategies are used by the target to regain or take back control over their online persona. These strategies may include changing one's profile picture or contact information.

Taken together, the early work that has been done on the topic of o-ORI points to the ease with which social media sites can provide a venue for would-be pursuers to conduct their unwanted pursuit, and it has revealed some specific strategies by which pursuers engage in o-ORI. The little research that is currently available suggests that such unwanted pursuit has deleterious implications for both targets and perpetrators, but that targets have strategies at their disposal to help them cope with the unwanted pursuit—and perhaps to thwart it before it becomes full-fledged stalking.

The similarities between unwanted pursuit behaviors and pursuit behaviors that are typically considered normative are obvious and beg the questions, "What distinguishes unwanted pursuit behaviors from more typical ones? Is it merely a matter of degree (e.g., "normal" amounts of con-tact with another are not seen as irritating or threatening, but "excessive" amounts are)? Are these same behaviors desired when relational goals are matched (e.g., I would also like to get back together with you) and undesired only when relational goals are mismatched (e.g., I no longer want to have any kind of relationship with you)? Is it only a problem if the behaviors persist past a certain point, such as after the pursuer has been rejected (e.g., the pursuer asked for a date, you politely declined, but they will not accept your decision as final or think you are playing hard to get)?" The point at which ordinary or normative relationship pursuit turns excessive, annoying, and unwanted is often hard to pin down, as relational development pro-cesses are complex. Conversely, it seems somewhat easier to distinguish when unwanted pursuit behaviors intensify from merely annoying (ORI) to downright threatening (stalking).

Stalking and Cyberstalking

Unlike ORI or o-ORI, stalking is illegal. Stalking was first criminalized in the United States in California in 1990; over the next decade, all 50 states and the federal government (as well as some Anglo countries other than the United States, such as Canada and Great Britain) had passed some form of legislation regarding stalking in various forms (McAnaney et al., 1993; Smartt, 2001). As a form of interpersonal aggression that may involve violence, stalking has received growing research attention from scholars representing a number of different disciplines. Although the research is still nascent, it has helped expand what is known about stalking from an empirical perspective.

Both legally and academically, stalking is conceptualized and operationalized in various ways. On the one hand, this flexible approach to conceptualizing stalking—which is victim defined—helps capture a wide range of behaviors and events that are experienced as stalking. On the other hand, the lack of agreement in conceptualizations and operationalizations of stalking have led to difficulties in drawing overarching conclusions and identifying basic knowledge claims. Of course, anything we think we know from research on stalking (e.g., how prevalent it is, who is most likely to perpetrate it and why, what the outcomes are) is based entirely on how the research in question defined the phenomenon of stalking to begin with.

In the literature, the term *ORI* is often used to encompass nonthreatening, annoying, unwanted pursuit behaviors as well as unwanted pursuit behaviors that are experienced as threatening and scary. To ensure that the distinction is clear in this chapter, the more specific term *stalking* will be used to refer to the latter. Although scholarly definitions vary, generally speaking, **stalking** is a pattern of unwanted, repeated, persistent, intrusive harassment directed toward a particular target over time that would cause a reasonable person to feel threatened, fearful, and/or in harm's way (Finch, 2001; Nicastro et al., 2000; Spitzberg & Hoobler, 2002; Westrup & Fremouw, 1998). As can be seen in Table 11.1, repeated harassment via telephone is thought to be the prototypical form of stalking, followed by actual pursuit behaviors such as following or lying in wait for the target.

FLIPPING THE SCRIPT

Is Facebook Stalking Really Stalking at All?

In popular culture it is common to hear people use the term *Facebook stalking* or *Instagram stalking*, along with a variety of other terms that have a similar meaning: *Facebook cyber-stalking, status creeping, profile stalking, Facestalking,* and *Stalkbook*. Yet, as we have determined in this chapter, stalking has a precise meaning that may render these colloquial terms inaccurate and misleading—or are they? Recall that repeated, unwanted, invasive pursuit behaviors must rise to the level of being perceived as reasonably threatening and/or fear inducing to be labeled stalking, and thus some scholars argue that true stalking behaviors enacted via online social networking sites are relatively rare (Chaulk & Jones, 2011). Although o-ORI appears to be quite common, these behaviors are not threatening or fear inducing enough to constitute stalking. Further, these passive behaviors may be best characterized as benign forms of basic, superficial information seeking (as discussed in Chapter 2). As such, this preliminary evidence suggests the term Facebook/Instagram stalking is a bit of a misnomer, strictly speaking.

Beyond this semantic issue, however, remains the question of whether online unwanted pursuit behaviors can cross the line—and cross contexts—into more traditional, face-to-face behavior. Although some research has shown only a minimal to moderate connection between the two (Spitzberg & Hoobler, 2002), at least one study with a college student sample has indeed demonstrated a link between o-ORI and offline stalking behaviors (Lyndon et al., 2011). More specifically, individuals who engage in online obsessive relational intrusion toward their former romantic partner (e.g., sending undesired tokens of affection through electronic means) were nearly six times more likely to also report enacting offline stalking behaviors (e.g., showing up at places—class, work, from behind a corner, from across the street, inside the ex's home—in a way that the target perceived as threatening). These results led the authors to conclude that, when it comes to college students and their former romantic partners, there is perhaps some truth to the idea of stalking on social media.

The advent and proliferation of new media and technologies have paved the way for stalking behaviors to be carried out via mediated modalities, potentially increasing the ease with which some stalking behaviors (e.g., surveillance) can be enacted (Tokunaga, 2011, 2016). The study of cyberstalking as a form of technological aggression is in its infancy, and as with stalking, conceptualization and operationalization discrepancies have characterized the research that purports to study it. As such, not much is yet known from an empirical perspective about the phenomenon of **cyberstalking**, which entails the use of electronic access and communication to stalk another person, including through email, instant messaging, chat rooms, blogs, social networking sites, cameras, spyware, GPS tracking, and listening devices (Sheridan & Grant, 2007; Shorey et al., 2015).

Considerations That Impact the Identification of Stalking

The "reasonable person" stipulation that is part of the conceptualization of stalking should foreshadow the idea that not everyone will perceive unwanted pursuit behavior in the same way. Some factors that help determine whether unwanted pursuit behaviors are recognized and identified as stalking include sex of the target, sex of the perpetrator, the target's prior history of stalking victimization, the nature of the target's relationship with the pursuer (i.e., a stranger or a former romantic partner), and—if/when relevant—who initiated the breakup of the romantic relationship.

As noted previously, female targets are more likely to perceive unwanted pursuit behaviors as stalking (i.e., as threatening and fear inducing; Cupach & Spitzberg, 2000; Spitzberg et al., 2010). Conversely, female pursuers are less likely to be perceived or identified as stalkers by male targets often because they do not tend to induce fear, even when their behaviors are excessive and extreme, as with Aliyah's behaviors toward Jayla in the vignette that opened this chapter (Sinclair & Frieze, 2000; Spitzberg et al., 2010). Male pursuers are generally found to engender more fear, although that may not be sufficient to cause targets to see them as stalkers (Kinkade et al., 2005; Phillips et al., 2004).

Perhaps surprisingly, having been stalked in the past does not seem to make targets more likely to acknowledge future unwanted pursuit behaviors as stalking (Kinkade et al., 2005; Spitzberg & Cupach, 2014). Further, there is no definitive case for the claim that strangers elicit more fear than former partners, although a few studies do show this pattern (e.g., Sheridan & Lyndon, 2012). Targets do, however, seem to more quickly acknowledge or recognize unwanted pursuit behaviors as stalking when these behaviors are perpetrated by former partners as compared to strangers (e.g., Cass & Rosay, 2012). Finally, in terms of stalking between former romantic partners, if the person who was broken up with (as compared to the person who did the breaking up) engages in unwanted pursuit behaviors with their ex, the person who initiated the breakup is more likely to be afraid and to label the behavior as stalking (Dennison & Thomson, 2002).

Prevalence of Stalking and Cyberstalking

In addition to issues of whether stalking is appropriately recognized and identified as stalking, the prevalence estimates of stalking naturally also depend on how stalking is defined in the research. As already discussed, these conceptualizations vary widely (Pathé, 2002). Thus, although prevalence estimates should be taken with a grain of salt, it is still informative to get a sense of how common stalking is. Evidence from a comprehensive review of studies that collectively examined the stalking experiences of over 1.2 million people yields lifetime female victimization prevalence ranges from 12%–22% and lifetime male victimization prevalence ranges from 7%–13% (Spitzberg & Cupach, 2014). About 74% of stalking victims are female, and about the same number of stalking perpetrators are male. Anywhere from 15%–22% of stalking cases are same-sex in nature, such as in the vignette that opened this chapter, wherein Aliyah was stalking Jayla. Yet, more same-sex stalking cases are male-male than are female-female.

There is evidence that in up to one quarter of cases, the same target is stalked multiple times by different stalkers, and further, that nearly the same amount of perpetrators are serial stalkers. The average duration of a stalking episode is approximately 15 months, and most people (78%) are acquainted with their stalker in some way (versus being completely unknown to their target). Previous romantic partners are the subgroup of "acquaintances" who are most likely to stalk their former partners (43%). Physical violence at the hands of the stalker is reported in 22%–31% of cases, with sexual violence reported in roughly 12% of cases. Violence is particularly likely when the stalker and target had a previous sexual relationship (Meloy et al., 2000). Fewer than half of targets who are victimized by stalking report contacting the police, and this number is closer to one third in some samples.

It is worth noting that the preceding prevalence estimates cut across various sample types, although differences in both prevalence and seriousness have emerged based on the types of samples under study. These include college student samples; clinical/forensic samples, which include cases of homicide and intimate partner violence that have resulted in mental health professionals or law enforcement officials intervening in some way; and general population samples, including both younger (e.g., adolescents) and older individuals in various contexts (Spitzberg & Cupach, 2014). Evidence from large-scale studies (i.e., those with samples greater than 2,000 people) reveal lower limits of overall lifetime stalking prevalence between 5%–7% for both general population and college student samples. Upper limits of stalking prevalence in these two groups vary more widely, at 28% for the general population and 56% for college student samples.

Estimating the prevalence of cyberstalking is in many ways fraught with more challenges than is estimating the prevalence of stalking, in part because operationalization of the former is difficult. In a study of approximately 65,000 adults in the United States, 26% of participants reported the experience of cyberstalking, primarily via repeated and harassing email (see Table 11.1; Baum et al., 2009). Preliminary evidence suggests that nearly three quarters of cyberstalking targets are female, 42% of cyberstalkers were former romantic partners, over 25% of cyberstalkers threatened to cause harm to the target in some offline capacity, and over one third of targets reported their cyberstalking experience to the police (Spitzberg & Cupach, 2014). Further, some other research suggests that females are more likely to report engaging in cyberstalking of former, current, or potential intimate partners (Smoker & March, 2017).

Taken together, these data suggest that stalking is a fairly common experience, seemingly more so for women than for men, that is often perpetrated by a former romantic partner following the breakup of a romantic relationship. While other forms of interpersonal aggression (e.g., intimate partner violence; see Chapter 10) appear to be decreasing in the United States, available data regarding stalking do not suggest systematic increases or decreases in this phenomenon (Catalano, 2012; Spitzberg & Cupach, 2014).

General Motives for Stalking

Beyond these wide-ranging prevalence rates, it is informative to consider the various factors that encourage the perpetration of stalking. Cupach and Spitzberg (2004, 2014) developed a typology of four basic motives underlying the perpetration of stalking. **Expressive motives** allow the stalker an outlet for their emotions and desires, be they positive (e.g., love, desire, an attempt to reconcile a romantic relationship, to ease loneliness) or negative (e.g., rage, envy, inability to let go and move on). **Instrumental motives** deal with the perpetrator's desire to negatively influence or control another person (e.g., to retaliate, punish, intimidate, humiliate). In the vignette that opened this chapter, Aliyah's motives are most likely instrumental in nature (i.e., to punish Jayla and perhaps to get her to end the relationship with

Andre), and her stalking behavior may also be motivated by the need to express her feelings of anger and inability to let go of Andre.

Personalogical motives stem from the perpetrator's character, personality, or psychological flaws and faults (e.g., mental disorders, social incompetence, destructive family-of-origin experiences, attachment style, a propensity to engage in antisocial and/or criminal behaviors). Finally, **contextual motives** deal with stressful external circumstances or situations that lead to stalking (e.g., breakups, job loss, the anniversary of a special day or event, activities that require ongoing contact such as working together, chance encounters that lead to unwanted pursuit).

Although these motives are not themselves recognized as predictors of the commission of stalking, they represent fundamental drives behind the act. In other words, one or more of the motives is implicated in the more specific predictors of stalking perpetration, which are discussed next.

Predictors of Stalking and Cyberstalking Perpetration

Although no specific profile of stalkers exists, some individual and situational factors have been associated with stalking perpetration. In addition, several theoretical explanations for stalking have been proposed.

Personal Characteristics

Many of the motives for these personal characteristics are personalogical in nature. For example, numerous studies reveal that some form of prior criminal history is associated with the commission of stalking, as is a history of violence and psychological abuse (Burgess et al., 1997; Davis et al., 2000; Kienlen et al., 1997; Meloy et al., 2001; Rosenfeld & Harmon, 2002). Physical or sexual abuse experienced in the family of origin is also a risk factor for later stalking perpetration (Kienlen et al., 1997). Those with poor social skills have difficulty initiating and sustaining relationships with others, and social incompetence has been associated with stalking (Babcock, 2000).

The personality trait of narcissism (having a grandiose sense of self-importance, exhibiting superiority and entitlement, seeking/needing excessive praise) has been linked to stalking (Mullen et al., 2000). Psychological disturbances have also been correlated with stalking perpetration, including mood disorders and psychotic disorders such as schizophrenia (Kienlen et al., 1997). Personality disorders such as borderline personality disorder, psychopathic personality disorder, obsessive compulsive disorder, and anti-social personality disorder have also been related to stalking, particularly in clinical samples (Morrison, 2001; Storey et al., 2009). **Erotomania**, a mental disorder, is linked with the perpetration of stalking in 10%–30% of cases (Rosenfeld, 2000). The inception of erotomania is sudden and has several qualities, including the perpetrator's delusional belief that the target of their stalking is passionately in love with them, the perpetrator's long-lasting fixation on a single target who is usually of higher social/socioeconomic status, the perpetrator's persistent attempts to come into contact with the target, and conduct on the part of the perpetrator that is illogical in nature (i.e., somehow reframing any denials on the part of the target as evidence of the target's love for the perpetrator; McAnaney et al., 1993; Cupach & Spitzberg, 2004). An erotomanic fantasizes about the perfect life they will have with the target, despite having never even met the person in some cases. Erotomanics are not usually dangerous and in fact evidence very little likelihood of becoming violent (Meloy, 1992).

Little research has investigated the predictors of cyberstalking, although presumably many of the same characteristics that encourage the perpetration of stalking would be implicated in cyberstalking as well. Several personality characteristics known as the **dark tetrad** have been linked to the perpetration of cyberstalking with current, former, or potential intimate partners (Smoker & March, 2017). The dark tetrad is a combination of four particularly noxious, interrelated subclinical personality traits: Machiavellianism, narcissism, psychopathy, and sadism. Machiavellianism is characterized by manipulation and exploitation of others by any means necessary in order to achieve one's own ends. Narcissism, as described previously, is marked by egotism, pride, entitlement, and grandiosity. Psychopathy is identified by selfish, antisocial, antagonistic behavior lacking in remorse and empathy. Sadism is characterized by taking pleasure in others' suffering, and a general enjoyment of aggression and cruelty. (Note that the dark tetrad builds off earlier work on the **dark triad**, as discussed in Chapter 8, which included subclinical psychopathy, narcissism, and Machiavellianism.) All the dark tetrad characteristics have been positively associated with increased intimate partner cyberstalking.

Situational Features

In addition to comparatively more permanent, internal features such as personality characteristics, stalking may be motivated by somewhat more transitory, external considerations. Stalkers are often unemployed and/or have a hard time maintaining steady employment, which may be related to personalogical or contextual motives. On the other hand, being employed is a risk factor for stalking victimization, given the predictability of routine and location that typically accompanies holding a steady job (Nicastro et al., 2001).

Being on the receiving end of an undesired breakup (a contextual motive) is perhaps the best predictor of stalking perpetration, as discussed previously in this chapter. Breakups are typically unilateral, meaning one person wants out of the relationship while the other person wants to continue the relationship. Studies suggest that the person who was broken up with may be especially likely to stalk the former partner, perhaps motivated by the desire to reestablish a romantic relationship with the target (an expressive motive; Tjaden & Thoennes, 1998). In such cases, as with ORI, there is a fundamental mismatch in the stalker's and the target's relationship goals. Further, the way you break up with someone may have implications for stalking. Breaking up with someone via social media (e.g., Facebook) can result in both stalking and cyberstalking victimization (Fox & Tokunaga, 2015).

Theoretical Explanations

Attachment theory. Beyond personal and situational elements that contribute to stalking perpetration, various theoretical perspectives have been shown to help explain the occurrence of stalking. Attachment theory provides a useful explanation for understanding who is more likely to engage in stalking and why (Bartholomew & Horowitz, 1991; Bowlby, 1969, 1973). Attachment theory was explained in some detail earlier in this textbook (see Chapter 2 for a review), but as a brief overview, recall that the four adult attachment styles are distinguished by two dimensions: an anxiety orientation, which is characterized by worries that the partner will not be accessible, attentive, and responsive; and an avoidance orientation, which is characterized by a reluctance to open up to others and to develop intimate relationships. Crossing these dimensions results in four adult attachment styles, which also differ according to an individual's positive or negative view or oneself and others. The adult attachment styles are *secure*, which is typified by low levels of both attachment anxiety and avoidance and with a positive view of self and others; *preoccupied*, which is illustrated by high levels of attachment anxiety but low levels of attachment avoidance and with a negative view of self but a positive view of others; *dismissive avoidant*, which is differentiated by low levels of attachment anxiety but high levels of attachment avoidance and a positive view of self but a negative view of others; and finally *fearful avoidant*, which is exemplified by high levels of both attachment anxiety and avoidance and a negative view of self and others.

Several studies have shown that individuals with high levels of attachment anxiety (i.e., preoccupieds, who are insecurely attached) are more likely to engage in stalking, perhaps because they are more upset about romantic relationship breakups and tend to experience more anger with regard to rejection and jealousy toward their former romantic partner (Brennan & Shaver, 1995; Davis et al., 2000). They also experience an increased need to control their partner, and intrusive pursuit such as stalking can help meet this goal (Davis et al., 2012). Preoccupieds, in particular, are more likely to perpetrate both ORI and stalking (Spitzberg & Cupach, 2014).

Coercive control theory. Coercive control theory, like attachment theory, was not developed to account for unwanted pursuit processes. As the name implies, its focus is on coercive controlling behaviors, yet the parallels between a coercive controlling person and those that perpetrate ORI and/or stalking are evident. For instance, individuals who use coercive control during a relationship are likely to then engage in unwanted, persistent pursuit when that relationship ends (Logan & Walker, 2009). To return to the vignette that opened this chapter, this evidence suggests the possibility that Aliyah may have relied on coercive control to dominate Andre during their marriage, before turning to stalking (as a means of continued control) after the relationship ended.

According to coercive control theory (Dutton & Goodman, 2005), the following are necessary in order to effectively control another person: (a) surveillance of the target, (b) making demands that include a credible threat of harm if the demands go unmet, (c) delivering on threatened consequences when necessary, (d) continuous control of the target's environment in order to reduce or eliminate the target's means of avoiding threatened consequences, and (e) isolating the target from sources of social network support. Interestingly, many of these coercive controlling behaviors and their motives are implicated in and/or reflective of conceptualizations and operationalizations of stalking (e.g., surveillance, credible threats). This makes clear the overlap between controlling, abusive individuals and the perpetration of stalking.

Although both attachment theory and coercive control theory can be used to provide partial explanations for unwanted pursuit (particularly stalking), neither of these theories was intended for this purpose. As such, a partial account is likely to be the most they can provide. For a more thorough explanation, we turn now to a theory that was developed with unwanted pursuit explicitly in mind.

Theory in Practice

Relational Goal Pursuit Theory

Relational goal pursuit theory (RGPT) originated from the communication discipline and was developed specifically to explain obsessive romantic pursuit, including both ORI and stalking (Cupach et al., 2000; Spitzberg & Cupach, 2001). RGPT posits that any relational pursuit is motivated by a person's goal to establish a relationship with a certain target. This lower order goal (e.g., to have a relationship with a particular person) becomes linked in the pursuer's mind to higher order goals of personal self-worth and overall life satisfaction. To return to the vignette that opened this chapter, this process of goal linking may be the root cause for Aliyah's persistent motivation to stalk her rival, Jayla. It is possible that Aliyah has tied the lower order goal of having a romantic relationship with Andre to higher order goals such as being happy with her life and feeling good about herself, and she sees Jayla as an obstacle to achieving those lower and higher order goals.

According to RGPT, this type of goal linking exacerbates and intensifies the original goal of establishing a relationship with the target even further, and makes it less likely that the pursuer will abandon the goal even in the face of stumbling blocks (e.g., the presence of Jayla as a romantic rival) or rejection (e.g., Andre asking Aliyah for a divorce). Instead, when obstacles or even rejection are encountered, the pursuer redoubles their efforts to "obtain" the relationship. The frustration associated with the goal being thwarted, coupled with the exaggerated importance of the goal in the pursuer's mind, leads to increased rumination (which increases over time until and unless the goal is achieved or abandoned); a "flood" of negative emotions such as anger, jealousy, frustration, and hurt; and rationalization (wherein the pursuer illogically and without just cause interprets their own and the target's behavior in ways that justify continued pursuit of the relational goal). It should be noted that the influences of rumination and emotional flooding are bidirectional in nature, such that rumination intensifies flooding and flooding aggravates rumination.

Because—in the pursuer's mind—achieving the ultimate goal of having a relationship with the person of interest is the only way to relieve the distress caused by this cycle of rumination and emotional flooding, the pursuer is encouraged to continue their unwanted pursuit. The pursuer is helped along in this process by their ability to rationalize the inappropriate, even obsessive, behavior as justifiable. This intrusive behavior is intensified by the pursuer's belief that the relationship/ultimate goal is eventually attainable (even when it is not), and the pursuer's self-efficacy and confidence with regard to their ability to successfully attain the goal.

Evidence exists to support the claim that the variables that comprise this theory, taken separately, influence obsessive pursuit. For example, stalkers have a higher propensity toward rumination. Further, it seems self-evident that stalkers experience various forms of negative affect, as they are ultimately not getting what they want, and much research exists to support the claims that self-efficacy and the anticipation of positive outcomes leads to the enactment of the behavior in question. In terms of post-breakup ORI, tests of RGPT have shown that—for both those who have been broken up with and those who initiated the breakup—determination to achieve the goal (i.e., to get the former partner back), rumination, and goal linkage are strong predictors of ORI. Further, for those who were rejected, emotional flooding was also predictive of ORI. Other research has shown that RGPT appears to be generally successful in predicting continued pursuit of a former partner, although perhaps less successful in predicting specific unwanted pursuit behaviors (Spitzberg et al., 2014).

Outcomes of Stalking and Cyberstalking

It hardly seems necessary to say that stalking is associated with a host of serious adverse consequences for the victim, and at times for the perpetrator as well. Victims may incur significant financial costs due to a variety of potential causes, including the repair of personal property damage, the need for therapy, the desire to relocate, and/or the necessity of legal aid (Sheridan & Lyndon, 2012). In addition, victims may experience negative physical effects by way of sleep disturbances, gaining or losing weight, feeling ill, and engaging in self-harm. Further, the psychological impact of stalking victimization can be quite severe in terms of stress, anxiety, and depression (Kuehner et al., 2012). Interestingly, stalking victims report experiencing more fear than cyberstalking victims, but cyberstalking victims take more protective actions than stalking victims (Nobles et al., 2014).

Because the deleterious effects of stalking could be listed ad nauseam with little coherence, Spitzberg and Cupach (2014) developed a typology that summarizes the various levels of trauma that may result from stalking victimization. Focusing on those that are identified as "first-order trauma effects" (i.e., those consequences that are experienced by the stalking victim directly, as opposed to effects that may be experienced by social network members or the broader community as a whole), the typology reveals just how far reaching the impact of stalking is likely to be (Spitzberg & Cupach, 2014, p. 196). In addition to those consequences discussed previously, being the victim of stalking may result in changing one's typical patterns of behavior (e.g., changing one's work schedule), changes in how one relates to others (e.g., becoming less trusting, losing friends), changes in spiritual beliefs (e.g., losing faith), changes in economic quality of life (e.g., costs of home security, loss of income due to changing jobs), and negative effects on the target's general quality of life (e.g., post-traumatic stress disorder, sleep disturbances).

Conclusion

In this chapter, you have learned about the commonalities and differences between ORI and stalking, and to a lesser extent, between stalking and cyberstalking. All constitute unwanted, even obsessive, relational pursuit behaviors, but ORI does not rise to the level of threat and fear that are elicited by stalking and cyberstalking. As you have seen here, stalking is relatively common and has a primarily male perpetrator/female victim dyadic gender composition. The perpetration of stalking is motivated by various desires and encouraged by a number of personal and contextual factors, perhaps the most important of which is locus of relationship breakup (or who broke up with whom). Various theoretical explanations for unwanted, persistent pursuit were discussed, before ending with a brief discussion of the damaging consequences of stalking, particularly for the victim. The knowledge you have gained from this chapter should help you more readily acknowledge the point at which unwanted pursuit behaviors become dangerous in nature, as well as give you a better understanding of what types of people are most likely to stalk and be stalked and why.

Discussion Questions

1. Is all stalking a form of obsessive relational intrusion, and is all obsessive relational intrusion a form of stalking? In answering this question, expand your discussion by identifying the similarities in and differences between obsessive relational intrusion and stalking.

2. As you can see from Table 11.1, there is considerable overlap between the most common obsessive relational intrusion and stalking behaviors. Based on what you have learned in this chapter, when are behaviors like persistent and repeated phone calls likely to be considered obsessive relational intrusion, and when are the same behaviors likely to be considered stalking, and why?

3. Discuss Facebook stalking or Instagram stalking based on what you now know about it from a scholarly perspective. Is it, indeed, stalking? Why or why not? How is online obsessive relational intrusion related to what is colloquially known as Facebook/Instagram stalking (if at all)?

4. How are the general motives for the perpetration of stalking linked to the more specific predictors of stalking?

5. Explain and discuss the attachment theory explanation and the relational goal pursuit theory explanation for obsessive relational intrusion/stalking as covered in this chapter. Summarize the findings regarding unwanted, obsessive pursuit that are related to these theories.

Chapter 12

Teasing, Bullying, and Cyberbullying

Tomio began college this year and decided to join a fraternity as a way to make friends and have a more active social life. The experience has been a good one for the most part, except that one of the fraternity members, Jin, often singles Tomio out to make fun of his expensive clothes, watch, or car. Jin works two jobs to put himself through school, and he seems to be envious of Tomio because he comes from a very wealthy family, as he often teases Tomio about being a spoiled brat who never has to work for anything. Tomio has coped with the teasing pretty well so far; it isn't anything he can't deal with, and his experiences in the fraternity have been mostly positive—until lately, when Jin escalated his behavior from teasing to outright bullying. Jin targets Tomio consistently, repeatedly, and aggressively. He is verbally abusive, he has spread rumors and lies about Tomio on social media, and he has attempted to ostracize Tomio from the other fraternity brothers. Things got even worse in the last week, when Jin threatened to hurt Tomio if he showed up at the next fraternity party. When Tomio attended, Jin became violent and shoved Tomio into a wall.

Teasing and bullying, as you see exemplified in this vignette, may occur in various types of relationships throughout the life span, from peer relationships in primary, secondary, and higher education to family relationships to workplace relationships. Bullying is most frequently seen in primary and secondary educational settings, although more recent research has begun to examine bullying at the college level. Teasing most often occurs in the context of close relationships, while bullying usually occurs between strangers, acquaintances, coworkers, or sometimes even friends and family members, but similar aggressive and/or violent behaviors that occur in close (i.e., romantic) relationships are not typically studied under the "bullying" moniker. As you learned in Chapter 10, comparable behaviors in the context of a romantic relationship are usually characterized as some form of aggression (e.g., physical, sexual, verbal) or intimate partner violence/physical abuse. Just as stalking was described as a form of interpersonal aggression in Chapter 11, here bullying and cyberbullying are understood as additional forms of interpersonal aggression—those that are often enacted outside of the context of close relationships.

In this chapter, we will discuss teasing, bullying, and cyberbullying, including distinctions from related concepts (some that were discussed in previous chapters). The prevalence of these negative behaviors will be probed, as will predictors and risk factors, and consequences of these behaviors (for the perpetrator, the victim, and bystanders) will be identified. The chapter concludes with some ways the destructive effects of bullying can be ameliorated, including a bullying intervention that has demonstrated national and international efficacy.

Teasing

As with almost any concept, various definitions of teasing exist across related disciplines (e.g., communication, psychology). Complicating this issue is that teasing is typically viewed quite differently by the perpetrator, who may have intended the teasing as a well-intentioned way to bond with the target, and the victim, who may interpret the teasing as a painful attack. In an early effort to conceptualize teasing, a three-component model of children's teasing was developed by Shapiro et al. (1991), which posited that teasing includes aggression, ambiguity, and humor. Later, the conceptualization was expanded to apply to teasing that occurs outside of childhood. In addition, Kowalski (2007) added a fourth crucial component to the conceptualization of teasing: identity confrontation. As such, today, most scholars agree that **teasing**—also sometimes known as permitted disrespect—is an aggressive type of peer victimization involving humor that includes some form of identity confrontation and is marked by some level of ambiguity (Kowalski, 2007; Pawluk, 1989; Shapiro et al., 1991).

Teasing always entails challenging someone else in a way that is intended to be humorous about some aspect of their identity; something that helps make the target who they are (Kowalski, 2004). This identity confrontation is one of the elements that distinguishes teasing from mere **joking,** which is not necessarily aggressive (unlike teasing, which is aggressive minimally because it is conducted at the target's expense) and can be accomplished with no or low identity confrontation (unlike teasing, which requires the presence of the target; Kowalski et al., 2001). Depending on how they are intended and/or perceived, teasing and joking may both be considered forms of hurtful communication (see Chapter 5). Note that identity confrontation does not have to focus on foundational, fundamental elements of the target's identity (e.g., religious values), as it may run the gamut from low, moderate, to high identity confrontation. Teasing often targets more superficial aspects of identity, such as a friend teasing you about the abysmal performance of your favorite sports team over the last few years and why you are still a die-hard fan. In the vignette that opened this chapter, the confrontation inherent in Jin's teasing of Tomio is Tomio's identity as the child of wealthy parents.

Teasing is typically ambiguous for the target and for any **bystanders** (those who witness teasing or bullying interactions but are not directly involved in them), in that it is delivered in a playful and lighthearted manner, yet it is also aggressive. Thus, targets (and bystanders) may never really know exactly what the perpetrator meant or how seriously the teasing should be taken. The perpetrator's motives for teasing are not always clear to others, as teasing may be enacted for relatively prosocial reasons (e.g., as a way of disclosing negative information in a less hurtful and threatening manner) or for more antisocial reasons (e.g., to demonstrate the perpetrator's power and dominance over the target). Research has shown that perpetrators and targets differ markedly in how they see teasing and how teasing affects them (Kowalski, 2000). "Good" or **prosocial teasing**—as opposed to cruel teasing—is actually funny (i.e., not just intended to be humorous), straightforward with little ambiguity, not very face threatening to the target, and is accompanied by some redressive action that is designed to reduce the face threat even further (Kowalski, 2007). For instance, following up a prosocial tease by saying "You know I'm just playing with you" is an example of a redressive action. "Cruel" or **antisocial teasing**, on the other hand, is not very funny, is more ambiguous than prosocial teasing, is more identity threatening than prosocial teasing, and is not accompanied by any redressive actions that would allow the target to perceive less face threat.

Prevalence of Teasing

Anecdotal evidence (as well as some research) suggests that teasing occurs more commonly than bullying—although both are so common as to have been labeled "ubiquitous" by some scholars and practitioners (e.g., Kowalski & Limber, 2007; Mooney et al., 1991). Most of the available research on prevalence estimates of teasing has been conducted with primary school children, revealing that nearly all of them recognize that teasing (e.g., calling names, insulting comments) has occurred in their school. Further, two thirds of them report having been the target of teasing while at least half of them admit to having teased others, with physical appearance being the most common type of identity confrontation (Eder, 1991; Mooney et al., 1991).

The little research that has been conducted regarding teasing prevalence in adulthood suggests that the pervasiveness of teasing becomes less common over the life span. In addition to prevalence estimates, the content of teasing appears to shift over time as well. Research has shown that although young adults may still be teased quite frequently about physical appearance elements such as weight, later adults are teased less often than children and young adults about aspects of their appearance. Instead, later adults appear to be most often teased about their behaviors (e.g., annoying or humorous habits like invading personal space or talking too loudly; Bias, 2005; Hooper et al., 2021).

Predictors of and Risk Factors for Teasing

Virtually everyone has engaged in teasing at some point in their lives, but some characteristics of persistent, frequent teasers have been identified in the literature. The personality trait of agreeableness has been positively associated with prosocial teasing, and romantic partners (whether agreeable or not) tend to tease each other more prosocially (Keltner et al., 1998). In terms of teasing more broadly (including antisocial forms of teasing), those with lower levels of conscientiousness and agreeableness, but higher levels of extroversion, tease others more frequently (Georgesen et al., 1999). People who tease—along with people who bully—have been shown to be more impulsive, less respectful, angrier, and less empathetic (Kowalski, 2007). In addition, their family of origin is often hostile and conflicted, and they frequently use aggression to resolve conflict (Mishna, 2003). In general, individuals with high self-esteem and an inflated ego/sense of self (e.g., narcissists) get aggressive when they are challenged and their ego is threatened, and this aggressiveness often takes the form of teasing and/or bullying (Bushman & Baumeister, 1998). Further, some evidence suggests that men may be more likely to tease than women, and that girls tease in a more playful way while boys tend to tease in a more aggressive way (Alberts, 1992; Eder, 1993).

Theory in Practice

Interactionist Model of Teasing Communication

Recognizing the limitations of a trait-based approach to determining who is likely to frequently tease others, some scholarship has pivoted to a more broadly pitched interactionist view (DiCioccio, 2010). An interactionist approach recognizes a number of different factors as impacting the phenomenon under scrutiny; in the case of teasing, those include certain personality characteristics of the perpetrator, resulting perpetrator predilections to communicate in particular ways, and the target's relational and situational judgments of the perpetrator's behavior.

The model begins with a focus on two perpetrator traits that were deemed most relevant: a secure attachment style (revisit Chapter 2 for a refresher on attachment theory, if necessary) and **hostility** (a negative trait evincing one's eagerness to behave aggressively toward someone else). These traits are thought to influence specific communication predispositions that are relevant to teasing perpetration. Generally speaking, a person with a secure attachment style is expected to be predisposed toward engaging in prosocial or affectionate teasing, while a person with elevated hostility is expected to be predisposed to enact aggressive teasing.

An improvement of this model over other explanations of teasing is that it goes beyond considerations of the various personality characteristics that influence the perpetration of teasing to a broader, more comprehensive consideration of relational and situational factors that will influence how the target makes sense of the teasing. More specifically, targets of teasing make judgments about whether the teasing is relationally appropriate (e.g., is this type of teasing appropriate given our relationship history, relationship type, and the closeness and quality of our relationship?). They also evaluate whether the teasing is situationally appropriate (e.g., is this type of teasing appropriate given the current situational norms, goals of both parties, formality/informality of the situation, and the broader audience of bystanders?).

The model concludes by proposing that these judgments of the relational and situational appropriateness of the tease will determine outcomes of the tease, such as relational (dis)satisfaction. If the tease is evaluated as relationally and situationally appropriate given the circumstances, then relational satisfaction with the perpetrator is likely to be increased (or minimally, it should not decrease). If the tease is judged as relationally and/or situationally inappropriate, then relational satisfaction with the perpetrator is likely to be decreased.

Consideration of these factors and the ways they interact with each other reveals how even an aggressive or antisocial tease may not have negative personal or relational implications by elucidating the processes that targets go through when interpreting another person's teasing behavior.

Although virtually anyone is at risk for being teased (just as anyone may perpetrate teasing—and most people do at some point in their lives), some characteristics appear to be associated with being the frequent object of others' teasing. In an early book written to assist parents of children who are being teased and bullied, Pearce (1989) wrote that people who are slightly—but not significantly—"different" in some way from what is considered typical or normative are prime targets for teasing. For example, people with minor physical differences (e.g., being slightly overweight, wearing glasses) might be targeted for teasing, whereas people with significant physical differences (e.g., being obese, being legally blind, using a wheelchair) are often not targeted in the same way. It seems clear that most people recognize from a fairly young age that some identity elements are not fair game for teasing.

Providing evidence to support the point that those who are perceived to be somehow "different" or atypical are more likely to be teased, research has found that adolescent boys and children with stigmatizing characteristics (e.g., learning disabilities, physical irregularities, speech impediments, etc.) seem to be especially vulnerable to teasing and bullying (Mishna, 2003; Storch et al., 2003). In general, anyone perceived to deviate from the "norm" may be at risk, even when those differences might be considered desirable in nature, such as being academically gifted, particularly attractive, or having substantial wealth.

Consequences of Teasing

As mentioned previously, teasing may be perceived in different ways (i.e., as positive or negative) by the target. Various factors impact this interpretation, including the frequency or persistence of teasing and considerations of where the teasing takes place (e.g., teasing that is persistent and that occurs in public appears to have a more negative impact on self-esteem; Hargreaves, 1967). Prosocial teasing may be interpreted as benign and as reflective of the relational solidarity between the perpetrator and the target, and the act of teasing can even serve to augment that solidarity (Eder, 1991). As noted previously, teasing (unlike bullying) typically occurs in the context of established relationships; thus, the mere fact that teasing is occurring can communicate to others that the people involved have some sort of relationship. The outcomes of teasing for perpetrators, victims, and bystanders are elaborated further here.

For perpetrators. Teasing has consequences for the perpetrator that are largely positive in nature. In other words, perpetrators typically feel good about their teasing, especially if that teasing is prosocial in nature and/or if that teasing has allowed the perpetrator to achieve their goals (whether positive or negative). Two exceptions to these generally positive outcomes are the experiences of embarrassment and guilt that may be experienced after teasing someone else or recalling having teased someone else (Kowalski, 2000).

For victims. When persistent teasing is not interpreted in a benign, prosocial manner, it can be experienced as hurtful and devaluing (Vangelisti, 1994). In the vignette that opened this chapter, Tomio does not appear to interpret Jin's teasing as benign or prosocial—and rightly so, as Jin's teases do not appear to be motivated by any camaraderie or closeness between the two. Teasing that is experienced as hurtful and devaluing leads to temporary undesirable outcomes, such as negative affect (e.g., embarrassment, shame; Kowalski, 2000). It may also lead to longer lasting negative consequences, such as decreased self-esteem, a poor self-image, and increased depression and anxiety.

Many people develop effective coping mechanisms for dealing with teasing, which allow them to cultivate a thick skin over time. On the other hand, people with high rejection sensitivity and/or those with internalizing problems such as depression, anxiety, emotionality, and/or low self-esteem do not react well to teasing (Hoover & Olson, 2000; Levy et al., 2001; Olweus, 1995). These individuals—called **passive victims** in older teasing and bullying research—are unfortunately recognized by teasing perpetrators as easy targets who are unlikely to retaliate (Coleman & Byrd, 2003). Passive victims tend to come from families that are **enmeshed** (i.e., overly close to the point that boundaries are unclear or nonexistent, usually precipitated by some sort of trauma that impacts the family system). Conversely, **proactive victims** respond aggressively in turn, believing that aggression will help them cope with the teasing behaviors by bringing an end to them (Tedeschi & Bond, 2001). Finally, **provocative victims** behave in ways that draw perpetrators' attention, acting in aggressive, offensive, and/or aggravating ways (e.g., displaying hyperactivity) that render them particularly likely to become targets (Perry et al., 2001).

Bearing in mind that appearance-based teasing is the most common type of teasing in childhood, numerous scholars have been interested in examining the longitudinal consequences of weight-based teasing, specifically. This program of research has demonstrated how weight-related teasing during adolescence is associated with a higher body mass index and obesity for both men and women 15 years later (Puhl et al., 2017). For women, weight-related teasing at the hands of peers and family members predicted both these outcomes 15 years later, while for men, only peer teasing was implicated as a significant predictor of long-term increases in body mass index and obesity. Further, for women, experiencing weight-related teasing during adolescence was associated with a range of unhealthy (or potentially unhealthy) weight control behaviors in adulthood, including binge eating, recent dieting, and eating to cope.

For bystanders. Teasing has implications for bystanders too, and as was true for targets, most of these outcomes are typically negative in nature. Bystanders have been shown to feel empathy for the person being targeted, and they sometimes try to put a stop to the teasing or otherwise defend the target (Kowalski, 2000). But because this is a risky choice, given that the bystander who enacts these behaviors may quickly find themselves becoming the perpetrator's new target, bystanders might instead go so far as to join in with the perpetrator, or of course they may do nothing at all other than simply observe the interaction. Bystanders will be discussed further in the second half of this chapter.

The focus of the first half of this chapter has appeared to be exclusively on teasing, but conceptually, teasing intersects with bullying such that it can be difficult at times to separate the two. Both can involve humor (although bullying does not always include attempts to be humorous) and both are face threatening. In addition, antisocial and cruel forms of teasing and bullying share predictors in common and may be functionally the same for victims in terms of impact (Alberts et al., 1996; Boxer & Cortés-Conde, 1997). As such, there is some overlap in predictors and consequences of both teasing and bullying. Further, bullying shares elements in common with cyberbullying as well, and some empirical research has identified traditional bullying as a warning sign of cyberbullying in terms of both perpetration and victimization (Kowalski, Morgan, & Limber, 2012). In the second half of this chapter, traditional bullying and cyberbullying are the focus.

Bullying and Cyberbullying

Along with teasing, traditional bullying and cyberbullying are aggressive forms of peer victimization. As is clear in the vignette that opened this chapter, Tomio is the victim of aggressive actions committed by one of his peers in his fraternity. Bullying is typically viewed as more severe than teasing, and although many definitions are available in extant literature, conceptualizations of **bullying** appear to share three major components across these definitions: it includes any number of aggressive behaviors, both physical and symbolic, that are used to intentionally inflict harm on the target (unlike teasing, which is confined to symbolic aggression); it is repeated over time; and the relationship between the perpetrator and the target is characterized by some sort of power imbalance (e.g., physical, psychological, social, or relational; Olweus, 1993, 1997). In the vignette that opened this chapter, Jin's teasing progressed to outright bullying (marked by an increase in aggression, including physical violence) and cyberbullying.

Even when there is no obvious or formal power differential between the perpetrator and the target—they may technically be peers, as is the case with Tomio and Jin—power may be derived from sources that are not formal in nature (e.g., social capital, popularity, etc.). When repeated, aggressive acts are perpetrated on a group instead of an individual (e.g., women, members of the LGBTQIAP community), this has been termed **bias bullying** (Smith, 2011).

Cyberbullying has been referred to as a "new" type of bullying that has been made possible by the advent of new technologies. It is typically defined using the same three components that are featured in most accepted definitions of traditional bullying: aggressive acts that are repeated over time against someone perceived to be lower in power, someone "who cannot easily defend him or herself" (Smith et al., 2008, p. 376). Yet, as the name implies, these unwanted, aggressive acts are carried out via electronic or mediated means. When Jin repeatedly used social media to spread defamatory lies about Tomio, he was engaging in cyberbullying.

Although bullying and cyberbullying are similar, two crucial differences have been identified that may be relevant. In cases of traditional bullying, both the perpetrator and the victim are known to each other. Conversely, in cases of cyberbullying, the perpetrator may maintain anonymity. This is a critical point, as this ability to remain anonymous may embolden people to commit online acts that they would not be willing to commit in traditional face-to-face settings (Kowalski & McCord, 2019). In addition, traditional bullying necessarily only occurs when the perpetrator and the target are together in the same location at the same time. Cyberbullying, though, may take place at any time, and in this way it has the potential to feel even more inescapable and pervasive than traditional bullying.

Prevalence of Bullying and Cyberbullying

Most of the research on traditional bullying and cyberbullying has been conducted with middle school-aged children, although considerable research exists on traditional bullying in contexts such as the workplace and senior living communities, and a more limited amount of research is available with students in elementary school, high school, and college (see West & Turner, 2018). Research on cyberbullying is beginning to focus on elementary and high school students and the workplace context as well (Kowalski & McCord, 2019).

Taken together, available prevalence estimates suggest that both traditional bullying and cyberbullying are especially common during the middle school years. A study of traditional bullying with a national sample of children in middle school revealed that 31% of them reported having bullied someone within the last 2 months while 39% of them reported having been bullied during the past 2 months (Kowalski & Limber, 2007). Across studies, bullying rates appear to be highest during middle school (specifically, grades 6–8), but more recently scholars have turned their attention to bullying among college students, where average prevalence rates ranging from 20%–25% have been reported (Lund & Ross, 2017; Williams & Guerra, 2007).

Cyberbullying appears to be even more common than traditional bullying, although global prevalence rates vary widely, likely due to differences in how scholars conceptualize and operationalize cyberbullying (e.g., some do not emphasize power differentials or the need for the behavior to be repeated for the behavior to "count" as cyberbullying). In a study of 12- to 17-year-olds, 72% reported at least once incident of online bullying in the past year (Juvonen & Gross, 2008). Studies of cyberbullying seem to demonstrate a pattern whereby cyberbullying increases from elementary to middle to high school years, where it appears to peak (Kowalski & McCord, 2019). However, in one study, more than 30% of college student participants said that their first ever experience with cyberbullying occurred while in college (Kowalski, Giumetti et al., 2012).

Predictors of and Risk Factors for Bullying and Cyberbullying

Numerous personal, internal and situational, and external characteristics and considerations have been implicated in identifying who is most likely to perpetrate bullying and who is most likely to fall victim to it. Because many of the same factors cut across both perpetration and victimization, as illustrated by the small subset of people who are **bully-victims**—those who both perpetrate bullying and are victimized by bullying, something that appears to be particularly common with cyberbullying—these predictors and risk factors will be discussed together (Mishna et al., 2012).

Personal characteristics. As previously discussed, both bullying and cyberbullying appear to peak during middle school, leading scholars to conclude that age is an internal quality that is predictive of both bullying and of being bullied. In addition, sex may also be a factor, as boys have been shown to perpetrate traditional bullying more often than girls (Olweus & Limber, 2010). With that said, a corpus of evidence shows no significant sex differences between girls and boys in cyberbullying perpetration or victimization (Hinduja & Patchin, 2008; Ybarra & Mitchell, 2004), and other research on traditional bullying suggests that girls and boys do not differ in their frequency of bullying perpetration as much as they differ in the nature of their bullying. That is, girls have been shown to enact more indirect forms of bullying (e.g., socially excluding the target) while boys have been shown to enact more direct forms of bullying (e.g., physically harming the target; Olweus, 1995). Bully-victims' perpetration of cyberbullying has been shown to be motivated by a desire to retaliate for being the victim of traditional bullying (Hemphill et al., 2012).

Other personal or internal predictors of traditional bullying perpetration include certain personality traits or characteristics, especially narcissism and **impulsivity** (van Geel et al., 2017). Decreased empathy has been associated with both traditional bullying and cyberbullying perpetration, as has the dark triad trait of psychopathy (Ang & Goh, 2010; Baughman et al., 2012; Goodboy & Martin, 2015; Mitsopoulou & Giovazolias, 2015). Overt narcissism has also been shown to predict cyberbullying perpetration and victimization (Fan et al., 2019). Finally, a general lack of social competence has been associated with both traditional bullying and cyberbullying victimization (Hunt et al., 2012).

Heightened depression and anxiety are characteristic of both perpetrators and victims of bullying and cyberbullying, as are lower levels of self-esteem (Kowalski & Limber, 2013; Tsaousis, 2016). Bully-victims have been shown to have the lowest self-esteem, as compared with perpetrators only and victims only (O'Moore & Kirkham, 2001). Hostility and anger have been associated with bullying perpetration as well as a general lack of respect for other people (Bosworth et al., 1999; Walters & Espelage, 2018).

Finally, those who morally approve of bullying have been shown to perpetrate both traditional bullying and cyberbullying (Williams & Guerra, 2007). **Moral disengagement**—a process wherein people reframe their aggressive actions toward others as being less harmful in terms of both their intent and the consequences for the target, or as being the fault of the target—has been related to traditional bullying perpetration, although the research is less definitive in terms the effect of moral disengagement on the perpetration of cyberbullying (Menesini et al., 2003).

Situational factors. In addition to the aforementioned personal characteristics that have been shown to impact bullying/cyberbullying perpetration and/or victimization, other research has identified situational or external features that impact these processes. Having been the victim of traditional bullying increases the likelihood of becoming a victim of cyberbullying (Kowalski & McCord, 2019). Both family and peer relationships are implicated in the perpetration of bullying and cyberbullying. More specifically, those who enact traditional bullying tend to come from families that are conflicted and hostile (Mishna, 2003). Conversely, those who enact cyberbullying tend to be weakly connected to their family, to be disciplined often, but to have their online activities monitored less frequently by their parents (Ybarra & Mitchell, 2004). Increased parental involvement in terms of monitoring and control of online activities has been associated with decreased cyberbullying victimization (Aoyama et al., 2012). Children who spend more time online have been shown to be at increased risk for both perpetration and victimization of cyberbullying (Kowalski, 2019).

Lack of social support from one's social network has been identified as a predictor of bullying as well, as increased social support from friends is associated with decreased perpetration and victimization (Fanti et al., 2012; Williams & Guerra, 2007). Children who feel supported by their peers appear to be less likely to become targets of cyberbullying (Kowalski, 2019).

Finally, feeling connected to one's school and perceiving that the school has a warm, welcoming climate is associated with decreased perpetration of bullying and cyberbullying (Williams & Guerra, 2007).

Theory in Practice

Social Interactionist Theory of Coercive Actions

Both bullying and cyberbullying can be approached and understood from various theoretical perspectives (e.g., stress and coping models), perhaps the most applicable of which is the social interactionist theory of coercive actions. This theory is concerned with the intrapersonal, interpersonal, and contextual reasons that encourage people to engage in **coercive behaviors**—those that are enacted with the intent to cause harm to someone else, or to force that person to comply with you—as opposed to noncoercive behaviors as a means to achieving their goals (Tedeschi & Felson, 1994). As such, the social interactionist theory of coercive actions lends itself naturally to a better understanding of bullying by allowing the possibility of isolating the most important elements and factors that give rise to bullying episodes.

According to the theory, bullying and cyberbullying would both constitute coercive acts intended to impose damage on another, to the extent that both these behaviors minimally harm the social standing of the target. The theory basically holds that perpetrators choose to use coercive behaviors when they believe those behaviors will facilitate goal achievement more effectively than the use of noncoercive behaviors. In this way, there is a practical or functional component to bullying and cyberbullying, which suggests that the types of outcomes a perpetrator is pursuing will influence how bullying plays out.

Coercive actions such as bullying may be proactive (i.e., motivated by the perpetrator's own self-interests and selfish motives) and/or reactive (i.e., motivated by the perpetrator's perception that the target has violated a norm). Perpetrators with proactive motives use bullying to feel better about themselves, to insult or otherwise tear down others (and perhaps look better themselves by comparison), or to impress bystanders. Conversely, perpetrators with reactive motives use bullying to encourage the target to adjust their non-normative behavior to be more in line with acceptable standards. Although research suggests that most bullying perpetration is proactively motivated, be aware that any given instance of bullying may reflect both motivations, contingent on the degree to which targets experience embarrassment and the extent to which perpetrators derive personal rewards from bullying (e.g., maintaining their position in the social hierarchy; Salmivalli & Nieminen, 2002).

Beyond recognizing that perpetrators' intentions impact the nature and consequences of bullying episodes, the social interactionist theory of coercive actions posits that a wide range of intrapersonal, interpersonal, and situational factors also combine to influence how bullying episodes unfold, how they are interpreted and made sense of, and their consequences. For instance, intrapersonally, the attributions that targets make for the perpetrator's actions are relevant, as discussed previously in this chapter. Targets who make benign attributions for the perpetrator's behavior will respond differently than targets who make malignant attributions for the behavior, with the latter resulting in more negative outcomes for the target. The personality characteristics or other individual qualities of the perpetrator and the target are relevant as well, as qualities such as hostility on the perpetrator's part and depression on the target's part will influence the bullying episode. In addition, the interpersonal history between perpetrators and targets and the nature of their relationships play a critical role in shaping bullying experiences (e.g., is the bullying perpetrated by a friend, a sibling, a coworker, a supervisor?), as do situational considerations such as whether the bullying episode takes place in the presence of others and the context in which it takes place (e.g., at a party, in a restroom, in the classroom, in the office, etc.).

As you can see, the social interactionist theory of coercive actions provides a comprehensive way of considering the bullying experience, as it takes into account qualities of both the perpetrator and the target, the relationship between the two, as well as the implications of the social environment in which the bullying episode occurs. Many of the factors that the social interactionist theory of coercive actions would expect to impact the bullying experience are discussed throughout this chapter.

Consequences of Bullying and Cyberbullying

It seems obvious to say that bullying and cyberbullying are associated with a host of negative outcomes, particularly for the targets. But research has identified consequences for perpetrators, bystanders, and bully-victims as well. In general, available research reveals that perpetrators experience more externalizing problems (i.e., expressing distress outwardly, perhaps by abusing alcohol or drugs or engaging in criminal activity) while targets experience more internalizing problems (i.e., turning distress inward, which may lead to anxiety disorders, low self-esteem, and other psychological difficulties; Kelly et al., 2015). These outcomes and others will be discussed.

For perpetrators. Although most research on bullying and cyberbullying outcomes naturally focuses on the victim of these episodes, some scholars have turned their attention to the implications for the perpetrators themselves. Although chronic bullies appear to experience few regrets, other bullies often feel guilt and remorse for their behavior (Kowalski, 2007). Perpetrators are also likely to experience depression and suicidal ideation (Rigby & Slee, 1999). They have difficulty in school, and they are more likely to abuse alcohol, tobacco, or controlled substances (Nansel et al., 2001). In addition, with regard to long-term effects, boys who were bullies are more likely to engage in criminal activity by early adulthood (Olweus, 1995).

For victims. Being the target of another's bullying or cyberbullying is associated with a wide variety of deleterious effects, including personal, relational, academic, and health-related problems. Targets of bullying and cyberbullying experience increased depression, loneliness, fear, and anxiety (Hawker & Boulton, 2000; Kowalski, Giumetti, et al., 2012; Olweus, 1995; Slee, 1995). Targets may come to blame themselves for repeated bullying or cyberbullying, which exacerbates these negative psychological consequences even further (Juvonen et al., 2000). Bullying and cyberbullying are also associated with inferior relationships with others and with poorer performance in, and a general dislike for, school (Gilmartin, 1987; Roberts & Coursol, 1996). Bullying and cyberbullying have also been linked to physical health problems, suicidal ideation, and even suicide (Rigby, 2003; Rigby & Slee, 1999; Wolke et al., 2001).

For bully-victims. Compared to perpetrator-only and victim-only groups, bully-victims experience some of the most severe negative outcomes. These include more mental health problems such as depression, psychotic experiences, and (to a lesser degree) anxiety by early adulthood (Lereya et al., 2015). Some studies have also linked increased internalizing problems (e.g., increased depression, lower self-esteem, increased anticipation of failure), more externalizing problems (e.g., alcohol/drug abuse), and suicidal ideation with bully-victims (Kelly et al., 2015; Nansel et al., 2003; Ozdemir & Stattin, 2011).

For bystanders. As is the case with teasing, bullying is typically enacted in public, and bystanders do not usually get involved or otherwise intervene despite feeling guilty about not doing so (O'Connell et al., 1999). The unwillingness of bystanders to act on behalf of the bullying victim has been attributed both to the fear of becoming the perpetrator's next target and to the expectation that someone else (e.g., a teacher) will and should intervene (DeRosier et al., 1994). Beyond bystander intervention concerns, witnesses of bullying have been found to experience some of the same negative consequences as perpetrators and targets do, including heightened anxiety and a dislike for school (Nishina & Juvonen, 2005).

Bullying Interventions

Despite the pervasiveness of teasing, bullying, and cyberbullying and their seemingly innumerable adverse effects, all hope is not lost—there are ways in which the harmful impact of bullying and cyberbullying may be ameliorated. For instance, research has shown that having just one close friend can help to buffer the impact of the especially deleterious psychological effects of teasing and bullying (Bollmer et al., 2005). Having a close friend gives targets someone to talk to when they are victimized, which is important as research reveals that targets who tell someone else about their experiences demonstrate enhanced mental and emotional functioning (Vernberg et al., 1995). In terms of cyberbullying, the same advent of new technologies that has provided the breeding ground for the proliferation of electronic bullying can perform the same function for putting an end to such behaviors. New technologies are currently being developed (e.g., apps) that can detect and help stop cyberbullying in real time (Kowalski, 2019).

In addition to these considerations, a sizeable amount of research has focused on school-based bullying interventions (given the prevalence of bullying in middle school), but these appear to have limited success. Perhaps the most efficacious and most comprehensive of these interventions is the Olweus Bullying Prevention Program (OBPP; Limber 2011; Olweus, 1993). The OBPP was developed by Dan Olweus, a pioneer of bullying research, to achieve three aims: decrease the incidence of bullying episodes at school, inhibit the development of new bullying episodes, and generally improve student relationships at school.

The OBPP promotes four basic guidelines for meeting these objectives, all of which are geared toward what adults in the school should be doing: (a) adults at school should demonstrate a genuine interest in their students and behave warmly toward them; (b) adults at school should be firm and set limits regarding unacceptable and inappropriate behavior; (c) there should be consequences for student rule violations, and these consequences should be nonhostile, nonphysical, and consistently implemented; and (d) it is up to adults to act as role models and positive authority figures for students.

Importantly, these four basic principles have been translated to a number of specific components that are necessary for schools who wish to adopt the OBPP. These components exist at the school level and include things like establishing a bullying prevention committee, conducting trainings for faculty and staff, developing and introducing the school rules regarding bullying (i.e., we will not bully others, we will try to help students who are bullied, we will try to include students who are left out, and if we know someone is being bullied we will tell an adult at school and an adult at home), holding a schoolwide program kickoff event, and making sure to involve the parents. Components have also been identified at the classroom level, including posting and enforcing the school rules regarding bullying, having weekly class meetings to discuss bullying and related topics, and involving the parents in some of these class meetings.

Individual-level components of the OBPP have been isolated as well, such as supervising and monitoring students, ensuring that all faculty and staff intervene immediately upon becoming aware of bullying, meeting with the perpetrators, victims, and their parents, and developing targeted intervention plans for each bullying episode. Finally, community-level components have been recognized, such as involving community members in the bullying prevention committee and asking community members to help disseminate the school's antibullying messages.

The OBPP has thus far been implemented in various primary and secondary schools in the United States, including schools across the states of South Carolina, Washington, California, and Pennsylvania. Evaluation data from these implementations demonstrates many different indicators of the program's positive outcomes, including a 16% decrease in bullying rates in intervention schools in South Carolina as compared to schools who did not implement the program. Using observational methods (during recess and lunch time) over a period of 4 years, implementation schools in Philadelphia, PA demonstrated a 45% decrease in bullying episodes from year 1 to year 4. In California, student self-reports of perpetrating and being the victim of bullying were used to assess program efficacy; these self-reports of being bullied decreased by 14% after 2 years while self-reports of bullying others decreased by 17% after 2 years. In summary, these results (and other results of national and international evaluations of the program that are not reported here) suggest the efficacy of the OBPP at various types of primary and secondary schools (e.g., both rural and urban) in and outside of the United States (Limber, 2011).

Conclusion

In this chapter, you have learned about the conceptualizations of teasing, bullying, and cyberbullying, including their similarities and points of departure. You are now aware of the prevalence of these aggressive behaviors, as well as the antecedents and risk factors for both perpetration and victimization. In addition, you have a better understanding of some of the more consistently identified consequences of these behaviors for perpetrators, victims, bully-victims, and bystanders. Finally, you have been exposed to some factors that may be helpful in combating the deleterious effects of teasing, bullying, and cyberbullying. What you have learned in this chapter should help you realize why and how teasing may be hurtful in ways that was not intended. It should also allow you to recognize instances of teasing, bullying, and cyberbullying when you see them occur, and hopefully to encourage you to intervene and/or take other steps to de-escalate the event and support the victim. Finally, you learned the importance of having at least one close friend if you are dealing with teasing, bullying, or cyberbullying—and more generally, the importance of sharing your experiences with others as a way of healing the hurt.

Discussion Questions

1. Identify and discuss the similarities and differences among teasing, joking, prosocial teasing, antisocial teasing, and hurtful communication you have learned in this and other chapters throughout this textbook. Based on what you have learned in this chapter, discuss the conditions under which various forms of teasing may be more and less harmful.

2. Discuss the predictors of and risk factors for teasing. Which of these are also predictors of and/or risk factors for bullying/cyberbullying?

3. Distinguish between bullying and cyberbullying, and discuss their prevalence rates. When are bullying and cyberbullying most prevalent?

4. Discuss the predictors of and risk factors for bullying and cyberbullying. Do some of these seem more important, in your opinion? Why or why not?

5. Identify and discuss the consequences of bullying and cyber-bullying for perpetrators, victims, and bystanders. Provide some suggestions for reducing their negative consequences.

Chapter 13

Destructive Conflict

Imani and Nasir have been dating for several years and recently moved in together. Living together has been an adjustment for both of them. Imani expected that sharing a residence translated to increasing the couple's commitment to each other, and this increased commitment would be reflected in changes such as how much time the couple spends together. Nasir, on the other hand, still seems to prefer spending most of his leisure time with his friends. This issue causes conflict between the couple, wherein Imani is very critical of this behavior and continually attempts to discuss the problem with Nasir to get him to change. For his part, Nasir does not see a problem with his behavior and does not agree that it should change just because the couple now live together. He becomes defensive when Imani raises the issue with him, and ultimately attempts to avoid these discussions, which inevitably turn into conflict episodes.

The destructive conflict pattern that Imani and Nasir are engaged in is not uncommon in romantic relationships and marriages. Conflict itself is a relatively common experience in the context of close relationships, although as the title of this chapter implies, not all conflict is inherently destructive in nature. Further, some conflicts are ongoing and may persist throughout the duration of close relationships, even functional and satisfying relationships. Because conflict is not innately negative, the ways in which individuals manage conflict—as opposed to the mere presence or even the frequency of conflict—in their close relationships becomes particularly impactful. This chapter will provide a basic overview of conflict and conflict management, including basic typologies of conflict strategies and styles as well as some of the more insidious patterns of destructive conflict. Although not all conflicts are considered dark side issues by default, here we will highlight particularly damaging patterns and outcomes of conflict, and we will close the chapter by identifying some ways to improve effective conflict management skills in close relationships.

Understanding Conflict

Numerous definitions of interpersonal conflict exist across related disciplines such as psychology and communication, and these definitions have various elements in common. In the communication field, the most widely accepted definition of an interpersonal conflict is "an expressed struggle between at least two interdependent parties who perceive incompatible goals, scarce resources, and interference from others in achieving their goals" (Hocker & Wilmot, 1995, p. 21). Harkening back to Chapter 1 of this textbook, you will recall that interdependence is a hallmark of interpersonal relationships, as well as a necessary but not sufficient condition of a close relationship. When we are interdependent with someone else in a relationship, we mutually influence each other. Note that the term *mutual* does not mean "equal" here; in other words, one person may be more influential than the other. Yet, interdependence suggests that what one partner does (or does not do) impacts the other person, and vice versa. If we were not interdependent with a close other, there would be little need to be concerned with their behaviors or decisions, as they would not affect us in meaningful, enduring ways.

Because people in close relationships are interdependent (among other things, including emotionally attached to each other), conflict management becomes especially relevant. When partners have competing goals that are valued or important, and they perceive that enough resources exist to satisfy only one goal, and that each partner is likely to attempt to exert their influence in order to ensure that their own personal goal is met, then an interpersonal conflict has arisen. Assume the (interdependent) characters in the vignette that opened this chapter are planning to take their vacation together this year. Nasir really wants to take a Caribbean cruise, while Imani has her heart set on visiting Tokyo. These "goals" are both important to each member of the couple, respectively, and yet they are not compatible with each other. Imani and Nasir only have enough money to take one vacation; further, they only have enough vacation days to plan one trip (scarce resources). Nasir assumes that Imani will be an obstacle in getting what he wants (i.e., to go on a cruise), and likewise Imani assumes that Nasir will interfere with her ability to get what she wants (i.e., to visit Tokyo). Thus, a conflict has emerged that the couple must resolve or otherwise manage.

Of course, not all conflicts are created equally, and not every conflict will have the same impact on partners and their close relationship. The previously described dissent about vacation destinations is probably rather superficial and less relationally impactful in the grand scheme of things, whereas the conflict pattern illustrated by Imani and Nasir in the vignette that opened this chapter could be repeated for the foreseeable future and may have serious adverse effects on their relationship if it is not resolved.

Scholars have distinguished between two basic foci of interpersonal conflict: disputes over task-related issues (e.g., who is going to do the grocery shopping this week) versus disagreements about relational matters (e.g., how much time should be spent together as a couple). Conflict about task-related issues, if it does not provoke negative affect, may help partners resolve the issue at hand and is less likely to have long-term negative implications for the relationship. However, relational-level conflict and interference from a close other regarding issues that are central to the relationship—as in the vignette that opened this chapter—typically engender negative emotions, and this type of conflict leads to negative consequences for the relationship.

Before moving on, a point about the term *expressed* from Hocker and Wilmot's (1995) definition of interpersonal conflict is warranted. More specifically, what is meant by this term? Must disagreements or struggles be explicitly verbally communicated in order to "count" as conflict? Other scholars have taken up this issue, differentiating between covert and overt conflict and indicating that conflict is not always voiced in overt ways that have typically been the focus of empirical study (e.g., arguments; Whittaker & Bry, 1991). Covert conflict behaviors may indeed be expressed in the form of negative types of nonverbal communication, including avoidant behaviors or vindictive actions (e.g., eye rolling, the silent treatment, slamming doors, leaving the field, etc.).

Prevalence and Consequences of Conflict

Conflict is common in interpersonal relationships, and even more so in close relationships such as romantic and family relationships as compared with friendship and coworker relationships (Argyle & Furnham, 1985; Canary et al., 1995; Cloven & Roloff, 1991; Sillars et al., 2004). The notion that close relationships—if they are as "good" as they should be—should not experience conflict episodes has been identified as an unrealistic belief about relationships, and it is one that could be detrimental to the health of the relationship. The negative affect that often accompanies disagreements is only compounded by the idealistic, impractical belief that the mere presence of conflict is in itself somehow a marker of a dysfunctional relationship or an indicator that the relationship will not last (Barki & Harwick, 2004). Overcoming an unrealistic belief that high-quality close relationships should not experience conflict is often one of the first steps to learning how to effectively manage inevitable relational disputes and disagreements.

Conflict can, of course, have negative effects, but these effects stem more from the way conflicts are managed than from the frequency of conflict in close relationships. Ineffectively handled conflict between romantic partners—especially when it is hostile, marked by negative behaviors, or otherwise destructive in nature—has been linked to a variety of physiological (e.g., stress hormones, cardiovascular responses, markers of inflammation) and psychological (e.g., depressive symptoms) health problems in both dating and married couples (e.g., Robles et al., 2014). It has been associated with negative implications both within the dyad/between partners (e.g., relationship dissatisfaction, domestic violence, relationship termination/divorce) and outside of it (e.g., parenting, performance at work; Booth et al., 2016).

Conflict in Mediated Contexts
Does Modality Impact Conflict in Romantic Relationships?

As you may recall from Chapter 4, individuals have a tendency to try to make sense of their own and other people's behavior by developing causal explanations for such behavior—in other words, to try to determine why something happened. As with other dark side behaviors such as infidelity, destructive conflict episodes naturally set the stage for attributions about our own and—possibly more importantly—a close other's behavior during the conflict. Attributions of responsibility generally fall along two types: internal/stable attributions for a behavior or event or external/

situational attributions for a behavior or event. Internal attributions are linked with some consistent, enduring, dispositional characteristic (e.g., my romantic partner became aggressive during conflict because they are a hostile person), whereas external attributions are associated with some inconsistent, temporary, context- or situation-driven explanation (e.g., my romantic partner became aggressive during conflict because they lost control of their emotions).

Although attributions are generally important across a wide variety of behaviors and circumstances, scholars have recently investigated attributions in the context of computer-mediated conflict discussions between dating and married partners, with an eye toward determining whether the synchronicity of the mediated discussion has an impact on conflict attributions (Kashian & Walther, 2020). Although some findings transcended the issue of synchronicity, interesting differences according to whether the conflict discussion was synchronous or asynchronous did emerge. For instance, partners who were more relationally satisfied tended to attribute their partner's positive conflict behaviors to more internal causes, particularly during asynchronous computer-mediated communication, leading the authors to conclude that it may be beneficial for satisfied couples to engage in conflict via asynchronous computer-mediated discussions when/if reasonable to do so.

Other research has shown that conflict in romantic relationships often moves from a mediated channel to the face-to-face context and/or from a face-to-face context to a mediated one. In other words, **channel switching** may occur during both asynchronous (e.g., text messaging, email) and synchronous (e.g., phone call) conflict episodes. Several motives have been identified for such channel switching, including to prevent escalation of the conflict, to better manage emotional states, to accommodate the partner's preferences, and to resolve the conflict (Scissors & Gergle, 2013). Interestingly, regardless of the channel switching that may occur during the conflict episode, romantic partners often feel they need to have a final face-to-face communication session in order to attain true closure for the conflict episode. This final face-to-face session often includes some sort of nonverbal behavior (e.g., a hug) that reassures the partners that the conflict has been resolved and the relationship has been reset. With that said, other research has found that romantic partners' conflict resolution in a face-to-face manner has no advantage over conflict resolution via computer-mediated communication (i.e., text messaging; Pollmann et al., 2020).

Conflict Strategies and Styles

Now that we have established a basic understanding of what conflict is, how it is conceptualized, its prevalence, and its typical consequences in close relationships, we move to a discussion of basic ways people can manage their interpersonal conflicts. Although various conflict management typologies exist in available literature, we will focus on two that are particularly prevalent in the close relationship context. Both these approaches are characterized as dual-concern models because they differentiate general conflict strategies and styles according to two dimensions: directness or indirectness (sometimes called assertiveness) and cooperativeness or uncooperativeness (Blake & Mouton, 1964; Rahim, 1983; Thomas & Kilmann, 1974). The directness or assertiveness dimension entails the extent to which conflict is explicitly discussed and engaged (versus the extent to which it is avoided or handled indirectly and nonassertively), while the cooperativeness dimension deals with the degree to which both parties' wants, needs, and goals are considered (versus the degree to which one or both parties have a more self-centered focus on "winning" the argument and achieving their own personal goals).

Conflict strategies. Sillars's (1980) early work with roommates revealed the presence of three basic conflict tactics, and these are still commonly used in empirical research today which investigates conflict strategies across a variety of close relationships (see also Sillars et al., 1982). As the name implies, **conflict strategies** are purposefully chosen tactics calculated to assist one in achieving their goals, and in that way they differ from conflict styles, which will be discussed later (Cai, 2016). The first of these conflict strategies is **integrative communication**, which reflects a high degree of concern for the needs and goals of both parties in the conflict (i.e., a high degree of cooperativeness) as well as a high degree of directness (i.e., a high degree of assertiveness) in terms of communication about the conflict issue. This type of conflict communication is constructive and prosocial in nature, focused on negotiating and collaborative problem solving in order to resolve the conflict in the best interest of both parties, all while demonstrating positive attitudes toward each other. Research suggests it is perceived as the most appropriate and effective conflict strategy, and it has been associated with both increased communication satisfaction and relationship satisfaction (Canary & Spitzberg, 1987, 1989).

The second of Sillars's (1980) strategies is **distributive communication**, which entails a high degree of concern for one's own (but not the other person's) wants and goals in the conflict (i.e., a low degree of cooperativeness) in addition to a high degree of directness (i.e., a high degree of assertiveness). Distributive communication strategies include threatening, blaming, and criticizing the other; making accusations; calling names; and generally behaving in a confrontational and even hostile way during conflict episodes (Sillars et al., 2004). This form of conflict communication is antisocial and destructive for the relationship, as relationship-level goals are subverted in the interest of asserting oneself in order to get what one wants, expressing a negative attitude toward the partner while doing so. Unsurprisingly, distributive communication is not perceived to be a competent conflict management tactic, and it has been related to both communication dissatisfaction and relationship dissatisfaction (Canary & Spitzberg, 1987, 1989).

The final strategy is **avoidant communication**, which is typically characterized as having a low degree of directness (i.e., a low degree of assertiveness) and a low degree of cooperativeness. It involves efforts to evade the conflict episode and conflict communication, including changing the subject, joking about the issue, denying the conflict, or leaving the conversation. Some evidence suggests that the avoidant strategy is used fairly often (i.e., by the roommates in Sillars's 1980 study) and that it is sometimes used by opposite-sex and same-sex friends who are generally quite satisfied with their relationship (Fitzpatrick & Winke, 1979). Although there may be conditions under which avoidance may not be negative for close relationships, and indeed may even be seen as beneficial for these relationships in some ways (e.g., when the conflict issue is not very important to either of the parties involved; Roloff & Ifert, 2000), there is also evidence that avoidance is associated with moderate decreases in communication satisfaction and satisfaction with one's partner (Canary & Cupach, 1988; Sillars, 1980). Because this conflict strategy precludes conflict resolution by its very nature, it appears to be ineffective in the long run.

Conflict styles. Beyond the strategic selection and usage of conflict tactics, other work has focused on more general **conflict styles**, which reflect relatively persistent predilections for responding to conflict in fairly consistent ways. Numerous conflict style typologies are available in extant research, which—as described previously—are distinguished according to cooperativeness and assertiveness dimensions. From this program of research, at least five major conflict styles have been identified: avoiding, accommodating, compromising, competing, and collaborating (Thomas, 1976; Thomas & Kilmann, 1974). These conflict styles are sometimes known by other names, as you will see, and the conflict styles can also be categorized according to their "win" or "lose" orientations.

Avoiding is the conflict management style that is low on both asser-tiveness and cooperativeness. It can involve numerous specific strategies that are all geared toward evading the conflict or any conflict communi-cation, including changing the topic, refusing to engage, or denying that a conflict even exists. The avoiding style is known as an "I lose, you lose" orientation to conflict—meaning the avoider loses as does the person who is attempting to initiate the conflict discussion—because of the refusal to discuss the issue and the resultant impossibility of actually resolving or bettering the conflict situation. This conflict style has been evaluated as both inappropriate and ineffective, and aside from some isolated circum-stances (e.g., when partners are too angry to discuss the issue productively), it does not appear to be a good approach to conflict in many situations (Gross & Guerrero, 2000).

Accommodating (also known as obliging) is low on assertiveness but high on cooperativeness, and it reflects an "I lose, you win" orientation to conflict. This conflict style is characterized by the person giving in to the wants and goals of their partner, demonstrating more concern for the other's needs than for one's own needs. Accommodating your partner's wishes may be a fine strategy under certain conditions, such as when you do not really care about the issue (but your partner does) or when a decision has to be made but the two parties are unable to come to an agreement (such as in the "choose where to go on vacation" example presented earlier). However, an accommodating style may be indicative of and serve to further perpetuate problems with the power dynamics in the relationship, given that it is typically the person who feels powerless (or the person who feels they have less power) who behaves in consistently accommodating ways toward a partner who is perceived to have higher power.

For instance, research on the **chilling effect** has demonstrated that individuals who perceive that they have less power in their romantic rela-tionship relative to their romantic partner are reluctant to initiate conflict with their partner for fear that their partner will react negatively and perhaps even end the relationship (Roloff & Cloven, 1990). Generally speaking, this type of relational power is determined by the **principle of least interest**, which states that in cases of unequal romantic involvement, the person who seems to care the least has more power in the relationship (Waller, 1938). It is likely that the chilling effect leads lower power partners to adopt an avoiding and/or accommodating conflict management style in their romantic relationship so as not to rock the boat and to hang on to a partner whose interest in the relationship is perceived to be tenuous. Some people are able to recognize that their conflict management style is less appropriate and effective when they take an accommodating approach to conflict (Gross & Guerrero, 2000). At minimum, the accommodating style is not effective in helping one achieve their own goals in conflict situations.

Compromising is moderately assertive and moderately cooperative; it represents a "we both win *and* we both lose" orientation. When two people compromise, they show concern for their own needs and for the other person's needs, as well as a willingness to work together to allow both people to get some of what they want, but neither of them gets everything they want. This orientation approaches conflict with the understanding that both parties have to give up something in order to get something. Compromising can be an appropriate, effective, and efficient means of resolving conflict, and it is generally perceived to be a fair way to deal with disputes as well (Gross & Guerrero, 2000). Yet, if the partners put their heads together, give it time, and think creatively, there may be better ways of approaching conflict.

Competing (also called dominating or competitive fighting) is a style that is high on assertiveness but low on cooperativeness, and it reflects an "I win, you lose" orientation to conflict. Individuals with competing conflict styles rely on distributive conflict strategies during conflict episodes, and they are motivated to do what is necessary in order to "win" the conflict and make sure their own needs are met—even at the cost of their partner's needs or the needs of the relationship. Some research has shown that this style is perceived as inappropriate by others, suggesting that although competing may help you get what you want in the short term, it seems to ultimately be harmful to close others and your relationships with them (Gross & Guerrero, 2000). Despite these negative consequences, some research has revealed that a competing approach to conflict is more common than cooperative approaches to conflict (Sillars, 1980).

Finally, **collaborating** is high on both assertiveness and cooperativeness, and it evinces an "I win, you win" orientation to conflict. Individuals with collaborating conflict styles use integrative communication in their conflict episodes, focusing on working together to create solutions that allow both parties to get what they want and achieve their goals without having to compromise or give anything up. A collaborating style is considered the "gold standard" of conflict styles; it has been evaluated as the most appropriate and the most effective style (Gross & Guerrero, 2000). With that said, collaborating is less efficient and requires more effort than other styles (e.g., compromising), as it takes time and ingenuity to develop new solutions to problems that do not make either party feel as if they are losing anything they really want.

Destructive Conflict Patterns

As has been stated repeatedly throughout this chapter, not all conflict is accurately characterized as negative (and therefore not all conflict is necessarily considered a dark side topic of study). Yet some of the conflict strategies and styles that were discussed in the previous section can clearly be considered from a dark side perspective. Further, evidence suggests that people often repeatedly enact maladaptive behaviors that cut across multiple conflict episodes—even when they do not intend to engage in these undesirable behaviors and when they have committed to changing their behaviors (Turk & Monahan, 1999). As such, the potential for conflict to become damaging and injurious is clear. Here, several conflict patterns that are recognized as (potentially) destructive are overviewed.

Serial Arguments

Some research has shown that arguments between romantic partners most often come to an end without actually resolving the conflict issue (W. L. Benoit & P. J. Benoit, 1987). For example, partners may simply change the subject or exit the interaction entirely, despite the lack of resolution. These unsettled disagreements can have negative relational consequences, and because the core conflict issue remains unresolved, these disputes are likely to emerge again in future (Hample et al., 1999; Turk & Monahan, 1999). These are known as **serial arguments**, wherein an unresolved issue spurs recurring conflict episodes between people (e.g., friends, romantic partners, family members) about that issue or a related one over a period of time (Bevan et al., 2004; Trapp & Hoff, 1985). The vignette that opened this chapter exemplifies a serial argument, given that Imani "continually" initiates the same dispute with Nasir regarding how much time he spends with her as compared with how much time he spends with friends.

While the duration of a serial argument may be relatively brief (e.g., until you and your partner decide where to go on vacation this year), it is also possible that such recurring arguments may endure over the course of many months, or even arise throughout the entire life span of a close relationship (Johnson & Roloff, 1998). Further, each recurring serial argument episode can incite the same frustrations, anger, and other negative affect every time it is raised. At some point, this negative cycle may encourage couples (or at least one of the partners) to attempt to avoid the issue that is at the root of the repeated disputes, as we see Nasir doing in the vignette that opened this chapter. One consideration that can render serial arguments less detrimental is romantic partners' perception that the disagreement can be resolved at some point. As such, **perceived resolvability** has a critical impact on the consequences of serial arguments in close relationships.

Theory in Practice

Serial Argument Process Model

Although research on serial arguments is still somewhat limited, the serial argument process model sheds some light on the inner workings of these recurring, unresolved disputes in close relationships (Bevan et al., 2008). This model is informed by earlier work by Trapp and Hoff (1985), who first provided a step-by-step outline of the serial argument process. More specifically, they argued that serial disputes are preceded by the perception of goal discordancy regarding the conflict issue and/or the perception of a larger incompatibility in the relationship at hand. Becoming aware of such incompatibilities may provoke a confrontation with the partner. The goal of such a confrontation is to settle the dispute by reaching an agreement.

During the argument, partners go through processes of "heating up" (where frustration and other negative affect grow stronger to the extent that partners are not able to persuade each other to agree and the conflict continues) and "simmering down" (a cooling off process where the partners recognize that their relationship with each other is more important than the negative affect caused by the argument). These processes may (re)occur any number of times over the life span of a serial argument, with typical outcomes being avoidance of the issue (particularly if it is perceived to be unresolvable) or eventual resolution.

Bevan and colleagues expanded these general ideas into a more formal theoretical statement regarding serial arguments, developing the serial argument process model. This model links perceptions of negative and positive goal importance with particular conflict management tactics, perceived resolvability of the serial argument, rumination about the serial argument, and ultimately the motivation to achieve one's goals within the context of the serial argument (Bevan, 2014). As noted, the goals that motivate people and that initiate the serial argument process may be negative or positive for the relationship. Positive goals include reaching a mutual understanding, expressing positive sentiments, and continuing the relationship. Negative goals, on the other hand, include establishing dominance/control, expressing negative sentiments, changing the partner's behavior, and hurting the partner in order to attain personal benefits. In both romantic and family relationships, negative goal importance and positive goal importance have each been connected with the use of particular conflict tactics (Bevan et al., 2008). Specifically, negative goal importance is linked with the use of more distributive (e.g., destructive conflict behaviors such as criticizing the other person) conflict tactics, while positive goal importance is associated with the use of more integrative (e.g., constructive conflict behaviors such as showing concern for the other person) conflict tactics. In turn, the use of particular conflict tactics is associated with the perceived resolvability of the unsettled dispute and with rumination about the serial argument. That is, the use of the integrative conflict tactic has been correlated with increased perceptions of resolvability, while the use of both integrative and distributive tactics has been shown to result in increased ruminative thoughts. Increased rumination about the serial argument has been linked with an increased motivation to achieve one's conflict goals in both family and dating contexts (Bevan et al., 2008).

These early results from tests of the serial argument process model provide some guidance for individuals with regard to how best to manage serial arguments in their own relationships. For example, because serial arguments are much less damaging to the relationship if they are perceived as (eventually) resolvable, and because the use of more constructive conflict tactics is related to increased perceptions of resolvability, individuals in close relationships should strive to use integrative conflict tactics in their own serial arguments.

Communication Danger Signs

Some patterns of conflict-related behavior may be present in a couple's relationship years before they begin to negatively impact satisfaction in that relationship. Markman (1979) proposed that spouses with certain communication risk factors (e.g., destructive conflict management, difficulty managing and expressing negative emotions) in combination with reduced protective factors (e.g., not enough positive communication, not enough social network support) are at risk for the development of problems in the relationship. More specifically, Markman et al. (2010) documented four harmful conflict management processes that make romantic partners feel insecure about their ability to discuss conflict issues with each other.

These communication danger signs include **escalation**, which occurs when partners respond to each other in ways that are increasingly nega- tive, thereby accelerating and intensifying already negative interactions. Another warning sign is **invalidation**, which may be accomplished more or less explicitly and entails putting down one's partner using sarcasm, mocking, insults, hostility, or by refuting or invalidating the partner's per- spective. A third warning sign is **withdrawal** and avoidance, or retreating from conflict interactions or even refusing to enter into any conflict discus- sions. The final communication danger sign is **negative interpretations**, which involve consistently presuming that the partner's motives are more negative than they really are.

Findings from this program of research led to the creation of marital erosion theory, which holds that some weaknesses in conflict management may be present from the very beginning in marriages (Stanley et al., 1999). These shortfalls become more impactful over time, as spouses naturally have to deal with stressors such as negotiating expectancies and resolv- ing problems over the course of the relationship. If these conflicts are not managed effectively, they will begin to wear away or erode the positive aspects of the marriage, which results in decreased relational quality and a greater likelihood of marital dissolution.

Demand-Withdraw Interaction Pattern

The **demand-withdraw pattern** of conflict management is both commonly used and significantly damaging for partners in close relationships (Chris- tensen & Heavey, 1990; Gottman & Levenson, 1988). In this pattern, one partner—the demander—is disapproving of the other partner's behavior and attempts to instigate a change in that behavior by discussing the problem. In the vignette that opened this chapter, Imani's behavior is typical of the demander in the demand-withdraw pattern. The other partner—the with- drawer—does not wish to change the behavior, becomes defensive when the issue is raised, and ultimately endeavors to withdraw or avoid the issue when it is brought up. The back-and-forth dynamic of the demand-withdraw pattern results in neither partner being able to achieve their goals (for the demander, solving the problem and effecting some sort of change; for the withdrawer, avoiding the problem and maintaining the status quo).

Although research has historically identified women as more likely to be the demanding partner in heterosexual romantic relationships, more recent research with same-sex couples suggests that a difference in gender is not necessary for demand-withdraw to occur (Holley et al., 2010). For example, the demand-withdraw pattern has also been observed in male same-sex relationships. These more recent findings have led scholars to propose alternative explanations for who is likely to make demands in relationships, suggesting that having a vested interest in the conflict topic is more likely to induce demands, as is having a strong desire for change in the relationship and/or the partner's behavior (Baucom et al., 2010; Klinetob & Smith, 1996). Those who make demands of their partner during conflict are most likely to experience cardiovascular reactivity, regardless of whether the "demander" is the husband or wife, establishing that the demand-withdraw pattern has negative physiological as well as psychological and relational ramifications (Newton & Sanford, 2003).

The Four Horsemen of the Apocalypse

Perhaps the most detrimental conflict pattern is Gottman's (1994) four horsemen of the apocalypse, so named because of the deleterious effects of the four behaviors on romantic relationships. The four horsemen occur in a pattern that includes (a) criticism, (b) contempt, (c) defensiveness, and (d) stonewalling. Unlike complaints, which are healthy and are focused on particular behaviors that could be changed in order to improve the couple's relationship, **criticisms** are unhealthy because they constitute personal attacks on another person. Criticisms often take the form of "You always ..." or "You never ...," but as Gottman points out, it is rare that people "always" or "never" engage in particular behaviors. Criticism represents the opposite of a soft startup to conflict, which has been recommended by Gottman and colleagues as the antidote to criticism. A soft startup entails beginning conflicts with complaints (rather than criticisms) that are couched in "I language" (e.g., in the vignette that opened this chapter, Imani might start a discussion with Nasir by saying something like "I feel like we are not spending as much time together lately"). Soft startup complaints should refrain from blaming or evaluating the other person, and instead simply describe what you see happening in a positive, polite way.

Contempt follows criticism in this particularly negative pattern of conflict and is perhaps the most damaging form of conflict communication in close relationships. Contempt goes beyond criticism by conveying scorn or disdain for the other person while at the same time communicating that you feel you are better than they are. It may entail insults, mocking, derision, or any other form of overt disapproval and disrespect. This behavior may be communicated verbally (e.g., put downs) or nonverbally (e.g., eye rolling). When romantic partners have experienced consistent problems throughout the duration of their relationship, it may result in eventually feeling this kind of contempt for each other. Gottman and colleagues recommend cultivating appreciation and gratitude for your partner's positive qualities as the antidote to contempt.

Following contempt is **defensiveness**, which attempts to divert blame from oneself to another person in an effort to defend oneself from attacks. Forms of defensiveness include denying responsibility, excuse making, cross complaining (i.e., instead of really listening to a close other's complaint, you counter their complaint about you with your own complaint about them), and making accusations. Although defensiveness is perhaps a rather natural reaction in conflict episodes, given people's tendency to respond to negativity in kind (i.e., people tend to respond to destructive acts that are done to them by reciprocating the negative behavior), Gottman and colleagues recommend taking responsibility and making amends for your own behavior when necessary as the antidote to defensiveness (Rusbult et al., 1991).

The last of the four horsemen is **stonewalling**, also known as withdrawing, which typically occurs after a pattern of criticism, contempt, and defensiveness have been established in the close relationship. When we stonewall, we shut down, which allows us to avoid the conflict episode by retreating from it. This stonewalling is a result of feeling physiologically and emotionally flooded or overwhelmed in the conflict situation, which prevents us from being able to discuss the conflict in a rational, effective way (Gottman, 1994). Although avoidance of conflict is not an overwhelmingly negative strategy—in other words, it can have its place under certain circumstances, as discussed previously in this chapter—it is usually the case that conflicts cannot be avoided indefinitely if the relationship is to endure. If you find yourself emotionally flooded and stonewalling during a conflict, Gottman and colleagues suggest putting the discussion on hold for at least 20 minutes while you do something that completely distracts you and calms you down as the antidote to stonewalling.

Improving Conflict Management Skills

As has been made clear throughout this chapter, conflict is to be expected in close, interdependent relationships. Fortunately, not all conflict is damaging to those relationships; unfortunately, not all conflicts are able to be resolved. It is clear, then, that the ways in which individuals manage conflicts that occur within their close relationships is crucial (Markman et al., 2010).

Toward this end, conflict interventions and relationship education programs have been developed recently that provide training for couples in ways to improve their conflict management skills, which sometimes includes accepting and forgiving the close other as opposed to trying to resolve each and every conflict. Interventions may be useful in mitigating harmful physiological responses to conflict such as increased stress hormones (e.g., cortisol); some evidence suggests that this effect may occur due to the improvement in relationship quality that is experienced post-intervention (Ditzen et al., 2011). Several of these conflict interventions will be discussed in an effort to help you improve your conflict management skills in your close relationships.

Handling Our Problems Effectively (HOPE) Intervention

Worthington and colleagues (Ripley & Worthington, 2014; Worthington et al., 2015) developed a communication and conflict resolution training targeted toward newlywed couples called HOPE: Handling Our Problems Effectively. One lesson from the HOPE intervention is the importance of learning better communication (including conflict resolution) skills early on in romantic relationships, before significant problems and relational difficulties develop (hence the focus on newlyweds, although beginning even earlier in the dating process would be ideal). Strong communication skills are useful not only during conflict episodes, of course; they contribute more broadly to the overall satisfaction and longevity of close relationships.

Throughout the HOPE program, participants are therapeutically assisted in developing improved communication skills such as active listening, expressing oneself appropriately and effectively, resolving differences by identifying areas of agreement, and breaking free of conflict. Longitudinal studies have demonstrated the effectiveness of the HOPE intervention in improving self-reports of marital quality, increasing empathy for one's partner, increasing positive communication, and improving physiological functioning (i.e., a reduction in stress hormones as assessed by salivary cortisol over time; Worthington et al., 2015). More information about the HOPE intervention and how to participate can be found at www.hopecouples.com.

No Conclusion Intervention

Interestingly—and perhaps controversially—an alternative therapeutic conflict intervention focuses instead on assisting couples in understanding that most conflicts simply cannot be satisfactorily resolved (Migerode,

2014). Over the course of 5 days in a group therapy setting, couples are guided through five steps: (1) each partner individually identifies several conflict issues; (2) each partner then evaluates their issues as "important" or "trivial;" and (3) the partners share their issues with each other, and each partner rates the other person's issues as "important" or "trivial" (p. 395). After the third step, the conflict issues identified by both partners can be categorized as follows: both partners feel the issue is important, both partners feel the issue is trivial, or one partner feels the issue is important while the other person considers it to be trivial. Categorizing the issues in terms of congruence or incongruence in partner ratings of importance/triviality leads to the next steps of the intervention: (4) deciding which conflict conversation to pursue and (5) going through the conflict conversation with the help of a coach.

Guidelines for three conversations are proposed by the intervention. If both partners feel the issue is trivial, then the partners are asked to solve the problem quickly (in about 5 minutes) with the overall attitude that "life is too short" to bother arguing over issues that both partners consider to be inconsequential (p. 396). If both partners have agreed that the issue is important, or if partners do not agree regarding the importance/triviality of the issue, then the conversation they are encouraged to have looks quite different. First, partners are encouraged to take their time in discussing the issue, including explaining why they classified the issue as important or trivial and engaging in good communication skills such as active listening and expressing understanding. However, the partners are explicitly encouraged to decide *not* to come to a definitive conclusion, and to instead end by putting the issue aside and—at some later point—beginning the process all over again. In this no conclusion intervention, the importance of conflict resolution is minimized while other processes (e.g., effective communication, evolution of the partners, changes in the way relational issues are perceived) are prioritized. Through the communicative processes of actively listening and openly discussing the reasons for evaluating the conflict issues as important (or not), perceptions can change and partners can become more understanding and accepting of each other. The no conclusion intervention certainly features some novel ideas on conflict resolution, but it should be noted that it has not yet received empirical support.

Prevention and Relationship Education Program (PREP)

The conflict intervention that currently has the strongest empirical evidence in its favor is PREP: the Prevention and Relationship Education

Program (Markman et al., 2010; Markman & Rhoades, 2012). As with other intervention and education approaches, PREP asks couples to identify warning signs that occur in conflict episodes and couples are then taught specific communication skills that allow them to manage—perhaps even resolve—the conflict more effectively. These communication skills include active listening, problem solving, and the speaker-listener technique. The **speaker-listener technique** takes a very structured approach to conflict discussions wherein partners are taught to take distinct turns as speaker and as listener (Markman et al., 1994). As the speaker, partners are instructed to communicate assertively using "I language" (e.g., "I feel frustrated when ...") rather than "you language" (e.g., "You make me feel frustrated when ..."). As the listener, partners are instructed to actively listen and engage in paraphrasing in order to ensure accuracy. The speaker-listener technique prioritizes active listening over conflict resolution, as the primary goal is to encourage a deeper understanding of the conflict issue before attempting to resolve it, ensuring that each partner feels heard, understood, and respected. The PREP appears to have significant potential in helping couples handle conflict more effectively, as meta-analyses have demonstrated the efficacy of PREP in improving conflict management skills, increasing relationship satisfaction, and even preventing divorce (Hawkins et al., 2008; Stanley et al., 2014).

Some key similarities across these interventions are obvious, even in the no conclusion intervention. Namely, the importance of communication skills such as expressing one's own position in a communicatively competent way, actively listening to the partner as they do the same, and feeling/expressing empathy and understanding for each other. **Communication competence**—expressing oneself effectively (in a way that accomplishes personal goals) *and* appropriately (without harming the other person; in a manner that is evaluated as legitimate by the other person)—is crucial in numerous contexts and situations, perhaps none more important than when managing conflict in close relationships (Spitzberg & Cupach, 1984). The "appropriateness" dimension of communication competence is especially implicated in conflict management, as destructive strategies, styles, and patterns such as distributive communication, a competitive style, demand-withdraw, and contempt are undesired by the other and may be perceived as damaging or otherwise hurtful. Thus, when managing conflict, it is not just about getting what you want, particularly if doing so comes at a cost to a close other.

Active listening is a communication skill that is specifically identified as a key component in each of the interventions discussed previously. Although various conceptualizations of active listening exist, and it goes by several different monikers in the literature (e.g., empathic listening), active listening is typically thought to have at least three components. The first component entails expressing attention and interest in what the other person is saying via **backchanneling** cues (i.e., nonverbal cues such as leaning forward or nodding your head and vocal cues such as saying "uh huh," which let the speaker know you are paying attention to and interested in what they are saying; McNaughton et al., 2007). Secondly, active listening involves refraining from judging the other person while listening, paraphrasing what the other has communicated (e.g., "So what I am hearing you say is …"), and confirming your understanding of what has been communicated (e.g., "I can see how you would feel angry when …;" Garland, 1981). This communicates **empathy** (i.e., putting yourself in another person's shoes in an effort to really understand their point of view) to the other and helps to build trust (Lester, 2002). Thirdly, active listening will likely require asking questions of the other person to encourage elaboration and to increase clarity for both parties (Paukert et al., 2004). Active listening can be particularly difficult to enact during conflict episodes, as we often think we know what the other person is thinking/will say, and we are typically focused on how best to formulate and represent our own responses, arguments, and agendas. Yet, it is so imperative in conflict situations for many reasons. As indicated by the interventions described, it may lead you to a better understanding of each other's perspective and a potential resolution to the conflict.

Conclusion

In this chapter, you have learned about interpersonal conflict and its impact in close relationships. Again, some conflict is inevitable and is not necessarily a negative or dark side occurrence. Whether conflict will have a negative impact (and how great a negative impact it will have) is determined by the ways in which people in close relationships manage their conflicts. Basic conflict strategies and tactics were discussed in this chapter, as was a commonly used typology of conflict styles. Several destructive conflict management patterns were identified as well, which tend to have negative consequences for close relationships and the people involved in them. Yet, good conflict management skills—often in the form of improved communication skills—can be taught, and people in close relationships can learn how to manage their conflicts in more effective and appropriate ways. The information you have learned in this chapter should allow you to recognize destructive methods of handling conflict when they arise in your own close relationships, and it should have provided you with some basic skills to enhance your own conflict management skills in your close relationships.

Discussion Questions

1. According to the definition that was presented in this chapter, can interpersonal conflict occur between strangers? As part of your response, make sure to thoroughly define and discuss the conceptualization of interpersonal conflict.

2. Discuss the five major conflict styles with an emphasis on establishing their pros and cons. Which of these conflict styles is most representative of how you typically engage in conflict in close relationships, such as dating or family relationships?

3. Although not all conflict is destructive, several damaging conflict patterns were overviewed in this chapter. Discuss these (potentially) destructive conflict patterns. Which appears to be the worst, in your opinion, and why?

4. Compare and contrast the three conflict interventions/education programs that were identified in this chapter. Do you think they would be as effective for family relationships as they are for dating or married relationships? Why or why not?

5. Numerous skills (many of them communicative in nature) that can help improve conflict management were presented in this chapter. Discuss these skills and rank order them in terms of how effective you perceive they are in more effectively negotiating conflicts in close relationships. Justify your rankings.

GLOSSARY

Accommodating – One of five major conflict styles; it is low in assertiveness but high in cooperativeness and involves giving in to the other person during conflict episodes.

Accommodation – Inhibiting our natural proclivity to respond to negative behaviors or communication "in kind" (i.e., in a reciprocal way) and instead respond in constructive, prosocial ways to another's relationship transgression.

Acquiescent responses – Reactions to hurtful events that make clear the communicator has hurt you. These include apologizing or otherwise trying to make amends, conceding or giving in, crying, etc.

Active listening – A multistage process that includes attentively listening in a nonjudgmental way; paraphrasing, validating, and empathizing with what the other has expressed; and asking questions in order to probe the issue and increase clarity. Active listening may be referred to as empathic listening.

Active uncertainty reduction strategy – Interacting with some third party (usually a member of the target's social network such as a friend) with the goal of gathering information about a target.

Active verbal responses – Reactions to hurtful events that involve some sort of confrontation with the hurtful communicator. Note that this confrontation can be prosocial (e.g., calmly asking for an explanation and attempting to talk through the issue) or antisocial (e.g., attacking the initiator, mocking or using sarcasm, or otherwise behaving in an aggressive fashion).

Affinity seeking – A social communicative process used to get others to like us and to feel positively toward us.

Agreeableness – One of the "big five" personality traits that reflects the tendency to be warm, trusting, altruistic, and affectionate.

Antisocial teasing – Also known as "cruel" teasing; it is characterized by decreased humor, more ambiguity/less straightforwardness than prosocial teasing, and more identity confrontation than prosocial teasing.

Anxious attachment orientation – A persistent positive view (i.e., a "mental model") of others that inclines one to strongly desire close connections and romantic relationships with others. This desire is so strong that anxiously attached people tend to become overly dependent on close relationships such as romantic relationships and their romantic partners. Yet, when involved in such romantic relationships, anxiously attached individuals experience a great deal of attachment-related anxiety (due to their negative perception of themselves) that causes them to greatly fear being abandoned by the close other.

Attachment – A bond or lasting psychological connectedness to another person that is formed through interactions, starting from infancy with interactions with primary caregivers.

Attributions – The explanations people make about the underlying causes of events and behaviors (their own and other people's).

Aversive interpersonal behaviors – Behaviors that deny people valued outcomes or cause people to experience adverse outcomes. These can run the gamut from major transgressions or violations of relational rules (e.g., infidelity) to more minor, mundane behaviors that do not rise to the level of relationship transgressions (e.g., not listening, acting moody, swearing, complaining, excessively seeking assurances, forgetting commitments, disappointing another).

Avoidant attachment orientation – An enduring negative view (i.e., a mental model) of others that inclines one to avoid close connections such as romantic relationships with others. Avoidantly attached individuals tend to believe that other people are not inherently reliable or trustworthy, and they do not wish to open up to others. They may fear rejection from others due to a negative perception of themselves, but when avoidantly attached people have positive perceptions of themselves, their avoidance of close relationships with others may be a function of their desire to focus their energies and attention elsewhere (e.g., on autonomous activities, such as work/career).

Avoidant communication – One of three major conflict management strategies; it is low in assertiveness and in cooperativeness and involves an individual's strategic choice to attempt to evade conflict communication in order to meet their goals.

Avoiding – One of five major conflict styles; it is low in assertiveness and low in cooperativeness and entails a person's general tendency to attempt to elude conflict communication.

Backchanneling – Providing encouraging verbal (e.g., uh-huh) and nonverbal (e.g., head nods, positive facial affect) feedback as another person is speaking.

These cues are intended to communicate that you are interested in the conversation and would like to continue it.

Behavioral familiarity – When you are familiar enough with the other person's baseline behavior (e.g., their normal pitch, how fluent their speech usually is) to render deviations from normal behavior meaningful in potentially deceptive interactions.

Behavioral jealousy – One of three interrelated components of jealousy; involves the detection (e.g., snooping) and/or prevention (e.g., disparaging the rival) behaviors that we use when a third-party rival is perceived in an effort to thwart our romantic partner's relationship with the rival.

Belongingness hypothesis – People have a driving need to "belong" or to form social attachments to others; we form these attachments readily and are typically disinclined to break them.

Bias bullying – When repeated, aggressive acts intended to cause harm are directed toward a group (rather than a particular person) who is perceived to be somehow lower in power than the perpetrator.

Bully-victim – A person who both perpetrates and is the victim of bullying or cyberbullying.

Bullying – Aggressive acts that are perpetrated by a person who has some type of power (e.g., physical, social) over another; these acts are repeated over time and are deliberately used for the purpose of causing harm.

Bystanders – People who bear witness to bullying and/or teasing but are not directly involved in the interaction.

Channel switching – Shifting between or among different modes of communication (e.g., face-to-face, text messaging, email, etc.) during a single communication episode.

Chilling effect – When a person who has less power in a close relationship does not bring up problems or complaints or conflict with the other person, who is perceived to have more power in the relationship. These perceptions of "who has the power" in the relationship are typically based on who cares the most, with the person who cares the least having more relational power.

Close relationships – Include all the elements of interpersonal relationships in addition to three more: (a) the ability to meet important psychological and interpersonal needs, (b) a degree of emotional attachment between the people involved, and (c) the perception of each other as difficult or impossible to easily replace.

Coercive behaviors – Actions that are used with the intent of causing harm to someone else or to force them to do what you want them to do.

Cognitive jealousy – One of three interrelated components of jealousy; includes negative thoughts such as suspicions and uncertainties about the threat of a rival third party.

Collaborating – One of five major conflict styles; it is high in both assertiveness and cooperativeness and entails working together to develop creative solutions to conflict issues that do not require either party to give up anything that is important to them.

Communication competence – Being communicatively competent requires a number of skills, including communicating in an effective way (i.e., a way that allows you to achieve your goals) while also ensuring that one's communication is appropriate (i.e., it is recognized by the other as reasonable and acceptable).

Communal coping – Occurs when two (or more) people in a relationship work together to cope with a problem or stressor cooperatively, as a unit.

Communication efficacy – An information-based motivation for topic avoidance/secret keeping whereby information control is motivated by the perception that one's own ability to successfully, effectively reveal the information or discuss the issue is low.

Communicative infidelity – Occurs when an individual strategically commits sexual infidelity in order to send a message to their romantic partner.

Compensatory restoration – A constructive communicative response to jealousy that entails behaviors that are directed toward improving yourself (e.g., trying to be a better romantic partner) or the relationship (e.g., using relational maintenance behaviors).

Competing – One of five major conflict styles; it is high in assertiveness but low in cooperativeness and involves acting in ways that allow you to "win" conflict episodes by getting what you want, even at the cost of the other person.

Compromising – One of five major conflict styles; it is moderate in both assertiveness and cooperativeness and includes approaching conflict as a give-and-take wherein both parties get some of the things they want but both parties also have to give up some of the things they want.

Conflict – An overtly or covertly expressed disagreement between at least two interdependent persons who perceive that their goals are incompatible, that there are only enough resources to satisfy one goal, and that the other person will attempt to interfere to thwart the achievement of one's personal goal.

Conflict strategies – Particular tactics that are strategically chosen in order to help one meet their conflict-related goals.

Conflict styles – Preferred, enduring tendencies to handle conflict in particular ways across conflict situations and contexts.

Conscientiousness – One of the "big five" personality traits that reflects the tendency to be responsible, rule abiding, hard-working, and goal oriented.

Contempt – A feeling of disdain or scorn for another person, accompanied by perceptions of one's own superiority.

Contextual motives – One of four motives for stalking; when stalking is motivated by external, situational circumstances that are possibly temporary in nature (e.g., stressors like a breakup or job loss).

Conventional secrets – One of three types of secrets that are specific to families; these things are kept secret because they are things that society at large typically deems inappropriate to reveal (e.g., information about family finances).

Counter-jealousy induction – A destructive communicative response to jealousy that entails purposeful attempts to make your romantic partner jealous because they first made you feel jealous.

Criticism – Personal attacks that place blame on another person for a problem.

Cyberbullying – A type of bullying (i.e., repeated, aggressive, symbolic acts against a target who has difficulty defending themself) that is carried out using electronic or mediated methods.

Cyberstalking – A form of technological aggression that includes talking another using methods of electronic access and communication. These range from more benign (e.g., email and social networking sites, such as Facebook) to much more nefarious (e.g., spyware and GPS tracking).

Dark side – A perspective or way of looking at things that draws attention to the inappropriate and destructive elements of all kinds of behaviors, even those that ostensibly begin as, are intended as, or are typically evaluated as positive.

Dark tetrad – The combination of four particularly malignant and destructive personality traits (i.e., narcissism, psychopathy, Machiavellianism, and sadism). People with this set of traits are more likely to take advantage of others, to be callous and manipulative, and to behave in ways that are cruel.

Dark triad – The original combination of three especially malicious and damaging personality traits (i.e., narcissism, psychopathy, and Machiavellianism). People with this set of traits are more likely to take advantage of others, to be callous and manipulative, and to behave in ways that benefit their own self-interests.

Deception – Purposely, knowingly misleading another person to believe something that the sender knows or believes to be false.

Deception detection – Accurately differentiating between true statements and deceptive ones.

Defensiveness – Attempting to avert blame as a means of defending oneself from another's attacks.

Demand-withdraw pattern – A push-pull, back-and-forth pattern in which one partner (the demander, who typically is most invested in the conflict issue) desires some type of change from the other partner (the withdrawer). To effect this change, the demander pursues conflict discussions with the withdrawer, who becomes defensive and attempts to avoid or retreat from such discussions.

Denial – An avoidant communicative response to jealousy that occurs when you do not admit that you are feeling jealous; instead, you pretend like you are not actually experiencing jealousy.

Depression – A mood disorder that entails frequent and long-lasting feelings of disinterest and sadness.

Devaluation – Feeling undervalued, unimportant, or easily replaceable as a result of a close other's communication or behavior; a common cause of hurt feelings.

Diagnostic utility – Prompting a potential deceiver to provide relevant information that will assist you in making an accurate judgment about whether they are lying.

Distributive communication – One of three major conflict management strategies; it is high in assertiveness but low in cooperativeness, and it involves antisocial and destructive conflict communication that is confrontational and perhaps openly hostile.

Double-shot hypothesis – Holds that people are most distressed anytime they believe that both emotional and sexual infidelity are co-occurring; explains how becoming aware of one type of infidelity (e.g., emotional) implies or suggests that the other type of infidelity (e.g., sexual) is also occurring.

Double-standard perspective – People tend to have a double standard for deception, such that we think our own deception is benign and justified but we judge others much more harshly if we discover they have deceived us.

Emotional infidelity – Occurs when a person invests emotional resources such as attention, social support, psychological intimacy, time, and love in someone other than their romantic partner.

Emotional jealousy – One of three interrelated components of jealousy; deals with the emotions that often accompany the jealousy experience, such as fear, anger, and sadness.

Empathy – The willingness and ability to understand and to share in someone else's feelings.

Enmeshed – A term often used to describe a family or relationship that is overly close in ways that are unhealthy, as boundaries between/among members are ambiguous or even lacking entirely.

Equivocations – Ambiguous, noncommittal statements that are indirect in that they do not actually express an opinion although they appear to have done so.

Erotomania – A mental disorder constituted by the persistent erotic delusion that one is loved by another.

Escalation – One of four communication danger signs; it entails accelerating and intensifying negative interactions and occurs when partners respond more and more negatively to each other, effectively "upping the ante."

Evolutionary explanations regarding infidelity – This perspective expects men and women to have different biological imperatives related to reproduction, and these concerns dictate (and explain differences in) which type of infidelity is most upsetting for heterosexual men and which type of infidelity is most upsetting for heterosexual women.

Exit – An active response to relational dissatisfaction that includes terminating the relationship permanently (e.g., divorcing or breaking up with the partner) or potentially temporarily (e.g., separating), or otherwise de-escalating the romantic relationship.

Exploitation risk – A potential dark side or drawback of forgiveness, wherein forgiving certain types of people can lead them to be more likely to reoffend or continue their offenses against you in future.

Expressive motives – One of four motives for stalking perpetration; when stalking is motivated by a need to express one's feelings, either positive (e.g., love for another person) or negative (e.g., rage toward another person).

External attributions – When we believe that an act was committed due to external, temporary, and uncontrollable reasons. External attributions encourage us to evaluate another's behavior as less blameworthy.

Extractive uncertainty reduction strategy – Mining online repositories of archived data that are maintained over time to get information about a target.

Extradyadic communication – Also known as extra-relational communication. In the context in which the term is used here, it means communication with someone outside of the primary romantic relationship (i.e., with a social network member such as a close friend or family member).

Extroversion – One of the "big five" personality traits that reflects the tendency to be sociable, outgoing, talkative, and energetic.

Falsifications – Outright lies; providing information to another that is false in the hopes that the person will believe it is true.

Forgiveness – Intrapersonal and interpersonal processes that are initiated by the receipt of an offense from another, to which the offended party reacts not with retaliation, but instead with a positive transformation of emotions, feelings, behavioral inclinations, and/or actual behaviors toward the offender, thereby extending undeserved mercy to the offender.

Forgiveness granting – How the offended party communicates forgiveness to an offender.

Forgiveness seeking – How the offender communicates with the offended party about the offense, including potentially apologizing or accepting responsibility for the offense.

Fundamental attribution error – A cognitive bias wherein we tend to blame another people personally for their actions (e.g., you did X because of something about you as a person), while we blame external circumstances for our own actions (e.g., I did X because I didn't have any other choice, not because I'm a bad person). In other words, we cut ourselves a break in terms of attributions, but we hold others fully accountable.

Futility of discussion – An information-based motivation for topic avoidance/ secret keeping wherein information control is motivated by the perception that revealing/discussing the issue with a close other will be pointless. Often, futility of discussion is perceived when the two parties are so entrenched in their opposite points of view that they are unable to take each other's perspective or otherwise fruitfully discuss the issue.

Gaslighting – A tactic of psychological manipulation that is common in abusive relationships, wherein the abuser undermines or contradicts the target's view of reality, making the target question their own sanity.

Gender harassment – Calling someone gay or lesbian in a malevolent way, in a way that is intended as an insult or slur, or using any pejorative term for homosexuality.

Gender symmetry – The idea that women and men experience and perpetrate intimate partner violence approximately equally.

Gender traditionalism – The belief in old-fashioned, conventional, stereotypical ideals concerning binary biological gender, including the types of roles that should be played by males (e.g., husbands take out the trash) versus females (e.g., wives take care of the children).

High-stakes lies – Falsehoods that have serious, potentially severe ramifications (e.g., legal, personal) if discovered.

Hostility – A destructive personality trait that indexes the eagerness or proclivity to behave aggressively toward others.

Human aggression – Any behavior that intends any kind of harm to another (who is motivated to avoid the harm), whether symbolic (e.g., emotional/psychological) or physical.

Hurt – A negative affective state experienced in response to some form of emotional damage, such as someone doing or saying something injurious, or someone not doing or saying something that was expected or desired.

Hurtful communication (or hurtful messages) – Things that people say or do (or neglect to say or do) that emotionally wound another and cause psychological/emotional pain.

Hyperaccessibility – When trying to suppress a thought (such as a secret) has the opposite effect of keeping the thought at the forefront of our minds.

Hyperintimacy – One of four types of obsessive relational intrusion; presumptuous behaviors that assume and imply that the relationship you have with the other person is closer and more intimate than it actually is.

Hyperpersonal – A name for computer-mediated relationships that are more intimate/close than they would be if the people involved were face-to-face.

Identity management – An individual-based motivation for topic avoidance/secret keeping that deals with the desire to limit the vulnerability that often emerges when information is discussed/shared. Identity concerns include the desire to avoid being criticized or judged by another, or to avoid being embarrassed by the disclosure or discussion of information.

Ideology of openness – The widely held belief that open, intimate communication is central to good communication and high-quality relationships with others.

Impersonal communication – Communication between people who do not have explanatory, psychological information about each other, and instead only have descriptive, sociological information based on superficial characteristics (e.g., demographic characteristics such as age, biological sex, etc.).

Impulsivity – The tendency to act without thinking through the consequences.

Infidelity – A violation of relational rules for partner behavior in terms of appropriate extradyadic interaction and exclusivity in a monogamous relationship.

Informational familiarity – When you are familiar enough with the other person's life to be privy to certain information about them.

Instrumental motives – One of four motives for stalking perpetration; when stalking is motivated by the desire to influence or control another person.

Integrative communication – A constructive communicative response to jealousy that involves helpful, nonaggressive discussion of the jealousy experience with your romantic partner that is focused on solving the problem at hand.

Interactive uncertainty reduction strategy – Interacting directly with the target of your uncertainty in an effort to acquire information about the target.

Intergenerational transmission – A process by which the propensity to perpetrate (and perhaps, to be victimized by) intimate partner violence is "passed down" through families as a result of seeing parental figures model violent behavior in the home.

Internal attributions – When we believe that an act was committed due to internal, stable, and controllable factors. Internal attributions encourage us to evaluate another's behavior as more blameworthy.

Interpersonal communication – The exchange of verbal and/or nonverbal messages between at least two people, regardless of the nature of the relationship between them. Perhaps the people involved have explanatory, psychological information about each other to use during interactions.

Interpersonal provocation – Being goaded into a response by someone else's aggressive or violent behavior.

Interpersonal relationships – Characterized by three major elements: (a) they are enduring, with repeated interactions over some period of time; (b) the people involved in them mutually influence each other—they are interdependent; and (c) the people involved have unique communication and other interaction patterns.

Intimacy – Feelings of being close and emotionally connected to another person.

Intimate partner violence – Physical (including sexual) harm that is committed within the context of a close, intimate, usually romantic relationship.

Intimate terrorism – A strategic, manipulative, repeated pattern of attempts to exert control over a romantic partner by using violence and a variety of coercive tactics such as threats, intimidation, continual surveillance, withholding of resources, etc.

Invalidation – One of four communication danger signs; it involves overtly or covertly putting down and insulting the partner, behaving in a hostile manner toward them, and/or negating their perspective or point of view.

Invulnerable responses – Reactions to hurtful events that are designed to convey the message that the recipient was not actually hurt by the initiator's message/behavior. These include laughing off the message, ignoring the hurtful event, or otherwise behaving in a stoic manner.

Jealousy – An interactive, interpersonal experience comprised of cognitive, affective, and communicative elements; it involves the need to protect and defend a valued relationship from the threat of a perceived or actual third-party rival.

Joking – Like teasing, joking is humorous and slightly ambiguous; yet unlike teasing, joking is low in identity confrontation and can be carried out without the target (if indeed there is a target) being present.

Low-stakes lies – Also known as "white lies," these types of deceptions are told in the interest of politeness, saving face, and social appropriateness; they have minimal consequences even if discovered.

Loyalty – A passive response to relational dissatisfaction wherein a person simply waits and hopes that relational difficulties will improve, all the while remaining devoted to the partner by supporting and standing by them.

Machiavellianism – A personality trait in which people use crafty manipulation to get what they want, espousing the phrase "any means to an end."

Magic Ratio – During conflict episodes, couples in stable and happy relationships exhibit 5 positive behaviors or interactions for every 1 negative behavior or interaction. According to a long program of research by John Gottman and his colleagues, adherence to this magic ratio is the difference between happy and unhappy couples (who tend to exhibit more negative behaviors relative to positive behaviors during conflict).

Mate poaching – Individuals who intentionally seek out other people who are not available, who are already in committed relationships, for romance and/or sex.

Message intensity – The potency or forcefulness with which a person communicates their attitude toward a topic or person.

Misogyny – Strongly negative feelings about and ingrained prejudices toward women.

Moral disengagement – Occurs when a person is able to rationalize behaviors that are inconsistent with their own or societal ethical standards; this is typically accomplished by downplaying one's own harmful intent, downplaying the effect of the behavior on others, or rationalizing that the behavior was justified by something the target did.

Motivational impairment effect – The heightened motivation that accompanies the telling of high-stakes lies comes with a concurrent increase in the amount of anxiety and nervous arousal we feel when lying, and because symptoms of such nervous arousal can be hard to control, it is more difficult to get away with these types of lies (despite the fact that we are much more motivated to do so, as compared to our motivation to get away with low-stakes lies).

Narcissism – A personality trait in which people admire themselves excessively, need lots of attention and admiration, display a sense of entitlement, and express a lack of empathy for others.

Narcissistic entitlement – The attitude that one deserves special, preferential treatment from other people even when these feelings of inflated self-worth are not warranted by one's achievements.

Neuroticism – One of the "big five" personality traits that reflects the tendency to be negatively biased to feel anxious and to experience the world as distressing (also called negative emotionality).

Negative communication – A destructive communicative response to jealousy that includes a wide range of direct (e.g., behaving in a hostile way) and indirect (e.g., giving the silent treatment) behaviors that are damaging and destructive but that stop short of violence or threats.

Negative interpretations – One of four communication danger signs; it occurs when partners consistently assume that each other's motives are more negative than they actually are.

Negativity effect – A documented phenomenon whereby negative elements of social interaction have a stronger, longer lasting impact than the positive events that occur in interpersonal and close relationships.

Neglect – A passive response to relational dissatisfaction that entails psychologically disengaging from the relationship, treating the partner badly, or allowing the relationship to deteriorate.

Object adaptors – Mindlessly manipulating objects such as clicking a pen or jangling keys, often when we are nervous, bored, or uncomfortable.

Obsessive relational intrusion – Repeated and unwanted pursuit and invasion of a target's sense of physical or symbolic privacy by another person who wants to have (or presumes to have) an intimate relationship with the target.

Omissions – Also known as concealment; leaving out information that you know is meaningful or relevant in order to leave another with a false impression of events.

On-again, off-again relationships – Committed, dating relationships that have broken up and renewed at least once.

Online obsessive relational intrusion – The online phenomenon of repeated and unwanted pursuit of another's sense of physical or symbolic privacy by someone who wants to have (or presumes to have) an intimate relationship with the target. Unlike ORI, o-ORI is carried out via online social networking sites such as Facebook. This phenomenon is also known as cyber obsessional pursuit.

Openness to new experiences – One of the "big five" personality traits that reflects the tendency to try new things and to be comfortable with novel experiences.

Overstatements – Also known as exaggerations; dramatizing, embellishing, or "stretching the truth," often to make oneself look better or to make a story more interesting.

Partner regulation behaviors – Communicative strategies that explicitly express opposition to a romantic partner's objectionable behavior (e.g., relationship transgressions), such as blaming the partner for their actions and requiring that they change.

Partner uncertainty – The doubts, questions, and insecurities that an individual perceives about their partner's participation in the relationship.

Partner unresponsiveness – An information-based motivation for topic avoidance/secret keeping whereby information control is motivated by perceptions that the close other will not be willing or able to discuss the issue in a productive manner, perhaps because the other thinks the issue is unimportant or because the other doesn't have the necessary knowledge to be helpful.

Partner-focused motives – Lies that are told for the benefit of (e.g., to protect) the person you are lying to.

Passive uncertainty reduction strategy – Merely observing the target of your uncertainty in an unobtrusive, inconspicuous, and discreet way in an effort to gain some knowledge about the target.

Passive victims – These individuals have elevated levels of rejection sensitivity, low self-esteem, and psychological difficulties such as anxiety and depression. They do not react well to being teased or bullied, and perpetrators begin to recognize them as easy targets who probably will not retaliate.

Pathological jealousy – An extreme, irrational, and unjustified experience of severe jealousy.

Perceived network involvement – An individual's perception of the behaviors that family members and close friends (i.e., social network members with whom one has a close relationship) enact toward the individual's romantic relationship.

Perceived resolvability – In the context of serial arguments, this refers to the belief that a particular conflict issue can at some point be settled or decided and that closure regarding the conflict issue is possible.

Personalogical motives – One of four motives for stalking perpetration; when a perpetrator has some sort of personal, mental, or character defect or difficulty that leads to stalking (e.g., mental disorders, insecure attachment style, social incompetence).

Physical aggression – Includes actions that cause another person bodily harm (e.g., slapping, shoving, punching, etc.).

Pitch – The high or low frequency of a sound.

Polyamory – Having sexual and/or emotional/romantic relationships with more than one person with the consent of every person involved.

Polyvictimization – Experiencing two or more types of abuse, such as sexual violence, physical violence, stalking, and psychological abuse.

Positive illusions – The tendency to see our romantic partner in a more positive light than is warranted by reality. This is achieved by minimizing our partner's flaws and exaggerating our partner's positive features.

Principle of least interest – The notion that unequal emotional involvement in a romantic relationship determines who has the most power in that relationship, with the person who is least interested in continuing the relationship having the most power.

Privacy management – An individual-based motivation for topic avoidance/ secret keeping that concerns the desire to protect one's private information and to maintain a degree of autonomy and control over private information.

Private information control – People value their ability to control their own private information, and they create and employ privacy rules to control the management of private information to potential co-owners. Once information is revealed to another, these rules must be negotiated between the co-owners of the information, and collective privacy boundaries are created.

Private information ownership – The notion that people own their own private information, have the right to choose to share that information (or not) with others, and that this sharing of private information does not give the target permission to disclose the information to others (i.e., the original owner of the information should have that right).

Private information turbulence – Maintaining collective privacy boundaries with co-owners of private information can be difficult and chaotic, which disrupts privacy regulation processes.

Proactive victims – These individuals respond to teasing and bullying with aggression of their own, thinking that is the best way to get the perpetrator to stop targeting them.

Prosocial teasing – Also known as "good" or effective teasing; it is characterized by actually being perceived as funny, as pretty straightforward, and as low in identity threat for the target.

Provocative victims – These individuals are thought to be frequent targets due to their likelihood of exhibiting attention-seeking aggressive behaviors that provoke perpetrators' aggression.

Psychopathy – An antisocial mental disorder that is characterized by manipulative and controlling behaviors, a lack of empathy for others, an inability to feel remorse or guilt, impulsivity, an inability to control oneself, and failure to take responsibility for one's actions.

Pupil dilation – When the pupils of your eyes expand and are larger than normal.

Pursuit – One of four types of obsessive relational intrusion; behaviors that let you know another person is romantically interested in you/attempting to form a close relationship with you (e.g., calling you frequently, leaving notes or gifts).

Putative secrets – Secrets that, unbeknownst to the secret keeper, have actually been discovered by a person(s) that the secret keeper was attempting to keep the information secret from.

Reactive jealousy – A more typical jealousy experience that is moderate, reasonable, and warranted.

Rejection sensitivity – An individual difference variable that reflects a defensive motivational system wherein some people have a chronic propensity to anticipate rejection in interpersonal situations; they are hypervigilant for possible cues to rejection and they tend to overreact to such cues.

Relational communication – The exchange of verbal and/or nonverbal messages in the context of close relationships.

Relational turbulence – A view of the relationship as in turmoil (chaotic, unstable, tumultuous) as a result of interpersonal encounters that are repeatedly and consistently characterized by extreme cognitions, emotions, and behaviors.

Relational uncertainty – An umbrella term that encompasses the three sources of uncertainty that are specific to close relationships: self, partner, and relationship uncertainties.

Relationship de-escalation – A destructive relationship-based motivation for topic avoidance/secret keeping wherein these behaviors are used to slow or stop the growth of a relationship or even to bring about the termination of a close relationship.

Relationship protection – A protective relationship-based motivation for topic avoidance/secret keeping wherein these behaviors are undertaken in order to shield the relationship with a close other from harm.

Relationship transgressions – Violations of implicit or explicit relational rules for appropriate behavior that significantly (perhaps irreparably) harm the victim and/or relationship.

Relationship uncertainty – The doubts, questions, and insecurities that an individual has regarding the nature and tenability of the relationship as its own entity, above and beyond self- or partner uncertainties.

Relationship-focused motives – Lies that are told for the benefit of (e.g., to protect) the relationship you have with the person you are lying to.

Revenge – A motive for communicative infidelity; when your desire to get back at your romantic partner for something they first did to you is your reason for committing sexual infidelity in order to send your partner a message.

Rival contact – A rival-focused communicative response to jealousy that includes direct contact with a third-party rival.

Rival derogation – A rival-focused communicative response to jealousy that entails efforts to put down or denigrate a third-party rival in an effort to make the rival seem less attractive to your romantic partner.

Romantic jealousy – One of several specific types of jealousy; occurs when the rival third party is interfering with the continuation or quality of your romantic relationship.

Rule violations – One of three types of secrets that are specific to families; these are secrets about things that break particular family rules (e.g., a family member's teenage/premarital pregnancy).

Rumination – A disadvantageous psychological process whereby one experiences repetitive, persistent, unwanted, intrusive thoughts about a negative emotional experience or event.

Sadism – The tendency to derive pleasure from inflicting physical and/or emotional pain on another.

Secret keeping – When a person purposely conceals information from another, sometimes even in cases where the other person is entitled to know the information, usually because the information is thought to be too risky to reveal or because the secret keeper has been told not to divulge the information.

Secret tests – Indirect, covert, strategic ways of acquiring information/reducing uncertainty about the nature of one's relationship with another, or the other person's commitment to you/the relationship.

Self-adaptors – Mindlessly engaging in self-touching behaviors (e.g., biting fingernails, scratching, cracking knuckles) as a result of feeling anxious, uncomfortable, or bored.

Self-focused motives – Lies that are told for the benefit of ourselves; to project a certain image, to avoid punishment or embarrassment, to achieve particular goals, etc.

Self-regulation – The processes by which the self changes its outward reactions or inner states to reduce perceived discrepancies between desired and current goal states. In other words, if I feel like engaging in excessive pursuit behaviors but also want to maximize my chances of successfully initiating a romantic relationship with a target, self-regulation allows me to control my outward behavior (which if left uncontrolled would compromise goal achievement) in order to maximize my chances for relationship development (which would allow me to meet my goal).

Self-uncertainty – The doubts, questions, and insecurities that an individual has about their own involvement in the relationship.

Serial arguments – Repetitive argumentative disputes that continue to recur over time with another person (e.g., a romantic partner) about a particular conflict issue that is not fully resolved.

Sex drive – A motive for communicative infidelity; when some element of sociosexuality, sexual adjustment, sexual self-esteem, sexual depression, and/or sexual preoccupation motivates your commission of sexual infidelity enacted to send a message to your romantic partner.

Sexual aggression – Nonconsensual sexual behaviors (e.g., rape, sexual assault) that cause another person physical harm.

Sexual coercion – Defined by the CDC as unwanted sexual penetration that occurs after being pressured in a nonphysical way (whereas rape is completed or attempted penetration that is accomplished via physical force). Sexual coercion can occur by pressuring another repeatedly to have sex, wearing the target down and showing dissatisfaction when they do not agree to sexual relations. It may also be accomplished by deception, false promises, threats on the part of the perpetrator (e.g., to end the relationship or to spread rumors about the target), or power plays (e.g., when the perpetrator is in a position of power over the target).

Sexual harassment – Unwanted sexual advances, requests for sexual favors, or a wide range of other verbal (e.g., making sexual comments), nonverbal (e.g., displaying sexual images), or physical contact (e.g., groping someone) that is sexual in nature.

Sexual infidelity – Occurs when a person devotes sexual resources to someone other than their romantic partner; has been defined rather broadly as extradyadic "sexual activity."

Signs of possession – A rival-focused communicative response to jealousy that involves public displays used to communicate to rivals that your romantic partner is already involved in a relationship with you (e.g., putting your arm around your partner's waist).

Silence – An avoidant communicative response to jealousy that entails being quiet, decreasing communication, and not talking about your experience of jealousy. This is done in order to meet your own needs rather than as an attempt to punish the romantic partner.

Situational couple violence – When conflict situations escalate too far, arguments become aggressive and violence (typically minor in nature) ensues. This type of violence is spontaneous, incited by the situation at hand, and is not part of an ongoing pattern of abuse.

Snooping – An intrusive act that entails examining another's private communications (e.g., text messages) secretly, without the other's knowledge or permission.

Social aggression – Similar to the concepts of indirect and relational aggression. Occurs when a target is injured in a roundabout, underhanded, and potentially subtle way, through some form of social manipulation or harm that is directed at their self-esteem and/or social standing. Examples include gossiping, spreading rumors, snubbing, excluding, and shunning.

Social pain – Experienced when one has been rendered vulnerable due to an actual or perceived separation from social relationships with others.

Social-cognitive theory of jealousy – Holds that differential mechanisms for reacting to emotional versus sexual infidelity would not have been adaptive for human beings; instead, general mechanisms for detecting any type of infidelity (either emotional or sexual) would have been more adaptive.

Speaker-listener technique – A structured approach to conflict discussions wherein partners take turns being the speaker and being the listener. Speakers are taught to communicate competently and to own their own feelings with the use of "I language." Listeners are taught to actively listen by paraphrasing and confirming/validating the speaker.

Speech errors – Accidental mistakes made when we are speaking, such as slips of the tongue, misspeaking, grammatical errors, stuttering, and dysfluencies that interrupt smooth speech delivery (e.g., filled pauses such as "uh").

Stalking – A form of interpersonal aggression that includes repeated, persistent, unwanted harassment that is perceived as threatening and/or fear inducing. Outside the United States, this may be referred to as criminal harassment.

Standards for openness hypothesis – The idea that topic avoidance is only relationally harmful to the extent that doing so is seen as a sign of a "bad" relationship.

Stonewalling – When a person shuts down and retreats or withdraws from a conflict episode.

Support deficit – Receiving less social support from social network members than you need or desire.

Support dilemmas – When the pros or advantages of receiving social support from a close other are offset by the costs or disadvantages of doing so.

Support gaps – When one receives more (i.e., a support surplus) or less (i.e., a support deficit) social support than is desired. Support deficits are especially problematic and lead to negative outcomes.

Support marshaling – The communicative behaviors and activities used by people to boost social support from social network members (or to limit interference from social network members) to augment the achievability of goals.

Support surplus – Receiving more social support from social network members than you need or desire.

Surveillance – A rival-focused communicative response to jealousy that is comprised of overt or covert activities intended to find out more about your romantic partner's relationship with the third-party rival.

Taboo secrets – One of three types of secrets that are specific to families; these secrets are considered taboo because they concern information or activities that are denounced by society in general (e.g., a family member's drug addiction).

Taboo topics – Topics that are acknowledge to be "off limits" for discussion, because such discussion is expected to result in negative outcomes.

Teasing – A humorous attempt to confront or challenge (e.g., make fun of) elements of someone else's identity that is slightly ambiguous in nature (e.g., it may be interpreted positively or negatively, depending on who you ask: the perpetrator, the target, or bystanders).

Thought suppression – Actively trying to keep from thinking about something, such as a secret.

Threat – One of four types of obsessive relational intrusion; fear-inducing behaviors that are intended to pressure and intimidate (e.g., warning that bad things might or will happen to you, physically harming you).

Tie signs – Behaviors or expressions (often nonverbal in nature) that make clear the nature or intimacy level of the relationship between two people (e.g., holding hands, gazing into each other's eyes).

Tolerance of ambiguity – How a person or group of people perceive and react to information or situations that are characterized by uncertainty or a lack of clarity.

Topic avoidance – A special case of privacy management in which a person deliberately, actively evades discussion of a topic. Unlike secret keeping, the other person may already know about the information that is being avoided.

Transgression-maximizing communication – Messages about a relationship transgression that highlight or play up the offensiveness of the transgression and/or the partner's direct personal responsibility for the transgression.

Transgression-minimizing communication – Messages about a relationship transgression that downplay or diminish the offensiveness of the transgression and/or the partner's direct personal responsibility for the transgression.

Transgression-related interpersonal motivations – A means of conceptualizing forgiveness as a set of three motivational changes that occur in response to a relationship transgression. These three motivation changes entail decreased motivation to avoid the transgressor, decreased motivation to retaliate against the transgressor, and increased benevolence or peacemaking motivations toward the transgressor.

Transitions – Broadly conceptualized as any change in identity, role, or circumstances that take place at the individual, relational, or situational level. Transitions represent a discontinuity in the relationship, and they require partners to alter how they coordinate their relationship and relate to each other.

Truth bias – The tendency to presume or believe that what other people tell us is true regardless of whether it actually is true.

Truth default – Passively presuming that someone else is being honest with us due to a failure to even consider the possibility that the person is being deceptive.

Uncertainty – The inability to predict or explain another person's attitudes or actions. Alternatively, insecurity regarding one's own amount of knowledge or about the amount of knowledge available about something or someone.

Understatements – Also known as minimizing; diminishing, weakening, or otherwise downplaying the truth, often to distance ourselves from something or to limit our perceived blameworthiness.

Unrequited love – A situation wherein one person has feelings for another person that the other person does not reciprocate.

Verbal aggression – Messages that are sent with the intent to psychologically/emotionally harm another person. Trait verbal aggression is a person's general tendency to attack another's self-concept (rather than their point of view on an issue) in an effort to symbolically hurt them.

Violation – One of four types of obsessive relational intrusion; disturbing encroachment behaviors that constitute a violation of privacy rules and some-times, a violation of laws (e.g., breaking into your home, taking photos of you without your consent/knowledge).

Violence – Any action or behavior intended to cause physical harm to another.

Violent communication – A destructive communicative response to jealousy that involves actual physical violence toward the romantic partner (e.g., hitting, shoving) and/or threats of physical harm to the partner.

Violent resistance – A retaliatory violent reaction used in response to another person's initial use of violence (i.e., when one person's perpetration of violence is met with the other person's violent response).

Voice – An active response to relational dissatisfaction wherein problems and potential solutions are discussed, help from third parties (e.g., therapists) may be sought, or efforts are undertaken to improve oneself or encourage the partner to improve themself.

Withdrawal – One of four communication danger signs; it occurs when conflict is avoided entirely or successfully sidestepped.

Wizards – A small group of deception detection experts in the forensic context who are able to accurately distinguish high-stakes lies from truths in more than 80% of cases.

REFERENCES

Abramowitz, J. S., Tolin, D. F., & Street, G. P. (2001). Paradoxical effects of thought suppression: A meta-analysis of controlled studies. *Clinical Psychology Review, 21*(5), 683–703.

Afifi, T. D., Caughlin, J. P., & Afifi, W. A. (2007). The dark side (and light side) of avoidance and secrets. In B. H. Spitzberg & W. R. Cupach (Eds.), *The dark side of interpersonal communication* (2nd ed., pp. 61–92). Routledge.

Afifi, T. D., & Joseph, A. (2009). The standards for openness hypothesis: A gendered explanation for why avoidance is so dissatisfying. In T. D. Afifi & W. A. Afifi (Eds.), *Uncertainty, information management, and disclosure decisions: Theories and applications* (pp. 341–362). Routledge.

Afifi, T. D., Olson, L. & Armstrong, C. (2005). The chilling effect and family secrets: Examining the role of self protection, other protection, and communication efficacy. *Human Communication Research, 31*, 564–598.

Afifi, T. D., & Schrodt, P. (2003). Uncertainty and the avoidance of the state of one's family in stepfamilies, post divorce single-parent families, and first-marriage families. *Human Communication Research, 29*, 516–532.

Afifi, T. D., & Steuber, K. (2009). The revelation risk model (RRM): Factors that predict the revelation of secrets and the strategies used to reveal them. *Communication Monographs, 76*, 144–176.

Afifi, W. A., & Burgoon, J. K. (1998). "We never talk about that": A comparison of cross-sex friendships and dating relationships on uncertainty and topic avoidance. *Personal Relationships, 5*, 255–272.

Afifi, W. A., & Caughlin, J. P. (2006). A close look at revealing secrets and some consequences that follow. *Communication Research, 33*, 467–488.

Afifi, W. A., Falato, W. L., & Weiner, J. L. (2001). Identity concerns following a severe relational transgression: The role of discovery method for the relational outcomes of infidelity. *Journal of Social and Personal Relationships, 18*, 291–308.

Afifi, W. A., & Guerrero, L. K. (1998). Some things are better left unsaid II: Topic avoidance in friendships. *Communication Quarterly, 46*, 231–249.

Afifi, W. A., & Guerrero, L. K. (2000). Motivations underlying topic avoidance in close relationships. In S. Petronio (Ed.), *Balancing the secrets of private disclosures* (pp. 165–179). Erlbaum.

Afifi, W. A., & Morse, C. R. (2009). Expanding the role of emotion in the theory of motivated information management. In T. D. Afifi & W. A. Afifi (Eds.),

Uncertainty, information management, and disclosure decisions: Theories and applications (pp. 87–105). Routledge.

Afifi, W. A., & Reichert, T. (1996). Understanding the role of uncertainty in jealousy experience and expression. *Communication Reports, 9,* 93–103.

Afifi, W. A., & Weiner, J. L. (2004). Toward a theory of motivated information management. *Communication Theory, 14,* 167–190.

Ainsworth, M. D. S. (1989). Attachments beyond infancy. *American Psychologist, 44,* 709–716.

Alberts, J. K. (1992). An inferential/strategic explanation for the social organization of teases. *Journal of Language and Social Psychology, 11,* 153–177.

Alberts, J. K., Kellar-Guenther, Y., & Corman, S. R. (1996). That's not funny: Understanding recipients' responses to teasing. *Western Journal of Communication, 60,* 337–357.

Albrecht, T. L., & Adelman, M. B. (1987). *Communicating social support.* SAGE.

Aldeis, D., & Afifi, T. D. (2015). Putative secrets and conflict in romantic relationships over time. *Communication Monographs, 82,* 224–251.

Allemand, M., Amberg, I., Zimprich, D., & Fincham, F. D. (2007). The role of trait forgiveness and relationship satisfaction in episodic forgiveness. *Journal of Social and Clinical Psychology, 26,* 199–217.

Allen, E. S., Atkins, D. C., Baucom, D. H., Snyder, D. K., Gordon, K. C., & Glass S. P. (2005). Intrapersonal, interpersonal, and contextual factors in engaging in and responding to extramarital involvement. *Clinical Psychology: Science and Practice, 12,* 101–130.

Allen, E. S., & Baucom, D. H. (2004). Adult attachment and patterns of extradyadic involvement. *Family Process, 43,* 467–488.

Allen, E. S., Rhoades, G. K., Stanley, S. M., Markman, H. J., Williams, T., Melton, J., & Clements, M. L. (2008). Premarital precursors of marital infidelity. *Family Process, 47,* 243–259.

Aloia, L. S., & Solomon, D. H. (2015). The physiology of argumentative skill deficiency: Cognitive ability, emotional competence, communication qualities, and responses to conflict. *Communication Monographs, 82,* 315–338.

Altman, I., & Taylor, D. (1973). *Social penetration: The development of interpersonal relationships.* Holt.

Amato, P. R., & Rogers, S. J. (1997). A longitudinal study of marital problems and subsequent divorce. *Journal of Marriage and the Family, 59,* 612–624.

Anderson, C. A., & Anderson, K. B. (2008). Men who target women: Specificity of target, generality of aggressive behavior. *Aggressive Behavior, 34,* 605–622.

Anderson, C. A., & Bushman, B. J. (2002). Human aggression. *Annual Review of Psychology, 53,* 27–51.

Andersen, P. A., Eloy, S. V., Guerrero, L. K., & Spitzberg, B. H. (1995). Romantic jealousy and relational satisfaction: A look at the impact of jealousy experience and expression. *Communication Reports, 8,* 77–85.

Andersen, P. A., Todd-Mancillas, W. R., & DiClemente, L. (1980). The effects of pupil dilation in physical, social, and task attraction. *Australian Scan: Journal of Human Communication, 7–8,* 89–95.

Ang, R. P., & Goh, D. H. (2010). Cyberbullying among adolescents: The role of affective and cognitive empathy, and gender. *Child Psychiatry and Human Development, 41,* 387–397.

Antheunis, M. L., Valkenburg, P. M., & Peter, J. (2010). Getting acquainted through social network sites: Testing a model of online uncertainty reduction and social attraction. *Computers in Human Behavior, 26,* 100–109.

Apostolou, M. (2019). The evolution of same-sex attraction in women. *Journal of Individual Differences, 40,* 104–110.

Archer, J. (2000). Sex differences in aggression between heterosexual partners: A meta-analytic review. *Psychological Bulletin, 126,* 651–680.

Argyle, M., & Furnham, A. (1983). Sources of satisfaction and conflict in long-term relationships. *Journal of Marriage and the Family, 45,* 481–493.

Aron, A., & Aron, E. (1986). *Love and the expansion of the self: Understanding attraction and satisfaction.* Hemisphere.

Asada, K. J., Lee, E., Levine, T. R., & Ferrara, M. H. (2004). Narcissism and empathy as predictors of obsessive relational intrusion. *Communication Research Reports, 21,* 379–390.

Atkins, D. C., Baucom, D. H., & Jacobson, N. S. (2001). Understanding infidelity: Correlates in a national random sample. *Journal of Family Psychology, 15,* 735–749.

Atwood, J. D. (2005). Cyber-affairs: "What's the big deal?" Therapeutic considerations. *Journal of Couple and Relationship Therapy: Innovations in Clinical and Educational Interventions, 4,* 117–134.

Aoyama, I., Utsumi, S., & Hasegawa, M. (2012). Cyberbullying in Japan: Cases, government reports, adolescent relational aggression, and parental monitoring roles. In Q. Li, D. Cross, & P. K. Smith (Eds.), *Cyberbullying in the global playground: Research from international perspectives* (pp. 183–201). Wiley.

Babcock, R. J. H. (2000). Psychology of stalking. In P. Infield & G. Platford (Eds.), *The law of harassment and stalking* (pp. 1–8). Butterworths.

Bachman, G. F., & Guerrero, L. K. (2006). Forgiveness, apology, and communicative responses to hurtful events. *Communication Reports, 19,* 45–56.

Baker, C. K., Cook, S. L., & Norris, F. H. (2003). Domestic violence and housing problems: A contextual analysis of women's help-seeking, received informal support, and formal system response. *Violence Against Women, 9,* 754–783.

Bancroft, L., Silverman, J. G., & Ritchie, D. (2012). *The batterer as parent* (2nd ed.). SAGE.

Bandura, A. (1977). Self-efficacy: Toward a unifying theory of behavior change. *Psychological Review, 84,* 191–215.

Bandura, A. (1978). *Social learning theory of aggression.* Prentice Hall.

Barbee, A. P., Derlega, V. J., Sherburne, S. P., & Grimshaw, A. (1998). Helpful and unhelpful forms of social support for HIV-positive individuals. In V. J. Derlega & A. P. Barbee (Eds.), *HIV and social interaction* (pp. 83–105). SAGE.

Barelds, D. P. H., & Barelds-Dijkstra, P. (2007). Relations between different types of jealousy and self and partner perceptions of relationship quality. *Clinical Psychology and Psychotherapy, 14*, 176–188.

Barelds, D. P. H., & Dijkstra, P. (2006). Reactive, anxious, and possessive forms of jealousy and their relation to relationship quality among heterosexuals and homosexuals. *Journal of Homosexuality, 51*, 183–198.

Barki, H., & Hartwick, J. (2004). Conceptualizing the construct of interpersonal conflict: *International Journal of Conflict Management, 15*, 216–244.

Barnlund, D. C. (1968). *Interpersonal communication: Survey and studies.* Houghton Mifflin.

Baron, R. A., Neuman, J. H., & Geddes, D. (1999). Social and personal determinants of workplace aggression: Evidence for the impact of perceived injustice and the Type A behavior pattern. *Aggressive Behavior, 25*, 281–296.

Bartholomew, K. (1990) Avoidance of intimacy: An attachment perspective. *Journal of Personal and Social Relationships, 7*, 147–178.

Bartholomew, K., & Horowitz, L. M. (1991). Attachment styles among young adults: A test of a four-category model. *Journal of Personality and Social Psychology, 61*, 226–244.

Bates, E. A. (2020). "No one would ever believe me": An exploration of the impact of intimate partner violence victimization on men. *Psychology of Men and Masculinities, 21*, 497–507.

Bauchner, J. E., Kaplan, E. P., & Miller, G. R. (1980). Detecting deception: The relationship of available information to judgmental accuracy in initial encounters. *Human Communication Research, 6*, 251–264.

Baucom, B. R., McFarland, P. T., & Christensen, A. (2010). Gender, topic, and time in observed demand-withdraw interaction in cross- and same-sex couples. *Journal of Family Psychology, 24*(3), 233–242.

Baum, K., Catalano, S., Rand, M., & Rose, K. (2009). *Stalking victimization in the United States.* U.S. Department of Justice.

Baughman, H. M., Dearing, S., Giammarco, E., & Vernon, P. A. (2012). Relationships between bullying behaviors and the Dark Triad: A study with adults. *Personality and Individual Differences, 52*, 571–575.

Baumeister, R. F., Exline, J. J., & Sommer, K. L. (1998). The victim role, grudge theory, and two dimensions of forgiveness. In E. J. Worthington (Ed.), *Dimensions of forgiveness: Psychological research and theoretical perspectives* (pp. 79–106). Templeton Press.

Baumeister, R. F., & Leary, M. R. (1995). The need to belong: Desire for interpersonal attachments as a fundamental human motivation. *Psychological Bulletin, 117*, 497–529.

Baumeister, R. F., Wotman, S. R., & Stillwell, A. M. (1993). Unrequited love: On heartbreak, anger, guilt, scriptlessness, and humiliation. *Journal of Personality and Social Psychology, 64*, 377–394.

Bavelas, J. B., Black, A., Chovil, M., & Mullett, J. (1990). *Equivocal communication.* SAGE.

Baxter, L. A. (1986). Gender differences in the heterosexual relationship rules embedded in breakup accounts. *Journal of Social and Personal Relationships, 3*, 289–306.

Baxter, L. A. (1990). Dialectical contradictions in relationship development. *Journal of Social and Personal Relationships, 7*, 69–88.

Baxter, L. A. (2006). Relational dialectics theory: Multivocal dialogues of family communication. In D. O. Braithwaite & L. A. Baxter (Eds.), *Engaging theories in family communication: Multiple perspectives* (pp. 130–145). SAGE.

Baxter, L. A., & Wilmot, W. W. (1984). "Secret tests": Social strategies for acquiring information about the state of the relationship. *Human Communication Research, 11*, 171–201.

Baxter, L. A., & Wilmot, W. W. (1985). Taboo topics in close relationships. *Journal of Social and Personal Relationships, 2*, 253–269.

Beatty, J. (1982). Task-evoked pupillary responses, processing load, and the structure of processing resources. *Psychological Bulletin, 91*, 276–292.

Becker, D. V., Sagarin, B. J., Guadagno, R. E., Millevoi, A., & Nicastle, L. D. (2004). When the sexes need not differ: Emotional responses to the sexual and emotional aspects of infidelity. *Personal Relationships, 11*, 529–538.

Bell, K. M., & Naugle, A. E. (2008). The role of emotion recognition skills in adult sexual revictimization. *The Journal of Behavioral Analysis of Offender and Victim: Treatment and Prevention, 1*, 93–118.

Bell, R. A., & Buerkel-Rothfuss, N. L. (1990). S(he) loves me, s(he) loves me not: Predictors of relational information-seeking in courtship and beyond. *Communication Quarterly, 38*, 64–82.

Bell, R. A., & Daly, J. A. (1984). The affinity-seeking function of communication. *Communication Monographs, 51*, 91–115.

Bellman, B. L. (1981). The paradox of secrecy. *Human Studies, 4*, 1–24.

Benoit, W. L., & Benoit, P. J. (1987). Everyday argument practices of naïve social actors. In J. W. Wenzel (Ed.), *Argument and critical practices* (pp. 465–473). SCA.

Berger, C. R. (1979). Beyond initial interaction: Uncertainty, understanding, and the development of interpersonal relationships. In H. Giles & R. N. St. Clair (Eds.), *Language and social psychology* (pp. 122–144). Basil Blackwell.

Berger, C. R. (1987). Communicating under uncertainty. In M. E. Roloff & G. R. Miller (Eds.), *Interpersonal processes: New directions in communication research* (pp. 39–62). SAGE.

Berger, C. R., & Bradac, J. J. (1982). *Language and social knowledge: Uncertainty in interpersonal relationships.* Edward Arnold.

Berger, C. R., & Calabrese, R. J. (1975). Some exploration in initial interaction and beyond: Toward a developmental theory of communication. *Human Communication Research, 1*, 99–112.

Berger, C. R., & Gudykunst, W. B. (1991). Uncertainty and communication. In B. Dervin & M. J. Voight (Eds.), *Progress in communication sciences* (pp. 21–66). Ablex.

Berkowitz, L. (1993). *Aggression: Its causes, consequences, and control.* McGraw-Hill.

Berkowitz, L., Cochran, S. T., & Embree, M. C. (1981). Physical pain and the goal of aversively stimulated aggression. *Journal of Personality and Social Psychology, 4,* 687–700.

Berry, J. W., Worthington, E. L., O'Connor, L. E., Parrott, L., & Wade, N. G. (2005). Forgivingness, vengeful rumination, and affective traits. *Journal of Personality, 73,* 183–225.

Berscheid, E., & Walster, E. (1974). Physical attractiveness. In L. Berkowitz (Ed.), *Advances in experimental social psychology* (pp. 158–216). Academic Press.

Betzig, L. (1989). Cases of conjugal dissolution: A cross-cultural study. *Current Anthropology, 30,* 654–676.

Bevan, J. L. (2006). Testing and refining a consequence model of jealousy across relational contexts and jealousy expression messages. *Communication Reports, 19,* 31–44.

Bevan, J. L. (2008). Experiencing and communicating romantic jealousy: Questioning the investment model. *Southern Communication Journal, 73,* 42–67.

Bevan, J. L. (2011). The consequence model of partner jealousy expression: Elaboration and refinement. *Western Journal of Communication, 75,* 523–540.

Bevan, J. L. (2013). *The communication of jealousy.* Peter Lang.

Bevan, J. L. (2014). Dyadic perceptions of goals, conflict strategies, and perceived resolvability in serial arguments. *Journal of Social and Personal Relationships, 31,* 773–795.

Bevan, J. L., Cameron, K. A., & Dillow, M. R. (2003). Compliance-gaining strategies associated with romantic reconciliation attempts. *Southern Communication Journal, 68,* 121–135.

Bevan, J. L., Finan, A., & Kaminsky, A. (2008). Modeling serial arguments in close relationships: The serial argument process model. *Human Communication Research, 34,* 600–624.

Bevan, J. L., Hale, J. L., & Williams, S. L. (2004). Identifying and characterizing goals of dating partners engaging in serial argumentation. *Argumentation and Advocacy, 41,* 28–40.

Bevan, J. L., & Samter, W. (2004). Toward a broader conceptualization of jealousy in close relationships: Two exploratory studies. *Communication Studies, 55,* 14–28.

Bias, J. P. (2005). *"Grow up, you big baby!": The experience and effects of teasing in adulthood* [Doctoral dissertation, Texas A&M University].

Bies, R. J., & Tripp, T. M. (2005). The study of revenge in the workplace: Conceptual, ideological, and empirical issues. In S. Fox and P. E. Spector (Eds.), *Counterproductive work behavior: Investigations of actors and targets* (pp. 65–81). American Psychological Association.

Birkley, E. L., & Eckhardt, C. I. (2015). Anger, hostility, internalizing negative emotions, and intimate partner violence perpetration: A meta-analytic review. *Clinical Psychology Review, 37,* 40–56.

Bjoerkqvist, K., Oesterman, K., & Lagerspetz, K. M. (1994). Sex differences in covert aggression among adults. *Aggressive Behavior, 20,* 27–33.

Black, M. C., Basile, K, C. Breiding, M. J., Smith, S. G., Walters, M. L., Merrick, M. T., Chen, J., & Stevens, M. R. (2011). *The National Intimate Partner and Sexual Violence*

Survey (NISVS): 2010 Summary Report. Centers for Disease Control and Prevention, National Center for Injury Prevention and Control.

Black, M. C., & Breiding, M. J. (2008). Adverse health conditions and health risk behaviors associated with intimate partner violence, United States, 2005. *Morbidity and Mortality Weekly Report, 57,* 113–117.

Blair, J. P., Levine, T. R., & Shaw, A. J. (2010). Content in context improves deception detection accuracy. *Human Communication Research, 36*(3), 423–442. https://doi.org/10.1111/j.1468-2958.2010.01382.x

Blake, R. R., & Mouton, J. S. (1964). *The managerial grid: The key to leadership excellence.* Gulf Publishing.

Blow, A. J., & Hartnett, K. (2005). Infidelity in committed relationships II: A substantive review. *Journal of Marital and Family Therapy, 31,* 217–233.

Blumstein, P., & Schwartz, P. (1983). *American couples: Money, work, sex.* William Morrow.

Bogaert, A. F., & Sadava, S. (2002). Adult attachment and sexual behavior. *Personal Relationships, 9,* 191–204.

Bok, S. (1983). *Secrets: On the ethics of concealment and revelation.* Vintage Books.

Bollmer, J. M., Milich, R., Harris, M. J., & Maras, M. A. (2005). A friend in need: The role of friendship quality as a protective factor in peer victimization and bullying. *Journal of Interpersonal Violence, 20,* 701–712.

Bond, C. F., & Atoum, A. O. (2009). International deception. *Personality and Social Psychology Bulletin, 26,* 385–395.

Bond, C. F., & DePaulo, B. M. (2006). Accuracy of deception detection judgments. *Personality and Social Psychology Review, 10*(3), 214–234. https://doi.org/10.1207/s15327957pspr1003_2

Bond, C. F., Howard, A. R., Hutchison, J. L., & Masip, J. (2013). Overlooking the obvious: Incentives to lie. *Basic Applied Social Psychology, 35,* 212–221.

Bond, C. F., Kahler, K. N., & Paolicelli, L. M. (1985). The miscommunication of deception: An adaptive perspective. *Journal of Experimental Social Psychology, 21,* 331–345.

Boon, S. D., Deveau, V. L., & Alibhai, A. M. (2009). Payback: The parameters of revenge in romantic relationships. *Journal of Social and Personal Relationships, 26,* 747–768.

Boon, S. D., & McLeod, B. A. (2001). Deception in romantic relationships: Subjective estimates of success at deceiving and attitudes toward deception. *Journal of Social and Personal Relationships, 18,* 463–476.

Boon, S. D., & Sulsky, L. M. (1997). Attributions of blame and forgiveness in romantic relationships: A policy-capturing study. *Journal of Social Behavior and Personality, 12,* 19–44.

Booth, A., Crouter, A. C., Clements, M. L., & Boone-Holladay, T. (2016). *Couples in conflict: Classic edition.* Routledge.

Bosworth, K., Espelage, D. L., & Simon, T. R. (1999). Factors associated with bullying behavior in middle school students. *Journal of Early Adolescence, 19,* 341–362.

Bouman, T. K. (2003). Intra- and interpersonal consequences of experimentally induced concealment. *Behaviour Research & Therapy, 41*(8), 959–968.

Bowlby, J. (1969). *Attachment and loss: Vol. 1, Attachment.* Basic Books.

Bowlby, J. (1973). *Attachment and loss: Vol. 2, Separation: Anxiety and anger.* Basic Books.

Bowlby, J. (1977). The making and breaking of affectional bonds. *British Journal of Psychiatry, 130,* 201–210.

Boxer, D., & Cortés-Conde, F. (1997). From bonding to biting: Conversational joking and identity display. *Journal of Pragmatics, 27,* 275–294.

Bradbury, T. N., & Fincham, F. D. (1990). Attributions in marriage: Review and critique. *Psychological Bulletin, 107,* 3–33.

Bradfield, M., & Aquino, K. (1999). The effects of blame attributions and offender likableness on forgiveness and revenge in the workplace. *Journal of Management, 25,* 607–631.

Brand, R. J., Markey, C. M., Mills, A., & Hodges, S. D. (2007). Sex differences in self-reported infidelity and its correlates. *Sex Roles, 57,* 101–109.

Brashers, D. E. (2001). Communication and uncertainty management. *Journal of Communication, 51,* 477–497.

Brashers, D. E., Neidig, J. L., & Goldsmith, D. J. (2004). Social support and the management of uncertainty for people living with HIV or AIDS. *Health Communication, 16,* 305–331.

Breiding, M. J. (2014). Prevalence and characteristics of sexual violence, stalking, and intimate partner violence victimization—National Intimate Partner and Sexual Violence Survey, United States, 2011. *Morbidity and Mortality Weekly Report Surveillance Summaries, 63,* 1–18.

Brennan, K. A., & Shaver, P. R. (1995). Dimensions of adult attachment, affect regulation, and romantic relationship functioning. *Personality and Social Psychology Bulletin, 21,* 267–283.

Bringle, R. G. (1991). Psychosocial aspects of jealousy: A transactional model. In P. Salovey (Ed.), *The psychology of jealousy and envy* (pp. 103–131). Guilford.

Brown, D. E. (1991). *Human universals.* McGraw-Hill.

Bryant, C. M., & Conger, R. D. (1999). Marital success and domains of social support in long-term relationships: Does the influence of network members ever end? *Journal of Marriage and the Family, 61,* 437–450.

Buel, S. M. (1999). Fifty obstacles to leaving, a.k.a., why abuse victims stay. *Family Violence, 28,* 19–28.

Buller, D. B., & Burgoon, J. K. (1994). Deception: Strategic and nonstrategic communication. In J. A. Daly & J. M. Wiemann (Eds.), *Strategic interpersonal communication* (pp. 191–224). Erlbaum.

Burgess, A. W., Baker, T., Greening, D., Hartman, C. R., Burgess, A. G., Douglas, J. E., & Halloran, R. (1997). Stalking behaviors within domestic violence. *Journal of Family Violence, 12,* 389–403.

Burgoon, J. K., Buller, D. B., Ebesu, A. S., & Rockwell, P. (2009). Interpersonal deception: V. Accuracy in deception detection. *Communication Monographs, 61*, 303–325.

Burgoon, J. K., Buller, D. B., & Floyd, K. (2001). Does participation affect deception success? A test of the interactivity principle. *Human Communication Research, 27*, 503–534.

Burgoon, J. K., Buller, D. B., & Woodall, G. B. (1996). *Nonverbal communication: The unspoken dialogue* (2nd edition). McGraw-Hill.

Burgoon, J. K., Guerrero, L. K., & Floyd, K. (2010). *Nonverbal communication*. Pearson.

Burgoon, J. K., Proudfoot, J. G., Schuetzler, R., & Wilson, D. (2014). Patterns of nonverbal behavior associated with truth and deception: Illustrations from three experiments. *Journal of Nonverbal Behavior, 38*, 325–354. doi: 10.1007/s10919-014-0181-5

Burgoon, J. K., Schuetzler, R., & Wilson, D. W. (2015). Kinesic patterning in deceptive and truthful interactions. *Journal of Nonverbal Behavior, 39*, 1–24.

Burgoon, J. K., Stern, L. A., & Dillman, L. (1995). *Interpersonal adaptation: Dyadic interaction patterns*. Cambridge University Press.

Burleson, B. R., & MacGeorge, E. L. (2002). Supportive communication. In M. E. Knapp & J. A. Daly (Eds.), *Handbook of interpersonal communication* (pp. 374–424). SAGE.

Burnette, J. L., McCullough, M. E., Van Tongeren, D. R., & Davis, D. E. (2012). Forgiveness results from integrating information about relationship value and exploitation risk. *Personality and Social Psychology Bulletin, 38*, 345–356.

Bushman, B. J., & Baumeister, R. F. (1998). Threatened egotism, narcissism, self-esteem, and direct and displaced aggression: Does self-love or self-hate lead to violence? *Journal of Personality and Social Psychology, 75*, 219–229.

Bushman, B. J., Baumeister, R. F., & Phillips, C. M. (2001). Do people aggress to improve their mood? Catharsis beliefs, affect regulation opportunity, and aggressive responding. *Journal of Personality and Social Psychology, 81*, 17–32.

Buss, D. M. (1988). Love acts: The evolutionary biology of love. In R. J. Sternberg & M. L. Barnes (Eds.), *The psychology of love* (pp. 100–117). Yale University Press.

Buss, D. M. (1989). Sex differences in human mate preferences: Evolutionary hypotheses tested in 37 cultures. *Behavioral and Brain Sciences, 12*, 1–49.

Buss, D. M. (1994). *The evolution of desire: Strategies of mate selection*. Basic Books.

Buss, D. M. (2000). *The dangerous passion: Why jealousy is as necessary as love and sex*. The Free Press.

Buss, D. M., Larsen, R. J., Westen, D., & Semmelroth, J. (1992). Sex differences in jealousy: Evolution, physiology, and psychology. *Psychological Science, 3*, 251–255.

Buss, D. M., & Shackelford, T. D. (1997). Susceptibility to infidelity in the first year of marriage. *Journal of Research in Personality, 31*, 193–221.

Buunk, B. P. (1982). Strategies of jealousy: Styles of coping with extramarital involvement of the spouse. *Family Relations, 31*, 13–18.

Buunk, B. P. (1987). Conditions that promote breakups as a consequence of extradyadic involvements. *Journal of Social and Clinical Psychology, 5*, 271–284.

Byrne, D. (1971). *The attraction paradigm.* Academic Press.

Cai, D. A. (2016). Conflict styles and strategies. In C. R. Berger, M. E. Roloff, & J. P. Caughlin (Eds.), *International encyclopedia of interpersonal communication.* Wiley.

Camden, C., Motley, M. T., & Wilson, A. (1984). White lies in interpersonal communication: A taxonomy and preliminary investigation of social motivations. *Western Journal of Communication, 48,* 309–325.

Cameron, J. J., Ross, M., & Holmes, J. G. (2002). Loving the one you hurt: Positive effects of recounting a transgression against an intimate partner. *Journal of Experimental Social Psychology, 38,* 307–314.

Canary, D. J., & Cupach, W. R. (1988). Relational and episodic characteristics associated with conflict tactics. *Journal of Social and Personal Relationships, 5,* 305–325.

Canary, D. J., Cupach, W. R., & Messman, S. J. (1995). *Relationship conflict.* SAGE.

Canary, D. J., & Spitzberg, B. H. (1987). Appropriateness and effectiveness perceptions of conflict strategies. *Human Communication Research, 14,* 93–120.

Canary, D. J., & Spitzberg, B. H. (1989). A model of the perceived competence of conflict strategies. *Human Communication Research, 15,* 630–649.

Card, N. A., Stucky, B. D., Sawalni, G. M., & Little, T. D. (2008). Direct and indirect aggression during childhood and adolescence: A meta-analytic review of gender differences, intercorrelations, and relations to maladjustment. *Child Development, 79,* 1185–1229.

Carpenter, C. J. (2012). Meta-analyses of sex differences in responses to sexual versus emotional infidelity: Men and women are more similar than different. *Psychology of Women Quarterly, 36,* 25–37.

Carpenter, C. J., & Spottswood, E. L. (2021). Extending the hyperpersonal model to observing others: The hyperperception model. *Journal of Communication Technology, 4,* 58–81.

Carpenter, C. J., & Spottswood, E. L. (2021). The hyperperception model: When your partner's new friends inspire jealousy and failing to use social distancing. *Cyberpsychology, Behavior, and Social Networking, 24,* 439–443.

Carr, J. L., & VanDeusen, K. M. (2004). Risk factors for male sexual aggression on college campuses. *Journal of Family Violence, 19,* 279–289.

Carson, C. L., & Cupach, W. R. (2000). Fueling the flames of the green-eyed monster: The role of ruminative thought in reaction to romantic jealous. *Western Journal of Communication, 64,* 308–329.

Caso, L., Maricchiolo, F., Bonaiuto, M., Vrij, A., & Mann, S. (2006). The impact of deception and suspicion on different hand movements. *Journal of Nonverbal Behavior, 30,* 1–19.

Cass, A. I., & Rosay, A. B. (2012). College student perceptions of criminal justice system responses to stalking. *Sex Roles, 66,* 392–404.

Catalano, S. (2012). *Intimate partner violence, 1993–2010.* U.S. Department of Justice.

Caughlin, J. P. (2010). A multiple goals theory of personal relationships: Conceptual integration and program overview. *Journal of Social and Personal Relationships, 27,* 824–848.

Caughlin, J. P., & Afifi, T. D. (2004). When is topic avoidance unsatisfying? Examining moderators of the association between avoidance and satisfaction. *Human Communication Research, 30*, 479–513.

Caughlin, J. P., Afifi, W. A., Carpenter-Theune, K. E., & Miller, L. E. (2005). Reasons for, and consequences of, revealing personal secrets in close relationships. *Personal Relationships, 12*, 43–59.

Caughlin, J. P., & Golish. T. D. (2002). An analysis of the association between topic avoidance and dissatisfaction: Comparing perceptual and interpersonal explanations. *Communication Monographs, 69*(4), 275–295.

Caughlin, J. P., & Petronio, S. (2004). Privacy in families. In A. L. Vangelisti (Ed.), *Handbook of family communication* (pp. 379–412). Erlbaum.

Caughlin, J. P., Scott, A. M., Miller, L. E., & Hefner, V. (2009). When information is supposedly a secret. *Journal of Social and Personal Relationships, 26*, 713–743.

Caughlin, J. P., & Vangelisti, A. L. (2009). Why people conceal or reveal secrets: A multiple goals theory perspective. In T. Afifi & W. Afifi (Eds.), *Uncertainty, information management, and disclosure decisions: Theories and applications* (pp. 279–299). Routledge.

Charny, I. W., & Parnass, S. (1995). The impact of extramarital relationships on the continuation of marriages. *Journal of Sex and Marital Therapy, 21*, 100–114.

Chaulk, K., & Jones, T. (2011). Online obsessive relational intrusion: Further concerns about Facebook. *Journal of Family Violence, 26*, 245–254.

Chory-Assad, R. M., & Booth-Butterfield, M. (2001). Secret test use and self-esteem in deteriorating relationships. *Communication Research Reports, 18*, 147–157.

Christensen, A., & Heavey, C. L. (1990). Gender and social structure in the demand/withdraw pattern of marital conflict. *Journal of Personality and Social Psychology, 59*(1), 73–81.

Cloven, D. H., & Roloff, M. E. (1991). Sense-making activities and interpersonal conflict: Communicative cures for the mulling blues. *Western Journal of Speech Communication, 55*, 134–158.

Cobb, J. (1979). Morbid jealousy. *British Journal of Hospital Medicine, 21*, 511–518.

Cody, M. J. (1982). A typology of disengagement strategies and an examination of the role intimacy, reactions to inequity, and relational problems play in strategy selection. *Communication Monographs, 49*, 148–170.

Cohen, D., & Nisbett, R. E. (1997). Field experiments examining the culture of honor: The role of institutions in perpetuating norms about violence. *Personality and Social Psychology Bulletin, 23*, 1188–1199.

Cohen, D., Nisbett, R. E., Bowdle, B. R., & Schwarz, N. (1996). Insult, aggression, and the Southern culture of honor: An experimental ethnography. *Interpersonal Relations and Group Processes, 70*, 945–960.

Cole, T. (2001). Lying to the one you love: The use of deception in romantic relationships. *Journal of Social and Personal Relationships, 18*, 107–129.

Coleman, P. K., & Byrd, C. P. (2003). Interpersonal correlates of peer victimization among young adolescents. *Journal of Youth and Adolescence, 32*, 301–314.

Comadena, M. E. (1992). Accuracy in detecting deception: Intimate and friendship relationships. In M. Burgoon (Ed.), *Communication yearbook 6* (pp. 446–472). SAGE.

Confer, J. C., & Cloud, M. D. (2011). Sex differences in response to imagining a partner's heterosexual or homosexual affair. *Personality & Individual Differences, 50,* 129–134.

Costa, P. T., & McCrae, R. R. (1992). Four ways five factors are basic. *Personality and Individual Differences, 13,* 653–665.

Crombag, H., Rassin, E., & Horselenberg, R. (2003). On vengeance. *Psychology, Crime, & Law, 94,* 333–334.

Crowley, J. P. (2012). Marshaling network support for romantic relationships: Towards the development of a typology. *Qualitative Communication Research, 1,* 315–346.

Crowley, J. P. (2015). Marshaling social support. In C. R. Berger & M. E. Roloff (Eds.), *International encyclopedia of interpersonal communication.* Wiley.

Crowley, J. P., Denes, A., Makos, S., & Whitt, J. (2018). Threats to courtship and the physiological response: Testosterone mediates the association between relational uncertainty and disclosure for dating partner recipients of relational transgressions. *Adaptive Human Behavior and Physiology, 4,* 264–282.

Crowley, J. P., & Faw, M. H. (2014). Support marshaling for romantic relationships: Empirical validation of a support marshaling typology. *Personal Relationships, 21,* 242–257.

Cunradi, C. B., Caetano, R., & Schafer, J. (2002). Socioeconomic predictors of intimate partner violence among White, Black, and Hispanic couples in the United States. *Journal of Family Violence, 17,* 377–389.

Cupach, W. R., & Metts, S. (1986). Accounts of relational dissolution: A comparison of marital and non-marital relationships. *Communication Monographs, 53,* 311–322.

Cupach, W. R., & Spitzberg, B. H. (Eds.) (1994). *The dark side of interpersonal communication.* Erlbaum.

Cupach, W. R., & Spitzberg, B. H. (1998). Obsessive relational intrusion and stalking. In B. H. Spitzberg & W. R. Cupach (Eds.), *The dark side of close relationships* (pp. 233–263). Erlbaum.

Cupach, W. R., & Spitzberg, B. H. (2000). Obsessive relational intrusion: Incidence, perceived severity, and coping. *Violence and Victims, 15,* 357–372.

Cupach, W. R., & Spitzberg, B. H. (2004). *The dark side of relationship pursuit: From attraction to obsession and stalking.* Erlbaum.

Cupach, W. R., Spitzberg, B. H., & Carson, C. L. (2000). Toward a theory of obsessive relational intrusion and stalking. In K. Dindia & S. Duck (Eds.), *Communication and personal relationships* (pp. 131–146). Wiley.

Dailey, R. M., Pfiester, A., Jin, B., Beck, G., & Clark, G. (2009). On-again, off-again dating relationships: How are they different from other dating relationships? *Personal Relationships, 16,* 23–47.

Daly, M., & Wilson, M. (1988). *Homicide.* Aldine de Gruyter.

Dank, M., Lachman, P., Zweig, J. M., & Yahner, J. (2014). Dating violence experiences of lesbian, gay, bisexual, and transgender youth. *Journal of Youth and Adolescence, 43,* 846–857.

Davis, K. E., Ace, A., & Andra, M. (2000). Stalking perpetrators and psychological maltreatment of partners: Anger-jealousy, attachment insecurity, need for control, and break-up context. *Violence and Victims, 15*, 407–425.

Davis, K. E., Swan, S. C., & Gambone, L. J. (2012). Why doesn't he just leave me alone? Persistent pursuit: A critical review of theories and evidence. *Sex Roles, 66*, 329–339.

Davis, L. E., & Strube, M. J. (1993). An assessment of romantic commitment among Black and White dating couples. *Journal of Applied Social Psychology, 23*, 212–225.

Davis, M., Markus, K., Walters, S. B., Vorus, N., & Connors, B. (2005). Behavioral cues to deception vs. topic incriminating potential in criminal confessions. *Law and Human Behavior, 29*, 483–704.

Denes, A., Dillow, M.R., Lannutti, P. J., & Bevan, J. (2020). Acceptable experimentation?: Investigating reasons for same-sex infidelity and women's anticipated responses to a male partner's hypothetical same-sex infidelity. *Personality & Individual Differences, 160*. https://doi.org/10.1016/j.paid.2020.109929

Denes, A., Lannutti, P. J., & Bevan, J. L. (2015). Same-sex infidelity in heterosexual romantic relationships: Investigating emotional, relational, and communicative responses. *Personal Relationships, 22*, 414–430.

Dennison, S. M., & Thomson, D. M. (2002). Identifying stalking: The relevance of intent in commonsense reasoning. *Law and Human Behavior, 26*, 543–561.

DePaulo, B. M., Ansfield, M. E., Kirkendol, S. E., & Boden, J. M. (2004). Serious lies. *Basic and Applied Social Psychology, 26*, 147–167.

DePaulo, B. M., & Kashy, D. A. (1998). Everyday lies in close and casual relationships. *Journal of Personality and Social Psychology, 74*, 63–79.

DePaulo, B. M., Kashy, D. A., Kirkendol, S. E., Wyer, M. M., & Epstein, J. A. (1996). Lying in everyday life. *Journal of Personality and Social Psychology, 70*, 979–995.

DePaulo B. M., & Kirkendol S.E. (1989). The motivational impairment effect in the communication of deception. In Yuille J. C. (Ed.) *Credibility assessment.* Nato Science (Vol. 47). Springer.

DePaulo, B. M., Lindsay, J. J., Malone, B. E., Muhlenbruck, L., Charlton, K., & Cooper, H. (2003). Cues to deception. *Psychological Bulletin, 129*, 74–118.

DePaulo, B. M., Stone, J. L., & Lassiter, G. D. (1985). Deceiving and detecting deceit. In B. R. Schlenker (Ed.), *The self and social life* (pp. 323–370). McGraw-Hill.

DePaulo, B. M., Zuckerman, M., & Rosenthal, R. (1980). Humans as lie detectors. *Journal of Communication, 30*, 129–139.

de Quervain, D. J. F., Fischbacher, U., Treyer, V., Schellhammer, M., Schnyder, U., Buck, A., & Fehr, E. (2004). The neural basis of altruistic punishment. *Science, 305*, 1254–1258.

Derby, K., Knox, D., & Easterling, B. (2012). Snooping in romantic relationships. *College Student Journal, 46*(2), 333–343.

Derlega, V. J., Metts, S., Petronio, S., & Margulis, S. T. (1993). *Self-disclosure.* SAGE.

DeRosier, M. E., Cillessen, A. H. N., Coie, J. D., & Dodge, K. A. (1994). Group social context and children's aggressive behavior. *Child Development, 65*, 1068–1079.

DeSteno, D. A., & Salovey, P. (1996). Evolutionary origins of sex differences in jealousy? Questioning the "fitness" of the model. *Psychological Science, 7,* 367–372.

deTurck, M. A., & Miller, G. R. (1985). Deception and arousal: Isolating the behavioral correlates of deception. *Human Communication Research, 12,* 181–201.

DeWall, C. N., MacDonald, G., Webster, G. D., Masten, C. L., Baumeister, R. L., Powell, C., Combs, D., Schurtz, D. R., Stillman, T. F., Tice, D. M., & Eisenberger, N. I. (2010). Acetaminophen reduces social pain: Behavioral and neural evidence. *Psychological Science, 21,* 931–937.

DiCioccio, R. D. (2010). The interactionist model of teasing communication. In T. A. Avtgis & A. S. Rancer (Eds.), *Arguments, aggression, and conflict: New directions in theory and research* (pp. 340–356). Taylor & Francis.

Dijkstra, P., Barelds, D. P. H., & Groothof, H. A. K. (2013). Jealousy in response to online and offline infidelity: The role of sex and sexual orientation. *Scandinavian Journal of Psychology, 54,* 328–336.

Dijkstra, P., Groothof, H. A. K., Poel, G. A., Laverman, T. T. G., Schrier, M. A., & Buunk, B. P. (2001). Sex differences in the events that elicit jealousy among homosexuals. *Personal Relationships, 8,* 41–54.

Dill, J. C., & Anderson, C. A. (1995). Effects of frustration justification on hostile aggression. *Aggressive Behavior, 21,* 359–369.

Dillow, M. R. (2016). Relationship transgressions. In C. R. Berger & M. E. Roloff (Eds.), *International encyclopedia of interpersonal communication.* Wiley.

Dillow, M R. (2019). Relational transgressions and forgiveness. In J. J. Ponzetti Jr. (Ed.), *Macmillan encyclopedia of intimate and family relationships: An interdisciplinary approach.* Macmillan.

Dillow, M. R., Afifi, W. A., & Matsunaga, M. (2012). Perceived partner uniqueness and communicative and behavioral transgression outcomes in romantic relationships. *Journal of Social and Personal Relationships, 29,* 28–51.

Dillow, M. R., Malachowski, C. C., Brann, M., & Weber, K. D. (2011). An experimental examination of the effects of communicative infidelity motives on communication and relational outcomes in romantic relationships. *Western Journal of Communication, 75,* 473–499.

Ditzen, B., Hahlweg, K., Fehm-Wolfsdorf, G., & Baucom, D. (2011). Assisting couples to develop healthy relationships: Effects of couples relationship education on cortisol. *Psychoneuroendocrinology, 36,* 597–607.

Drigotas, S. M., & Rusbult, C. E. (1992). Should I stay or should I go? A dependence model of breakups. *Journal of Personality and Social Psychology, 62,* 62–87.

Drigotas, S. M., Safstrom, C. A., & Gentilia, T. (1999). An investment model prediction of dating infidelity. *Journal of Personality and Social Psychology, 77,* 509–524.

Driscoll, R., Davis, K. E., & Lipetz, M. E. (1972). Parental interference and romantic love: The Romeo and Juliet effect. *Journal of Personality and Social Psychology, 24,* 1–10.

Dobash R. E., & Dobash, R. P. (2015). *When men murder women.* Oxford University Press.

Dobash, R. P., Dobash, R. E., Cavanaugh, K., & Lewis, R. (1998). Separate and intersecting realities: A comparison of men's and women's accounts of violence against women. *Violence Against Women, 4*, 382–414.

Donne, M. D., DeLuca, J., Pleskach, P., Bromson, C., Mosley, M. P., Perez, E. T., Mathews, S. G., Stephenson, R., & Frye, V. (2018). Barriers and facilitators of help-seeking among men who experience sexual violence. *American Journal of Men's Health, 12*, 189–201.

Duck, S. (1994). Stratagems, spoils, and a serpent's tooth: On the delights and dilemmas of personal relationships. In W. R. Cupach & B. H. Spitzberg (Eds.), *The dark side of interpersonal communication* (pp. 3–24). Erlbaum.

Duck, S. W. (1992). *Human relations* (2nd ed.). SAGE.

Dunn, J. (1983). Sibling relationships in early childhood. *Child Development, 54*, 787–811.

Dutton, D. G., & Karakanta, C. (2013). Depression as a risk marker for aggression: A critical review. *Aggression and Violent Behavior, 18*, 310–319.

Dutton, M. A., & Goodman, L. A. (2005). Coercion in intimate partner violence: Toward a new conceptualization. *Sex Roles, 52*, 743–756.

Eaton, J. (2013). The effects of third-party validation and minimization on judgments of the transgressor and the third party. *British Journal of Social Psychology, 52*, 273–289.

Eaton, J. & Sanders, C. B. (2012). A little help from our friends: Informal third parties and interpersonal conflict. *Personal Relationships, 19*, 623–643.

Eder, D. (1991). The role of teasing in adolescent peer group culture. *Sociological Studies of Child Development, 4*, 181–197.

Eder, D. (1993). "Go get ya a French!": Romantic and sexual teasing among adolescent girls. In D. Tannen (Ed.), *Gender and conversational interaction* (pp. 17–31). Oxford University Press.

Eisenberger, N. I., Lieberman, M. D., & Williams, K. D. (2003). Does rejection hurt? An fMRI study of social exclusion. *Science, 302*, 290–292.

Ekman, P. (1981). Mistakes when deceiving. *Annals of the New York Academy of Sciences, 364*, 269–278.

Ekman, P. (1985). *Telling lies: Clues to deceit in the marketplace, politics, and marriage.* Norton.

Ekman, P. (1988). Lying and nonverbal behavior: Theoretical issues and new findings. *Journal of Nonverbal Behavior, 12*, 163–175.

Ekman, P. (1992). *Telling lies: Clues to deceit in the marketplace, marriage, and politics.* Norton.

Ekman, P., & Friesen, W. V. (1969). Nonverbal leakage and clues to deception. *Psychiatry, 32*, 88–106.

Ekman, P., Friesen, W. V., & O'Sullivan, M. (1988). Smiles when lying. *Journal of Personality and Social Psychology, 54*, 414–420.

Elphinston, R. A., Feeney, J. A., & Noller, P. (2011). Measuring romantic jealousy: Validation of the multidimensional jealousy scale in Australian samples. *Australian Journal of Psychology, 63*, 243–251.

Elphinston, R. A., & Noller, P. (2011). Time to face it! Facebook intrusion and the implications for romantic jealousy and relationship satisfaction. *Cyberpsychology, Behavior, and Social Networking, 14*, 631–635.

Elshout, M., Nelissen, R. M. A., & van Beest, I. (2015). A prototype analysis of vengeance. *Personal Relationships, 22*, 502–523.

Emmers-Sommer, T. M. (2003). When partners falter: Repair after a transgression. In D. J. Canary & M. Dainton (Eds.), *Maintaining relationships through communication: Relational, contextual, and cultural variations* (pp. 185–205). Erlbaum.

Epstein, R. (2007). The truth about online dating. *Scientific American Mind, 18*, 28–35.

Exline, J. J., Baumeister, R. F., Bushman, B. J., Campbell, W. K., & Finkel, E. J. (2004). Too proud to let go: Narcissistic entitlement as a barrier to forgiveness. *Journal of Personality and Social Psychology, 87*, 894–912.

Fan, C., Chu, X., Zhang, M., & Zhou, Z. (2019). Are narcissists more likely to be involved in cyberbullying? Examining the mediating role of self-esteem. *Journal of Interpersonal Violence, 34*, 3127–3150.

Fanti, K. A., Demetriou, G. G., & Hawa, V. V. (2012). A longitudinal study of cyberbullying: Examining risk and protective factors. *European Journal of Developmental Psychology, 9*, 168–181.

Faw, M. H., & Pederson, J. R. (2018). Network member support marshaling in response to another's relational transgression experience. *Qualitative Research Reports in Communication, 19*, 86–93.

Feeney, J. A. (2004). Hurt feelings in couple relationships: Towards integrative models of the negative effects of hurtful events. *Journal of Social and Personal Relationships, 21*, 487–508.

Feeney, J. A. (2005). Hurt feelings in couple relationships: Exploring the role of attachment and perceptions of personal injury. *Personal Relationships, 12*, 253–271.

Feeney, J. A., & Hill, A. (2006). Victim-perpetrator differences in reports of hurtful events. *Journal of Social and Personal Relationships, 23*, 587–608.

Fehr, B., & Baldwin, M. (1996). Prototype and script analysis of laypeople's knowledge of anger. In G. J. O. Fletcher & J. Fitness (Eds.), *Knowledge structures in close relationships: A social psychological approach* (pp. 219–245). Erlbaum.

Fehr, R., Gelfand, M. J., & Nag, M. (2010). The road to forgiveness: A meta-analytic synthesis of its situational and dispositional correlates. *Psychological Bulletin, 136*, 894–914.

Fife, S. T., Weeks, G. R., & Stellberg-Filbert, J. (2013). Facilitating forgiveness in the treatment of infidelity: An interpersonal model. *Journal of Family Therapy, 35*(4), 343–367.

Finch, E. (2001). *The criminalization of stalking: Constructing the problem and evaluating the solution.* Cavendish.

Fincham, F. D. (2000). The kiss of the porcupines: From attributing responsibility to forgiving. *Personal Relationships, 7*(1), 1–23.

Fincham, F. D., & Bradbury, T. (1989). Attribution of responsibility in close relationships: Egocentric bias or partner-centric bias? *Journal of Marriage and the Family, 51*, 27–35.

Finkel, E. J., Rusbult, C. E., Kumashiro, M., & Hannon, P. A. (2002). Dealing with betrayal in close relationships: Does commitment promote forgiveness? *Journal of Personality and Social Psychology, 82,* 956–974.

Finkenauer, C., Frijns, T., Engels, R. C. M. E., & Kerkhof, P. (2005). Perceiving concealment in relationships between parents and adolescents: Links with parental behavior. *Personal Relationships, 12,* 387–406.

Finkenauer, C., Kerkhof, P., Righetti, F., & Branje, S. (2009). Living together apart: Perceived concealment as a signal of exclusion in marital relationships. *Personality and Social Psychology Bulletin, 35,* 1410–1422.

Fitness, J. (2001). Betrayal, rejection, revenge, and forgiveness: An interpersonal script approach. In M. R. Leary (Ed.), *Interpersonal rejection* (pp. 73–103). Oxford University Press.

Fitzpatrick, M. A. & Winke, J. (1979). You always hurt the one you love: Strategies and tactics in interpersonal conflict. *Communication Quarterly, 27,* 3–11.

Fleuriet, C., Cole, M., Guerrero, L. K. (2014). Exploring Facebook: Attachment style and nonverbal message characteristics as predictors of anticipated emotional reactions to Facebook postings. *Journal of Nonverbal Behavior, 38,* 429–450.

Fleischmann, A. A., Spitzberg, B. H., Andersen, P. A., & Roesch, S. C. (2005). Tickling the monster: Jealousy induction in relationships. *Journal of Social and Personal Relationships, 22,* 49–73.

Folkes, V. S. (1982). Communicating the reasons for social rejection. *Journal of Experimental Social Psychology, 18,* 235–252.

Forste, R., & Tanfer, K. (1996). Sexual exclusivity among dating, cohabiting, and married women. *Journal of Marriage and the Family, 58,* 33–47.

Fox, J., & Anderegg, C. (2014). Romantic relationship stages and social networking sites: Uncertainty reduction strategies and perceived relational norms on Facebook. *Cyberpsychology, Behavior, and Social Networking, 17,* 685–691.

Fox, J., & Tokunaga, R. A. (2015). Romantic partner monitoring after breakups: Attachment, dependence, distress, and post-dissolution online surveillance via social networking sites. *Cyberpsychology, Behavior, and Social Networking, 18,* 491–498.

Fox, J., & Warber, K. M. (2014). Social networking sites in romantic relationships: Attachment, uncertainty, and partner surveillance on Facebook. *Cyberpsychology, Behavior, and Social Networking, 17,* 3–7.

Fraley, R. C., & Shaver, P. R. (1997). Adult attachment and the suppression of unwanted thoughts. *Journal of Personality and Social Psychology, 73,* 1080–1091.

Franklin, C. A. (2016). Sorority affiliation and sexual assault victimization: Assessing vulnerability using path analysis. *Violence Against Women, 22,* 895–922.

Frederick, D. A., & Fales, M. R. (2016). Upset over sexual versus emotional infidelity among gay, lesbian, bisexual, and heterosexual adults. *Archives of Sexual Behavior, 45,* 175–191.

Frenkel-Brunswick, W. (1948). Intolerance of ambiguity as an emotional and perceptual personality variable. *Journal of Personality, 18,* 108–123.

Frenkel-Brunswick, W. (1949). Tolerance toward ambiguity as a personality variable. *American Psychologist, 3,* 268.

Frijda, N. H. (1994). The lex talionis: On vengeance. In S. H. M. van Goozen, N. E. Van de Poll, & J. A. Sergeant (Eds.), *Emotions: Essays on emotion theory* (pp. 263–289). Erlbaum.

Funk, F., McGeer, V., & Gollwitzer, M. (2014). Get the message: Punishment is satisfactory if the transgressor responds to its communicative intent. *Personality and Social Psychology Bulletin, 40,* 986–997.

Furnham, A., & Marks, J. (2013). Tolerance of ambiguity: A review of recent literature. *Psychology, 4,* 717–728.

Gabriels, J. B., & Strelan, P. (2018). For whom we forgive matters: Relationship focus magnifies, but self- focus buffers against the negative effects of forgiving an exploitative partner. *British Journal of Social Psychology, 57*(1), 154–173.

Galen, B. R., & Underwood, M. K. (1997). A developmental investigation of social aggression among children. *Developmental Psychology, 3,* 589–600.

Garland, D. R. (1981). Training married couples in listening skills: Effects on behavior, perceptual accuracy, and marital adjustment. *Family Relations, 30,* 297–307.

Garrard, E., & McNaughton, D. (2010). *Forgiveness.* Routledge.

Geen, R. G. (2001). *Human aggression* (2nd ed.). Taylor and Francis.

George, J. F., & Robb, A. (2008). Deception and computer-mediated communication in daily life. *Communication Reports, 21,* 92–103.

Georgesen, J. C., Harris, M. J., Milich, R., & Young, J. (1999). "Just teasing …": Personality effects on perceptions and life narratives of childhood teasing. *Personality and Social Psychology Bulletin, 25,* 1254–1267.

Gibbs, J. L., Ellison, N. B., & Lai, C. H. (2011). First comes love, then comes Google: An investigation of uncertainty reduction strategies and self-disclosure in online dating. *Communication Research, 38,* 70–100.

Gilmartin, B. G. (1987). Peer group antecedents of severe love-shyness in males. *Journal of Personality, 55,* 467–489.

Glass, S. P. (2003). *Not "just friends": Protect your relationship from infidelity and heal the trauma of betrayal.* The Free Press.

Glass, S. P., & Wright, T. (1985). Sex differences in type of extramarital involvement and marital dissatisfaction. *Sex Roles, 12,* 1101–1120.

Glass, S. P., & Wright, T. (1992). Justifications for extramarital relationships: The association between attitudes, behaviors, and gender. *Journal of Sex Research, 29,* 361–387.

Govier, T. (1999). Forgiveness and the unforgivable. *American Philosophical Quarterly, 36,* 59–75.

Goldsmith, D. J. (2004). *Communicating social support.* Cambridge University Press.

Goodboy, A. K., Bolkan, S., Brisini, K., & Solomon, D. H. (2021). Relational uncertainty within the relational turbulence theory: The bifactor exploratory structural equation model. *Journal of Communication, 71*(3), 403–430.

Goodboy, A. K., Bolkan, S., Sharabi, L. L., Myers, S. A., & Baker, J. P. (2020). The relational turbulence model: A meta-analytic review. *Human Communication Research, 46,* 229–249.

Goodboy, A. K., & Martin, M. M. (2015). The personality profile of a cyberbully: Examining the dark triad. *Computers in Human Behavior, 49*, 1–4.

Goodman, L. A., Salyers, M. P., Mueser, K. T., Rosenberg, S. D., Swartz, M., Essock, S. M., Osher, F. C., Butterfield, M. I., & Swanson, J. (2001). Recent victimization in women and men with severe mental illness: Prevalence and correlates. *Journal of Traumatic Stress, 14*, 615–632.

Gottman, J. M. (1994). *What predicts divorce?* Erlbaum.

Gottman, J. M., & Levenson, R. W. (1988). The social psychophysiology of marriage. In P. Noller & M. A. Fitzpatrick (Eds.), *Perspectives on marital interaction* (pp. 182–200). Multilingual Matters.

Gould, S. J. (2002). *The structure of evolutionary theory.* Harvard University Press.

Gouldner, A. W. (1960). The norm of reciprocity: A preliminary statement. *American Sociological Review, 25*, 161–178.

Gracia, E., Rodriguez, C. M., & Lila, M. (2015). Preliminary evaluation of an analog procedure to assess acceptability of intimate partner violence against women: The partner violence acceptability movie task. *Frontiers in Psychology, 6*, 1–7.

Gray, J. D., & Silver, R. C. (1990). Opposite sides of the same coin: Former spouses' divergent perspectives in coping with their divorce. *Journal of Personality and Social Psychology, 59*, 1180–1191.

Greeff, A. P. (2000). Characteristics of families that function well. *Journal of Family Issues, 21*, 948–962.

Green, J. D., Burnette, J. L., & Davis, J. L. (2008). Third-party forgiveness: (Not) forgiving your close other's betrayer. *Personality and Social Psychology Bulletin, 34*(3), 407–418.

Grimes, W. (2017, March 31). Francine Hughes Wilson, 69, domestic violence victim who took action, dies. *The New York Times.* https://www.nytimes.com/2017/03/31/us/francine-hughes-wilson-dead-burning-bed-defendant.html

Gross, M. E., & Guerrero, L. K. (2000). Managing conflict appropriately and effectively: An application of the competence model to Rahim's organizational conflict styles. *International Journal of Conflict Management, 11*, 200–226.

Groothof, H. A. K., Dijkstra, P., & Barelds, D. P. H. (2009). Sex differences in jealousy: The case of internet infidelity. *Journal of Social and Personal Relationships, 26*, 1119–1129.

Gruber, J., & Fineran, S. (2007). The impact of bullying and sexual harassment victimization on the mental and physical health of adolescents. *Violence Against Women, 13*, 627–643.

Guadagno, R. E., & Sagarin, B. J. (2010). Sex differences in jealousy: An evolutionary perspective on online infidelity. *Journal of Applied Social Psychology, 40*, 2636–2655.

Guerrero, L. K. (1998). Attachment style differences in the experience and expression of romantic jealousy. *Personal Relationships, 5*, 273–291.

Guerrero, L. K. (2012). Communicative responses to jealousy: How to cope with the green-eyed monster. In A. K. Goodboy & K. Shultz (Eds.), *Introduction to communication studies* (pp. 209–216). Kendall Hunt.

Guerrero, L. K. (2014). Jealousy and relational satisfaction: Actor effects, partner effects, and the mediating role of destructive communication responses to jealousy. *Western Journal of Communication, 78*, 586–611.

Guerrero, L. K. (2015). Attachment theory: A communication perspective. In D. O. Braithwaite & P. Schrodt (Eds.), *Engaging theories in interpersonal communication: Multiple perspectives* (2nd ed.). SAGE.

Guerrero, L. K., & Afifi, W. A. (1995a). Some things are better left unsaid: Topic avoidance in family relationships. *Communication Quarterly, 43*, 276–296.

Guerrero, L. K., & Afifi, W. A. (1998a). Communicative responses to jealousy as a function of self-esteem and relationship maintenance goals: A test of Bryson's dual motivation model. *Communication Reports, 11*, 111–122.

Guerrero, L. K., & Afifi, W. A. (1998b). What parents don't know: Topic avoidance in parent-child relationships. In T. J. Socha & G. H. Stamp (Eds.), *Parents, children, and communication: Frontiers of theory and research* (pp. 219–245). Erlbaum.

Guerrero, L. K., & Andersen, P. A. (1998a). The dark side of jealousy and envy: Desire, delusion, desperation, and destructive communication. In B. H. Spitzberg & W. R. Cupach (Eds.), *The dark side of relationships* (pp. 33–70). Erlbaum.

Guerrero, L. K., & Andersen, P. A. (1998b). Jealousy experience and expression in romantic relationships. In P. A. Andersen & L. K. Guerrero (Eds.), *Handbook of communication and emotion: Research, theory, applications, and contexts* (pp. 155–158). Academic Press.

Guerrero, L. K., Andersen, P. A., Jorgensen, P. F., Spitzberg, B. H., & Eloy, S. V. (1995). Coping with the green-eyed monster: Conceptualizing and measuring communicative responses to romantic jealousy. *Western Journal of Communication, 59*, 270–304.

Guerrero, L. K., & Bachman, G. F. (2008). Communication following relational transgressions in dating relationships: An investment model explanation. *Southern Communication Journal, 73*, 4–23.

Guerrero, L. K., & Bachman, G. F. (2010). Forgiveness and forgiving communication: An expectancy-investment model. *Journal of Social and Personal Relationships, 27*, 801–823.

Guerrero, L. K., & Eloy, S. V. (1992). Jealousy and relational satisfaction across marital types. *Communication Reports, 5*, 23–31.

Guerrero, L. K., Farinelli, L., & McEwan, B. (2009). Attachment and relational satisfaction: The mediating effect of emotional communication. *Communication Monographs, 76*, 487–514.

Guerrero, L. K., Hannawa, A. F., & Babin, E. A. (2011). The communicative responses to jealousy scale: Revision, empirical validation, and associations with relational satisfaction. *Communication Methods and Measures, 5*, 223–249.

Guerrero, L. K., & Jones, S. M. (2003). Differences in one's own and one's partner's perceptions of social skills as a function of attachment style. *Communication Quarterly, 51*, 277–295.

Guerrero, L. K., & Reiter R. L. (1998). Expressing emotion: Sex differences in social skills and communicative responses to anger, sadness, and jealousy. In D. J. Canary

& K. Dindia (Eds.), *Sex differences and similarities in communication* (pp. 321–350). Erlbaum.

Guerrero, L. K., Trost, M. L., & Yoshimura, S. M. (2005). Emotion and communication in the context of romantic jealousy. *Personal Relationships, 12,* 233–252.

Guthrie, J., & Kunkel, A. (2013). Tell me sweet (and not-so-sweet) little lies: Deception in romantic relationships. *Communication Studies, 64,* 141–157.

Hall, E. T. (1976). *Beyond culture.* Doubleday.

Hall, J. H., & Fincham, F. D. (2006). Relationship dissolution following infidelity. In M. A. Fine & J. A. Harvey (Eds.), *Handbook of divorce and relationship dissolution* (pp. 153–168). Routledge.

Hamby, S. L. (2018). Are women really as violent as men? The "gender symmetry" controversy. In C. M. Renzetti, J. L. Edleson, & R. K. Bergen (Eds.), *Sourcebook on violence against women* (3rd ed., pp. 49–71). SAGE.

Hample, D. (1980). Purposes and effects of lying. *The Southern Speech Communication Journal, 46,* 33–47.

Hample, D., Benoit, P. J., Houston, J., Purifoy, G., & Van Hyfte, V., & Wardwell, C. (1999). Naïve theories of argument: Avoiding interpersonal arguments or cutting them short. *Argumentation and Advocacy, 35,* 130–140.

Hancock, J. T., & Toma, C. L. (2009). Putting your best face forward: The accuracy of online dating photographs. *Journal of Communication, 59,* 367–386.

Haney, C., Banks, W. C., & Zimbardo, P. G. (1973). A study of prisoners and guards in a simulated prison. *Naval Research Review, 30,* 4–17.

Hansen, G. L. (1987). Extra-dyadic relations during courtship. *Journal of Sex Research, 23,* 382–390.

Hargreaves, D. (1967). *Social relations in a secondary school.* Routledge and Kegan Paul.

Harrigan, J. A., & O'Connell, D. M. (1996). Facial movements during anxiety states. *Personality and Individual Differences, 21,* 205–212.

Harris, C. (2003). A review of sex differences in sexual jealousy, including self-report data, psychophysiological responses, interpersonal violence, and morbid jealousy. *Personality and Social Psychology Review, 7,* 102–128.

Hartwig, M., & Bond, C. F. (2011). Why do lie-catchers fail? A lens model analysis of human lie judgments. *Psychological Bulletin, 137,* 643–659.

Hartwig, M., & Bond, D. F. (2014). Lie detection from multiple cues: A meta-analysis. *Applied Cognitive Psychology, 28,* 661–676.

Hartwig, M., Granhag, P. A., Stromwall, L. A., & Vrij, M. (2005). Detecting deception via strategic disclosure of evidence. *Law and Human Behavior, 29,* 469–484. https://doi.org/10.1007/s10979-005-5521-x

Harvey, J. H. (1987). Attributions in close relationships: Research and theoretical developments. *Journal of Social & Clinical Psychology, 5*(4), 420–434.

Hawk, S. T., Becht, A., & Branje, S. (2015). "Snooping" as a distinct parental monitoring strategy: Comparisons with overt solicitation and control. *Journal of Research on Adolescence, 26*(3), 443–458.

Hawker, D. S. J., & Boulton, M. J. (2000). Twenty years' research on peer victimization and psychosocial maladjustment: A meta-analytic review of cross-sectional studies. *The Journal of Child Psychology and Psychiatry and Allied Disciplines, 41,* 441–455.

Hayashi, A., Abe, N., Ueno, A., Shigemune, Y., Mori, E., Tashiro, M., & Fujii, T. (2010). Neural correlates of forgiveness for moral transgressions involving deception. *Brain Research, 1332,* 90–99.

Hays, R. B., Magee, R. H., & Chauncey, S. (1994). Identifying helpful and unhelpful behaviours of loved ones: The PWA's perspective. *AIDS Care, 6,* 379–392.

Heider, F. (1958). *The psychology of interpersonal relations.* Wiley.

Hemphill, S. A., Kotevski, A., Tollit, M., Smith, R., Herrenkohl, T. I., Toumbourou, J. W., & Catalano, R. F. (2012). Longitudinal predictors of cyber and traditional bullying perpetration in Australian secondary school students. *Journal of Adolescent Health, 51,* 59–65.

Henline, B. H., Lamke, L. K., & Howard, M. D. (2007). Exploring perceptions of online infidelity. *Personal Relationships, 14,* 113–128.

Hill, C. T., Rubin, Z., & Peplau, L. A. (1976). Breakups before marriage: The end of 103 affairs. *Journal of Social Issues, 32,* 147–168.

Hinduja, S., & Patchin, J. W. (2008). Cyberbullying: An exploratory analysis of factors related to offending and victimization. *Deviant Behavior, 29,* 129–156.

Hines, D. A., & Douglas, E. M. (2010). Intimate terrorism by women towards men: Does it exist? *Journal of Aggression, Conflict, and Peace Resolution, 2,* 36–56.

Hocker, J. L., & Wilmot, W. W. (1995). *Interpersonal conflict* (4th ed.). William C. Brown.

Hofstede, G. (1980). *Culture's consequences: International differences in work-related values.* SAGE.

Holland, M. K., & Tarlow, G. (1972). Blinking and mental load. *Psychological Reports, 31,* 119–127.

Holland, M. K., & Tarlow, G. (1975). Blinking and thinking. *Psychological Reports, 41,* 403–406.

Holley, S. R., Sturm, V. E., & Levenson, R. W. (2010). Exploring the basis for gender differences in the demand-withdraw pattern. *Journal of Homosexuality, 57*(5), 666–684.

Holmes, J. G., & Rempel, J. K. (1989). Trust in close relationships. In C. Hendrick (Ed.), *Close relationships* (pp. 187–220). SAGE.

Hooper, L., Puhl, R., Eisenberg, M. E., Crow, S., & Neumark-Sztainer, D. (2021). Weight teasing experienced during adolescence and young adulthood: Cross-sectional and longitudinal associations with disordered eating behaviors in an ethnically/racially and socioeconomically diverse sample. *International Journal of Eating Disorders, 54,* 1449–1462.

Hoover, J. H., & Olson, G. (2000). Sticks and stones may break their bones: Teasing as bullying. *Reclaiming Children and Youth, 9,* 87–91.

Horan, S. M., & Dillow, M. R. (2009). Deceivers and emotion: The relationships among deceptive message type, relational qualities, and guilt and shame. *Atlantic Journal of Communication, 17,* 149–165.

Hudson, M. B., Nicolas, S. C., Howser, M. E., Lipsett, K. E., Robinson, I. W., Pope, L. J., Hobby, A. F., & Friedman, D. R. (2015). Examining how gender and emoticons influence Facebook jealousy. *Cyberpsychology, Behavior, and Social Networking, 18*, 87–92.

Hunt, C., Peters, L., & Rapee, R. M. (2012). Development of a measure of the experience of being bullied in youth. *Psychological Assessment, 24*, 156–165.

Hurlbert, D. F., Apt, C., Gasar, S., Wilson, N. E., & Murphy, Y. (1994). Sexual narcissism: A validation study. *Journal of Sex and Marital Therapy, 20*, 24–34.

Infante, D. A. (1987). Aggressiveness. In J. C. McCroskey and J. A. Daly (Eds.), *Personality and interpersonal communication* (pp. 157–192). SAGE.

Infante, D. A., Chandler, T. A., & Rudd, J. E. (1989). Test of an argumentative skill deficiency model of interspousal violence. *Communication Monographs, 56*, 163–177.

Infante, D. A., & Rancer, A. S. (1996). Argumentativeness and verbal aggressiveness: A review of recent theory and research. *Annals of the International Communication Association, 19*, 319–352.

Jin, B. (2013). Hurtful texting in friendships: Satisfaction buffers the distancing effects of intention. *Communication Research Reports, 30*, 148–156.

Johnson, K. L., & Roloff, M. E. (1998). Serial arguing and relational quality: Determinants and consequences of perceived resolvability. *Communication Research, 25*, 327–343.

Johnson, M. P. (1995). Patriarchal terrorism and common couple violence: Two forms of violence against women. *Journal of Marriage and the Family, 57*, 283–294.

Johnson, M. P. (2008). *A typology of domestic violence: Intimate terrorism, violent resistance, and situational couple violence.* Northeastern University Press.

Johnson, M. P. (2011). Gender and types of intimate partner violence: A response to an anti-feminist literature review. *Aggression and Violent Behavior, 16*, 289–296.

Johnson, M. P., & Ferraro, K. J. (2000). Research on domestic violence in the 1990s: Making distinctions. *Journal of Marriage and the Family, 62*, 948–963.

Johnson, M. P., & Leone, J. M. (2005). The differential effects of intimate terrorism and situational couple violence: Findings from the National Violence Against Women Survey. *Journal of Family Issues, 26*, 322–349.

Jonason, P. K., Li, N. P., & Buss, D. M. (2010). The costs and benefits of the dark triad: Implications for mate poaching and mate retention tactics. *Personality and Individual Differences, 48*, 373–378.

Jonason, P. K., Luevano, V. X., & Adams, H. M. (2012). How the dark triad traits predict relationship choices. *Personality and Individual Differences, 53*, 180–184.

Jones, W. H., & Burdette, M. P. (1994). Betrayal in relationships. In A. L. Weber & J. H. Harvey (Eds.), *Perspectives on close relationships* (pp. 243–262). Allyn & Bacon.

Jones, W. H., Moore, D. S., Schratter, A., & Negel, L. A. (1999). Interpersonal transgressions and betrayals. In J. M. Adams & W. H. Jones (Eds.), *The handbook of interpersonal commitment and relationship stability* (pp. 233–256). Plenum.

Julien, D., & Markman, H. J. (1991). Social support and social networks as determinants of individual and marital outcomes. *Journal of Social and Personal Relationships, 8*, 549–568.

Juvonen, J., & Gross, E. F. (2008). Extending the school grounds? Bullying experiences in cyberspace. *Journal of School Health, 78*, 496–505.

Juvonen, J., Nishina, A., & Graham, S. (2000). Peer harassment, psychological adjustment, and school functioning in early adolescence. *Journal of Educational Psychology, 92*, 349–359.

Kachadourian, L. K., Fincham, F. D., & Davila, J. (2004). The tendency to forgive in dating and married couples: The role of attachment and relational satisfaction. *Personal Relationships, 11*, 373–393.

Kann, L., Kinchen, S., Shanklin, S. L., Flint, K. H., Hawkins, J., Harris, W. A., Lowry, R., Olsen, E. O., McManus, T., Chyen, D., Whittle, L., Taylor, E., Demissie, Z., Brener, N., Thornton, J., Moore, J., & Zaza, S. (2014). Youth risk behavior surveillance—United States, 2013. *Morbidity and Mortality Weekly Report, 63*.

Karney, B. R., Bradbury, T. N., Fincham, F. D., & Sullivan, K. T. (1994). The role of negative affectivity in the association between attributions and marital satisfaction. *Journal of Personality and Social Psychology, 66*, 413–424.

Kashian, N., & Walther, J. B. (2020). The effect of relational satisfaction and media synchronicity on attributions in computer-mediated conflict. *Communication Research, 47*(5), 647–668.

Kashy, D. A., & DePaulo, B. M. (1996). Who lies? *Journal of Personality and Social Psychology, 70*, 1037–1051.

Kellermann, K. (1984). The negativity effect and its implications in initial interaction. *Communication Monographs, 51*, 37–55.

Kelley, H. H. (1983). Love and commitment. In H. H. Kelley, E. Berscheid, A. Christensen, J. H. Harvey, T. L. Huston, G. Levinger, E. McClintock, L. A. Peplau, & D. R. Peterson (Eds.). *Close relationships* (pp. 89–115). SAGE.

Kelley, H. H. (1986). Personal relationships: Their nature and significance. In R. Gilmour & S. Duck (Eds.), *The emerging field of personal relationships* (pp. 3–19). Erlbaum.

Kelley, D. L. (1998). Communication of forgiveness. *Communication Studies, 49*, 255–271.

Kelley, D. L., & Waldron, V. R. (2005). An investigation of forgiveness-seeking communication and relational outcomes. *Communication Quarterly, 53*, 339–358.

Kelly E. V., Newton, N. C., Stapinski, L. A., Slade, T., Barrett, E. L., Conrad, P. J., & Teesson, M. (2015). Suicidality, internalizing problems and externalizing problems among adolescent bullies, victims, and bully-victims. *Preventive Medicine, 73*, 100–105.

Kelly, J. B., & Johnson, M. P. (2008). Differentiation among types of intimate partner violence: Research update and implications for interventions. *Family Court Review, 46*, 476–499.

Keltner, D., Young, R. C., Heerey, E. A., Oemig, C., & Monarch, N. D. (1998). Teasing in hierarchical and intimate relations. *Journal of Personality and Social Psychology, 75*, 1231–1247.

Kienlen, K. K., Birmingham, D. L., Solberg, K. B., O'Regan, J. T., & Meloy, J. R. (1997). A comparative study of psychotic and nonpsychotic stalking. *Journal of the American Academy of Psychiatry and Law, 25*, 317–334.

Kimberg, L. S. (2008). Addressing intimate partner violence with male patients: A review and introduction of pilot guidelines. *Journal of General Internal Medicine, 23,* 2071–2078.

Kimmel, M. S. (2002). "Gender symmetry" in domestic violence: A substantive and methodological review. *Violence Against Women, 8,* 1332–1363.

King, M. E., & Theiss, J. A. (2016). The communicative and physiological manifestations of relational turbulence during the empty-nest phase of marital relationships. *Communication Quarterly, 64,* 495–517.

Kinkade, P., Burns, R., & Fuentes, A. I. (2005). Criminalizing attractions: Perceptions of stalking and the stalker. *Crime & Delinquency, 51,* 3–25.

Kirkwood, C. (1993). *Leaving abusive partners: From the scars of survival to the wisdom for change.* SAGE.

Kjaervik, S. L., & Bushman, B. J. (2021). The link between narcissism and aggression: A meta-analytic review. *Psychological Bulletin, 147,* 477–503.

Klinetob, N. A., & Smith, D. A. (1996). Demand-withdraw communication in marital interaction: Test of interspousal contingency and gender role hypotheses. *Journal of Marriage and the Family, 58,* 945–957.

Knapp, M. L. (1978). *Social intercourse: From greeting to goodbye.* Allyn & Bacon.

Knapp, M. L., & Comadena, M. E. (1979). Telling it like it isn't: A review of theory and research on deceptive communications. *Human Communication Research, 5,* 270–285.

Knapp, M. L., & Daly, J. A. (2011). Background and current trends in the study of interpersonal communication. In M. L. Knapp & J. A. Daly (Eds.), *The SAGE handbook of interpersonal communication* (4th ed., pp. 3–22). SAGE.

Knapp, M. L., Hart, R. P., & Dennis, H. S. (1974). An exploration of deception as a communication construct. *Human Communication Research, 1,* 15–29.

Knobloch, L. K. (2007a). The dark side of relational uncertainty: Obstacle or opportunity? In B. H. Spitzberg & W. R. Cupach (Eds.), *The dark side of interpersonal communication* (2nd ed.). Routledge.

Knobloch, L. K. (2007b). Perceptions of turmoil within courtship: Associations with intimacy, relational uncertainty, and interference from partners. *Journal of Social and Personal Relationships, 24,* 363–384.

Knobloch, L. K. (2008a). Extending the emotions-in-relationships model to conversation. *Communication Research, 35,* 822–848.

Knobloch, L. K. (2008b). The content of relational uncertainty within marriage. *Journal of Social and Personal Relationships, 25,* 467–495.

Knobloch, L. K., & Carpenter-Theune, K. E. (2004). Topic avoidance in developing romantic relationships: Associations with intimacy and relational uncertainty. *Communication Research, 31,* 173–205.

Knobloch, L. K., & Donovan-Kicken, E. (2006). Perceived involvement of network members in courtships: A test of the relational turbulence model. *Personal Relationships, 13,* 281–302.

Knobloch, L. K., & Knobloch-Fedders, L. M. (2010). The role of relational uncertainty in depressive symptoms and relationship quality: An actor-partner interdependence model. *Journal of Social and Personal Relationships, 27*, 137–159.

Knobloch, L. K., Knobloch-Fedders, L. M., & Durbin, C. E. (2011). Depressive symptoms and relational uncertainty as predictors of reassurance seeking and negative feedback seeking in conversation. *Communication Monographs, 78*, 437–462.

Knobloch, L. K., Miller, L. E., & Carpenter, K. E. (2007). Using the relational turbulence model to understand negative emotion within courtship. *Personal Relationships, 14*, 91–112.

Knobloch, L. K., Solomon, D. H., & Cruz, M. G. (2001). The role of relationship development and attachment in the experience of romantic jealousy. *Personal Relationships, 8*, 205–224.

Knobloch, L. K., & Theiss, J. A. (2010). An actor-partner interdependence model of relational turbulence: Cognitions and emotions. *Journal of Social and Personal Relationships, 27*, 595–619.

Kowalski, R. M. (1997). Aversive interpersonal behaviors: An overarching framework. In R. M. Kowalski (Ed.), *Aversive interpersonal behaviors: The Springer series in social/clinical psychology*. Springer.

Kowalski, R. M. (2000). "I was only kidding!": Victims' and perpetrators' perceptions of teasing. *Personality and Social Psychology Bulletin, 26*, 231–241.

Kowalski, R. M. (2001). Aversive interpersonal behaviors: On being annoying, thoughtless, and mean. In R. M. Kowalski (Ed.), *Behaving badly: Aversive behaviors in interpersonal relationships* (pp. 3–25). American Psychological Association.

Kowalski, R. M. (2004). Proneness to, perceptions of, and responses to teasing; The influence of both intrapersonal and interpersonal factors. *European Journal of Personality, 18*, 331–349.

Kowalski, R. M. (2007). Teasing and bullying. In B. H. Spitzberg & W. R. Cupach (Eds.), *The dark side of interpersonal communication* (2nd ed., pp. 161–197). Routledge.

Kowalski, R. M., Giumetti, G. W., Schroeder, A. N., & Reese, H. (2012). Cyberbullying among college students: Evidence from multiple domains of college life. In C. Wankel & L. Wankel (Eds.), *Misbehavior online in higher education* (pp. 293–321). Emerald.

Kowalski, R. M., Howerton, E., & McKenzie, M. (2001). Permitted disrespect: Teasing in interpersonal interactions. In R. M. Kowalski (Ed.), *Behaving badly: Aversive behaviors in interpersonal relationships* (pp. 177–202). American Psychological Association.

Kowalski, R. M., & Limber, S. P. (2007). Electronic bullying among middle school students. *Journal of Adolescent Health, 41*, 522–530.

Kowalski, R. M., & McCord, A. (2019). Cyberbullying. In D. L. Merskin (Ed.), *The SAGE international encyclopedia of mass media and society*. SAGE.

Kowalski, R. M., Morgan, C. A., & Limber, S. P. (2012). Traditional bullying as a potential warning sign of cyberbullying. *School Psychology International, 33*, 505–519.

Kowalski, R. M., Walker, S., Wilkinson, R., Queen, A., & Sharpe, B. (2003). Lying, cheating, complaining, and other aversive interpersonal behaviors: A narrative examination of the darker side of relationships. *Journal of Social and Personal Relationships, 20*, 471–490.

Kuehner, C., Gass, P., & Dressing, H. (2012). Mediating effects of stalking victimization on gender differences in mental health. *Journal of Interpersonal Violence, 27*, 199–221.

Lane, J. D., & Wegner, D. M. (1995). The cognitive consequences of secrecy. *Journal of Personality and Social Psychology, 69*, 237–253.

Laumann, E. O., Gagnon, J. H., Michael, R. T., & Michaels, S. (1994). *The social organization of sexuality: Sexual practices in the United States.* University of Chicago Press.

Lazarus, R. S. (1982). Thoughts on the relations between emotion and cognition. *American Psychologist, 37*, 1019–1024.

Leary, M. R., Springer, C., Negel, L., Ansell, E., & Evans, K. (1998). The causes, phenomenology, and consequences of hurt feelings. *Journal of Personality and Social Psychology, 74*, 1225–1237.

Leff, J., & Vaughn, C. (1985). *Expressed emotion in families: Its significance for mental illness.* Guilford.

Lemay, E. P., Overall, N. C., & Clark, M. S. (2012). Experiences and interpersonal consequences of hurt feelings and anger. *Journal of Personality and Social Psychology, 103*, 982–1006.

Lereya, S. T., Copeland, W. E., Zammit, S., & Wolke, D. (2015). Bully/victims: A longitudinal, population-based cohort study of their mental health. *European Child and Adolescent Psychiatry, 24*, 1461–1471.

Leslie, L. A., Huston, T. L., & Johnson, M. P. (1986). Parental reactions to dating relationships: Do they make a difference? *Journal of Marriage and Family, 48*, 57–66.

Levine, T. R. (2014). Truth-default theory (TDT): A theory of human deception and deception detection. *Journal of Language and Social Psychology, 33*, 378–392.

Levine, T. R. (2015). New and improved accuracy findings in deception detection research. *Current Opinion in Psychology, 6*, 1–5.

Levine, T. R. (2020). *Duped: Truth-default theory and the social science of lying and deception.* The University of Alabama Press.

Levine, T. R., Blair, J. P., & Clare, D. D. (2014). Diagnostic utility: Experimental demonstrations and replications of powerful question effects and smaller question by experience interactions in high-stakes deception detection. *Human Communication Research, 40*(2), 262–289. https://doi.org/10.1111/hcre.12021

Levine, T. R., Clare, D. D., Blair, J. P., McCornack, S. A., Morrison, K., & Park, H. S. (2014). Expertise in deception detection involves actively prompting diagnostic information rather than passive behavioral observation. *Human Communication Research, 40*(4), 442–462. https://doi.org/10.1111/hcre.12032

Levine, T. R., & Knapp, M. L. (2018). Lying and deception in close relationships. In A. L. Vangelisti & D. Perlman (Eds), *The Cambridge handbook of personal relationships* (2nd ed., pp. 329–340). Cambridge University Press.

Levine, T. R., & McCornack, S. A. (1992). Linking love and lies: A formal test of the McCornack and Parks model of deception detection. *Journal of Social and Personal Relationships, 9*, 143–154.

Levy, S. R., Ayduk, O., & Downey, G. (2001). The role of rejection sensitivity in people's relationships with significant others and valued social groups. In M. R. Leary (Ed.), *Interpersonal rejection* (pp. 251–290). Oxford University Press.

Lewis, C. C., & George, J. F. (2008). Cross-cultural deception in social networking sites and face-to-face communication. *Computers in Human Behavior, 24,* 2945–2964.

Lieberman, B. (1988). Extra-premarital intercourse: Attitudes toward a neglected sexual behavior. *Journal of Sex Research, 24,* 291–299.

Limber, S. P. (2011). Development, evaluation, and future directions of the Olweus Bullying Prevention Program. *Journal of School Violence, 10,* 71–87.

Lin, Y. H. W., & Rusbult, C. E. (1995). Commitment to dating relationships and cross-sex friendships in America and China: The impact of centrality of relationship, normative support, and investment model variables. *Journal of Social and Personal Relationships, 12,* 7–26.

Liu, C. (2000). A theory of marital sexual life. *Journal of Marriage and the Family, 62,* 363–374.

Logan, T. K., & Walker, R. (2009). Partner stalking: Psychological dominance or "business as usual?" *Trauma, Violence, & Abuse, 10,* 247–270.

Luchies, L. B., Finkel, E. J., McNulty, J. K., & Kumashiro, M. (2010). The doormat effect: When forgiving erodes self-respect and self-concept clarity. *Journal of personality and social psychology, 98*(5), 734–749.

Lund, E. M., & Ross, S. W. (2017). Bullying perpetration, victimization, and demographic differences in college students: A review of the literature. *Trauma, Violence, & Abuse, 18,* 348–360.

Lyndon, A., Bonds-Raacke, J., & Cratty, A. D. (2011). College students' Facebook stalking of ex-partners. *Cyberpsychology, Behavior, and Social Networking, 14,* 711–716.

Lyons, R. F. Mickelson, K. D., Sullivan, M. J. L., & Coyne, J. C. (1998). Coping as a communal process. *Journal of Social and Personal Relationships, 15,* 579–605.

Malachowski, C. C., & Frisby, B. N. (2015). The aftermath of hurtful events: Cognitive, communicative, and relational outcomes. *Communication Quarterly, 63,* 187–203.

Marcus-Newhall, A., Pedersen, W. C., Carlson, M., & Miller, N. (2000). *Journal of Personality and Social Psychology, 78,* 670–689.

Markman, H. J. (1979). Application of a behavioral model of marriage in predicting relationship satisfaction of couples planning marriage. *Journal of Consulting and Clinical Psychology, 47,* 743–749.

Markman, H. J., & Rhoades, G. K. (2012). Relationship education research: Current status and future directions. *Journal of Marital and Family Therapy, 38*(1), 169–200.

Markman, H. J., Stanley, S. M., & Blumberg, S. L. (2010). *Fighting for your marriage: A deluxe revised edition of the classic best-seller for enhancing marriage and preventing divorce.* Wiley.

Marshall, T. C. (2012). Facebook surveillance of former romantic partners: Associations with postbreakup recovery and personal growth. *Cyberpsychology, Behavior, and Social Networking, 15,* 521–526.

Martin, S. L., Macy, R. J., & Young, S. K. (2011). Health and economic consequences of sexual violence. In J. W. White, M. P. Koss, & A. E. Kazdin (Eds.), *Violence against women and children, Volume 1: Mapping the terrain* (pp. 173–195). American Psychological Association.

McAnaney, K. G., Curliss, L. A., & Abeyta-Price, C. E. (1993). From imprudence to crime: Anti-stalking laws. *Notre Dame Law Review, 68,* 819–909.

McCornack, S. A., & Levine, T. R. (1990a). When lies are uncovered: Emotional and relational outcomes of discovered deception. *Communication Monographs, 57,* 119–138.

McCornack, S. A., & Levine, T. R. (1990b). When lovers become leery: The relationship between suspicion and accuracy in detecting deception. *Communication Monographs, 57,* 219–230.

McCornack, S. A., & Parks, M. R. (1986). Deception detection and relationship development: The other side of trust. In M. L. McLaughlin (Ed.), *Communication yearbook 9* (pp. 377–389). SAGE.

McCullough, M. E., Bellah, C. G., Kilpatrick, D. S., & Johnson, J. L. (2001). Vengefulness: Relationships with forgiveness, rumination, well-being, and the Big Five. *Personality and Social Psychology Bulletin, 27,* 601–610.

McCullough, M. E., Bono, G., & Root, L. M. (2007). Rumination, emotion, and forgiveness: Three longitudinal studies. *Journal of Personality and Social Psychology, 92,* 490–505.

McCullough, M. E., Fincham, F. D., & Tsang, J. A. (2003). Forgiveness, forbearance, and time: Temporal unfolding of transgression-related interpersonal motivations. *Journal of Personality and Social Psychology, 84,* 540–557.

McCullough, M. E., Kurzban, R., & Tabak, B. A. (2013). Cognitive systems for revenge and forgiveness. *Behavioral and Brain Sciences, 36,* 1–58.

McCullough, M. E., Pargament, K. I., Thoresen, C. E. (2000). The psychology of forgiveness: History, conceptual issues, and overview. In M. E. McCullough, K. I. Pargament, & C. E. Thoresen (Eds.), *Forgiveness: Theory, research, and practice* (pp. 1–14). Guilford.

McCullough, M. E., Rachal, K., Sandage, S., Worthington, E., Brown, S., & Hight, T. (1998). Interpersonal forgiving in close relationships II: Theoretical elaboration and measurement. *Journal of Personality and Social Psychology, 75,* 1586–1603.

McCullough, M. E., Worthington, E. L., & Rachal, K. C. (1997). Interpersonal forgiving in close relationships. *Journal of Personality and Social Psychology, 73,* 321–336.

McEwen, W. J., & Greenberg, B. S. (1970). The effects of message intensity on receiver evaluations of source, message, and topic. *Journal of Communication, 20,* 340–350.

McLaren, R. M., & Solomon, D. H. (2008). Appraisals and distancing responses to hurtful messages. *Communication Research, 35,* 339–357.

McLaren, R. M., & Solomon, D. H. (2014). Victim and perpetrator accounts of hurtful messages: An actor-partner interdependence model. *Human Communication Research, 40,* 291–308.

McLaren, R. M., Solomon, D. H., & Priem, J. S. (2011). Explaining variation in contemporaneous responses to hurt in premarital romantic relationships: A relational turbulence model perspective. *Communication Research, 38,* 543–564.

McLaren, R. M., Solomon, D. H., & Priem, J. S. (2012). The effect of relationship characteristics and relational communication on experiences of hurt from romantic partners. *Journal of Communication, 62,* 950–971.

McNaughton, D., Hamlin, D., McCarthy, J., Head-Reeves, D., & Schreiner, M. (2007). Learning to listen: Teaching an active listening strategy to pre-service education professionals. *Topics in Early Childhood Special Education, 27,* 223–231.

McNulty, J. K. (2008). Forgiveness in marriage: Putting the benefits into context. *Journal of Family Psychology, 22*(1), 171–175.

McNulty, J. K. (2010). Forgiveness increases the likelihood of subsequent partner transgressions in marriage. *Journal of Family Psychology, 24*(6), 787–790.

McNulty, J. K., & Russell, V. M. (2016). Forgive and forget, or forgive and regret? Whether forgiveness leads to less or more offending depends on offender agreeableness. *Personality and Social Psychology Bulletin, 42*(5), 616–631.

McWhirter, D. P., & Mattison, A. M. (1984). *The male couple: How relationships develop.* Prentice Hall.

Meloy, J. R. (1992). *Violent attachments.* Jason Aronson.

Meloy, J. R., Davis, B., & Lovette, J. (2001). Risk factors for violence among stalkers. *Journal of Threat Assessment, 1,* 3–16.

Meloy, J. R., Rivers, L., Siegel, L., Gothard, S., Naimark, D., & Nicolini, J. R. (2000). A replication study of obsessional followers and offenders with mental disorders. *Journal of Forensic Sciences, 45,* 147–152.

Menesini, E., Sanchez, V., Fonzi, A., Ortega, R., Costabile, A., & Lo Feudo, G. (2003). Moral emotions and bullying: A cross-national comparison of differences between bullies, victims and outsiders. *Aggressive Behavior, 29,* 515–530.

Merolla, A. J. (2008). Communicating forgiveness in friendships and dating relationships. *Communication Studies, 59,* 114–141.

Merolla, A. J. (2017). Forgiveness following conflict: What it is, why it happens, and how it's done. In J. A. Samp (Ed.), *Communicating interpersonal conflict in close relationships: Contexts, challenges, and opportunities* (pp. 227–249). Routledge.

Merolla, A. J., & Zhang, S. (2011). In the wake of transgressions: Examining forgiveness communication in personal relationships. *Personal Relationships, 18,* 79–95.

Messman-Moore, T. L., Ward, R. M., & Brown, A. L. (2009). Substance use and PTSD symptoms impact the likelihood of rape and revictimization in college women. *Journal of Interpersonal Violence, 24,* 499–521.

Metts, S. (1989). An exploratory investigation of deception in close relationships. *Journal of Social and Personal Relationships, 6,* 159–179.

Metts, S. (1994). Relational transgressions. In W. R. Cupach & B. H. Spitzberg (Eds.), *The dark side of interpersonal communication* (pp. 217–239). Erlbaum.

Metts, S., & Cupach, W. R. (2007). Responses to relational transgressions: Hurt, anger, and sometimes forgiveness. In B. H. Spitzberg & W. R. Cupach (Eds.), *The dark side of interpersonal communication* (2nd ed., pp. 243–276). Erlbaum.

Migerode, L. (2014). The no conclusion intervention for couples in conflict. *Journal of Marital & Family Therapy, 40*, 391–401.

Milgram, S. (1963). Behavioral study of obedience. *Journal of Abnormal and Social Psychology, 67*, 371–378.

Miller, C. W., & Roloff, M. E. (2005). Gender and willingness to confront hurtful messages from romantic partners. *Communication Quarterly, 53*, 323–337.

Miller, C. W., & Roloff, M. E. (2014). When hurt continues: Taking conflict personally leads to rumination, residual hurt and negative motivations toward someone who hurt us. *Communication Quarterly, 62*, 193–213.

Miller, G. R., & Steinberg, M. (1975). *Between people: A new analysis of interpersonal communication.* Science Research Associates.

Miller, G. R., & Stiff, J. B. (1993). *Deceptive communication.* Sage.

Miller, L. C., & Fishkin, S. A. (1997). On the dynamics of human bonding and reproductive success: Seeking windows on the adapted-for-human-environmental interface. In J. A. Simpson & D. T. Kenrick (Eds.), *Evolutionary social psychology* (pp. 197–235). Erlbaum.

Mishna, F. (2003). Peer victimization: The case for social work intervention. *Families in Society, 84*, 513–522.

Mishna, F., Khoury-Kassabri, M., Gadalla, T., & Daciuk, J. (2012). Risk factors for involvement in cyberbullying: Victims, bullies, and bully-victims. *Children and Youth Services Review, 34*, 63–70.

Mitsopoulou, E., & Giovazolias, T. (2015). Personality traits, empathy and bullying behavior: A meta-analytic approach. *Aggression and Violent Behavior, 21*, 61–72.

Mongeau, P. A., Hale, J. L., & Alles, M. (1994). An experimental investigation of accounts and attributions following sexual infidelity. *Communication Monographs, 61*, 326–343.

Mongeau, P. A., & Schulz, B. E. (1997). What he doesn't know won't hurt him (or me): Verbal responses and attributions following sexual infidelity. *Communication Reports, 10*, 143–152.

Mooney, A., Cresser, R., & Blatchford, P. (1991). Children's views on teasing and fighting in junior schools. *Educational Research, 33*, 103–112.

Morrison, K. A. (2001). Predicting violent behavior in stalkers: A preliminary investigation of Canadian cases in criminal harassment. *Journal of Forensic Sciences, 46*, 1403–1410.

Muise, A., Christofides, E., & Desmarais, S. (2009). More information than you ever wanted: Does Facebook bring out the green-eyed monster of jealousy? *Cyberpsychology, Behavior, and Social Networking, 12*, 441–444.

Mullen, P. E. (1991). Jealousy: The pathology of passion. *British Journal of Psychiatry, 158*, 593–601.

Mullen, P. E., Pathé, M., & Purcell, R. (2000). *Stalkers and their victims.* Cambridge University Press.

Murray, S. L., Holmes, J. G., & Griffin, D. W. (2003). Reflections on the self-fulfilling effects of positive illusions. *Psychological Inquiry, 14*, 289–295.

Murrell, A. R., Christoff, K. A., & Henning, K. R. (2007). Characteristics of domestic violence offenders: Associations with childhood exposure to violence. *Journal of Family Violence, 22,* 523–532.

Nansel, T, R., Haynie, D. L., & Simons-Morton, B. (2003). The association of bullying and victimization with middle school adjustment. In M. J. Elias & J. E. Zins (Eds.), *Bullying, peer harassment, and victimization in the schools: The next generation of prevention* (pp. 45–61). Haworth.

Nansel, T. R., Overpeck, M., Pilla, R. S., Ruan, W. J., Simons-Morton, B., & Scheidt, P. (2001). Bullying behaviors among U.S. youth: Prevalence and association with psychosocial adjustment. *Journal of the American Medical Association, 25,* 2094–2100.

Neubeck, G., & Schletzer, V. M. (1969). A study of extramarital relationships. In G. Neubeck (Ed.), *Extramarital relations* (pp. 146–151). Prentice Hall.

Newton, T. L., & Sanford, J. M. (2003). Conflict structure moderates associations between cardiovascular reactivity and negative marital interactions. *Health Psychology, 22,* 270–278.

Nicastro, A., Cousins, A., & Spitzberg, B. H. (2000). The tactical face of stalking. *Journal of Criminal Justice, 28,* 69–82.

Nishina, A., & Juvonen, J. (2005). Daily reports of witnessing and experiencing peer harassment in middle school. *Child Development, 76,* 435–450.

Nobles, M. R., Reyns, B. W., Fox, K. A., & Fisher, B. S. (2014). Protection against pursuit: A conceptual and empirical comparison of cyberstalking and stalking victimization among a national sample. *Justice Quarterly, 31,* 986–1014.

Norlander, B., & Eckhardt, C. (2005). Anger, hostility, and male perpetrators of intimate partner violence: A meta-analytic review. *Child Psychology Review, 25(2),* 119–152.

O'Connell, P., Pepler, D., & Craig, W. (1999). Peer involvement in bullying: Insights and challenges for intervention. *Journal of Adolescence, 22,* 437–452.

O'Hair, H. D., & Cody, M. J. (1994). Deception. In W. R. Cupach & B. H. Spitzberg (Eds.), *The dark side of interpersonal communication* (pp. 181–213). Erlbaum.

O'Hearn, H. G., & Margolin, G. (2000). *Cognitive Therapy and Research, 24,* 159–174.

O'Leary, K. D., & Schumacher, J. A. (2003). The association between alcohol use and intimate partner violence: Linear effect, threshold effect, or both? *Addictive Behaviors, 28,* 1575–1585.

O'Moore, M., & Kirkham, C. (2001). Self-esteem and its relationship to bullying behaviour. *Aggressive Behavior, 27,* 269–283.

O'Sullivan, M., & Ekman, P. (2004). The wizards of deception detection. In P. A. Granhag & L. A. Stromwall (Eds.), *The detection of deception in forensic contexts* (pp. 269–286). Cambridge University Press.

Oka, S. C., Chapman, R., & Jacobson, R. C. (2000). Phasic pupil dilation response to noxious stimulation: Effects of conduction distance, sex, and age. *Journal of Psychophysiology, 14,* 97–105.

Olson, M. M., Russell, C. S., Higgins-Kessler, M., & Miller, R. B. (2002). Emotional processes following disclosure of an extramarital affair. *Journal of Marital and Family Therapy, 28,* 423–434.

Olweus, D. (1993). *Bullying at school.* Wiley.

Olweus, D. (1995). Bullying or peer abuse at school: Facts and intervention. *Psychological Science, 4,* 196–200.

Olweus, D. (1997). Bully/victim problems in school: Facts and intervention. *European Journal of Psychology of Education, 12,* 495–510.

Olweus, D., & Limber, S. P. (2010). Bullying in school: Evaluation and dissemination of the Olweus Bullying Prevention Program. *American Journal of Orthopsychiatry, 80,* 124–134.

Orzeck, T., & Lung, E. (2005). Big-five personality differences of cheaters and non-cheaters. *Current Psychology, 24,* 274–286.

Osgood, C. E. (1952). The nature and measurement of meaning. *Psychological Bulletin, 49,* 197–237.

Osgood, C. E., & Suci, G. J. (1955). Factor analysis of meaning. *Journal of Experimental Psychology, 50,* 325–338.

Overall, N. C., & McNulty, J. K. (2017). What type of communication during conflict is beneficial for intimate relationships? *Current opinion in psychology, 13,* 1–5.

Ozdemir, M., & Stattin, H. (2011). Bullies, victims, and bully-victims: A longitudinal examination of the effects of bullying-victimization experiences on youth well-being. *Journal of Aggression, Conflict and Peace Research, 3,* 97–102.

Park, H. S., Levine, T. R., McCornack, S. A., Morrison, K., & Ferrara, M. (2002). How people really detect lies. *Communication Monographs, 69,* 144–157.

Parks, M. R. (1982). Ideology in interpersonal communication: Off the couch and into the world. In M. Burgoon (Ed.), *Communication yearbook 6* (pp. 79–107). SAGE.

Parks, M. R. (2011). Social networks and the life of relationships. In M. L. Knapp & J. A. Daly (Eds.), *The SAGE handbook of interpersonal communication* (pp. 355–388). SAGE.

Parks, M. R., & Adelman, M. B. (1983). Communication networks and the development of romantic relationships: An expansion of uncertainty reduction theory. *Human Communication Research, 10,* 55–79.

Parks, M. R., Stan, C. M., & Eggert, L. L. (1983). Romantic involvement and social network involvement. *Social Psychology Quarterly, 46,* 116–131.

Pathé, M. (2002). *Surviving stalking.* Cambridge University Press.

Patterson, B., & O'Hair, D. (1992). Relational reconciliation: Toward a more comprehensive model of relational development. *Communication Research Reports, 9,* 117–129.

Paukert, A., Stagner, B., & Hope, K. (2004). The assessment of active listening skills in helpline volunteers. *Stress, Trauma, and Crisis, 7,* 61–76.

Paul, L., Foss, M. A., & Galloway, J. (1993). Sexual jealousy in young women and men: Aggressive responses to a partner and rival. *Aggressive Behavior, 19,* 401–420.

Pawluk, C. J. (1989). Social construction of teasing. *Journal for the Theory of Social Behavior, 19,* 145–167.

Pearce, J. (1989). *Fighting, teasing and bullying: Simple and effective ways to help your child.* Thorsons.

Pearce, Z. J., & Halford, W. (2008). Do attributions mediate the association between attachment and negative couple communication? *Personal Relationships, 15*, 155–170.

Pederson, J. R., & Faw, M. (2019). Communal coping following relational transgressions: Perceptions of third-party personal network members. *Communication Reports, 32*, 112–124.

Pederson, J. R., High, A., & McLaren, R. M. (2020). Support gaps surrounding conversations about coping with relational transgressions. *Western Journal of Communication, 84*, 204–226.

Pederson, J. R., & McLaren, R. M. (2017). Indirect effects of supportive communication during conversations about coping with relational transgressions. *Personal Relationships, 24*, 804–819.

Pennebaker, J. W. (1995). *Emotion, disclosure, and health.* American Psychological Association.

Pérez, Z. J., & Hussey, H. (2014). *A hidden crisis: Including the LGBT community when addressing sexual violence on college campuses.* Center for American Progress. https://files.eric.ed.gov/fulltext/ED564604.pdf

Perlman, D., & Carcedo, R. J. (2011). Overview of the dark side of relationships research. In W. R. Cupach & B. H. Spitzberg (Eds.), *The dark side of close relationships II* (pp. 1–37). Routledge.

Perry, D. G., Hodges, E. V. E., & Egan, S. K. (2001). Determinants of chronic victimization by peers: A review and new model of family influence. In J. Juvonen & S. Graham (Eds.), *Peer harassment in school: The plight of the vulnerable and victimized* (pp. 73–104). Guilford.

Petrie, K. J., Booth, R. J., & Pennebaker, J. W. (1998). The immunological effects of thought suppression. *Journal of Personality and Social Psychology, 75*(5), 1264–1272.

Petronio, S. (1991). Communication boundary management: A theoretical model of managing disclosure of private information between marital couples. *Communication Theory, 1*, 311–335.

Petronio, S. (2000). *Balancing the secrets of private disclosures.* Erlbaum.

Petronio, S. (2002). *Boundaries of privacy: Dialectic of disclosure.* SUNY Press.

Petronio, S. (2016). Communication privacy management theory. In C. R. Berger, M. E. Roloff, & J. P. Caughlin (Eds.), *International encyclopedia of interpersonal communication.* Wiley.

Petronio, S., Reeder, H. M., Hecht, M. L., & Ros-Mendoza, T. M. (1996). Disclosure of sexual abuse by children and adolescents. *Journal of Applied Communication Research, 24*, 181–199.

Pfeiffer, S. M., & Wong, P. T. P. (1989). Multidimensional jealousy. *Journal of Social and Personal Relationships, 6*, 181–196.

Phillips, L., Quirk, R., Rosenfeld, B., & O'Connor, M. (2004). Is it stalking? Perceptions of stalking among college undergraduates. *Criminal Justice and Behavior, 31*, 73–96.

Pines, A. M. (1992). *Romantic jealousy: Understanding and conquering the shadow of love.* St. Martin's.

Pollmann, M. M. H., Crockett, E. E., Vanden Abeele, M. M. P., & Schouten, A. P. (2020). Does attachment style moderate the effect of computer-mediated versus face-to-face conflict discussions? *Personal Relationships, 27,* 939–955.

Priem, J. S., & Solomon, D. H. (2011). Relational uncertainty and cortisol responses to hurtful and supportive messages from a dating partner. *Personal Relationships, 18,* 198–223.

Prins, K. S., Buunk, B. P., & VanYperen, N. W. (1993). Equity, normative disapproval, and extramarital relationships. *Journal of Social and Personal Relationships, 10,* 39–53.

Puhl, R., Wall, M. M., Chen, C., Austin, S. B., Eisenberg, M. E., & Neumark-Sztainer, D. (2017). Experiences of weight teasing in adolescence and weight-related outcomes in adulthood: A 15-year longitudinal study. *Preventative Medicine, 100,* 173–179.

Raghavan, C., Mennerich, A., Sexton, E., & James, S. E. (2006). Community violence and its direct, indirect, and mediating effects on intimate partner violence. *Violence Against Women, 12,* 1132–1149.

Rahim, M. A. (1983). A measure of styles of handling interpersonal conflict. *Academy of Management Journal, 26,* 368–376.

Ramirez, A., Walther, J. B., Burgoon, J. K., & Sunnafrank, M. (2006). Information-seeking strategies, uncertainty, and computer-mediated communication: Toward a conceptual model. *Human Communication Research, 28,* 213–228.

Rasmussen, K. R. (2016). Entitled vengeance: A meta-analysis relating narcissism to provoked aggression. *Aggressive Behavior, 42,* 362–379.

Rawlins, W. (1983). Openness as problematic in ongoing friendships: Two conversational dilemmas. *Communication Monographs, 50,* 1–13.

Reed, L. A., Tolman, R. M., & Ward, L. M. (2016). Snooping and sexting: Digital media as a context for dating aggression and abuse among college students. *Violence Against Women, 22*(13), 1556–1576.

Reinhard, M., Sporer, S. L., & Scharmach, M. (2013). Perceived familiarity with a judgmental situation improves lie detection ability. *Swiss Journal of Psychology, 72,* 43–52.

Rennison, C. M. (2002). *Rape and sexual assault: Reporting to police and medical attention.* U.S. Department of Justice, Bureau of Justice Statistics.

Rennison, C. M. (2018). Current controversies: Disadvantage as a catalyst for sexual victimization. In C. M. Renzetti, J. L. Edleson, & R. K. Bergen (Eds.), *Sourcebook on violence against women* (3rd ed., pp. 102–108). SAGE.

Rennison, C. M., & Planty, M. (2003). Nonlethal intimate partner violence: Examining race, gender, and income patterns. *Violence and Victims, 18,* 433–443.

Renzetti, C. M. (1992). *Violent betrayal: Partner abuse in lesbian relationships.* SAGE.

Reuter, T. R., Newcomb, M. E., Whitton, S. W., & Mustanski, B. (2017). Intimate partner violence victimization in LGBT young adults: Demographic differences and associations with health behaviors. *Psychology of Violence, 7,* 101–109.

Rigby, K. (2000). Effects of peer victimization in schools and perceived social support on adolescent well-being. *Journal of Adolescence, 23,* 57–68.

Rigby, K., & Slee, P. (1999). Suicidal ideation among adolescent school children, involvement in bully-victim problems, and perceived social support. *Suicide and Life-Threatening Behavior, 29,* 119–130.

Ripley, J. S., & Worthington, E. L. Jr. (2014). *Couple therapy: A new hope-focused approach.* InterVarsity Press.

Roberts, W. B., & Coursol, D. H. (1996). Strategies for intervention with childhood and adolescent victims of bullying, teasing, and intimidation in school settings. *Elementary School Guidance and Counseling, 30,* 204–212.

Robles, T. F., Slatcher, R. B., Trombello, J. M. & McGinn, M. M. (2014). Marital quality and health: A meta-analytic review. *Psychological Bulletin, 140,* 140–187.

Roloff, M. E., & Cloven, D. H. (1990). The chilling effect in interpersonal relationships: The reluctance to speak one's mind. In D. D. Cahn (Ed.), *Intimates in conflict: A communication perspective* (pp. 49–76). Erlbaum.

Roloff, M. E., & Ifert, D. (1998). Antecedents and consequences of explicit agreements to declare a topic taboo in dating relationships. *Personal Relationships, 5,* 191–205.

Roloff, M. E., & Ifert, D. E. (2000). Conflict management through avoidance: Withholding complaints, suppressing arguments, and declaring topics taboo. In S. Petronio (Ed.), *Balancing the secrets of private disclosures* (pp. 151–163). Erlbaum.

Roloff, M. E., Soule, K. P., & Carey, C. M. (2001). Reasons for remaining in a relationship and responses to relational transgressions. *Journal of Social and Personal Relationships, 18,* 362–385.

Rook, K. S. (1984). The negative side of social interaction: Impact on psychological well-being. *Journal of Personality and Social Psychology, 46,* 1097–1108.

Rook, K. S. (1998). Investigating the positive and negative sides of personal relationships: Through a lens darkly? In B. H. Spitzberg & W. R. Cupach (Eds.), *The dark side of close relationships* (pp. 369–393). Erlbaum.

Roscoe, B., Cavanaugh, L. E., & Kennedy, D. R. (1988). Dating infidelity: Behaviors, reasons, and consequences. *Adolescence, 23,* 35–43.

Rosenfeld, B. (2000). Assessment and treatment of obsessional harassment. *Aggression and Violent Behavior, 5,* 529–549.

Rosenfeld, B., & Harmon, R. (2002). Factors associated with violence in stalking and obsessional harassment cases. *Criminal Justice and Behavior, 29,* 671–691.

Ross, L. D. (1977). The intuitive psychologist and his shortcomings: Distortions in the attribution process. In L. Berkowitz (Ed.), *Advances in experimental social psychology* (Vol. 10, pp. 173–220). Academic Press.

Rote, W. M., & Smetana, J. G. (2018). Within-family dyadic patterns of parental monitoring and adolescent information management. *Development Psychology, 54*(12), 2302–2315.

Rotunda, R. J., Kass, S. J., Sutton, M. A., & Leon, D. T. (2003). Internet use and misuse: Preliminary findings a new assessment instrument. *Behavior Modification, 27,* 484–504.

Rusbult, C. E. (1980). Commitment and satisfaction in romantic associations: A test of the investment model. *Journal of Experimental Social Psychology, 16,* 172–186.

Rusbult, C. E. (1983). A longitudinal test of the investment model: The development (and deterioration) of satisfaction and commitment in heterosexual involvements. *Journal of Personality and Social Psychology, 45*, 101–117.

Rusbult, C. E., Bissonnette, V. I., Arriaga, X. B., & Cox, C. L. (1998). Accommodation processes during the early years of marriage. In T. N. Bradbury (Ed.), *The developmental course of marital dysfunction* (pp. 74–113). Cambridge University Press.

Rusbult, C. E., Johnson, D. J., & Morrow, G. D. (1986a). Determinants and consequences of exit, voice, loyalty, and neglect: Responses to dissatisfaction in adult romantic involvements. *Human Relations, 39*, 45–63.

Rusbult, C. E., Johnson, D. J., & Morrow, G. D. (1986b). Predicting satisfaction and commitment in adult romantic involvements: An assessment of the generalizability of the investment model. *Social Psychology Quarterly, 49*, 81–89.

Rusbult, C. E., Martz, J. M., & Agnew, C. R. (1998). The investment model scale: Measuring commitment level, satisfaction level, quality of alternatives, and investment size. *Personal Relationships, 5*, 357–391.

Rusbult, C. E., Morrow, G. D., & Johnson, D. J. (1987). Self-esteem and problem-solving behaviour in close relationships. *British Journal of Social Psychology, 26*, 293–303.

Rusbult, C. E., Olsen, N., Davis, J. L., & Hannon, P. A. (2001). Commitment and relationship mechanisms. In J. H. Harvey & A. Wenzel (Eds.), *Close romantic relationships: Maintenance and enhancement* (pp. 87–113). Erlbaum.

Rusbult, C. E., Verette, J., Whitney, G. A., Slovik, L. F., & Lipkus, I. (1991). Accommodation processes in close relationships: Theory and preliminary empirical evidence. *Journal of Personality and Social Psychology, 60*(1), 53–79.

Rusbult, C. E., Zembrodt, I. M., & Gunn, L. K. (1982). Exit, voice, loyalty, and neglect: Responses to dissatisfaction in romantic involvements. *Journal of Personality and Social Psychology, 43*, 1230–1242.

Rusbult, C. E., Zembrodt, I. M., & Iwaniszek, J. (1986). The impact of gender and sex-role orientation on responses to dissatisfaction in close relationships. *Sex Roles, 15*, 1–20.

Russell, V. M., Baker, L. R., McNulty, J. K., & Overall, N. C. (2018). "You're forgiven, but don't do it again!" Direct partner regulation buffers the costs of forgiveness. *Journal of Family Psychology, 32*(4), 435–444.

Sabini, J., & Green, M. (2004). Emotional responses to sexual and emotional infidelity: Constants and differences across genders, samples, and methods. *Personality and Social Psychology Bulletin, 30*, 1375–1388.

Sagarin, B. J., Becker, D. V., Guadagno, R. E., Nicastle, L. D., & Millevoi, A. (2003). Sex differences (and similarities) in jealousy: The moderating influence of infidelity experience and sexual orientation of the infidelity. *Evolution and Human Behavior, 24*, 17–23.

Salmivalli, C., Kaukiainen, A., & Lagerspetz, K. (2000). Aggression and sociometric status among peers: Do gender and type of aggression matter? *Scandinavian Journal of Psychology, 41*, 17–24.

Salmivalli, C., & Nieminen, E. (2002). Proactive and reactive aggression among school bullies, victims, and bully-victims. *Aggressive Behavior, 28*, 30–44.

Salovey, P., & Rodin, J. (1989). Envy and jealousy in close relationships. In C. Hendrick (Ed.), *Close relationships* (pp. 221–246). SAGE.

Schutz, W. C. (1958). *The interpersonal underworld.* Science and Behavior Books.

Scissors, L. E., & Gergle, D. (2013). "Back and forth, back and forth": Channel switching in romantic couple conflict. *CSCW, 13,* 237–248.

Seiter, J. S., & Bruschke, J. (2007). Deception and emotion: The effects of motivation, relationship type, and sex on expected feelings of guilt and shame following acts of deception in United States and Chinese samples. *Communication Studies, 58,* 1–16.

Seiter, J. S., Bruschke, J., & Bai, C. (2002). The acceptability of deception as a function of perceivers' culture, deceiver's intention, and deceiver-deceived relationship. *Western Journal of Communication, 66,* 158–180.

Serota, K. B., & Levine, T. R. (2015). A few prolific liars: Variation in the prevalence of lying. *Journal of Language and Social Psychology, 34,* 138–157.

Serota, K. B., Levine, T. R., & Boster, F. J. (2010). The prevalence of lying in America: Three studies of reported deception. *Human Communication Research, 36,* 1–24.

Shackelford, T. K., & Buss, D. M. (1997). Cues to infidelity. *Personality and Social Psychology Bulletin, 23,* 1034–1045.

Shapiro, J. P., Baumeister, R. F., & Kessler, J. W. (1991). A three-component model of children's teasing: Aggression, humor, and ambiguity. *Journal of Social and Clinical Psychology, 10,* 459–472.

Sheridan, L. P., & Grant, T. (2007). Is cyberstalking different? *Psychology, Crime and Law, 13,* 627–640.

Sheridan, L. P., & Lyndon, A. E. (2012). The influence of prior relationship, gender, and fear on the consequences of stalking victimization. *Sex Roles, 66,* 340–350.

Shorey, R. C., Cornelius, T. L., & Strauss, C. (2015). Stalking in college student dating relationships: A descriptive investigation. *Journal of Family Violence, 30,* 935–942.

Shorey, R. C., McNulty, J. K., Moore, T. M., & Stuart, G. L. (2015). Emotion regulation moderates the association between proximal negative affect and intimate partner violence perpetration. *Prevention Science, 16,* 873–880.

Sillars, A. L. (1980). Attributions and communication in roommate conflicts. *Communication Monographs, 47,* 180–200.

Sillars, A. L., Canary, D. J., & Tafoya, M. (2004). Communication, conflict, and the quality of family relationships. In A. L. Vangelisti (Ed.), *Handbook of family communication* (pp. 413–446). Erlbaum.

Sillars, A. L., Coletti, S. F., Parry, D., & Rogers, M. A. (1982). Coding verbal conflict tactics: Nonverbal and perceptual correlates of the "avoidance-distributive-integrative" distinction. *Human Communication Research, 9,* 83–95.

Simpson, J. A., & Gangestad, S. W. (1991). Individual differences in sociosexuality: Evidence for convergent and discriminant validity. *Journal of Personality and Social Psychology, 60,* 870–883.

Sinclair, H. C., & Frieze, I. H. (2000). Initial courtship behavior and stalking: How should we draw the line? *Violence and Victims, 15,* 23–40.

Sinclair, H. C., Ladny, R. T., & Lyndon, A. E. (2011). Adding insult to injury: Effects of interpersonal rejection types, rejection sensitivity, and self-regulation on obsessive relational intrusion. *Aggressive Behavior, 37*, 503–520.

Slee, P. T. (1995). Bullying: Health concerns of Australian secondary school students. *International Journal of Adolescence and Youth, 5*, 215–224.

Slomkowski, C. L., & Killen, M. (1992). Young children's conceptions of transgressions with friends and nonfriends. *International Journal of Behavioral Development, 15*, 247–258.

Smartt, U. (2001). The stalking phenomenon: Trends in European and international stalking and harassment litigation. *European Journal of Crime, Criminal Law and Criminal Justice, 9*, 209–232.

Smith, P. K. (2011). Bullying in schools: Thirty year of research. In C. P. Monks & I. Coyne (Eds.), *Bullying in different contexts* (pp. 36–60). Cambridge University Press.

Smith, P K., Mahdavi, J., Carvalho, M., Fisher, S., Russel, S., & Tippett, N. (2008). Cyberbullying: Its nature and impact in secondary school pupils. *The Journal of Child Psychology and Psychiatry, 49*, 376–385.

Smoker, M., & March, E. (2017). Predicting perpetration of intimate partner cyberstalking: Gender and the dark tetrad. *Computers in Human Behavior, 72*, 390–396.

Snell, W. E., & Papini, D. R. (1989). The sexuality scale: An instrument to measure sexual self-esteem, sexual depression, and sexual preoccupation. *Journal of Sex Research, 26*, 256–263.

Solomon, D. H. (2016). Relational turbulence model. In C. R. Berger & M. E. Roloff (Eds.), *International encyclopedia of interpersonal communication*. Wiley-Blackwell.

Solomon, D. H., & Knobloch, L. K. (2004). A model of relational turbulence: The role of intimacy, relational uncertainty, and interference from partners in appraisals of irritations. *Journal of Social and Personal Relationships, 21*, 795–816.

Solomon, D. H., Knobloch, L. K., Theiss, J. A., & McLaren, R. M. (2016). Relational turbulence theory: Explaining variation in subjective experiences and communication within romantic relationships. *Human Communication Research, 42*, 507–532.

Solomon, D. H., & Theiss, J. A. (2008). A longitudinal test of the relational turbulence model of romantic relationship development. *Personal Relationships, 15*, 339–357.

Solomon, D. H., Weber, K. M., & Steuber, K. R. (2010). Turbulence in relationship transitions. In S. W. Smith & S. R. Wilson (Eds.), *New directions in interpersonal communication research* (pp. 115–134). SAGE.

Sommers, T. (2009). The two faces of revenge: Moral responsibility and the culture of honor. *Biology and Philosophy, 24*, 35–50.

Spanier, G. B., & Margolis, R. L. (1983). Marital separation and extramarital sexual behavior. *The Journal of Sex Research, 19*, 23–48.

Spencer, C. M., Stith, S. M., & Cafersky, B. (2019). Risk markers for physical intimate partner violence victimization: A meta-analysis. *Aggression and Violent Behavior, 44*, 8–17.

Spitzberg, B. H., & Chou, H. (2005, May). *I did it on purpose: A model of strategic infidelity*. Paper presented at the annual convention of the International Communication Association, New York, NY.

Spitzberg, B. H., & Cupach, W. R. (1984). *Interpersonal communication competence.* SAGE.

Spitzberg, B. H., & Cupach, W. R. (Eds.) (1998). *The dark side of close relationships.* Erlbaum.

Spitzberg, B. H., & Cupach, W. R. (2001). Paradoxes of pursuit: Toward a relational model of stalking-related phenomena. In J. Davis (Ed.), *Stalking crimes and victim protection: Prevention, intervention, threat assessment, and case management* (pp. 97–136). CRC Press.

Spitzberg, B. H., & Cupach, W. R. (Eds.) (2007). *The dark side of interpersonal communication.* Erlbaum.

Spitzberg, B. H., & Cupach, W. R. (2014). *The dark side of relationship pursuit: From attraction to obsession and stalking* (2nd ed.). Routledge.

Spitzberg, B. H., Cupach, W. R., & Ciceraro, L. D. L. (2010). Sex differences in stalking and obsessive relational intrusion: Two meta-analyses. *Partner Abuse, 1,* 259–285.

Spitzberg, B. H., Cupach, W. R., Hannawa, A. F., & Crowley, J. P. (2014). A preliminary test of a relational goal pursuit theory of obsessive relational intrusion and stalking. *Studies in Communication Sciences, 14,* 29–36.

Spitzberg, B. H., & Hoobler, G. (2002). Cyberstalking and the technologies of interpersonal terrorism. *New Media & Society, 4,* 71–92.

Spitzberg, B. H., Marshall, L., & Cupach, W. R. (2001). Obsessive relational intrusion, coping, and sexual coercion victimization. *Communication Reports, 14,* 19–30.

Spitzberg, B. H., Nicastro, A. M., & Cousins, A. V. (1998). Exploring the interactional phenomenon of stalking and obsessive relational intrusion. *Communication Reports, 11,* 33–47.

Spitzberg, B. H., & Rhea, J. (1999). Obsessive relational intrusion and sexual coercion victimization. *Journal of Interpersonal Violence, 14,* 3–20.

Spitzberg, B. H., & Tafoya, M. A. (2005, May). *Further explorations in communicative infidelity: Jealousy, sociosexuality, and vengefulness.* Paper presented at the annual meeting of the International Communication Association, New York, NY.

Sporer, S. L., & Schwandt, B. (2006). Paraverbal indicators of deception: A meta-analytic synthesis. *Applied Cognitive Psychology, 20,* 421–446.

Sporer, S. L., & Schwandt, B. (2007). Moderators of nonverbal indicators of deception: A meta-analytic synthesis. *Psychology, Public Policy, and Law, 13,* 1–34.

Sprecher, S., & Felmlee, D. (1992). The influence of parents and friends on the quality and stability of romantic relationships: A three-wave longitudinal investigation. *Journal of Marriage and the Family, 54,* 888–900.

Sprecher, S., & Felmlee, D. (2000). Romantic partners' perceptions of social network attributes with the passage of time and relationship transitions. *Personal Relationships, 7,* 325–340.

Sprecher, S., Felmlee, D., Orbuch, T. L., & Willetts, M. C. (2002). Social networks and change in personal relationships. In A. L. Vangelisti, H. T. Reis, & M. A. Fitzpatrick (Eds.), *Stability and change in relationships* (pp. 257–282). Cambridge University Press.

Spring, J. A. (1996). *After the affair.* HarperCollins.

Stanley, J. L., Bartholomew, K., Taylor, T., Oram, D., & Landolt, M. (2006). Intimate violence in male same-sex relationships. *Journal of Family Violence, 21,* 31–41.

Stanley, S. M., Blumberg, S. L., & Markman, H. J. (1999). Helping couples fight for their marriages: The PREP approach. In R. Berger & M. T. Hannah (Eds.), *Preventive approaches in couples therapy* (pp. 279–303). Brunner/Mazel.

Starr, L. R., & Davila, J. (2008). Excessive reassurance seeking, depression, and interpersonal rejection: A meta-analytic review. *Journal of Abnormal Psychology, 117,* 762–775.

Stearns, P. N. (1989). *Jealousy: The evolution of an emotion in American history.* University Press.

Stiles, W. B. (1987). I have to talk to somebody: A fever model of disclosure. In V. J. Derlega & J. H. Berg (Eds.), *Self-disclosure: Theory, research, and therapy* (pp. 257–282). Plenum.

Storch, E. A., Brassard, M. R., & Masia-Warner, C. L. (2003). The relationship of peer victimization to social anxiety and loneliness in adolescence. *Child Study Journal, 33,* 1–18.

Storey, J. E., Hart, S. D., Meloy, J. R., & Reavis, J. A. (2009). Psychopathy and stalking. *Law and Human Behavior, 33,* 237–246.

Straus, M. A., & Gelles, R. J. (1986). Societal change and change in family violence from 1975 to 1985 as revealed by two national surveys. *Journal of Marriage and the Family, 48,* 465–479.

Straus, M. A., Gelles, R. J., & Steinmetz, S. K. (1980). *Behind closed doors: Violence in the American family.* Doubleday.

Strelan, P., Crabb, S., Chan, D., & Jones, L. (2017). Lay perspectives on the costs and risks of forgiving. *Personal Relationships, 24*(2), 392–407.

Strube, M. J., & Barbour, L. S. (1984). Factors related to the decision to leave an abusive relationship. *Journal of Marriage and the Family, 46,* 837–844.

Stuckless, N., & Goranson, R. (1992). The vengeance scale: Development of a measure of attitudes toward revenge. *Journal of Social Behavior and Personality, 7,* 25–42.

Sturgeon, J. A., & Zautra, A. J. (2016). Social pain and physical pain: Shared paths to resilience. *Pain Management, 6,* 63–74.

Sugarman, D. B., & Frankel, S. L. (1996). Patriarchal ideology and wife-assault: A meta-analytic review. *Journal of Family Violence, 11,* 13–40.

Sugarman, D. B., & Hotaling, G. T. (1989). Dating violence: Prevalence, context, and risk markers. In M. A. Pirog-Good & J. E. Stets (Eds.), *Violence in dating relationships: Emerging social issues* (pp. 3–32). Praeger.

Swan, S. C., Gambone, L. J., Fields, A. M., Sullivan, D. P., & Snow, D. L. (2005). Women who use violence in intimate relationships: The role of anger, victimization, and symptoms of posttraumatic stress and depression. *Violence and Victims, 20,* 267–285.

Tafoya, M. A., & Spitzberg, B. H. (2007). The dark side of infidelity: Its nature, prevalence, and communicative functions. In B. H. Spitzberg & W. R. Cupach (Eds.), *The dark side of interpersonal communication* (2nd ed., pp. 201–242). Erlbaum.

Tarrier, N., Beckett, R., Harwood, S., & Bishay, N. (1990). Morbid jealousy: A review and cognitive-behavioural formulation. *British Journal of Psychiatry, 157*, 319–326.

Tedeschi, J. T., & Felson, R. B. (1994). *Violence, aggression, and coercive actions.* American Psychological Association.

Theiss, J. A. (2018). *The experience and expression of uncertainty in close relationships.* Cambridge University Press.

Theiss, J. A., & Knobloch, L. K. (2009). An actor-partner interdependence model of irritations in romantic relationships. *Communication Research, 36*, 510–536.

Theiss, J. A., Knobloch, L. K., Checton, M. G., & Magsamen-Conrad, K. (2009). Relationship characteristics associated with the experience of hurt in romantic relationships: A test of the relational turbulence model. *Human Communication Research, 35*, 588–615.

Theiss, J. A., & Solomon, D. H. (2006a). A relational turbulence model of communication about irritations in romantic relationships. *Communication Research, 33*, 391–418.

Theiss, J. A., & Solomon, D. H. (2006b). Coupling longitudinal data and multilevel modeling to examine the antecedents and consequences of jealousy experiences in romantic relationships: A test of the relational turbulence model. *Human Communication Research, 32*, 469–503.

Thomas, K. W., & Kilmann, R. H. (1974). *Thomas-Kilmann conflict mode instrument.* Xicom.

Thompson, A. P. (1983). Extramarital sex: A review of the research literature. *Journal of Sex Research, 19*, 1–22.

Tjaden, P., & Thoennes, N. (1998). *Stalking in America: Findings from the National Violence Against Women Survey.* National Institute of Justice.

Tjaden, P., & Thoennes, N. (2000). Prevalence and consequences of male-to-female and female-to-male intimate partner violence as measured by the National Violence against Women Survey. *Violence Against Women, 6*, 142–161.

Tokunaga, R. S. (2007). *Cyber-intrusions: Strategies of coping with online obsessive relational intrusion* [Doctoral dissertation, *University of Hawai'i*]. http://hdl.handle.net/10125/20905

Tokunaga, R. S. (2011). Social networking site or social surveillance site? Understanding the use of interpersonal electronic surveillance in romantic relationships. *Computers in Human Behavior, 27*, 705–713.

Tokunaga, R. S. (2016). Interpersonal surveillance over social network sites: Applying a theory of negative relational maintenance and the investment model. *Journal of Social and Personal Relationships, 33*, 171–190.

Toma, C. L., Hancock, J. T., & Ellison, N. B. (2008). Separating fact from fiction: An examination of deceptive self-presentation in online dating profiles. *Personality and Social Psychology Bulletin, 34*, 1023–1036.

Tong, S. T. (2013). Facebook use during relationship termination: Uncertainty reduction and surveillance. *Cyberpsychology, Behavior, and Social Networking, 16*, 788–793.

Trapp, R., & Hoff, N. (1985). A model of serial arguments in interpersonal relationships. *Journal of the American Forensic Association, 22*, 1–11.

Treas, J., & Giesen, D. (2000). Sexual infidelity among married and cohabiting Americans. *Journal of Marriage and the Family, 62*, 48–60.

Trivers, R. (2011). *The folly of fools: The logic of deceit and self-deception in human life.* Basic Books.

Truman, J. L., & Langton, L. (2015). *Criminal victimization, 2014.* U.S. Department of Justice, Bureau of Justice Statistics.

Tsang, J. A., & Stanford, M. S. (2007). Forgiveness for intimate partner violence: The influence of victim and offender variables. *Personality and Individual Differences, 42*(4), 653–664.

Tsapelas, I., Fisher, H. E., & Aron, A. (2011). Infidelity: When, where, why. In W. R. Cupach & B. H. Spitzberg (Eds.), *The dark side of close relationships II* (pp. 175–195). Routledge.

Tsaousis, I. (2016). The relationship of self-esteem to bullying perpetration and peer victimization among schoolchildren and adolescents: A meta-analytic review. *Aggression and Violent Behavior, 31*, 186–199.

Turk, D. R., & Monahan, J. L. (1999). "Here I go again": An examination of repetitive behaviors during interpersonal conflict. *Southern Communication Journal, 65*, 232–244.

Turner, R. E., Edgley, C., & Olmstead, G. (1975). Information control in conversations: Honesty is not always the best policy. *Kansas Journal of Sociology, 11*, 69–89.

Ullman, S. E., & Najdowski, C. J. (2011). Vulnerability and protective factors for sexual assault. In J. W. White, M. P. Koss, & A. E. Kazdin (Eds.), *Violence against women and children, Volume 1: Mapping the terrain* (pp. 151–172). American Psychological Association.

U.S. Department of Education. (2010). *Dear colleague letter: Harassment and bullying.* Office for Civil Rights. https://www2.ed.gov/about/offices/list/ocr/docs/dcl-fact-sheet-201010.pdf

Utz, S., Muscanell, N., & Khalid, C. (2015). Snapchat elicits more jealousy than Facebook: A comparison of Snapchat and Facebook use. *Cyberpsychology, Behavior, and Social Networking, 18*, 141–146.

Vallade, J. I., & Dillow, M. R. (2014). An exploration of extradyadic communicative messages following relational transgressions in romantic relationships. *Southern Communication Journal, 79*, 94–113.

Vallade, J. I., Dillow, M. R., & Myers, S. A. (2016). A qualitative exploration of romantic partners' motives for and content of communication with friends following negative relational events. *Communication Quarterly, 64*, 348–368.

van Geel, M., Toprak, F., Goemans, A., Zwaanswijk, W., & Vedder, P. (2017). Are youth psychopathic traits related to bullying? Meta-analysis on callous-unemotional traits, narcissism, and impulsivity. *Child Psychiatry and Human Development, 48*, 768–777.

Vangelisti, A. L. (1994a). Family secrets: Forms, functions, and correlates. *Journal of Social and Personal Relationships, 11*, 113–135.

Vangelisti, A. L. (1994b). Messages that hurt. In W. R. Cupach & B. H. Spitzberg (Eds.), *The dark side of interpersonal communication* (pp. 53–82). Erlbaum.

Vangelisti, A. L. (2001). Making sense of hurtful interactions in close relationships. In V. Manusov & J. H. Harvey (Eds.), *Attribution, communication behavior, and close relationships* (pp. 38–58). Cambridge University Press.

Vangelisti, A. L. (2007). Communicating hurt. In B. H. Spitzberg & W. R. Cupach (Eds.), *The dark side of interpersonal communication* (2nd ed., pp. 121–142). Erlbaum.

Vangelisti, A. L. (2015). Hurtful communication. In C. R. Berger & M. E. Roloff (Eds.), *International encyclopedia of interpersonal communication*. Wiley.

Vangelisti, A. L., & Brody, N. (2021). The physiology of social pain: Examining, problematizing, and contextualizing the experience of social pain. In L. S. Aloia, A. Denes, & J. P. Crowley (Eds.), *The Oxford handbook of the physiology of interpersonal communication*. Oxford University Press.

Vangelisti, A. L., & Caughlin, J. P. (1997). Revealing family secrets: The influence of topic, function, and relationships. *Journal of Social and Personal Relationships, 14,* 679–706.

Vangelisti, A. L., Caughlin, J. P., & Timmerman, L. (2001). Criteria for revealing family secrets. *Communication Monographs, 68,* 1–27.

Vangelisti, A. L., & Crumley, L. P. (1998). Reactions to messages that hurt: The influence of relational contexts. *Communication Monographs, 65,* 173–196.

Vangelisti, A. L., Maguire, K. C., Alexander, A. L., & Clark, G. (2007). Hurtful family environments: Links with individual and relationship variables. *Communication Monographs, 74,* 357–385.

Vangelisti, A. L., Pennebaker, J. W., Brody, N., & Guinn, T. D. (2014). Reducing social pain: Sex differences in the impact of physical pain relievers. *Personal Relationships, 21,* 349–363.

Vangelisti, A. L., & Young, S. L. (2000). When words hurt: The effects of perceived intentionality on interpersonal relationships. *Journal of Social and Personal Relationships, 17,* 393–424.

Vangelisti, A. L., Young, S. L., Carpenter-Theune, K. E., & Alexander, A. L. (2005). Why does it hurt? The perceived causes of hurt feelings. *Communication Research, 32,* 443–477.

Vaughan, D. (1986). *Uncoupling: Turning points in intimate relationships.* Oxford University Press.

Vernberg, E. M., Ewell, K. K., Beery, S. H., Freeman, C. M., & Abwender, D. A. (1995). Aversive exchanges with peers and adjustment during early adolescence: Is disclosure helpful? *Child Psychiatry and Human Development, 26,* 43–59.

Villar, G., Arciuli, J., & Paterson, H. (2013). Vocal pitch production during lying: Beliefs about deception matter. *Psychiatry, Psychology, and Law, 20,* 123–132.

Vinkers, C. D. W., Finkenauer, C., & Hawk, S. T. (2011). Why close partners snoop? Predictors of intrusive behavior in newlywed couples. *Personal Relationships, 18*(1), 110–124.

Vrij, A. (2007). Deception: A social lubricant and a selfish act. In K. Fiedler (Ed.), *Social communication* (pp. 309–342). Psychology Press.

Vrij, A., Edward, K., Roberts, K. P., & Bull, R. (2000). Detecting deceit via analysis of verbal and nonverbal behavior. *Journal of Nonverbal Behavior, 24,* 239–263.

Waldron, V. R., & Kelley, D. L. (2005). Forgiving communication as a response to relational transgressions. *Journal of Social and Personal Relationships, 22,* 723–742.

Waldron, V. R., & Kelley, D. L. (2008). *Communicating forgiveness.* SAGE.

Waller, W. (1938). *The family: A dynamic interpretation.* Cordon.

Walters, G. D., & Espelage, D. L. (2018). From victim to victimizer: Hostility, anger, and depression as mediators of the bullying victimization-bullying perpetration association. *Journal of School Psychology, 68,* 73–83.

Walters, M. L., Chen, J., & Breiding, M. J. (2013). The National Intimate Partner and Sexual Violence Survey (NISVS): 2010 findings on victimization by sexual orientation. *National Center for Injury Prevention and Control and Centers for Disease Control and Prevention, 648*(73), 6.

Walther, J. B. (1996). Computer-mediated communication: Impersonal, interpersonal, and hyperpersonal interaction. *Communication Research, 3,* 3–43.

Webb, A. K., Honts, C. R., Kircher, J. C., Bernhardt, P., & Cook, A. E. (2009). Effectiveness of pupil diameter in a probable-lie comparison question test for deception. *Legal and Criminological Psychology, 14,* 279–292.

Wegner, D. M. (1989). *White bears and other unwanted thoughts: Suppression, obsession, and the psychology of mental control.* Penguin.

Wegner, D. M., Schneider, D. J., Carter, S. R., & White, T. L. (1987). Paradoxical effects of thought suppression. *Journal of Personality and Social Psychology, 53*(1), 5–13.

Weiner, B. (1985). An attributional theory of achievement motivation and emotion. *Psychological Review, 92,* 548–573.

Weiner, B. (1995). *Judgments of responsibility.* Guilford.

West, R., & Turner, L. H. (2018). Coming to terms with bullying: A communication perspective. In R. West & C. S. Beck (Eds.), *The Routledge handbook of communication and bullying* (pp. 3–12). Routledge.

Westrup, D., & Fremouw, W. J. (1998). Stalking behavior: A literature review and suggested functional analytic assessment technology. *Aggression and Violent Behavior: A Review Journal, 3,* 255–274.

Whisman, M. A., Gordon, C. C., & Chatav, Y. (2007). Predicting sexual infidelity in a population-based sample of married individuals. *Journal of Family Psychology, 21,* 320–324.

White, G. L. (1980). Inducing jealousy: A power perspective. *Personality and Social Psychology Bulletin, 6,* 222–227.

White, G. L. (1981a). A model of romantic jealousy. *Motivation and Emotion, 5,* 295–310.

White, G. L. (1981b). Some correlates of romantic jealousy. *Journal of Personality, 49,* 129–147.

White, G. L. (1981c). Jealousy and partner's perceived motives for attraction to a rival. *Social Psychology Quarterly, 44,* 24–30.

White, G. L., & Mullen, P. E. (1989). *Jealousy: Theory, research, and clinical strategies.* Guilford.

Whittaker, S., & Bry, B. H. (1991). Overt and covert parental conflict and adolescent problems: Observed marital interaction in clinic and nonclinic families. *Adolescence, 26,* 865–876.

Whitty, M. T. (2003). Pushing the wrong buttons: Men's and women's attitudes toward online and offline infidelity. *Cyberpsychology and Behavior, 6,* 569–579.

Whitty, M. T. (2005). The realness of cybercheating: Men's and women's representations of unfaithful Internet relationships. *Social Science Computer Review, 23,* 57–67.

Widmer, E. D., Treas, J., & Newcomb, R. (1998). Attitudes toward nonmarital sex in 24 countries. *Journal of Sex Research, 35,* 349–358.

Wiederman, W. W. (1997). Extramarital sex: Prevalence and correlates in a national survey. *Journal of Sex Research, 34,* 167–174.

Wiederman, W. W., & Allgeier, E. R. (1993). Gender differences in sexual jealousy: Adaptionist or social learning explanation? *Evolution and Human Behavior, 14,* 115–140.

Wiederman, W. W., & Hurd, C. (1999). Extradyadic involvement during dating. *Journal of Social and Personal Relationships, 16,* 265–274.

Wiederman, W. W., & LaMar, L. (1998). "Not with him you don't!": Gender and emotional reactions to sexual infidelity during courtship. *The Journal of Sex Research, 35,* 288–297.

Wiggins, J. D., & Lederer, D. A. (1984). Differential antecedents of infidelity in marriage. *American Mental Health Counselors Association Journal, 6,* 152–161.

Williams, K. R., & Guerra, N. G. (2007). Prevalence and predictors of Internet bullying. *Journal of Adolescent Health, 41,* 514–521.

Wolke, D., Woods, S., Bloomfield, L., & Karstadt, L. (2001). Bullying involvement in primary school and common health problems. *Archives of Disease in Childhood, 85,* 197–201.

Worthington, E. L. Jr., Berry, J. W., Hook, J. N., Davis, D. E., Scherer, M., Griffin, B. J., & Campana, K. L. (2015). Forgiveness-reconciliation and communication-conflict-resolution interventions versus retested controls in early married couples. *Journal of Counseling Psychology, 62,* 14–27.

Ybarra, M. L., & Mitchell, K. J. (2004). Youth engaging in online harassment: Associations with caregiver-child relationships, Internet use, and personal characteristics. *Journal of Adolescence, 27,* 319–336.

Yoshimura, S. M. (2004a). Emotional and behavioral responses to romantic jealousy expressions. *Communication Reports, 17,* 85–101.

Yoshimura, S. M. (2004b). *Fifteen types of revenge activities enacted against current and past romantic partners.* Paper presented at the annual meeting of the International Communication Association, Madison, WI.

Yoshimura, S. M. (2007). Goals and emotional outcomes of revenge activities in interpersonal relationships. *Journal of Social and Personal Relationships, 24,* 87–98.

Yoshimura, S. M., Anderson, C., Curran, T., & Allen, N. (2013). *The aspects, boundaries, and limitations of interpersonal revenge: The intimate revenge behavior measure.* Paper presented at the annual meeting of the National Communication Association, Washington, DC.

Yoshimura, S. M., & Boon, S. D. (2018). *Communicating revenge in interpersonal relationships.* Lexington Books.

Young, S. L. (2004). Factors that influence recipients' appraisals of hurtful communication. *Journal of Social and Personal Relationships, 21,* 291–303.

Young, S. L., & Bippus, A. M. (2001). Does it make a difference if they hurt you in a funny way? Humorously and non-humorously phrased hurtful messages in personal relationships. *Communication Quarterly, 49,* 35–42.

Zhang, S., & Merolla, A. J. (2006). Communicating dislike of close friends' romantic partners. *Communication Research Reports, 23,* 179–186.

Zuckerman, M., DePaulo, B. M., & Rosenthal, R. (1981). Verbal and nonverbal communication of deception. In L. Berkowitz (Ed.), *Advances in experimental social psychology* (Vol. 14, pp. 1–59). Academic Press.

INDEX

A

accommodating, 242
accommodation, 55
acquiescent responses, 80
active information acquisition strategies, 29–30
active listening, 252–253
active verbal responses, 80
activity jealousy, 86
adult attachment styles, 22
affective reactions, 25
affinity-seeking strategies, 197
aggression, 174
    human, 174–175
    interpersonal provocations, 186
    physical, 175
    relatively stable predictors, 182–184
    role of communication skills in, 186–187
    sexual, 175
    situational predictors, 186
    types of, 174–176
    verbal, 186–187
aggressive behaviors, 4
agreeableness, 137
alcohol addiction, 9
ambiguity tolerance, 20
antisocial personality disorder, 207
antisocial teasing, 217
anxious attachment orientation, 75
attachment styles in close relationships, 20–22
attachment theory, 208
attribution theory, 57
aversive interpersonal behaviors, 7, 53
aversive social behaviors, 7
avoidant attachment orientation, 74
avoidant communication, 98–99, 241
avoiding, 242

B

backchanneling cues, 253
behavioral familiarity, 122
behavioral jealousy, 94, 149
behavioral norms, 17–18
belongingness hypothesis, 1
bias bullying, 223
blameworthiness, 57
blinking, 122
body movements, 123
borderline personality disorder, 206
bullying, 4, 68, 216, 223–232
    bias, 223
    bully-victims experience, 229
    bystanders, implications for, 229–230
    definition, 223
    interventions, 230–232
    perpetrators, implications for, 229
    predictors of and risk factors for, 225–227
    prevalence of, 224–225
    situational factors, 226
    victims, implications for, 229
bully-victims, 225, 229
The Burning Bed, 184, 189
bystanders, 217, 222–223, 229–230

C

channel switching, 239
chilling effect, 242
close relationships, 4–5, 9–12, 68
    attachment styles in, 20–22
    benefits of openness in, 34
    deception in, 106–108
    infidelity in, 132–133
    intimacy in, 22–23
    topic avoidance in, 39
coercive behaviors, 227
coercive control theory, 209
cognitive jealousy, 91, 149

Printed in the USA
CPSIA information can be obtained
at www.ICGtesting.com
LVHW010318170824
788501LV00022B/75